THE ART OF ILLUSION

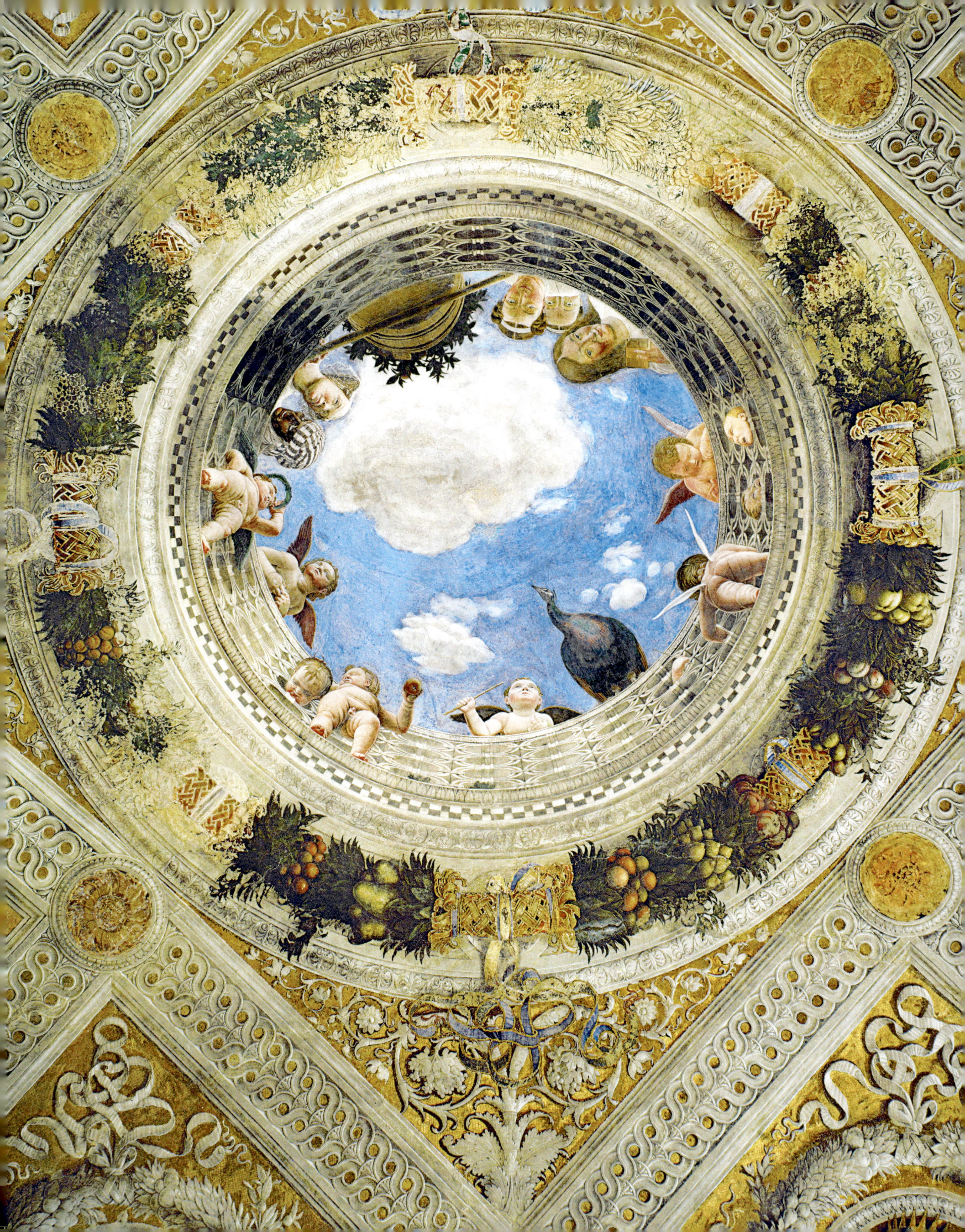

FLORIAN HEINE

THE ART OF ILLUSION

PRESTEL

Munich · London · New York

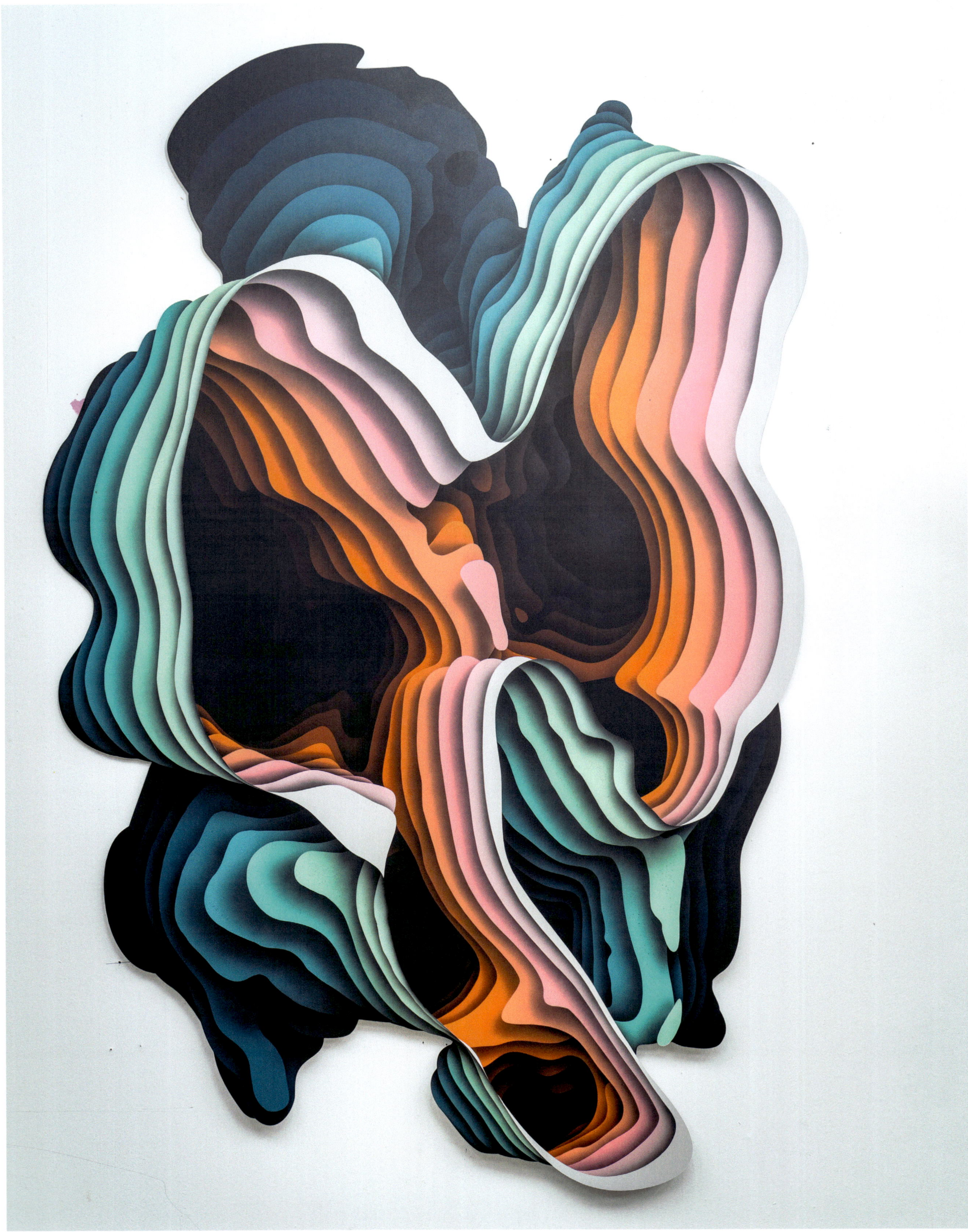

◀ *Implicate_03,* 2019, UV and acrylic on aluminum composite panel, 190 × 140 cm

CONTENTS

INTRODUCTION

Is Seeing Believing?

Everything we see is real. But not everything we perceive actually corresponds to that which we believe we see. "Art is magic delivered from the lie of being truth", wrote the German philosopher Theodor W. Adorno (1903–1969).[1] And indeed, some things that artists create appear to be magic in the sense that a three-dimensional world is created before our very eyes on a flat canvas or a real wall. We are perfectly aware of its creation, and yet, all the same, we not only accept the 'pretence' but sometimes also find it difficult to see it for what it really is: paint on wall or canvas. The art here lies in the ability to imitate nature in the most deceptively real way. We see a painted object, as flat as paint on canvas is, yet we perceive it three-dimensionally. Trompe l'œil (French for 'trick of the eye') is a phenomenon. Painters trick us into believing that an object exists before us, and yet it does not. The only thing that exists is the two-dimensional image, when we finally recognise it as such. However, if one does not grasp the illusion and continues to assume that this object is actually present, then how real is it in our perception? If we assume that it is present, is it actually present, at least in our minds? In the special genre of the 'optical illusion', art manages to make things real that are not – at least for that short moment between seeing and perceiving, between perception and '(dis)enchantment'.

In painting, we see pictures, and it is clear to us that they are likenesses of reality or else of fantasy. This is the same case in sculpture, although sculpture possesses the greater closeness to that three-dimensional reality and thus the sculptors' 'attempts to deceive' take

▶ Jean-Léon Gérôme, *Pygmalion and Galatea*, c. 1890

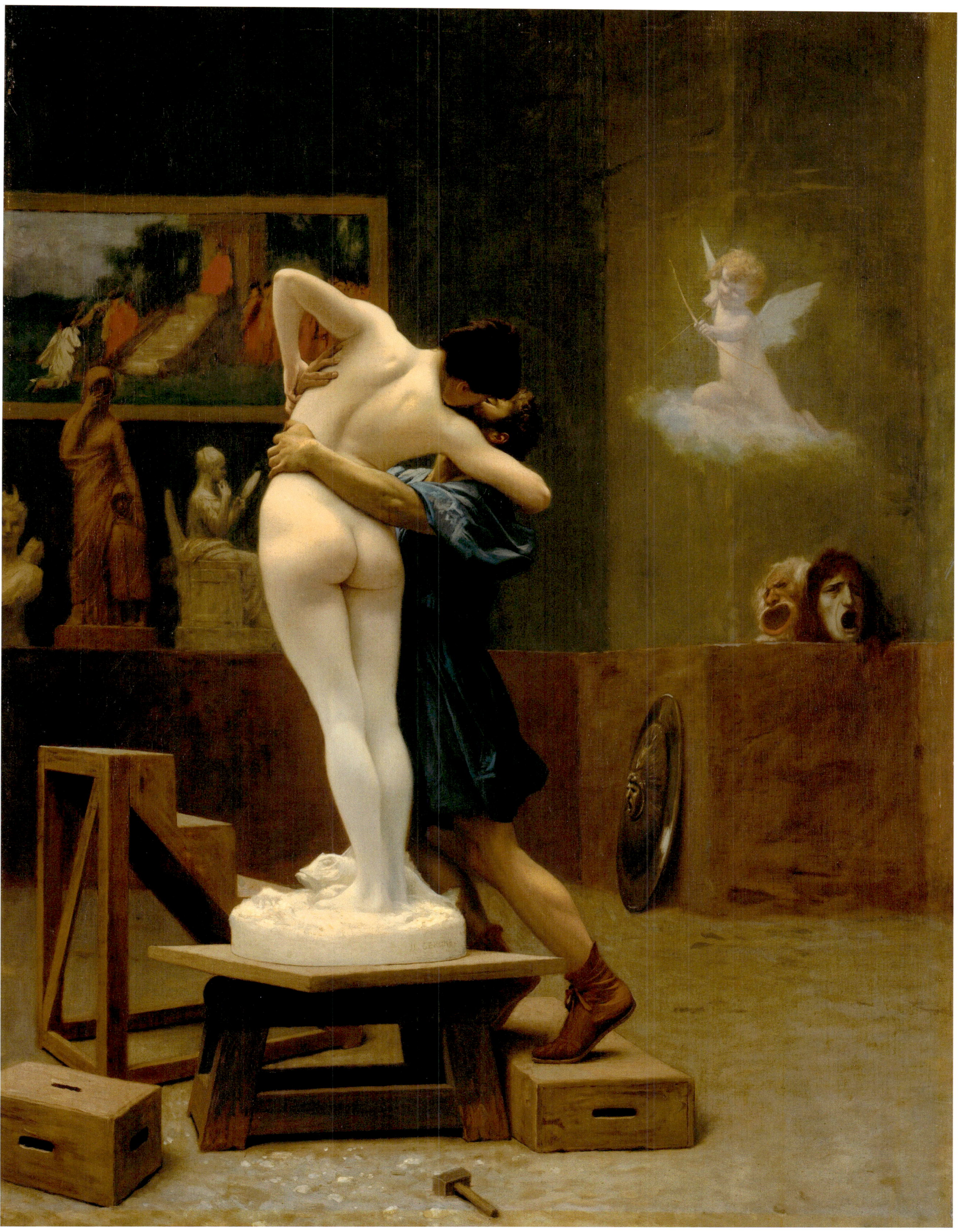

place on another level. In photography, deception is also dealt with differently than in painting. Photography is traditionally attributed a high degree of credibility, which seems to be increasingly easy to undermine in these days of digital image manipulation. Photography therefore carries out its deceptions in more subtle ways.

It has always been an endeavour of artists to depict the world around us, to engage with it and thereby grasp it. From the very beginning, painting and sculpture, as well, have provided a way of understanding the world, of explaining it and of helping find one's way in it. In antiquity, the highest aspiration was to imitate nature, and the painter who succeeded in this most convincingly, who created work most deceptively real, was considered to be the most gifted. The Roman historian and author Pliny the Elder (c. AD 23–79) reports in his *Natural History* (*Naturalis historia*), the first work of art history, on a famous competition in 397 BC between two of the stars of painting at the time, Parrhasius and Zeuxis. After Zeuxis had finished his picture of grapes, birds came and attempted to peck at them. Thus, sure of victory, he went to his competitor to see his work, but it was hidden behind a curtain. As Zeuxis tried to pull the curtain aside, he realised that he had been the victim of a perfect illusion. The curtain itself was the painting and Zeuxis could do nothing but acknowledge Parrhasius as the victor. Some elements of this story are still used in art today, and the motifs return over the course of the centuries in the most diverse variations

▼ Left
False Door of Heneni, c. 2250 BC
▼ Right
Casa della Farnesina, c. 20 BC

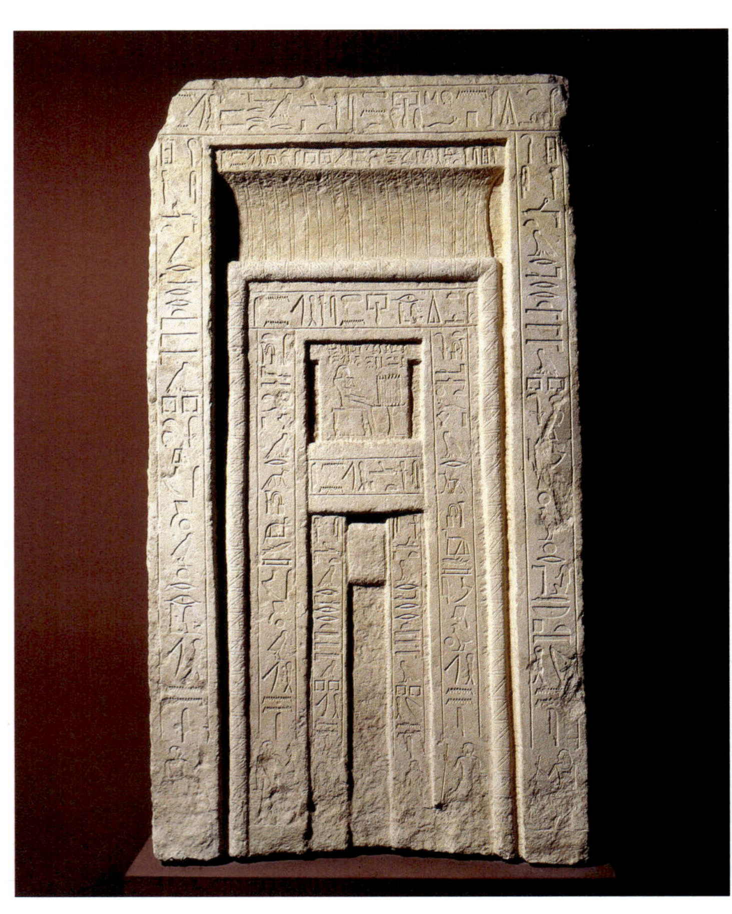

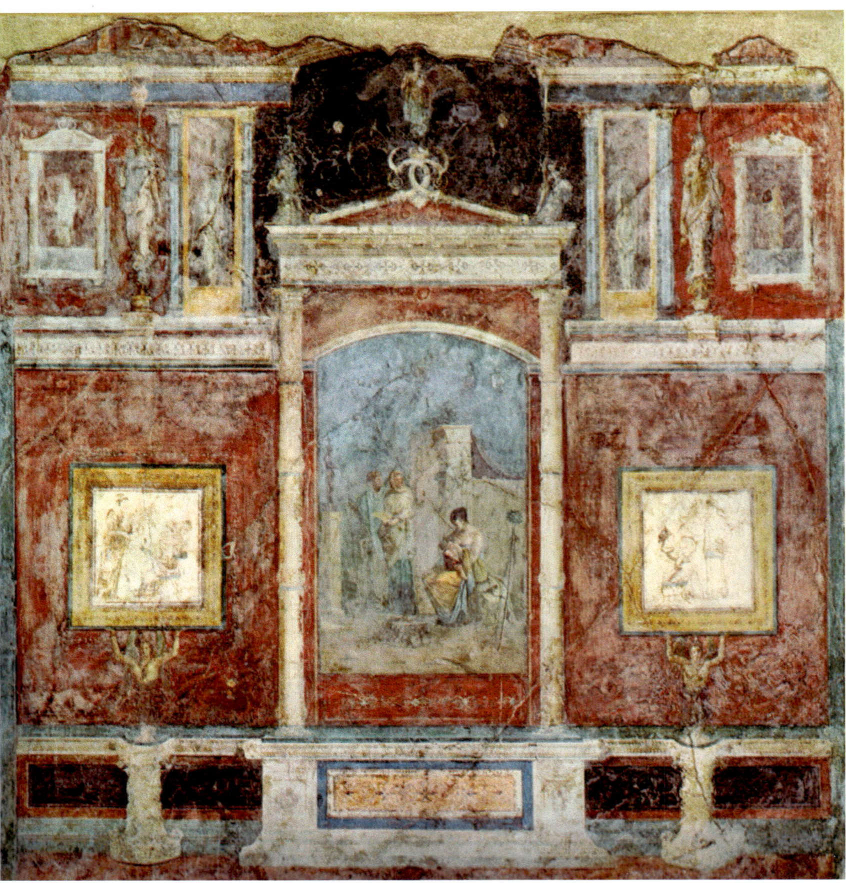

(fig. pp. 88/89): the grapes, the curtain, the power of judgement of man and beast and, above all, the astonishment at the moment of realising that there is a world of difference between sight and perception. Yet perhaps Zeuxis would have been the more suitable winner, since he had completely impartial, neutral test subjects and adjudicators in the birds that wanted to snack on his grapes. With his curtain, Parrhasius introduced an element into the competition that was not unusual at the time, and thus Zeuxis probably had no doubt that a precious painting – especially in such a competition – might be protected by a curtain. So, it was not only art, but also a play on expectations that made Parrhasius the winner. For, in the end, we only see with our eyes; perception, which involves more than just the physio-optical absorption of stimuli, takes place in the brain.

Fascination with such a perfect imitation was a constant theme throughout antiquity, and the deception of the audience which resulted was tested with ever new variations: be it in architecture, where people were sometimes misled by fake doors and corridors (fig. p. 8 left), or in sculpture, where – according to legend – the sculptor Pygmalion fell in love with his extremely realistic female statue, which then came to life (an event which, as far as we know, remained an isolated incident; fig. p. 7). However, painting supplied the broadest field for attempts at deception of all kinds, whether it was intended to make a room appear larger and more splendid, as can be seen in Roman villas (fig. pp. 10/11); wall decorations in which framed pictures were simulated (fig. p. 8 right); or for the amazement and amusement of guests when it seemed that fragments of crockery or pieces of leftover food littered an elegant floor (fig. pp. 14/15). The latter variant even received its own term as a genre: 'rhyparography' (art that is engaged with distasteful and sordid subjects). The art of illusion was also used in the theatre, where the stage's architectural background, for example, led the audience to believe that it was seeing a real city, even though its boundaries did not extend beyond the stage apron. All of this was created with the greatest skill and artistry. However, little has survived. Of Greek panel painting, made so famous in the writings of Pliny, nothing is extant and of the architectural painting only very little. It was only from the middle of the 18th century onwards that much of such works from antiquity became once again known, with the excavations of the cities of

▶ **Overleaf**
A frescoed wall in the House of Marcus Lucretius Fronto, between 50 BC and AD 15

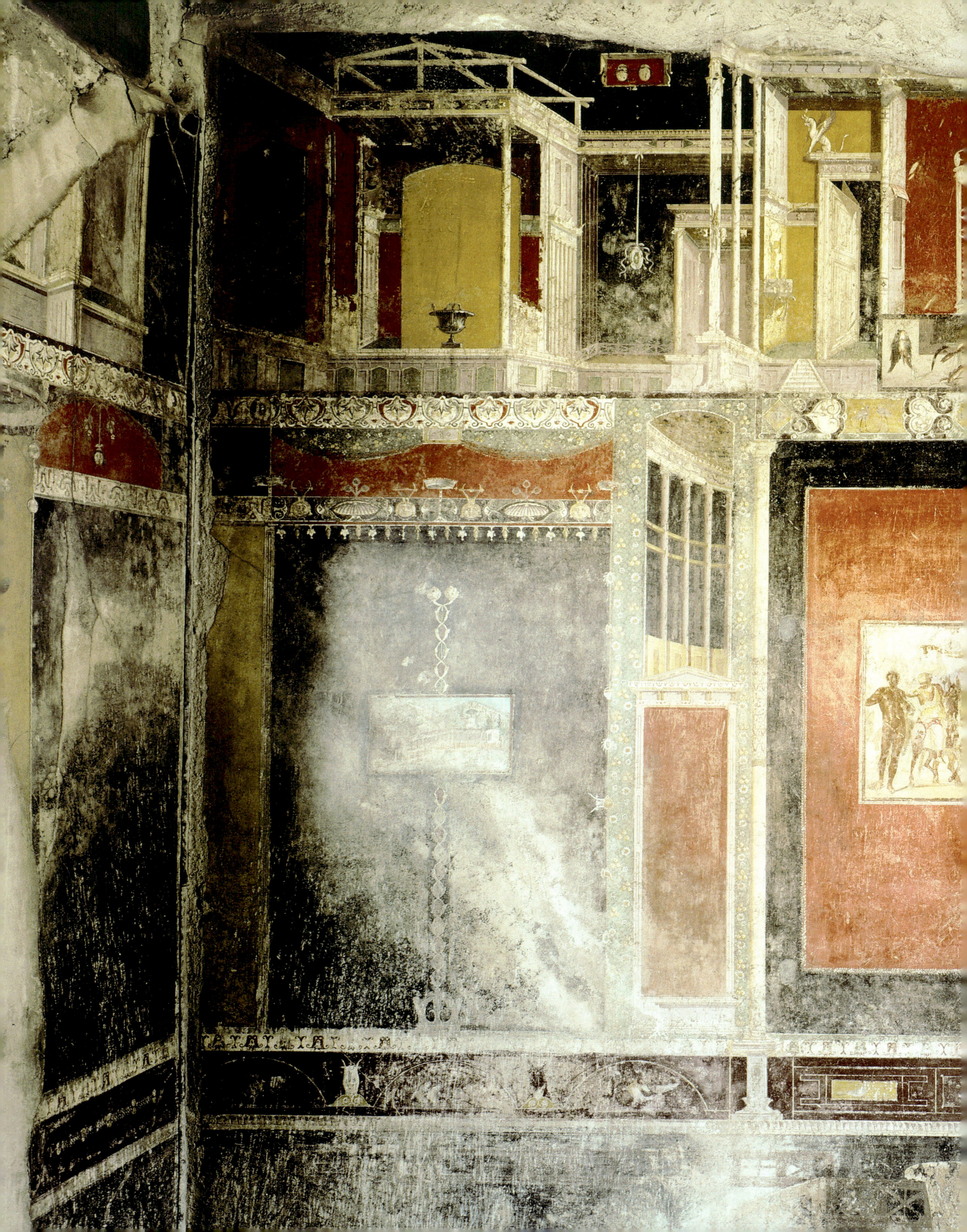

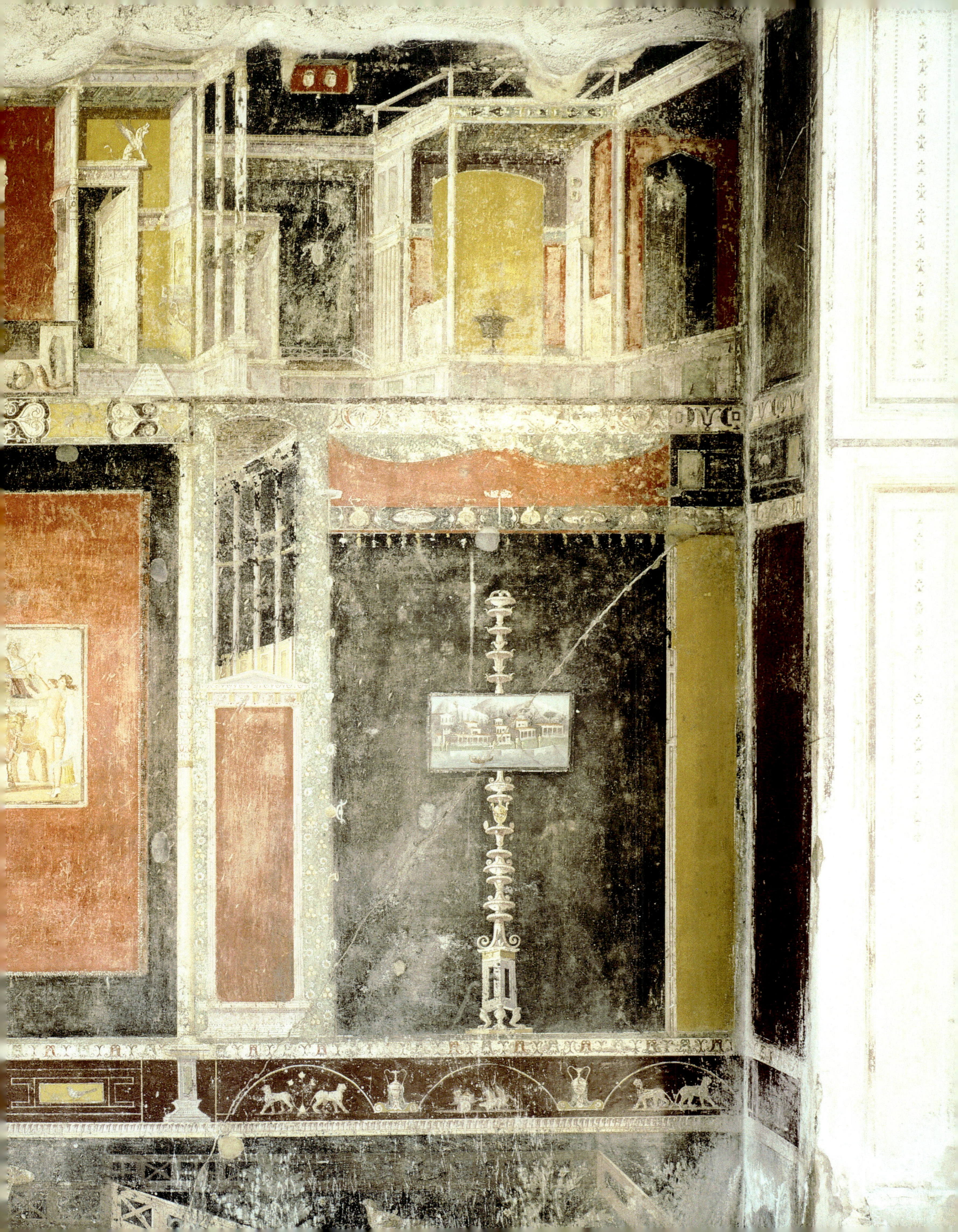

Herculaneum and Pompeii, which were buried by the eruption of Mount Vesuvius in AD 79.

With the Fall of the Roman Empire in the 5th century and the years of mass migrations that followed, Christianity not only established itself as the religion of the people but also as the new, all-encompassing power structure. The world became a different one and so did art. To depict the world faithfully or even to provoke optical illusions was no longer desired. For Christianity, the temporal world, although God's creation, was considered sinful. The visible world receded behind the ideal one. Amongst the influences on medieval theology was the ancient philosopher Plato (427 – 347 BC), who referred to painters as "copyists of a copy",[2] because for Plato the material world was nothing more than the mere likeness of the ideal world.

In the 13th century, the scholasticists that formed around Albertus Magnus (c. 1200 – 1280) and Thomas Aquinas (c. 1225 – 1274) appeared on the scene, and the times changed again. They reconciled the Christian faith with Aristotelian thought and declared that it would be quite pleasing in the sight of God to explore this earthy world scientifically and artistically – to put it simply.

And so, after the allegedly 'dark' Middle Ages, in which little attention was paid to a realistic representation of the visible world and all its elements, in the 14th century people began to rediscover old artistic techniques and to develop new ones. Art changed once again, this time back to the direction of nature. An important new beginning was made by the young Italian painter Giotto di Bondone (c. 1266 – 1337) around 1300 with the painting of the Basilica of Saint Francis in Assisi and the Scrovegni Chapel in Padua around 1304. The architectural theorist Filarete (1400 – 1469) wrote about Giotto in his *Treatise on Architecture* (*Trattato di architettura,* c. 1460), saying that the artist began studying nature very closely and painting it from a young age. Indeed, Giotto once played a practical joke on his teacher Cimabue (1240 – 1302) by painting a fly on the nose of a figure on which his master was working. It was so lifelike that Cimabue tried to sweep it away. A tiny beginning, but one of the first artistic attempts at illusion in the early modern era …

With Giotto's innovations and the discovery of linear perspective in the Italian Renaissance, artists were provided new tools that enabled them to open spaces where there were none, to create objects where there was only paint and to create movement where only stillness may be found. Artists such as Masaccio (1401–1428), Bramante (1444–1514) and Giovanni Battista Tiepolo (1696–1770) can astonish viewers today almost as much as they did in their own times (figs. pp. 38, 43, 50). The same is true of the Dutch painters, such as Samuel van Hoogstraten (1627–1678) and Cornelis Norbertus Gysbrechts (c. 1610–after 1675), whose trompe l'œils are peak examples of artistic illusion (figs. pp. 62, 64, 86/87). In the 19th century, some American painters such as John Haberle (1856–1933) and Nicholas Alden Brocks (1840–1904) even went too far with the art of deception, which brought them several studio visits from the police (figs. pp. 67, 94/95). In the 20th century, illusion at the hand of art became itself a theme, and painters like René Magritte (1898–1967) and other surrealists questioned art and perception in completely new ways (figs. pp. 70/71, 96/97).

Sculptors, too, have at times desired – and still desire – to get deceptively close to reality with their figures, as can be seen particularly well in the *Miracle Man* of Saxony from 1500, the wax portrait of Louis XIV and in the works of Duane Hanson (1925–1996; figs. pp. 151, 159, 161). Hyperrealist sculptors such as Ron Mueck (b. 1958) and Patricia Piccinini (b. 1965) not only come extremely close to reality, but they also surpass it, as it were, with their works – while at the same time retaining a dimension of believability (figs. pp. 152, 164/165, 166/167).

Newer genres such as photography and street art are shaping the art of illusion today. Photographers like Andreas Gursky (b. 1955) and Pelle Cass (b. 1954) succeed in exaggerating reality in a deceptively real way (figs. pp. 129, 130/131, 133–135). And while Liu Bolin (b. 1973) disappears in his photographs, the French photographer JR (b. 1983) even succeeds at making entire buildings disappear through photographic trompe l'œils and then reappear as anamorphoses (figs. pp. 122/123, 138). Ultimately, with street art, the focal point of art is shifting with new forms and new means of expression from museums and gallery spaces into the street, where it can be seen by everyone and stands every chance of being spread around the world in an instant.

The Art of Illusion takes you on a journey through the world of art and deception, beauty and illusion. This book is intended to whet your appetite for art. But more than that, it should give you the urge to see and discover, to perceive, to marvel and to be amazed.

▶ **Overleaf**
The Unswept Floor, AD 2

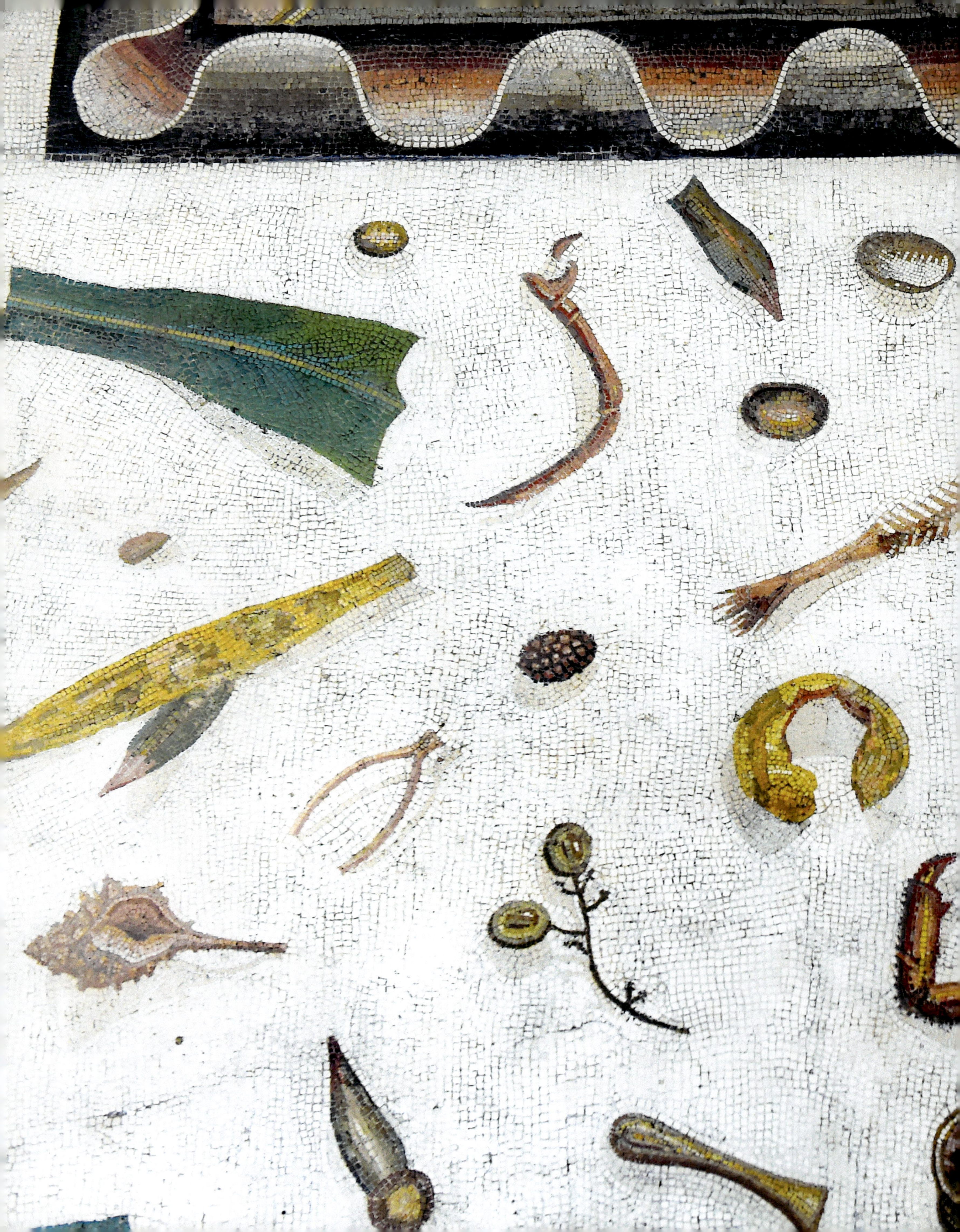

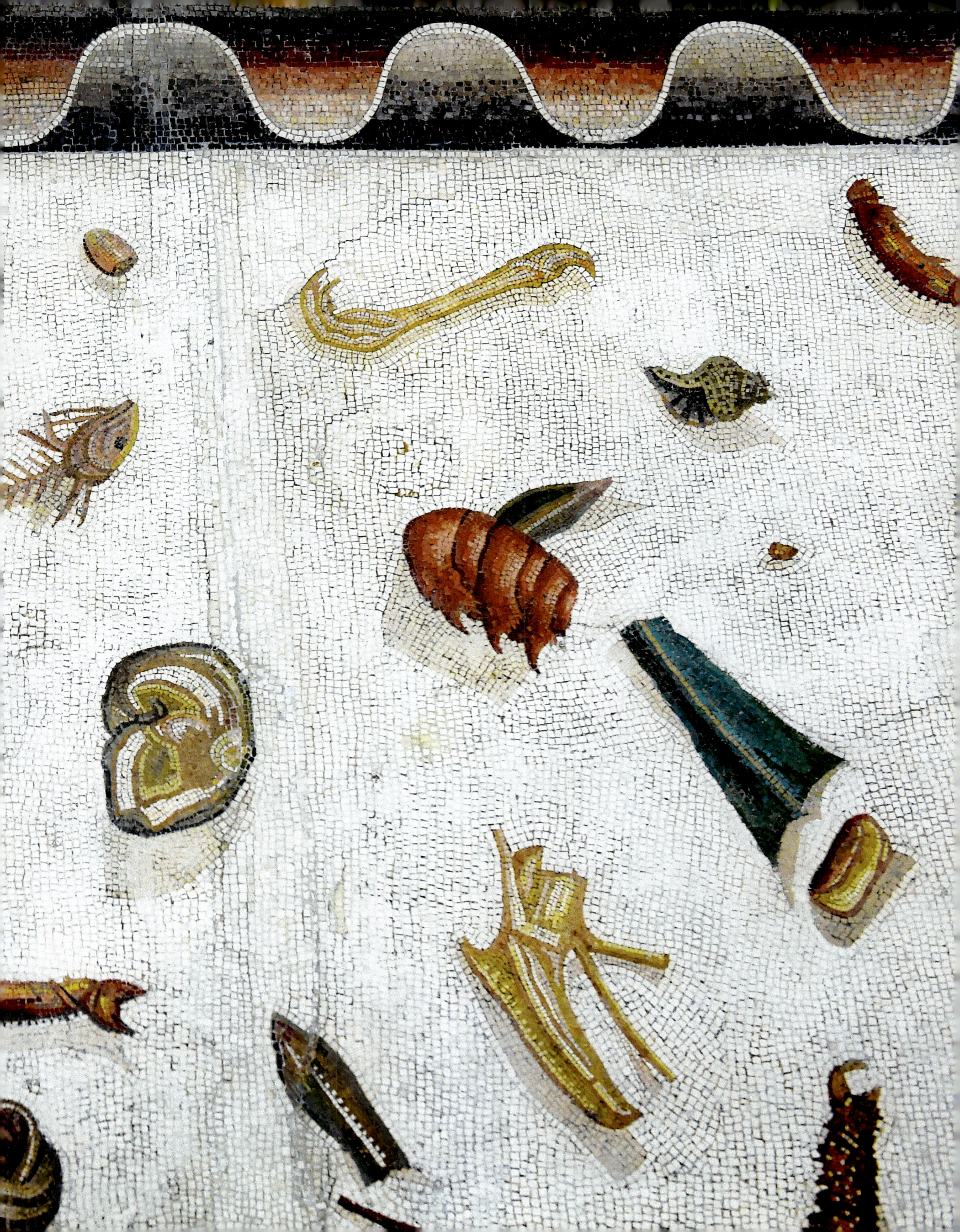

ARCHITECTURE

Space Made Real

The Renaissance began in 14th-century Italy across various fields, including literature, the sciences, religion and, of course, architecture and painting. The 'rebirth' of painting, in fact, already began when, in Padua and Assisi, Giotto di Bondone (c. 1266 – 1337) engaged artistically with the life and work of Francis of Assisi, who had died in 1226 and was already canonised in 1228. Since Francis was a 'contemporary' saint, for Giotto it was simply not an option to depict his life using established forms belonging to the Middle Ages. In his frescoes, Giotto shunned the tradition of creating symbolic landscapes and topographies, and instead bestowed his figures with individual character and a physical mass. While formerly, painted figures seemed almost to stand on tiptoe or to float before some undefined background, Giotto chose to place them 'right' on the soles of their feet. The topographies, too, became more concrete. While in the Middle Ages it had been sufficient to 'suggest' an entire forest through the depiction of two or three trees, or a palace through a few columns, now the relevant building was brought into the picture – an example being the church of Santa Maria sopra Minerva in Assisi, before which an important event in the life of St Francis had taken place (fig. right). What Giotto did not yet know, however, was how buildings and figures might be represented correctly in relation to each other. Even Giotto's figures stand all on a line, parallel to the viewer, with the effect that the picture lacks depth and the figures in the painted scene lack a stage on which to perform.

The Renaissance had begun, and Giotto's frescoes were widely praised, even by the likes of Dante Alighieri (1265 – 1321) and later

▶ Giotto di Bondone, A commoner pays homage to St Francis in the market square of Assisi, c. 1295/1300

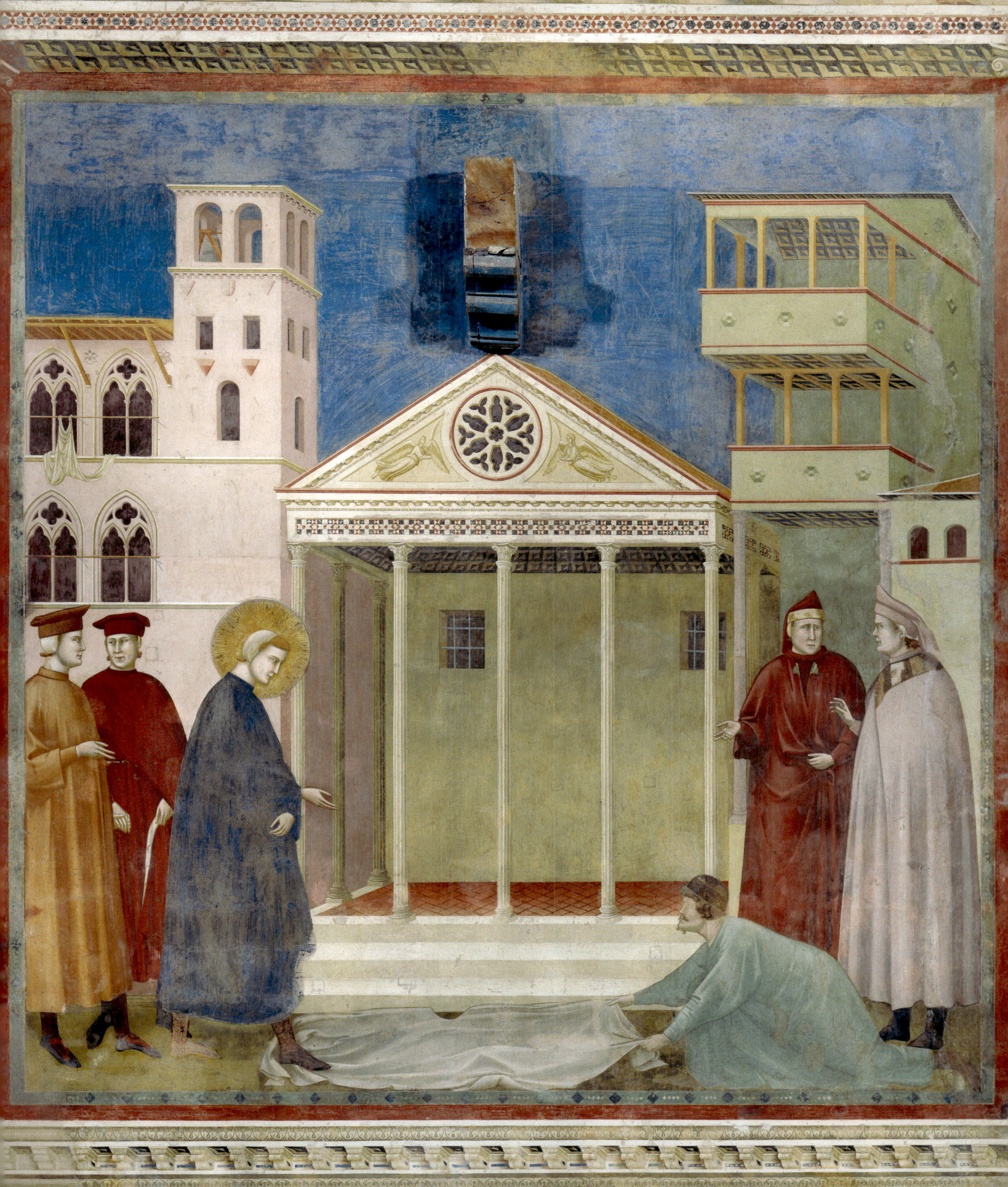

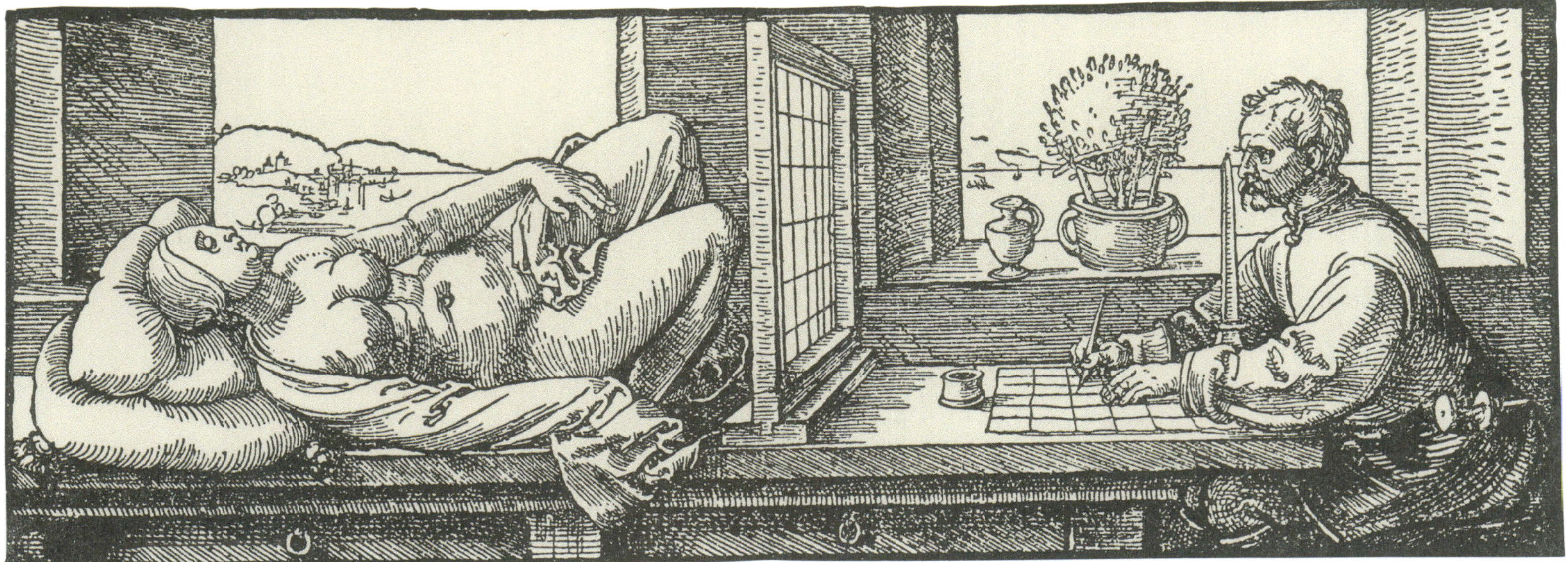

▲ Albrecht Dürer, *Draughtsman Making a Perspective Drawing of a Reclining Woman*, print from 1538

Giorgio Vasari (1511–1574) in his famous *The Lives of the Artists* (*Le vite*), published in 1568. But it was still only a beginning, and nearly a hundred years would pass before the real revolution in painting was to take place, when in Florence the sculptor, painter, goldsmith and architect Filippo Brunelleschi (1377–1446) first understood the rules governing linear perspective and went on to formulate these in a way that could be used by painters. The picture that most likely started Brunelleschi on this path was a representation of the Florence Baptistery – although the picture, unfortunately, no longer exists today. Brunelleschi painted the building in the years between 1415 and 1420, so convincingly and with such realism that those who saw it, such as his biographer Antonio Manetti, are said to have almost believed that they were viewing the real Baptistery.

It is no longer entirely clear how Brunelleschi painted this picture. Manetti reports that Brunelleschi stood two metres inside the cathedral opposite, with a particular apparatus, and drew the picture from this vantage point. Vasari assumed the architect had produced the picture using a grid, as Leon Battista Alberti described in his 1435 treatise *On Painting* (*De pictura*). According to this, Brunelleschi developed a system which Alberti described as a view through a window, capturing a particular section of space; if one looks with one eye from a fixed point through a pane of glass every point of space or the object one might wish to depict comes to lie on a certain point on the pane. If one connects those points, allowing the parallel lines to remain parallel, the lines run away from the viewer to intersect at the so-called vanishing point, and one obtains an image in linear perspective. The lines running into the distance appear foreshortened. The size of the objects becomes proportionally smaller the further into the distance they go, exactly as when one looks down a straight road, it seems to narrow the further it reaches towards the horizon. It is perhaps no coincidence, when one takes into account the streets of Florence, that this discovery was made in a city that has long straight streets and not in the countryside in some village full of nooks and crannies and corners, where such observations would be far more difficult to make. Alberti therefore assumed that Brunelleschi used a frame with a grid, probably similar to that known to us from a woodcut by Albrecht Dürer (fig. left).

In 1999, the British painter David Hockney (b. 1937) demonstrated through an experiment that Brunelleschi had perhaps instead used a much simpler and more elegant method to paint this view – a mirror projection. To achieve this, Hockney also positioned himself on the porch of the cathedral and projected the inverted image of the Baptistery onto his paper ground with a concave mirror. By tracing this projection, he obtained an image that was in accurate perspective. For such an imaginative and brilliant artist as Brunelleschi, who would go on to create the Florentine cathedral dome and help shape Renaissance architecture, it would only be a small step to draw the correct conclusions from the projection and establish the rules of linear perspective. Yet, the creation of a view in correct perspective was one thing; it was a more interesting challenge, however, for architects and painters to construct new spaces and paint pictures that seemed real. How ever Brunelleschi ultimately painted his picture, the fact is that it has been lost, and so the first painting known to us which was created according to these new rules of linear perspective is the *Holy Trinity* fresco in Santa Maria Novella in Florence, created by Brunelleschi's friend Masaccio (1401–1428) around 1427 (see pp. 38–39).

With Masaccio's fresco of the Trinity, both the idea and technique of linear perspective had come into the world and with it the idea of creating spaces and objects that only appear to exist. The world of painting had changed in one fell swoop. Everyone did their best to learn and master these new rules. Paolo Uccello (1397–1475) was extremely determined to do so, and it is said that he hardly ate or slept because he was so busy working on mastering perspective. Around 1436, Uccello

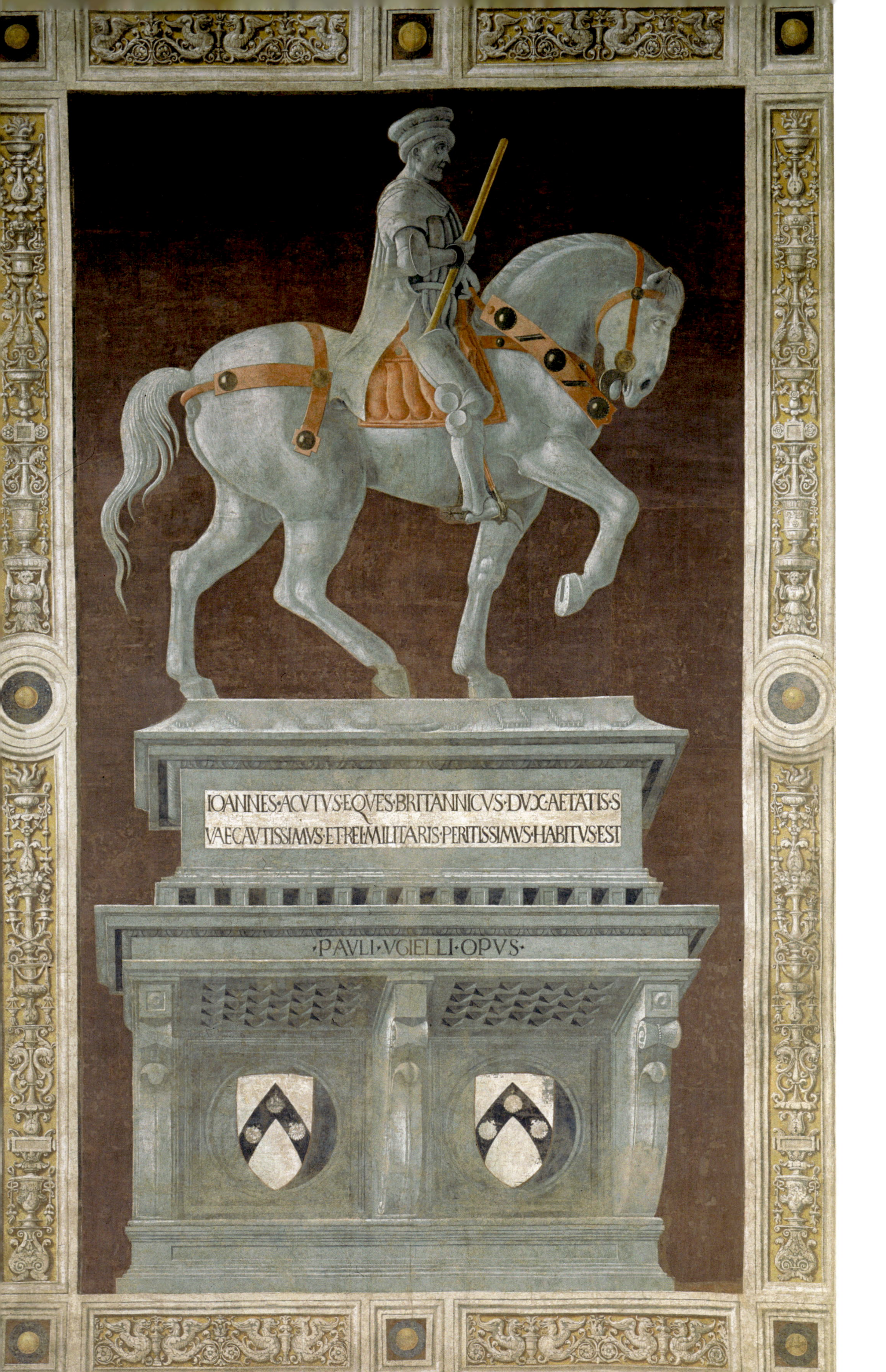
IOANNES·ACVTVS·EQVES·BRITANNICVS·DVX·AETATIS·S
VAE·CAVTISSIMVS·ET·REI·MILITARIS·PERITISSIMVS·HABITVS·EST
·PAVLI·VGIELLI·OPVS·

was commissioned to create an equestrian statue in the Florence Cathedral of the English mercenary captain John Hawkwood, who was in Florentine service (fig. left). Since a real equestrian statue was too expensive, a painted version was chosen that should be made to look like a real sculpture. Vasari described this in his biography of Uccello: "Paolo drew in perspective a large sarcophagus, supposed to contain the corpse, and over this he placed the image of him in his Captain's armour, on horseback."[3] One can assume that this kind of illusionistic painting achieved its desired effect, at least at the time.

The court painter of the Gonzaga in Mantua was even more successful and convincing with the new technique; Andrea Mantegna (1431–1506) was a fervent admirer of the rediscovery of antiquity. His passion was also for perspective painting. His father-in-law, the Venetian painter Jacopo Bellini, father of the famous artists Gentile and Giovanni Bellini, was the forerunner of linear perspective in Venice and dealt extensively with various spatial constructions in his sketchbooks. From 1461 to 1474, Mantegna created the first illusionistic ceiling painting in the so-called Camera degli Sposi in the Palace of the Gonzaga (see pp. 40–41). Here, Mantegna managed to open up a new dimension in perspective and illusionist painting: the ceiling. This would become the field in which artists, over the next centuries, repeatedly surpassed each other with ever new illusions and works meant to astound.

Michelangelo (1475–1564) also used the height and the increased distance to viewers in the Sistine Chapel in Rome when Pope Julius II commissioned him to decorate the ceiling of this high, box-shaped space. Michelangelo, who saw himself primarily as a sculptor, had actually come to Rome to design the pope's huge marble tomb. But first it was required of him that he paint the vaulted ceiling of the 20-metre-high chapel. What Michelangelo created here between 1508 and 1512 is legendary, and it had an immense influence on the artists of his time and those of future generations (fig. pp. 22/23). *The Creation of Adam* is probably one of the most famous works of art in history. Yet, God's posterior, depicted in another central panel, has so far been seldom reproduced. For our context, however, the ceiling's interest lies less in the figures than in the architecture, or more accurately, the illusionistic architecture. Michelangelo divided the 41-metre-long and 13-metre-wide ceiling into five pairs of transverse ribs and four pendentives. Like

◀ Paolo Uccello, *Funerary Monument to Sir John Hawkwood*, 1436

▶ **Overleaf**
Michelangelo, Ceiling of the Sistine Chapel, 1508–1512

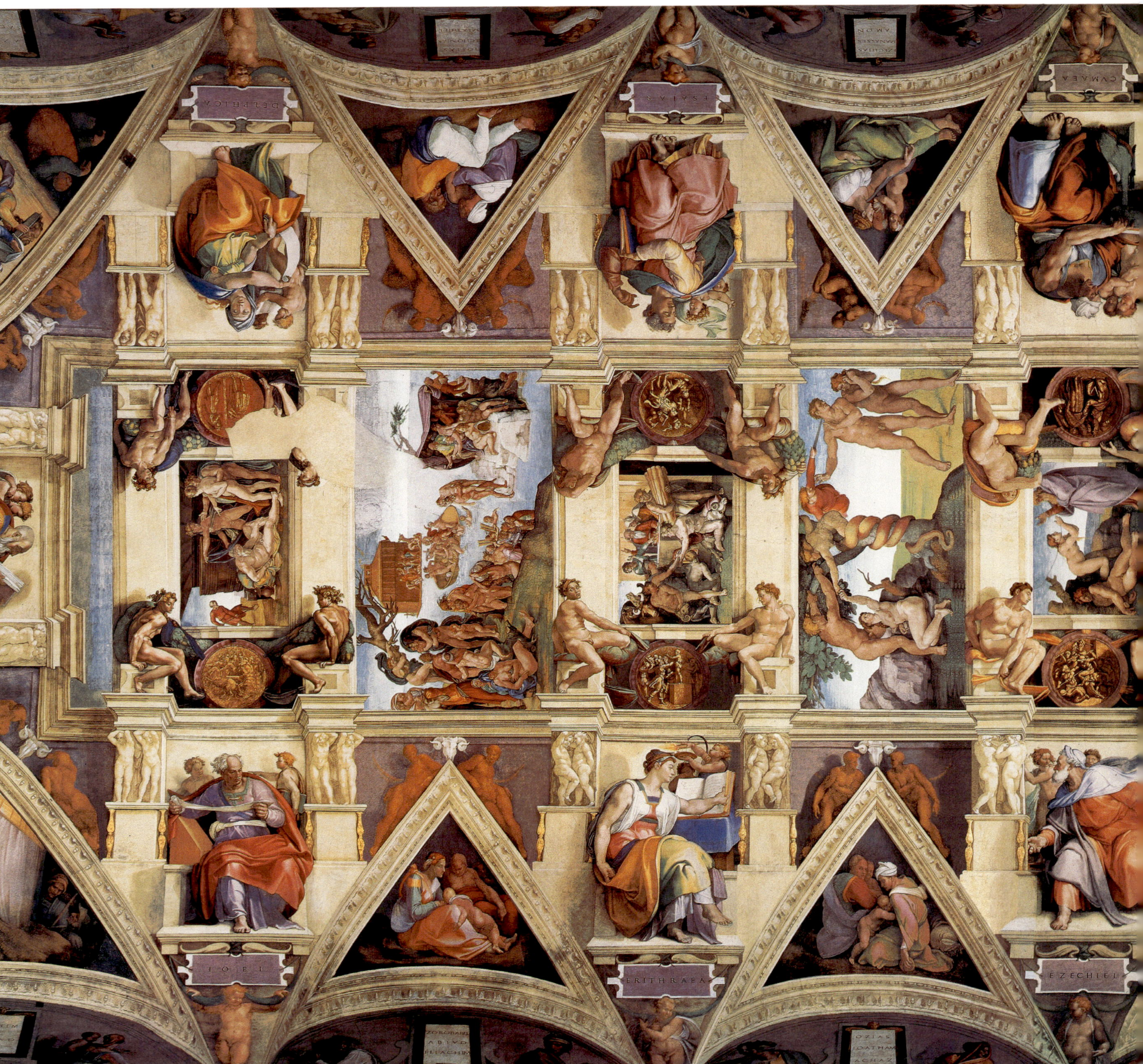
IOEL
ERITHRAEA
EZECHIEL

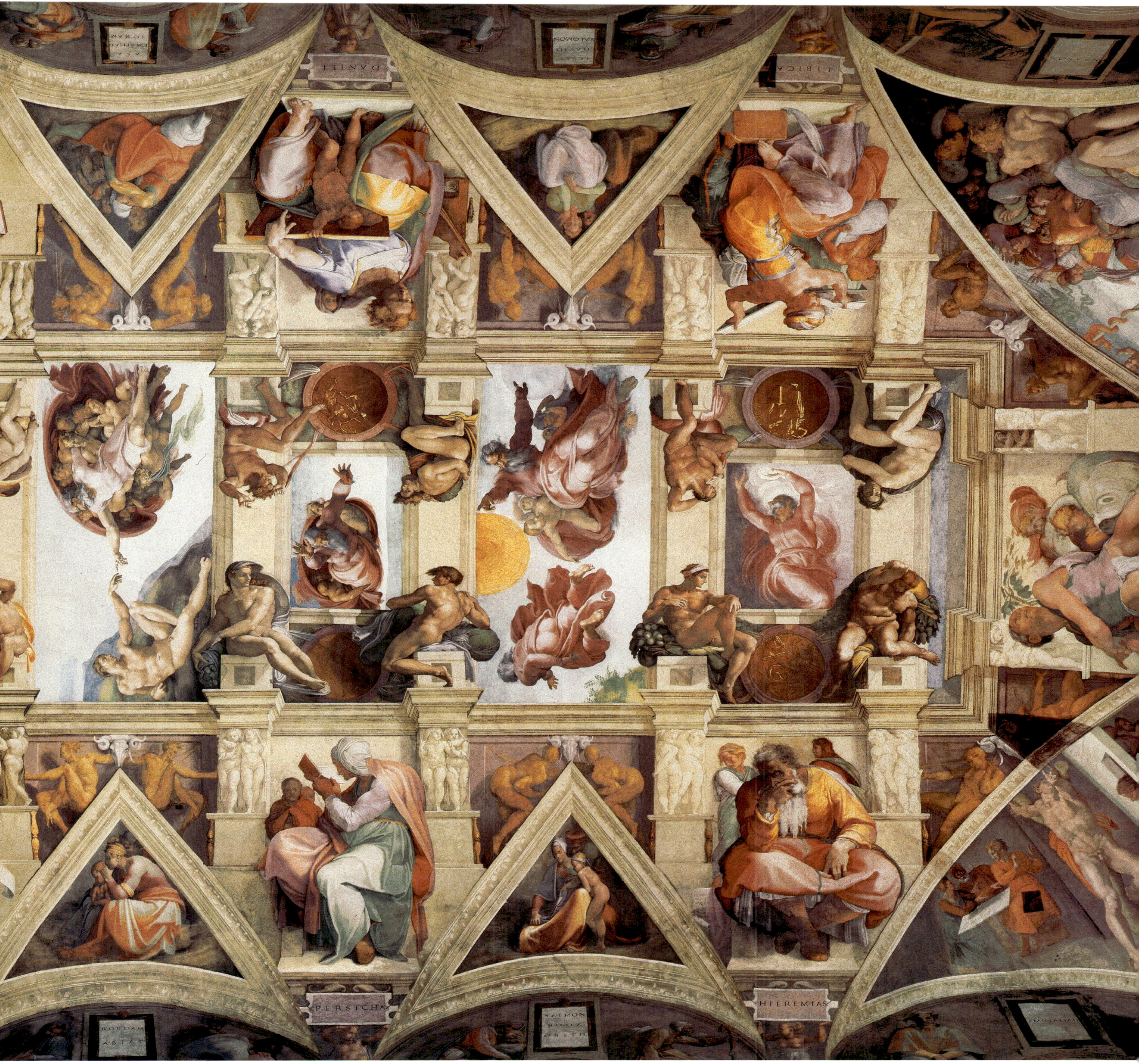
PERSICHA
HIEREMIAS

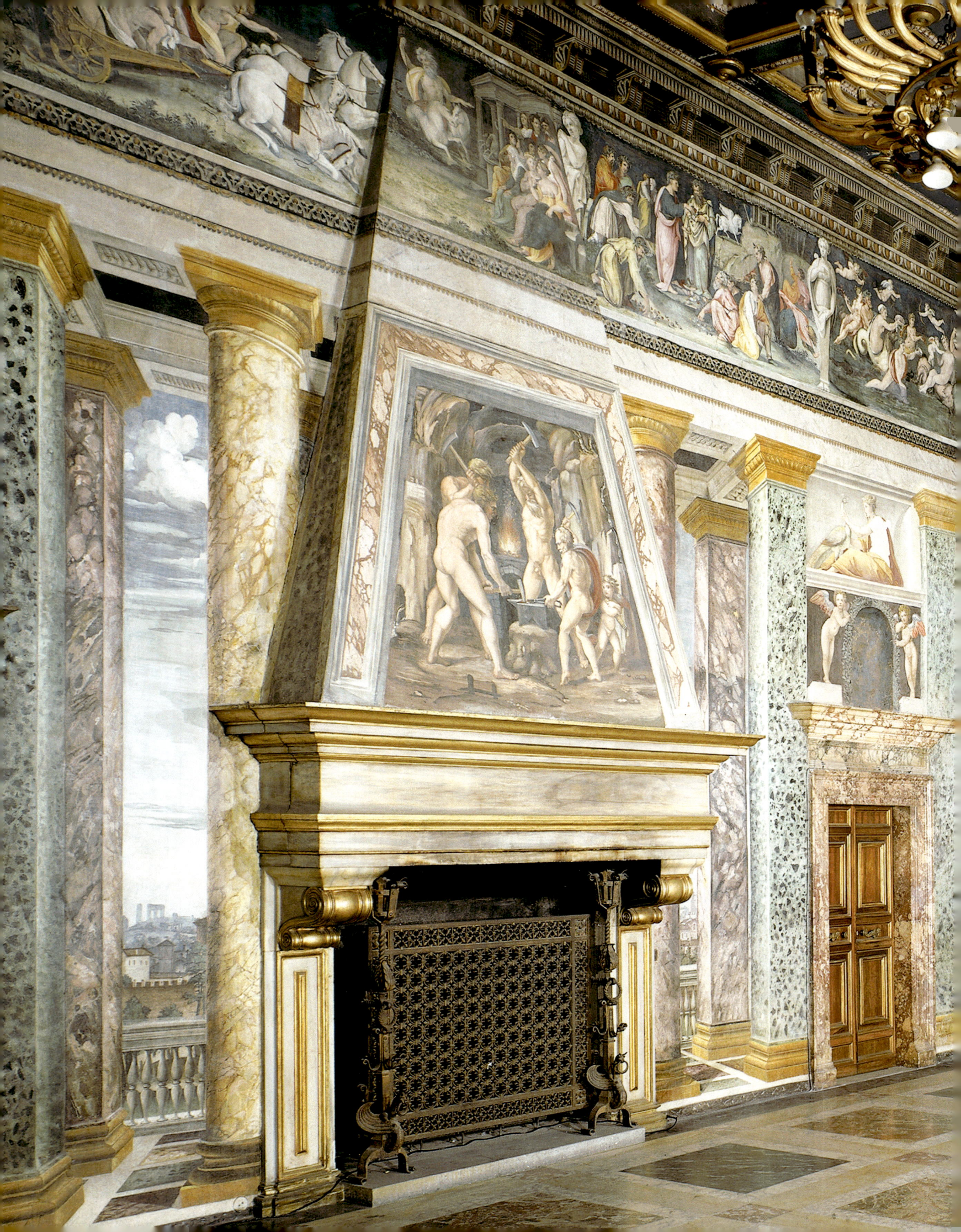

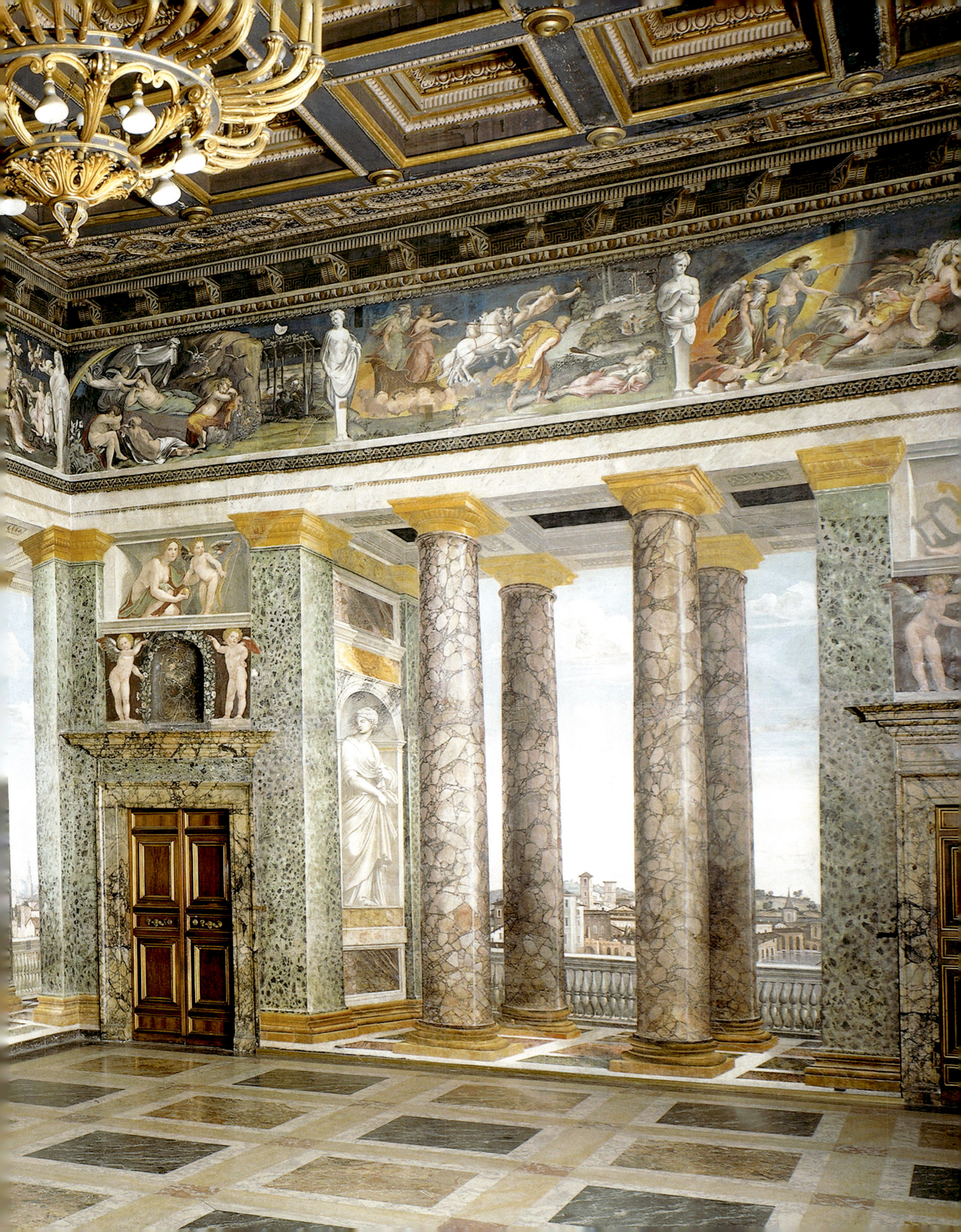

Mantegna in Mantua, Michelangelo creates his own illusory architectural framework, into which he fits his pictorial narratives from the Old Testament. Michelangelo suggests to the viewer a vault which raises the already very high chapel with a steeply curved ceiling.

Within real architecture, as well, the illusion that could be created by means of linear perspective was repeatedly used with a great degree of success, to the astonishment of the observer or even to make the reality of the thing unrecognisable. For, why should a technique that can credibly depict a three-dimensional space on a two-dimensional surface not also work in three-dimensional space, no matter how flat it may be? Donato Bramante (1444–1514), the later master builder of St Peter's Basilica in Rome, showed in the church of Santa Maria presso San Satiro in Milan just how this works (see pp. 42–43). The further away from the viewer, the more convincing the illusion becomes. And, of course, it is also an advantage to enter a space designed in this way without prior knowledge of what one is about to see.

The Venetian painter Titian probably had this same experience when he and Vasari visited the Villa Farnesina in Rome, which, from 1510, the architect and painter Baldassare Peruzzi (1481–1536) built and partly decorated. The highlight of this magnificent palace, built on top of an ancient villa, is the Sala delle Prospettive, the Hall of Perspectives (fig. pp. 24/25). Here, Peruzzi managed to create, with this illusionistic architecture, the quite disorientating impression of a huge loggia with a supposed garden view, which Vasari described by saying that "nothing more beautiful can be imagined."[4] All around, one sees a diorama, as it were, of Rome at that time. One can recognise the Arch of Septimius Severus, the Torre delle Milizie and parts of the Ospedale di Santo Spirito between the various architectural elements. In order to properly appreciate the effects of perspective, it is necessary to view the space from different viewpoints. With the whole room decorated in perspective using stucco and imitation marble, one is more than happy to fall for the illusion. According to Vasari, it was Titian who "would by no means believe that it was painted, until he had changed his point of view, when he was struck with amazement."[5] Titian would certainly have had a similar reaction if he had visited the Villa Barbaro by Andrea Palladio (1508–1580) and allowed himself to be overwhelmed by the frescoes of Paolo Veronese (1528–1588; see pp. 44–45).

◀ Previous spread
Baldassare Peruzzi, Hall of Perspectives at the Villa Farnesina, c. 1515

Illusions are one of the specialties of theatre. There, a world is created that, ideally, allows the people in the audience to recognise themselves but seen from a completely different perspective. Poets are responsible for its content; the task of ensuring that their words are also accentuated in visual form is left to stage designers and architects. In 1580, one of the most influential architects in history, Andrea Palladio, planned and built the first free-standing theatre building since antiquity, the Teatro Olimpico in Vicenza (fig. below). Andrea Palladio incorporated all his thoughts on ancient theatre into this building, right up to the sky-blue ceiling intended to evoke the illusion of an open-air theatre, as was customary during antiquity. In Palladio's time, up to eight hundred people could follow the staged spectacles from the fourteen stepped rows of seats. They saw – and still see today – a three-storey scenery flat with three portals that provide a view onto five streets. If one follows the streets with only one's eyes, one may imagine wandering down long urban canyons; but if one were actually to walk into this city of scenery, one would come up against its limits after a

▼ Andrea Palladio and Vincenzo Scamozzi, stage and scenery of the Teatro Olimpico, 1580 – 1584

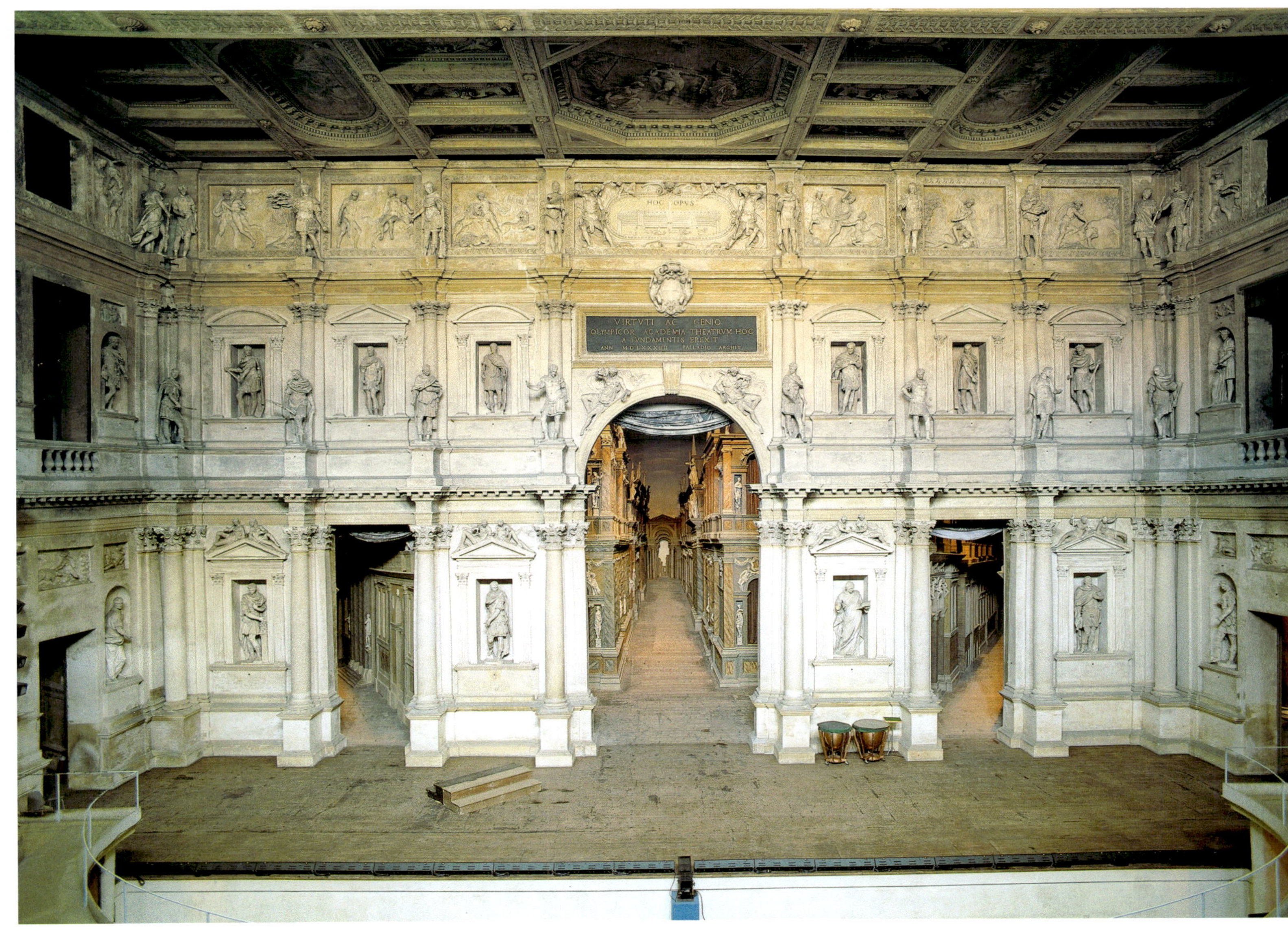

short 12 metres. Andrea Palladio and above all his successor Vincenzo Scamozzi (1548–1616) created this stage area after the Accademia Olimpica, to which Palladio belonged at the time, had acquired further building land and were thus able to enlarge the theatre. The view into this fictitious city is drawn by the raked stage floor as well as the perspective foreshortening of the houses into a distance that, in reality, does not exist. The Teatro Olimpico became a model for many theatres, from the Swedish Drottningholm to the Ekhof Theatre in Gotha, to the many small historical municipal theatres of Northern Italy.

It is likely that Francesco Borromini (1599–1667), who completed an apprenticeship as a stone sculptor in Milan, had Bramante's architectural illusion of Santa Maria presso San Satiro in mind when he took over the restoration of the Palazzo Spada in Rome in 1635. The ingenious baroque master builder, who with his complex architectural language created such astounding churches as San Carlo alle Quattro Fontane, also indulged in architectural trompe l'œil when he built a gallery in the courtyard of the Palazzo Spada (fig. right). Confusion arises as one passes through the courtyards of the palace only to come to a sudden stop before a long gallery. The barrel-vaulted colonnade, supported by double columns, ends in a further courtyard, in which a statue may be seen. One must look twice to realise that this arcade is not, as one may have initially assumed, over 20 metres long, but instead a mere eight. Estimating the real size of the statue is even more difficult. In fact, it measures only 65 centimetres. This foreshortened passage, in perfect perspective, must have been even more confusing at the time of its construction, when sunlight still shone through the thrice intersected colonnade of arches. Borromini succeeded in this trick, just like Palladio in his theatre, by elevating the floor, sinking the ceiling and making the columns continuously smaller, as the rules of a corresponding drawing in linear perspective would dictate. His great rival, Gian Lorenzo Bernini (1598–1680), certainly knew this gallery when, around 1665, he used the same illusory technique for the Scala Regia in the Vatican, completed, however, in the more monumental baroque style typical of his work (fig. p. 30).

Like theatres, churches also provide a kind of stage, one on which Holy Mass is celebrated. And here, too, illusion sometimes plays a not insignificant role – especially in the Baroque era. Churches were

▶ Francesco Borromini, Perspective Gallery, built after 1632

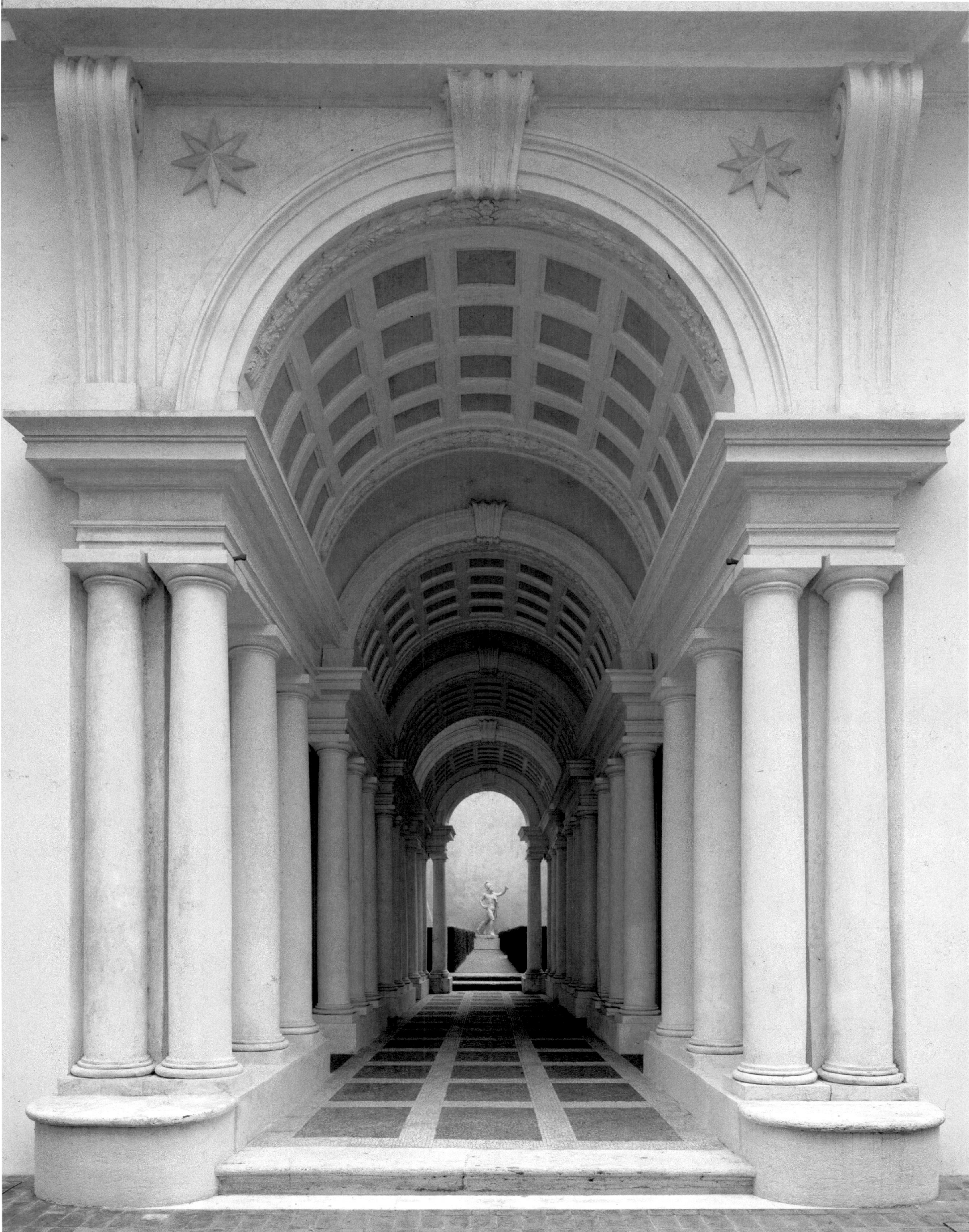

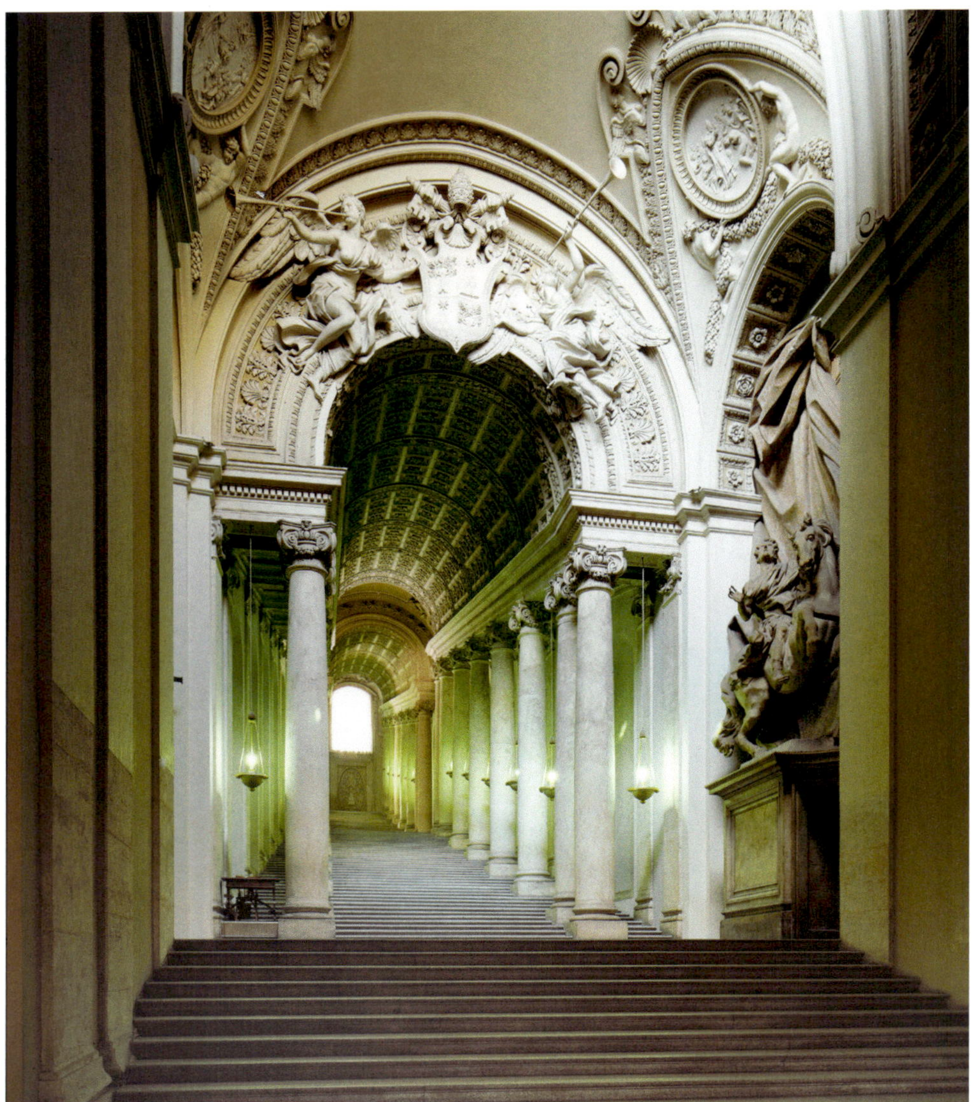

◂ Gian Lorenzo Bernini, Scala Regia, 1663–1666

well-nigh predestined for such art. In private buildings, illusionistic representations served to amuse the guests; in churches, the stakes soon rose concerning much more. Protestantism challenged the church not only on theological, spiritual and moral grounds but also, with its hostility towards sacred imagery, in the artistic arena. The response to the Reformation was the Counter-Reformation, which struck back powerfully – powerfully also in relation to visual imagery. Crucial was the visualisation of the Kingdom of God – the faithful should embrace the Good News, more through their emotions than

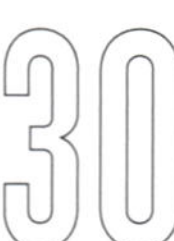

through reason, with each of their senses, so to speak. This opened up completely new possibilities for artists. People were to be emotionally overwhelmed through art and its use in churches, not didactically, but through the sensuous power of the Baroque. With church ceilings, the Counter-Reformation had found the ideal canvas for its 'propaganda'. Following Mantegna, Michelangelo and Correggio (c. 1489–1534), who was amongst the first to portray the heavenly sphere as a subject worthy of illusionist works, church ceilings became 'emotionalised'.

One of the pinnacles of *quadrature* painting, as the art of perspective ceiling painting is also known, and in terms of its programmatic use by the Counter-Reformation, is the ceiling of the Church of Sant'Ignazio in Rome, created by Andrea Pozzo (1642–1709; see pp. 46–49). As with Masaccio, the illusion of faux, painted architecture works perfectly only from a certain point, which in Sant'Ignazio – as in Florence – is especially marked on the floor. As soon as the viewpoint is changed, the illusion dissolves. Yet, as churchgoers do tend to move around, the painters needed to take this into consideration and further develop their art. So that the illusion could be seen properly from more than just a single point, they implemented multiple vanishing points for large ceilings. This meant that there was no perfect central linear perspective, yet a workable illusion, not completely correct from any one point, but convincing enough from several points.

One of the greatest masters of ceiling painting and illusionism was the Venetian Giovanni Battista Tiepolo (1696–1770), who created important fresco cycles in Venice and Northern Italy, such as in I Gesuati and the Church of the Scalzi, as well as in many palaces from Udine to Venice and Milan. In 1750, the Würzburg Prince-Bishop Carl Philipp von Greiffenclau was able to lure Tiepolo across the Alps for the first time, not least through means of the prospect of an extremely princely fee, where he was to improve upon the Würzburg Residence of Balthasar Neumann with his art (see pp. 50–51). With the palace's stairway fresco as its high point, the great era of illusionistic ceiling and architectural painting came slowly to an end. In classicism, which can seem a little cool in comparison, the urge for illusion and deception ceased to play a major role – apart from in some theatres and opera houses, where illusion was and remains, simply, a part of the programme.

Styles change, as does society, its needs, and its uses and access to art. Illusionistic gimmicks became history, at the latest, with the Bauhaus and the developments that followed on from there. It was not until the 1970s that walls began, once more, to be designed to include experiments in perspective. Influenced by the Mexican murals of Diego Rivera (1886–1957), José Clemente Orozco (1883–1949) and David Alfaro Siqueiros (1896–1974), artists in the USA began seemingly to break open entire building facades and show what lay within. Or they broke through walls optically, as in the case of Warren Edward Johnson (b. 1938), known as Blue Sky, in order to offer a glimpse at a virtual landscape. The 15 × 23 metre mural *Tunnelvision* (fig. below) was created in 1975 as one of the first of its kind in the USA, in Columbia, South Carolina, on the wall of a bank. It can still be seen there today. In the 1970s, the USA launched a national programme which funded around 2,500 murals in public spaces. Art was to be brought out of the museums and into the streets. The advantage of working with entire

▶ Richard Haas, *Homage to Cincinnatus*, 1983

▼ Blue Sky, *Tunnelvision*, 1975

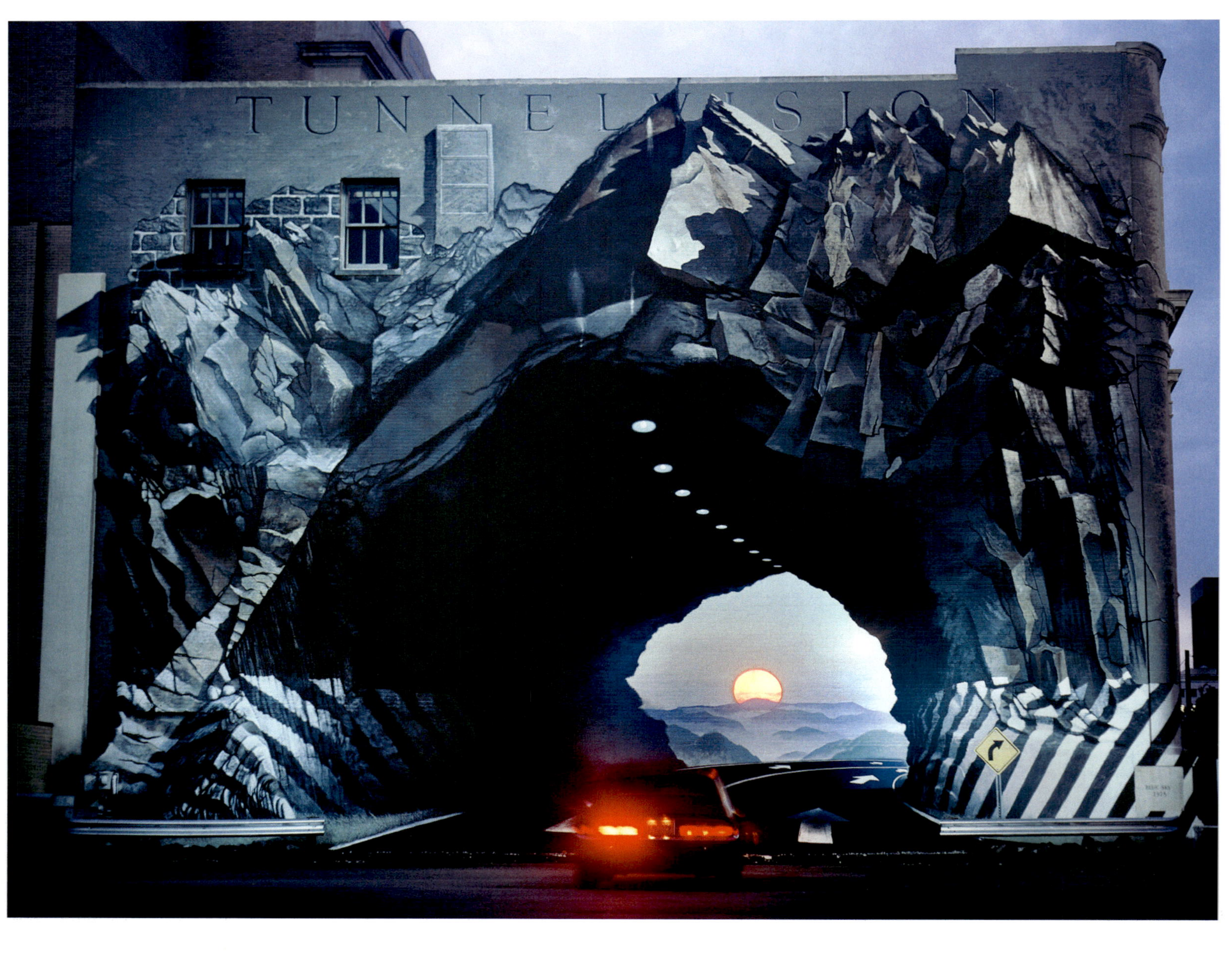

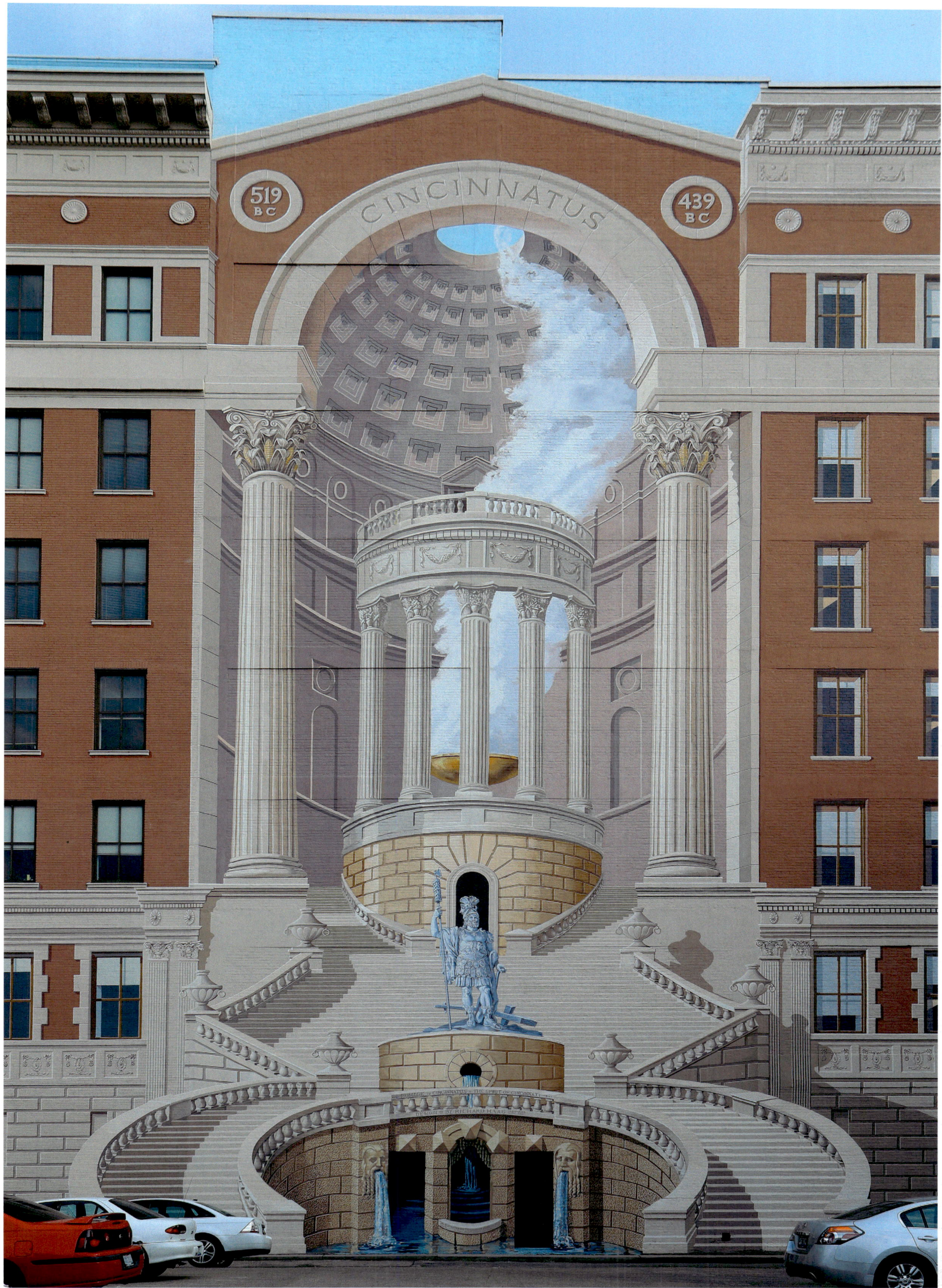

519 BC
CINCINNATUS
439 BC
HOMAGE TO CINCINNATUS · THE SPIRIT OF CINCINNATI
DESIGNED BY RICHARD HAAS

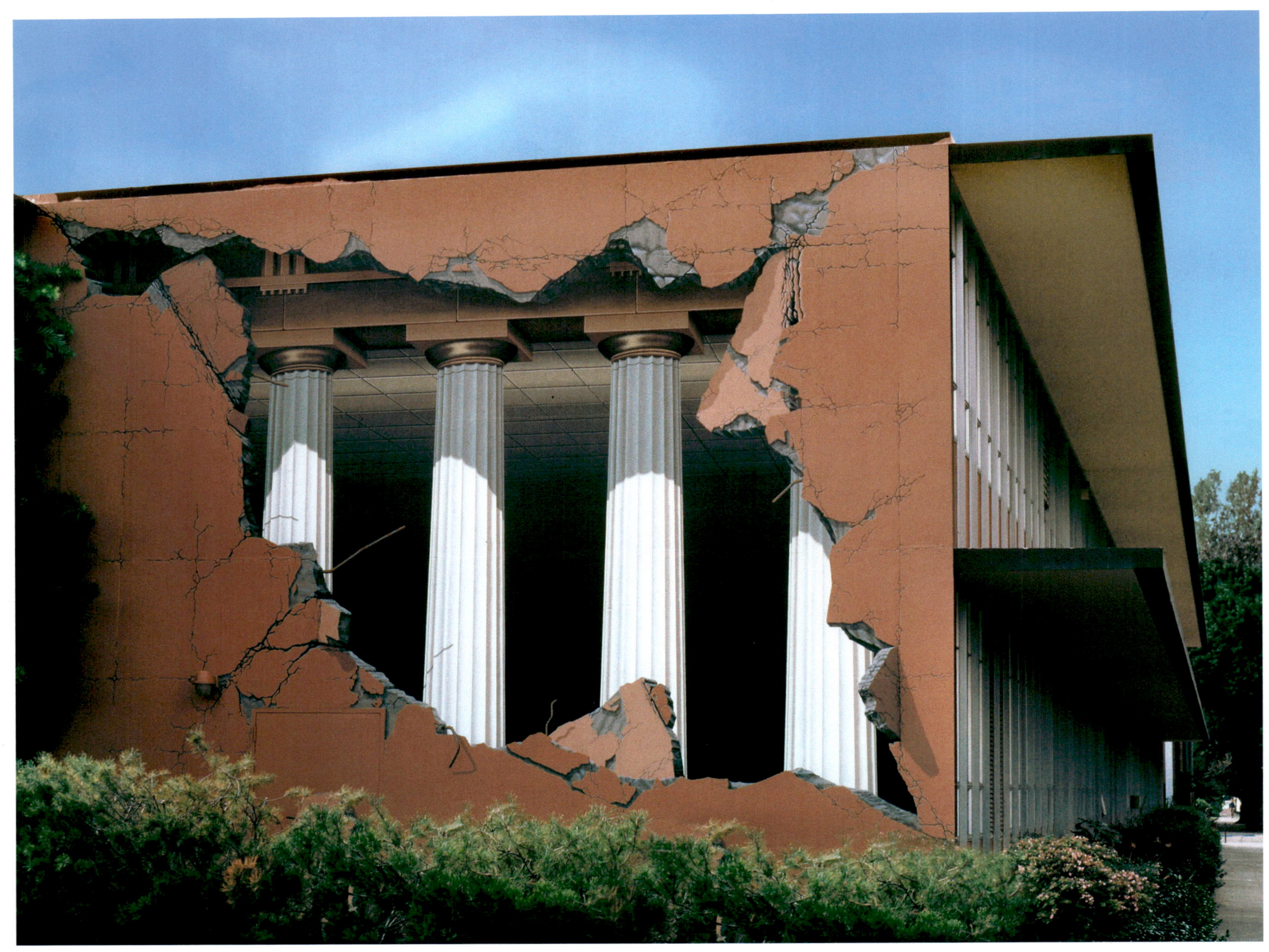

▲ John Pugh, Taylor Hall, California State University, Chico, 1981

walls is the possibility of being able to create life-size depictions of larger objects.

This is what Richard Haas (b. 1936) did with his desire to create the impression of realistic architecture through his murals. In *Homage to Cincinnatus* from 1983 (fig. p. 33), the artist references the ancient Roman statesman whose lifestyle made him a symbol of simplicity, humility and virtue. The Society of the Cincinnati was founded in 1783 to preserve these ideals, ideals for which the movement for American independence also strove. The society's first president was George

Washington. The city of Cincinnati, Ohio, where Richard Haas created the mural, was, in fact, named after the order and not the statesman of antiquity. In 2015, the seven-storey mural was restored with the help of the artist, having become one of the most beloved symbols of the city. Haas created many more murals but only one outside the USA. This was created in 1984 in Munich's Zwingerstrasse which ended up being covered by a building constructed in 2010.

For many painters, being able to create work in public spaces is, above all, a powerful form for communicating with the public. Ultimately, the principle today is still the same as the one pursued by the Jesuits in the Counter-Reformation: People should be overwhelmed. People desire to be overwhelmed and beguiled. The methods and motives become ever more sophisticated and the results correspondingly ever more impressive. One great master of illusion is the American John Pugh (b. 1957; fig. left). He succeeds in drawing the viewer into the picture through the means of perfectly realised trompe l'œil effects, while telling stories, which, after the first surprise, inspire further reflection. Pugh designs his pictures in such a way that, following the initial sense of astonishment, there is a second level to discover which draws one still deeper into the picture. Beyond this, he also wants to create a sense of community. First of all, murals are bound to a certain location and, because of their size alone, have an element of attraction, an attraction that draws the attention of observers within the context of their actual environment. This fact, coupled with a sharpened perception, is intended to evoke something of a sense of community in the environment. A mural "can link people together, stimulate a sense of pride within the community, and introduce the viewer to new ideas and perspectives."[6]

The Italian Manuel di Rita (b. 1980), known as Peeta (fig. p. 37), also pursues the creation of new perspectives and questioning perception, albeit with a completely different pictorial language. In contrast to classic trompe l'œil, which invests existing walls with a new reality, Peeta works abstractly. With his geometric forms, he not only unsettles the architectural principles of support and load, but simultaneously breaks up inherent, rigid points of view. Peeta's walls seem to burst under the force of his geometric forms. One hardly recognises where the real walls, corners and edges actually run. They seem to have dissolved completely in order to make room for his new structures. As Peeta himself puts it, a "temporary interruption of normality" emerges.[7] His forms seem to reach out from the wall into their surroundings and thus create a new fictitious space, one that our perception proves itself all too willing to accept. Even those forms from the real buildings, which the artist leaves visible, such as doors or windows, develop a dynamic life of their own and detach themselves from their previous contexts. Peeta breaks open the walls, and the completely unexpected emerges. It seems as if a completely different inner life had been hidden within these buildings, of which one had no idea before, previous to Peeta's 'treatment'. The painter seems to have given buildings a new structure, one that separates them completely from their original essence. This new structure, however, seems so complex that the artist himself is unable to completely expose it.

For centuries, painted walls have exerted a special allure. They cast a spell over the viewer, who is then seduced into giving in to illusion, and to being inspired, knowing full well that what they see in front of them cannot be real – at least, probably not … It is an art of seduction that, at least initially, demands nothing from the viewer other than the pure pleasure of looking and recognising.

▸ Peeta, Zehntstrasse, Mannheim, 2019

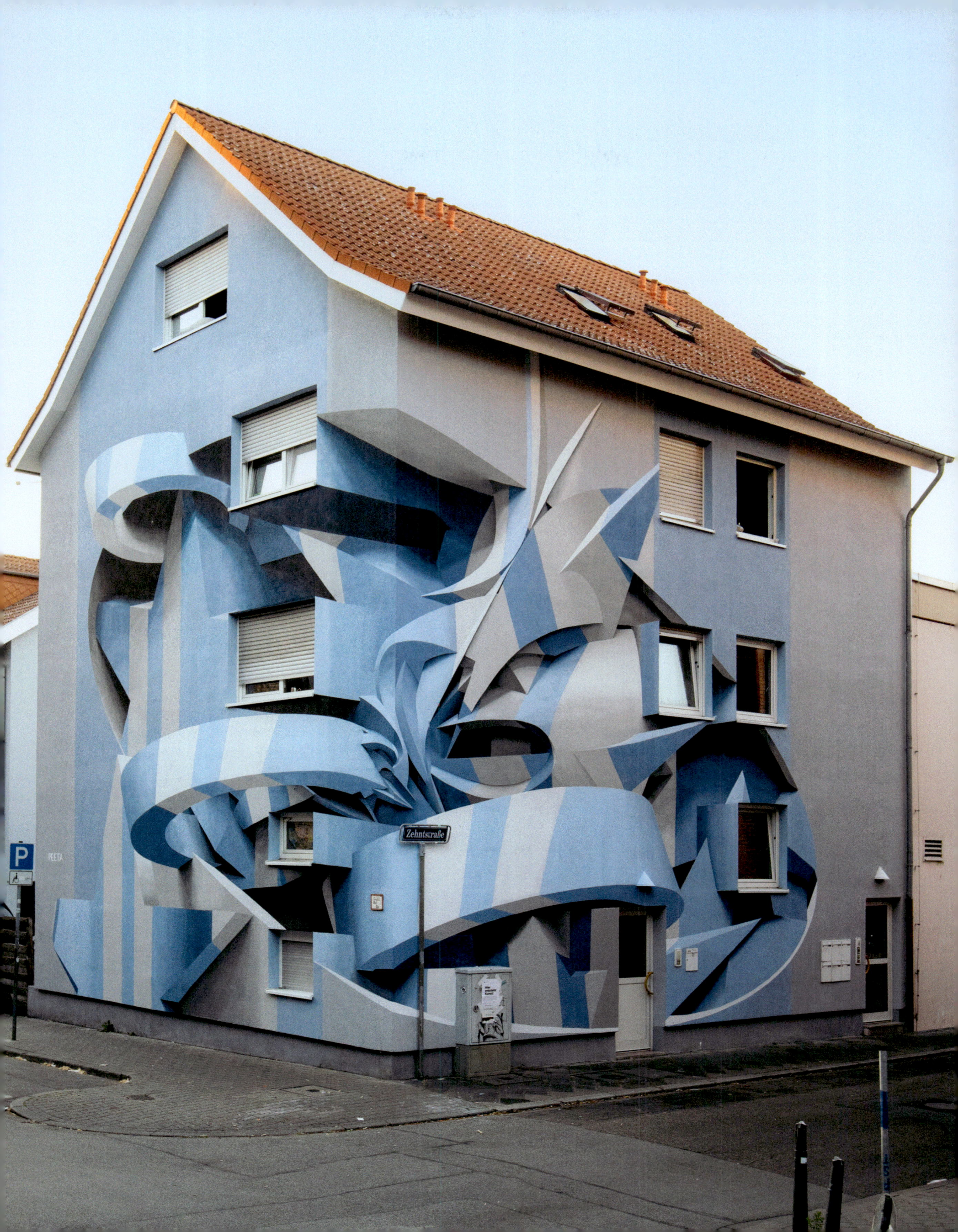
Zehntstraße
P

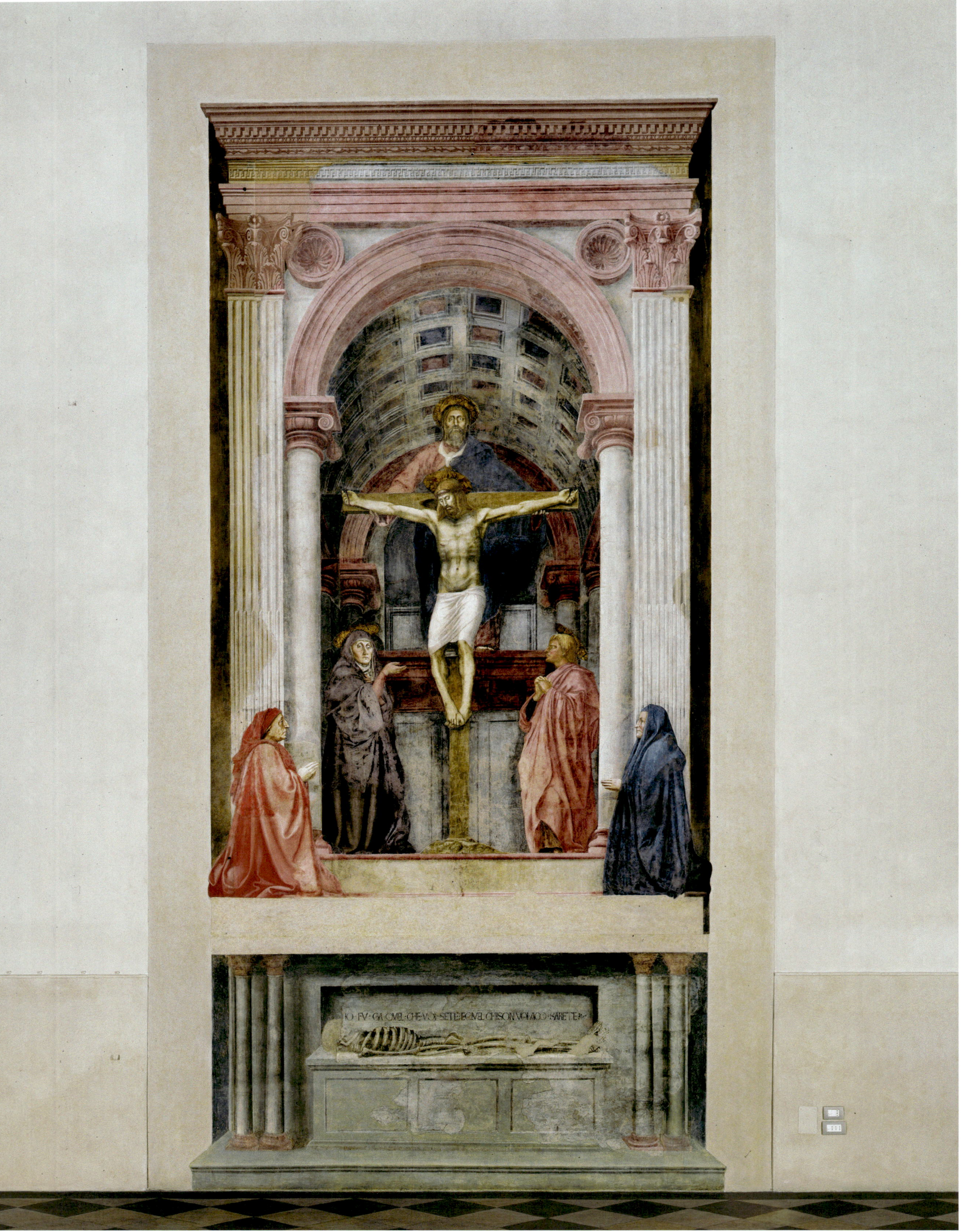
IO·FV·GIA·QVEL·CHE·VOI·SETE·E·QVEL·CH'IO·SON·VOI·ANCO·SARETE

Masaccio
Holy Trinity, c. 1427

Fresco, 667 × 317 cm
Santa Maria Novella, Florence

The earliest three-dimensional image that we know today was painted by a close friend of Filippo Brunelleschi, Tommaso di ser Giovanni Cassai, known as Masaccio (1401–1428), who created a chapel with a view of the *Holy Trinity* for the church of Santa Maria Novella around 1427. In front of the observer the space of a chapel seems to open up, in the centre of which is the crucified Christ, God the Father and a dove, the symbolic representation of the Holy Spirit. Beside the cross stand John the Apostle and the Virgin Mary, who, with a simple gesture, draws our attention to Christ. In front of the supposed chapel, the two donors who commissioned it kneel on the left and right.

Viewing the fresco today, we are no longer deceived by this alleged chapel. We understand and recognise immediately that it is a flat wall. At the time of its creation, however, things were obviously somewhat different. The people looked into the illusionistic chapel and saw a space flanked by pilasters and columns, the vaulted coffered ceiling of which draws the eye into the depths of the room. It is very likely that Brunelleschi designed the architectural template. Masaccio applied the rules of linear perspective in an exemplary manner. Using a vanishing point and intersecting vanishing lines, he constructed a system of lines that he scratched into the fresh plaster and which is still, to some extent, visible today.

With illusionistic spaces such as these, what counts is the surprise of the observer, and this would have been achieved here, since something comparable had never been seen before, neither the architecture nor this kind of linear perspectival representation. Masaccio's intention, however, was not to entertain the public; quite the contrary, he wanted to show the story being depicted as realistically as possible in order to make the Passion of Christ even more tangible.

To further enhance the three-dimensional effect of the chapel space, Masaccio positioned it above a niche framed by short columns, in which a sarcophagus may be seen, upon which a skeleton seems to lie. Here, too, the faithful would have looked a second time in amazement, for it was not uncommon for some priests to display such real desiccated corpses for the edification of their flock. Masaccio's skeleton surpassed everything that had ever been painted before: It is, in fact, the first skeleton painted according to all the rules of anatomy and illusionist art, more than half a century before Leonardo da Vinci's anatomical drawings. People would have been frightened by their initial sight of it, especially since one must not forget the original freshness of the colours and thus the high degree of realism. The not exactly encouraging inscription on the sarcophagus, "I once was what you are and what I am you also shall be", will have done the rest.

Of course, even then, viewers quickly understood that no new chapel had been built here, but that they were dealing with an illusion. But even in his *Lives of the Artists*, Giorgio Vasari still reports on Masaccio's chapel, which after more than a century was already obscured by newer altars, but still gave him the impression that the wall had been "pierced".[8]

Andrea Mantegna

Camera degli Sposi, 1461–1474

Fresco, room floor area c. 8 × 8 m,
height c. 7 m
Palazzo Ducale, Mantua

▶ **Facing page and frontispiece**

Andrea Mantegna (1431–1506), like many of his peers, was an admirer of antiquity. He knew coffered ceilings, and those with other classical designs, from historical buildings, such as the Pantheon in Rome, and the churches of Brunelleschi in Florence. In Mantua, as court painter to the Gonzaga, he was also responsible for the 'image' of the family. Between 1461 and 1474, in the course of these responsibilities, he took charge of painting the Camera degli Sposi, or 'bridal chamber', the ceiling design of which was to fundamentally change architectural painting.

The name of the room is somewhat misleading as it is no romantic bower, but instead a prestigious reception hall kept for official occasions. The entire space is covered with a painted, illusionistic architecture that appears to open towards the exterior landscape. In the arcades represented on the walls, the family members of the Gonzaga are immortalised, with the room's pictorial decorations also serving the allegorical glorification of the family. Of course, the guests will have immediately noticed that not only the figures but also the architecture of the arcades are only painted, as perfect and convincing as the illusion may be. If one looks up to the ceiling, however, it is all too easy to lose sense of whether what one is looking at is in fact all just paint. The faux arcades merge into vaulted ribs that cover the entire ceiling. The painted figurative designs look as if they are made of stucco. In the centre, the ceiling seems to open up, similar to the Roman Pantheon, revealing a view of a partially clouded sky – with the essential difference, however, that the aperture in Rome is real. The height of the room, some 7 metres, is not insignificant for the success of the illusion. The room appears even higher due to the painted arches, while the illusion becomes all the more credible the further the distance between the artwork and its observer becomes. The ostensible ceiling opening is surrounded by a stone balustrade, giving the impression that there is a kind of roof terrace above. On the balustrade, nine putti clamber about (the arm of a tenth is just visible), logically, painted from an extreme angle as if seen from below. Their plentiful rolls of baby fat help to underline the foreshortening effect. To increase the illusion of the oculus, a flowerpot balances over the edge and is only prevented from falling by a wooden stick placed across the parapet. A peacock and five young ladies complete the scene, happily observing the fine company in the room below. The atmosphere on this roof terrace exudes quite a merry impression, with the figures expressing the family's claim to sovereignty by playfully reinterpreting classical insignia; sceptre and orb are replaced by a stick and apple, and one of the putti holds a laurel wreath over his own head. This casual treatment is an allusion to the good reputation that the government of the Gonzaga enjoyed, or at least believed itself to enjoy. The effect of the ceiling is quite astonishing, and it takes a few moments to see it for the illusion that it is. The supposed stucco moulding is so perfectly executed through a use of grisaille, with its effects of light and shadow, that we doubt ourselves all over again.

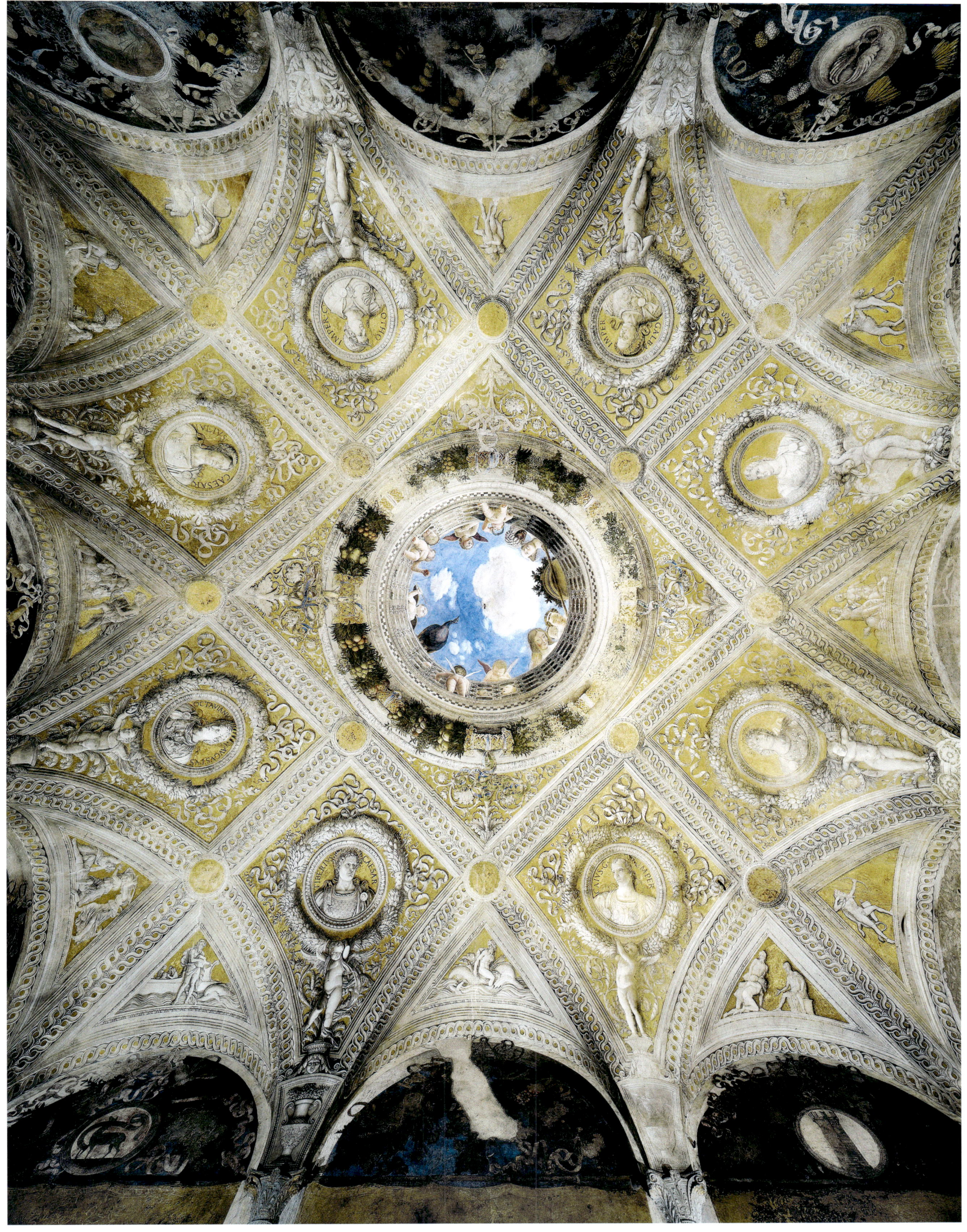

Donato Bramante

Apse of Santa Maria presso San Satiro, Milan, c. 1480

Santa Maria presso San Satiro is a complex of several sacred structures in the centre of Milan, the oldest part of which, a small central building, dates back to the 9th century. This building, dedicated to St Satyrus, was to be extended by Bramante to include a Marian chapel and a sacristy. The structure's history has been somewhat lost to us in its entirety, but it is clear that there was, at some point, a change in orientation, with the former nave becoming instead the transept and the new nave ending at what was previously the south wall. This, however, created the problem of a lack of space for the new choir apse, as there was a thoroughfare behind the church over which nothing could be built. Put bluntly, the future architect of St Peter's Basilica, the largest church in all of Christendom, was left with a space of no more than 90 centimetres for the apse. Bramante shone, however, coming up with an ingenious solution that is still striking today. Why should a technique that can so credibly reproduce a three-dimensional space on a two-dimensional surface not also work in three-dimensional space? Even if the space available is only 90 centimetres deep.

One enters the church from the north and looks down its three naves into the choir, which seems to have a depth of three arcades and is covered by a coffered barrel vault. Walking through the church, which is somewhat small with its length of only 30 metres, even an attentive visitor would fail to notice anything unusual until almost directly in front of the altar, where they would notice that there is in fact no deep apse opening up before them, but that instead the church ends abruptly. The choir apse, which according to the original plans should have been almost 10 metres deep, was shrunk to less than a metre by Bramante. The ingenious architect and 'artist of illusion', with his arcades, niches and the painted, coffered ceiling, succeeded in creating one of the first – and still one of the most amazing – architectural trompe l'œils that follows all the rules of linear perspective and which, even with today's powerful camera technology, is hard to recognise.

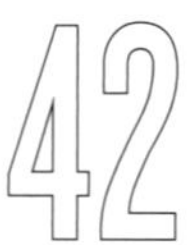

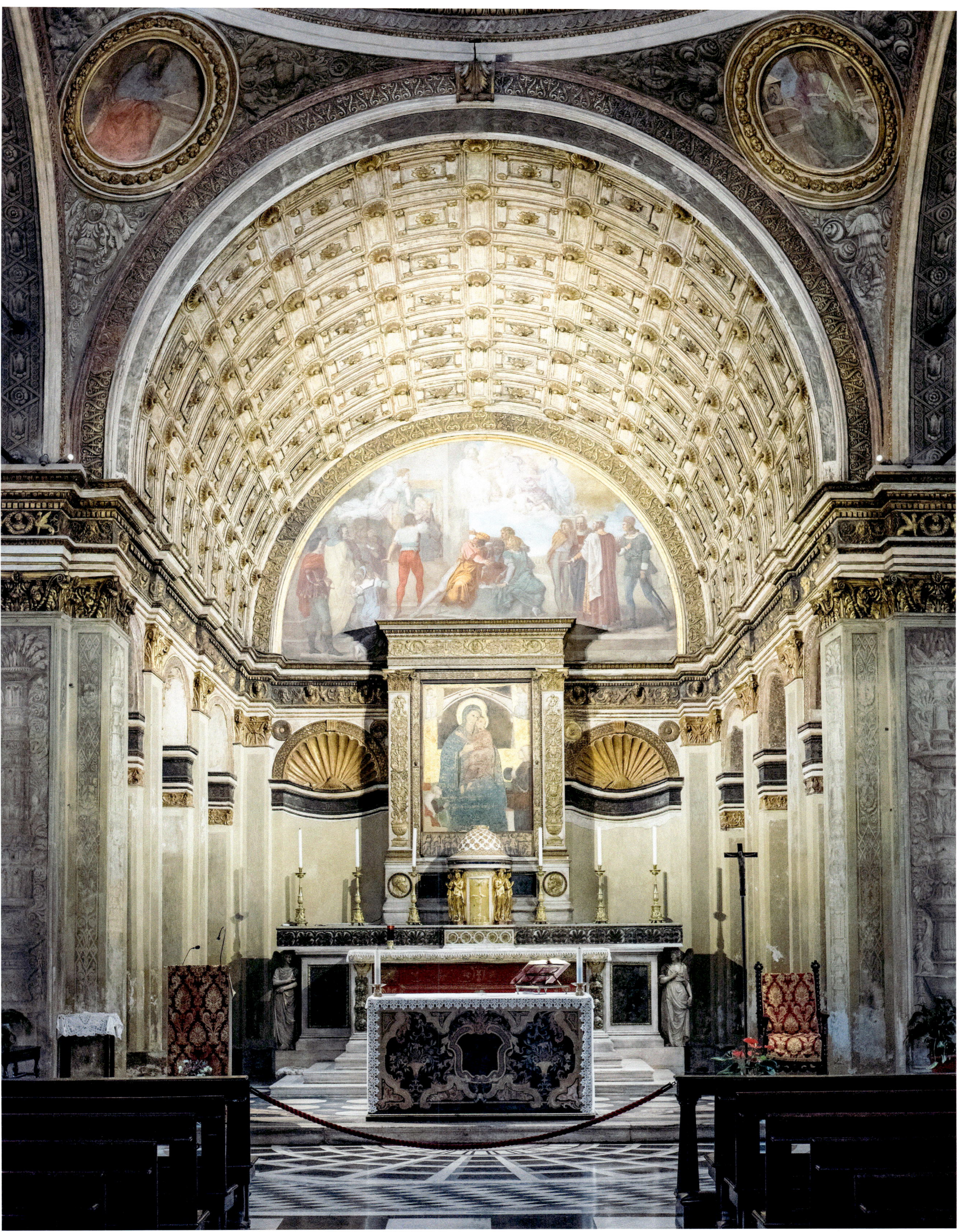

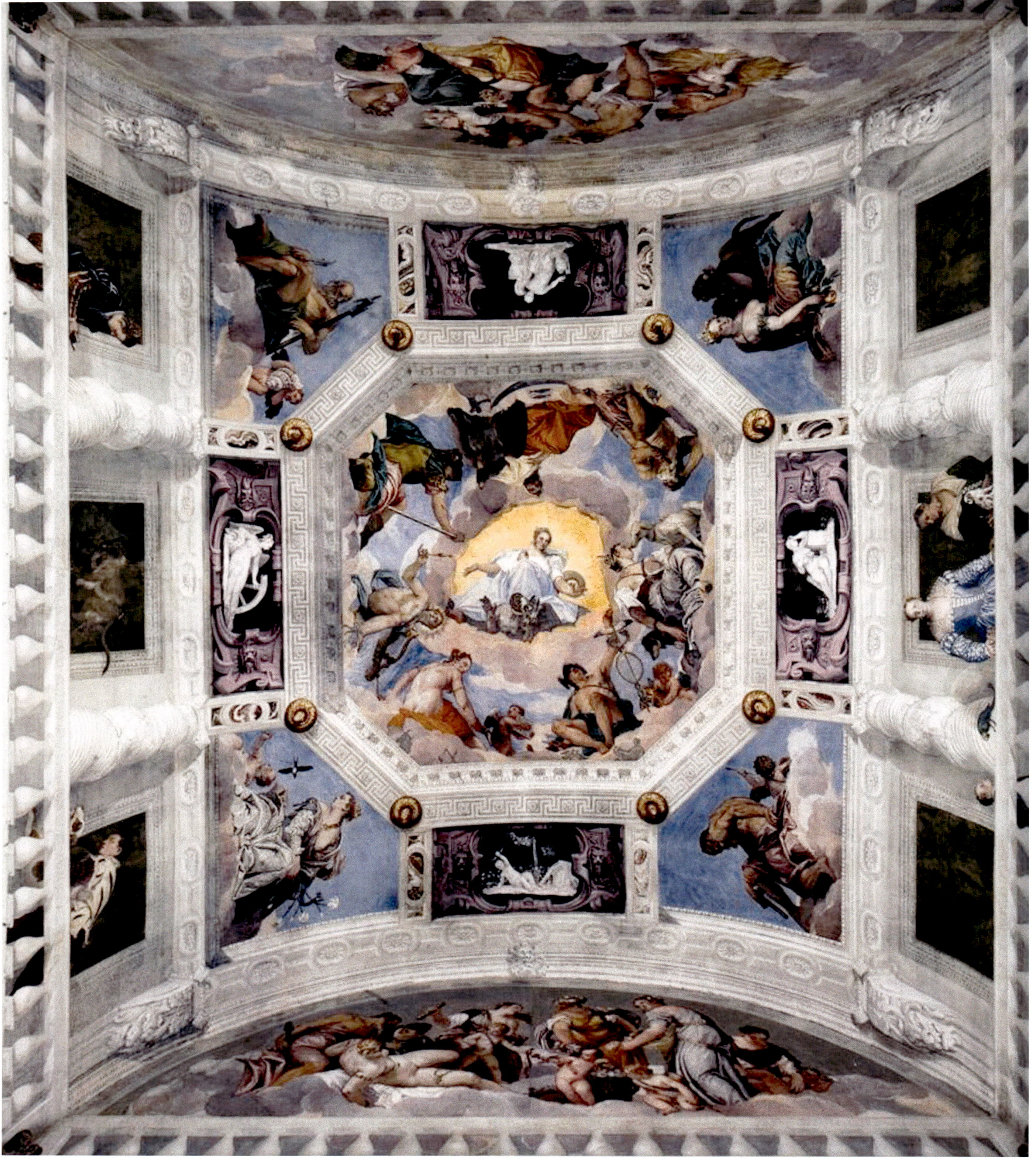

Paolo Veronese

Fresco cycle for Andrea Palladio's Villa Barbaro at Maser, c. 1561

From 1554 to 1558, at Maser in the Veneto, Andrea Palladio (1508–1580) built one of his famous villas for his friend and patron Daniele Barbaro and Barbaro's brother Marcantonio – possibly his most famous villa. At that time, these villas served as both a retreat and prestigious country estate for wealthy Venetians, while also functioning as the centre of a well-organised agricultural industry, modelled on the 'villa rustica' of antiquity. Villa Barbaro is particularly special because it involved two masters working together at the height of their creativity: Alongside Palladio, in around 1561, the painter Paolo Veronese (1528–1588) created one of the most important fresco cycles in the Veneto here, an extraordinary artistic creation which remains an example to many artists.

Veronese designed six rooms in the 'piano nobile' of the villa with such wit and lightness of touch that, at times, one hardly knows what is real and what is painted. It is a constant interplay between architecture, stucco and painting, as if one were observing an ongoing contest between reality and illusion. In the central vestibule, between the actual windows and balustrades, are painted 'vistas' onto illusionist landscapes, which at the same time preserve a relationship to the surrounding region. The columns which flank the doors – with their real frames and gables – are also only frescoes, which, let us not forget, also happen to be a lot cheaper than building real columns. Amidst both the real and the illusionistic architecture, figures appear here and there, seemingly entering through doorways, peering around corners or even hiding between pairs of painted columns. And as if that were not extraordinary enough, in niches along the wall, an array of assorted weaponry, standards and medals are to be found, as well as dogs and cats, and even old shoes and brooms. The house gives the impression of being frantically busy, even if it happens that nobody is present.

In the largest room, the Sala dell'Olimpo, Veronese's interplay with illusion takes a step further still, extending up to the ceiling where the ancient world of the gods is gathered. Below, behind the surrounding parapet, life-size figures in contemporary dress can be seen, amongst them a young man, completely immersed in his reading, and what seems to be the lady of the house, who, accompanied by her maid, looks off to the right. Harmony plays an important role in the architecture of the villa as well as in its decoration: harmony between inside and out, illusion and reality, the profane and the sacred and finally between Christianity and ancient paganism, as brought together in this Hall of Olympus. It is an ideal image of the Renaissance, which felt itself bound to the ideas and ideals of antiquity, but was nevertheless anchored in the Christian faith, as can be seen in the villa's Stanza della Lucerna. In Venetian painting, in particular, a lightness of harmony seems to predominate, despite everything, even in the crisis-ridden times of the Reformation and all its political upheavals.

Andrea Pozzo

Dome and nave frescoes of Sant'Ignazio, Rome, 1685/1694

▶ **Facing page and overleaf**

One of the highlights of *quadratura*, another term for illusionistic ceiling painting, can be found in the Church of Sant'Ignazio in Rome, completed in 1662. It is the second Jesuit church in Rome, after the mother church Il Gesù, and is dedicated to Ignatius of Loyola (1491–1556), the founder of the order, who was canonised in 1622. For reasons of cost, construction of the new building dragged on for quite some time, and in the end, it could not be completed as originally planned. The reason was not only a lack of money, however, but also – and above all – the neighbouring Dominicans, who protested against the large dome, claiming that its size would block the light from their library.

The architect, painter and Jesuit lay brother Andrea Pozzo (1642–1709) came up with a brilliant, inexpensive and very neighbourly solution: He painted the dome instead of building it. Pozzo designed the mock cupola to face the entrance of the church, so that when entering what is one of Rome's largest churches, one has, at least briefly, the impression of an immense crossing dome. Pozzo was so successful in this that he was then commissioned to create a fresco to decorate the entirety of the nave. The theme of the ceiling is the apotheosis of the order's founder and of the missionary successes of the Jesuits, which had been founded in 1534. Similar to Correggio, in Parma, one and a half centuries earlier, Pozzo opened up the church roof for the faithful and presented them with a view of an almost infinite sky. But unlike Correggio, whose faux architecture ended with the cupola, Pozzo continued his construction a few storeys higher. It does not end on the level where the actual ceiling construction ends, but instead continues the church's real architecture upwards – in bold foreshortened form – through the medium of paint. The view seems almost to shoot up into the air, as one perceives an almost unimaginably high space which finally opens onto the infinity of the Kingdom of Heaven.

Andrea Pozzo was not only successful as an architect and painter – in 1703, Emperor Leopold I called him to Vienna, where he rebuilt the city's Jesuit Church and also created a magnificent mock dome for it – he also wrote a two-volume textbook (*Perspectiva pictorum atque architectorum*) as an introduction into perspective, architectural painting and the science of illusionistic architecture. The work, published in Latin in 1693 and 1700, was immediately translated into every major European language. It was even translated into Chinese in 1729, which may say more about the international network of the Jesuit Order than of the interest the Chinese felt for illusionistic architectural painting.

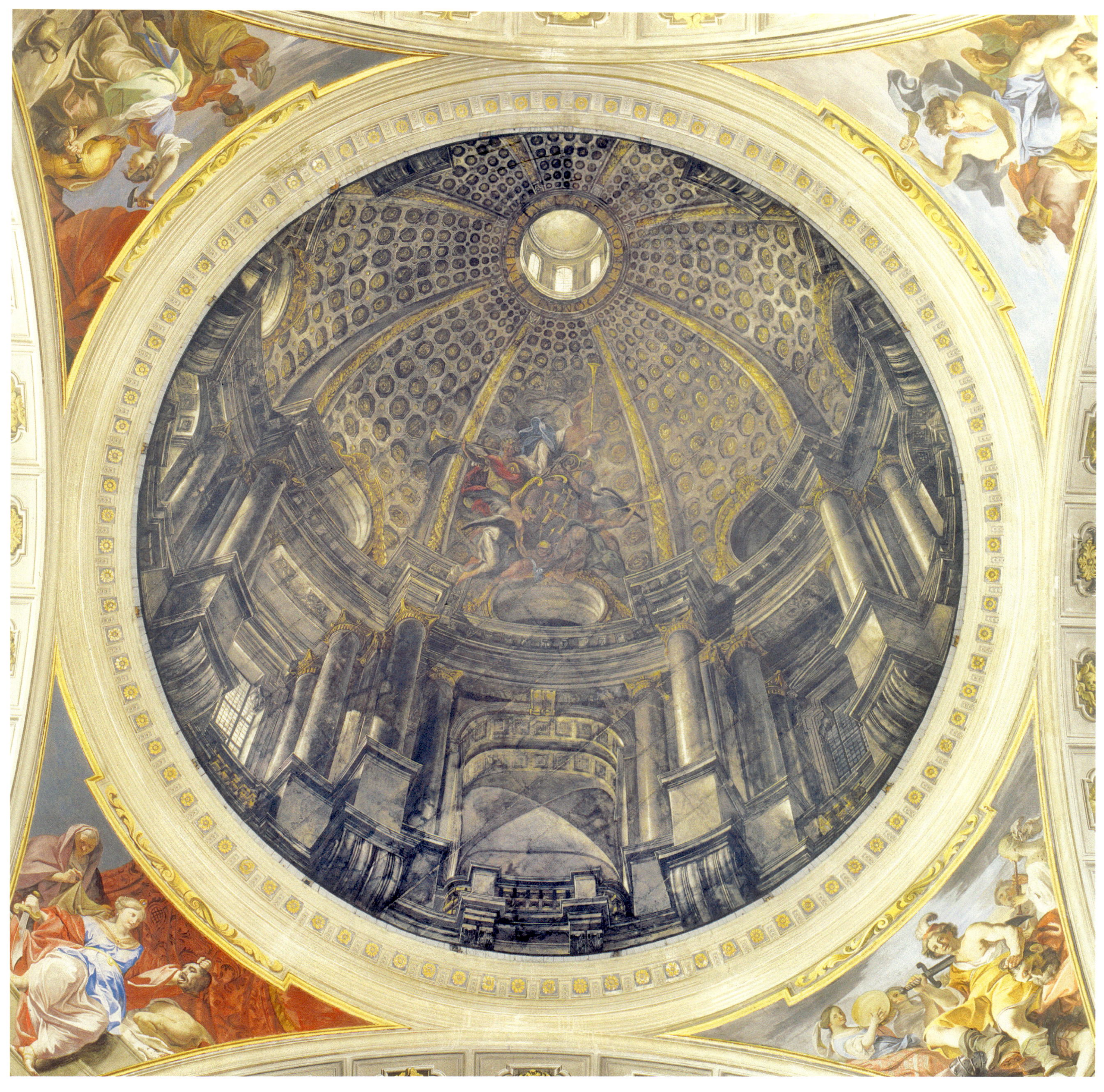

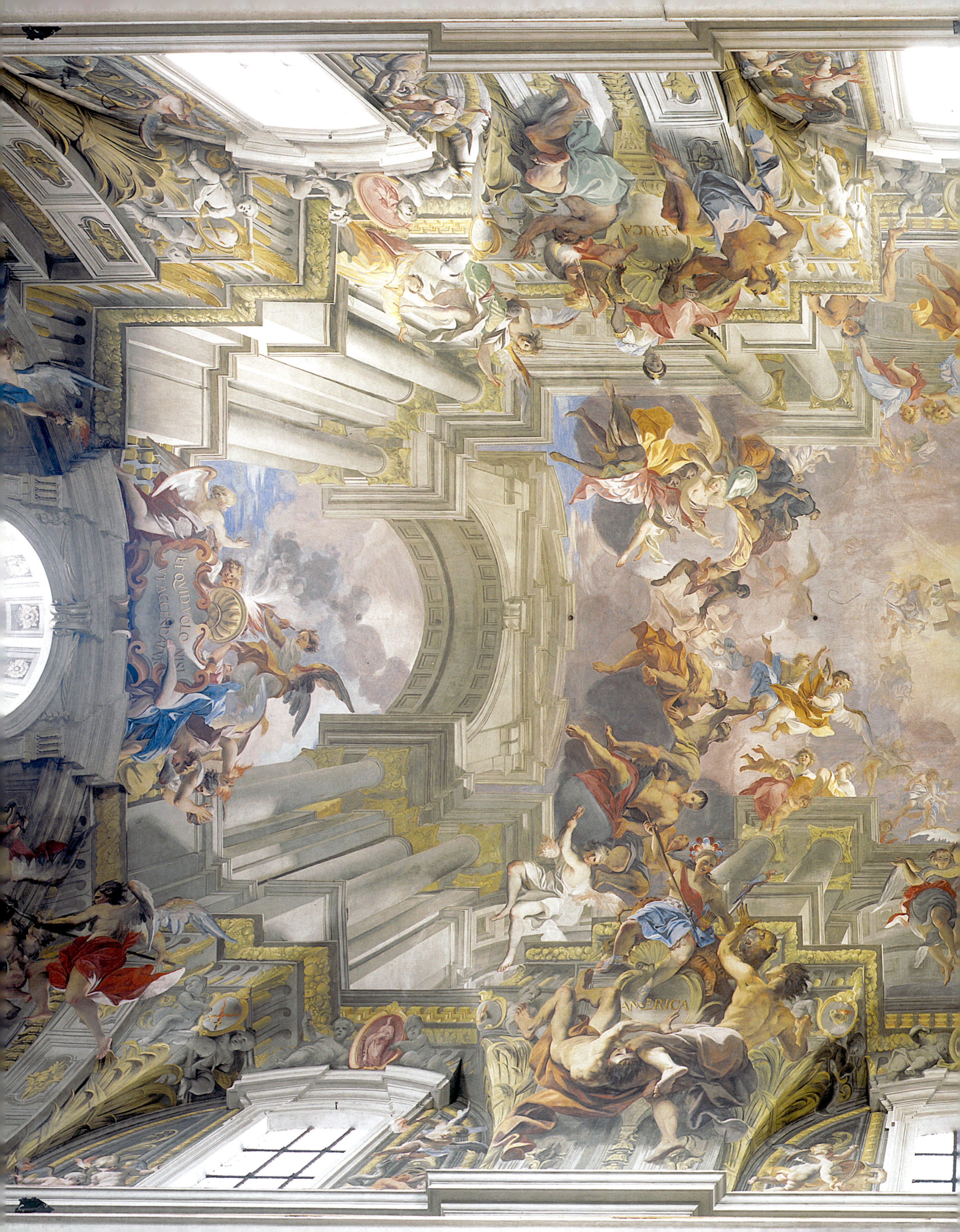
AMERICA

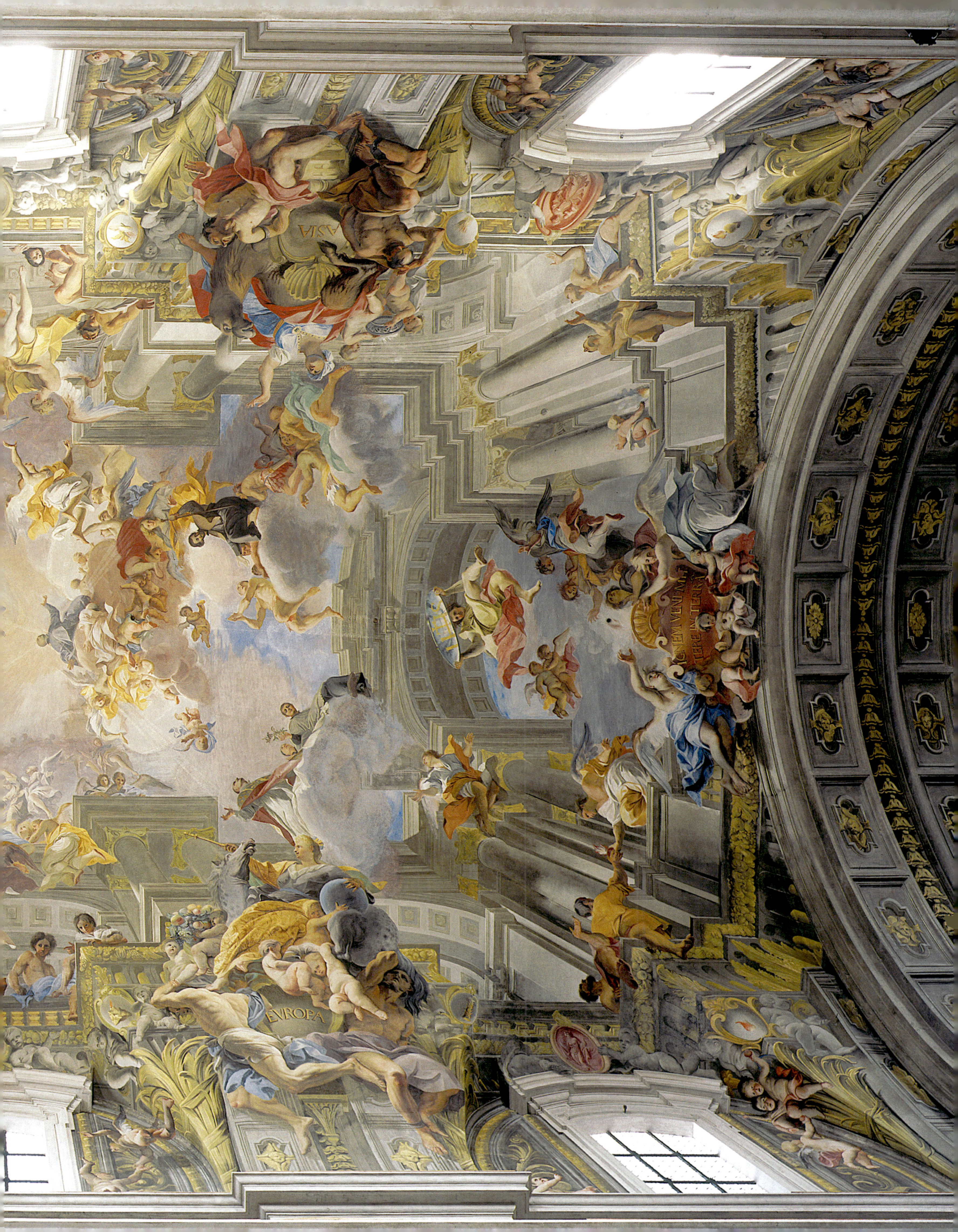

ASIA
EVROPA

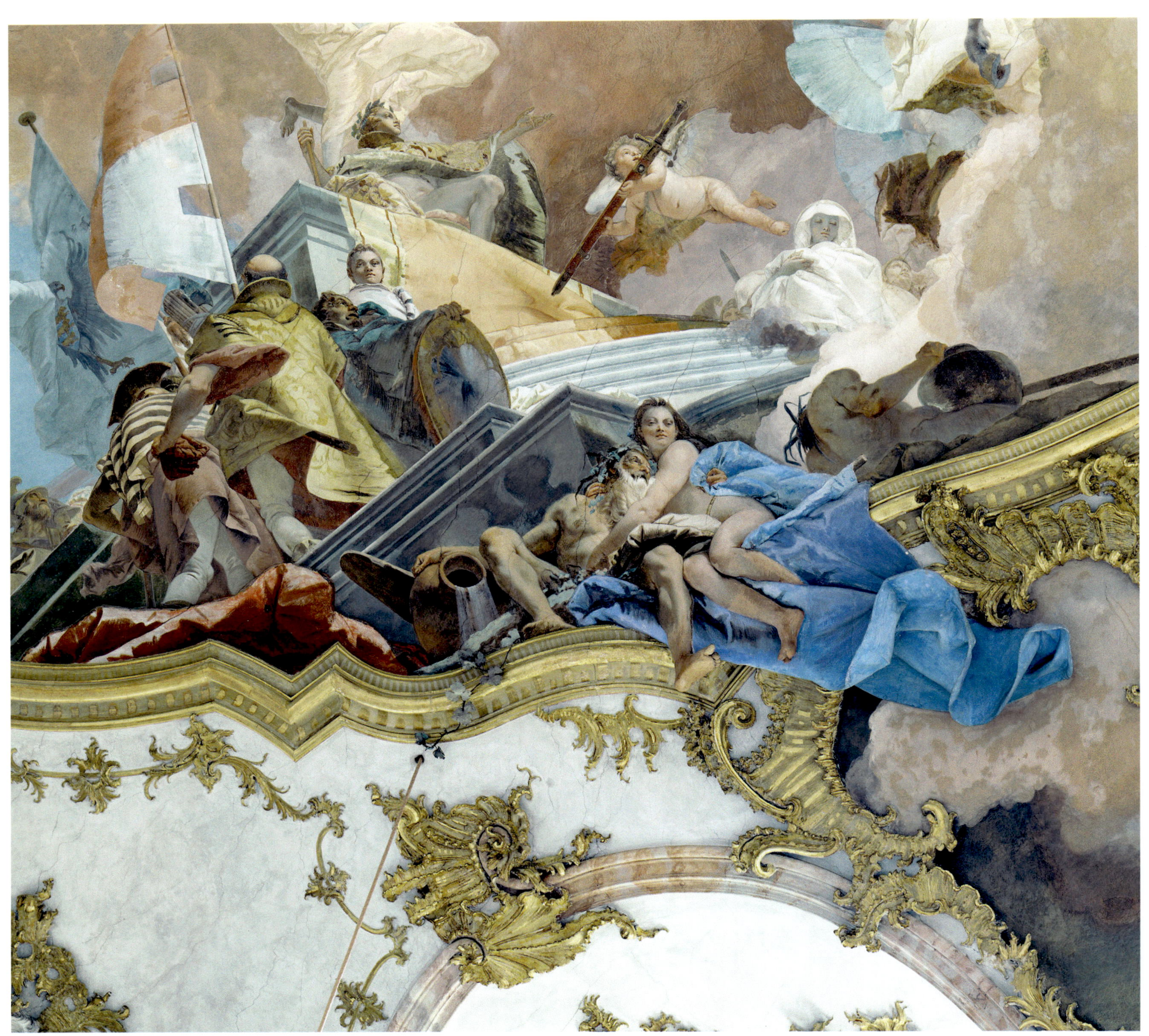

Giovanni Battista Tiepolo

Imperial Hall and Staircase of the Würzburg Residence, 1750 – 1753

The entire Würzburg Residence is a harmonious union of architecture, stucco work and painting. For the visitor, this *Gesamtkunstwerk*, or 'total work of art', presents itself as a magnificent sequence of rooms that ultimately culminates, beyond the grand staircase and vestibule, in the so-called Kaisersaal (Imperial Hall). The designs for the building were drawn by the ingenious architect Balthasar Neumann (1687 – 1753), who began construction in 1720. From 1750 to 1753, Giovanni Battista Tiepolo (1696 – 1770) painted three ceiling frescoes here, which were intended to show the history of the Würzburg Bishopric during the reign of Emperor Frederick Barbarossa. In the 9-metre-high hall, the transitions between art forms are fluid. It is often difficult to be certain of what is real and what has been painted. Beginning with the columns, which, with their reddish stucco, give the impression of being made of real marble, up to the architectural transitions, where it is apparent that the painter Tiepolo and the stuccoist Antonio Bossi (1699 - 1764) complement each other's work perfectly. It is not so much a question of illusionistic architecture as of a deliberate, artistic-intellectual confusion of illusion and reality. Looking from any commonplace viewpoint, it is sometimes impossible to say whether an architectural detail is perhaps only stucco, or whether the leg of a figure is painted or if it actually protrudes from the wall.

Tiepolo concluded the painting of the Imperial Hall to the complete satisfaction of his client and received, in response, a subsequent commission, for which, without a doubt, he was called personally to Würzburg, to create a fresco for the quite unique staircase. With an area of 19 × 32 metres and an average height of 5.5 metres, Tiepolo was about to create, without any help, the largest, thematically coherent ceiling fresco in the world, across a surface of over 600 square metres. The theme was (and how could it be otherwise) the apotheosis of the prince-bishop, surrounded by the ancient heaven of gods and allegories of the four continents that were known at that time. Here, too, Tiepolo managed to combine painted architecture with the real in such a way that makes it difficult to accurately estimate the height of the ceiling. In contrast to the Imperial Hall, in which the frescoes are partially framed by stucco moulding, here the painter has begun directly above the main cornice – barely visible from the stairs below – and extends the actual three-dimensional step around the entire space as an illusionistic painting on which stuccoed figures sit at the corners. And so it continues with many details, some of which hang over the parapet, sometimes painted, sometimes made of stucco. This constant changing, back and forth, confuses the eye and delights the intellect. The figures too make it difficult for the viewer to decide in just which dimension they belong.

Such grand staircases were a speciality of baroque palace construction. They offered an ostentatious stage on which the guests – but above all the hosts – could present themselves accordingly. The whole ceremony of arriving, of escorting and of receiving could be excellently stage-managed here. Largely through the frescoes of Tiepolo, the staircase of the Würzburg Residence is an ideal example of this kind of late Baroque *mise en scène* in architecture.

PAINTING

Seeing and Perceiving

Theological reform was accompanied by a renewal in painting. After the end of the Middle Ages, during which the Church had kept artists in check, so to speak, some time was needed to rediscover old skills and techniques, as well as develop new ones. A period of artistic experimentation and research began to catch up to, or even surpass, the artistic developments that had come before during the period of antiquity, or what was considered 'antiquity'. Painters tried, once more, to reconnect their art to nature.

The Italian painter Giotto di Bondone (c. 1266–1337) was an artist with fundamentally new ideas. He put an end to the flat, rigid painting style of the Middle Ages and turned towards nature, which he could depict like no other before him. The poet Dante Alighieri (1265–1321) praised him in his *Divine Comedy*, and Giovanni Boccaccio (1313–1375) wrote in his *Decameron*, "[One of our fellow citizens,] whose name was Giotto, was so very skilful that there was nothing created by nature [...] that he could not copy, with a stylus or a pen or a brush, so closely that it seemed not like, but rather the thing itself".[9] If one looks at Giotto's paintings today, one can only truly understand this sense of astonishment by also comparing them with the contemporary art of the time. Giotto did not copy the standard models and formulas, but instead translated his personal observations into pictures. He gave his figures a new kind of physicality and weight. A skilful use of light and shadow also plays an essential role in this. The frescoes along the dado of the Scrovegni Chapel in Padua, from 1304, show this particularly well. Here, Giotto painted figures as symbolic representations of the Virtues and

▶ Giotto di Bondone, *Faith*, c. 1306

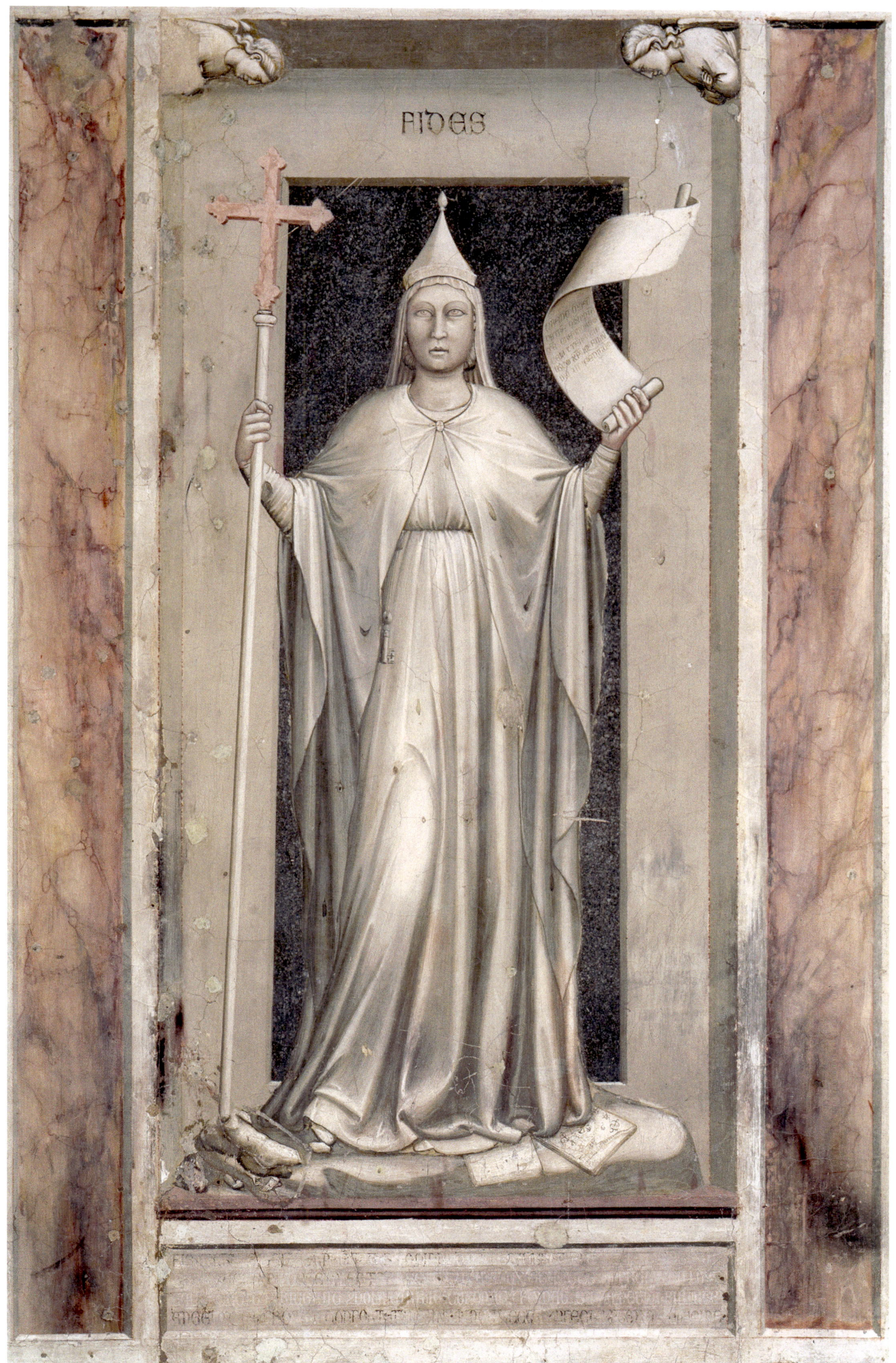
FIDES

Vices, in shades of grey (fig. p. 53). Giotto had come so far in how he lent his figures mass and volume through the use of light and shadow that he was the first to try to simulate stone sculpture by using this grisaille technique. He was thus also the first artist since antiquity to create the illusion of spatial depth on a flat surface, and he did this so convincingly that "indeed, it was often found that men were deceived by his productions into thinking them real", as Boccaccio writes.[10]

This was the beginning of a contest between the arts within aesthetic theory known as 'paragone' (Italian for 'comparison'), which came up again and again over the next centuries: Which is the more suitable art form to represent life, painting or sculpture? One might think that sculpture would have the advantage because of its inherent three-dimensionality, if there were not painters like Giotto and the many others who have occupied themselves with optical illusions and who have been so successful with their 'tricks' of conjuring spatial depth and realistic surfaces to the point of being able to completely deceive their audience. The Flemish painter Jan van Eyck (c. 1390–1441) was an undisputed master in this, as well as in grisaille painting (see pp. 82–83).

The imitation of statues, especially those from antiquity, was also fashionable in 15th-century Italy. One of the greatest admirers of

▼ Andrea Mantegna, *The Introduction of the Cult of Cybele at Rome*, 1505/1506

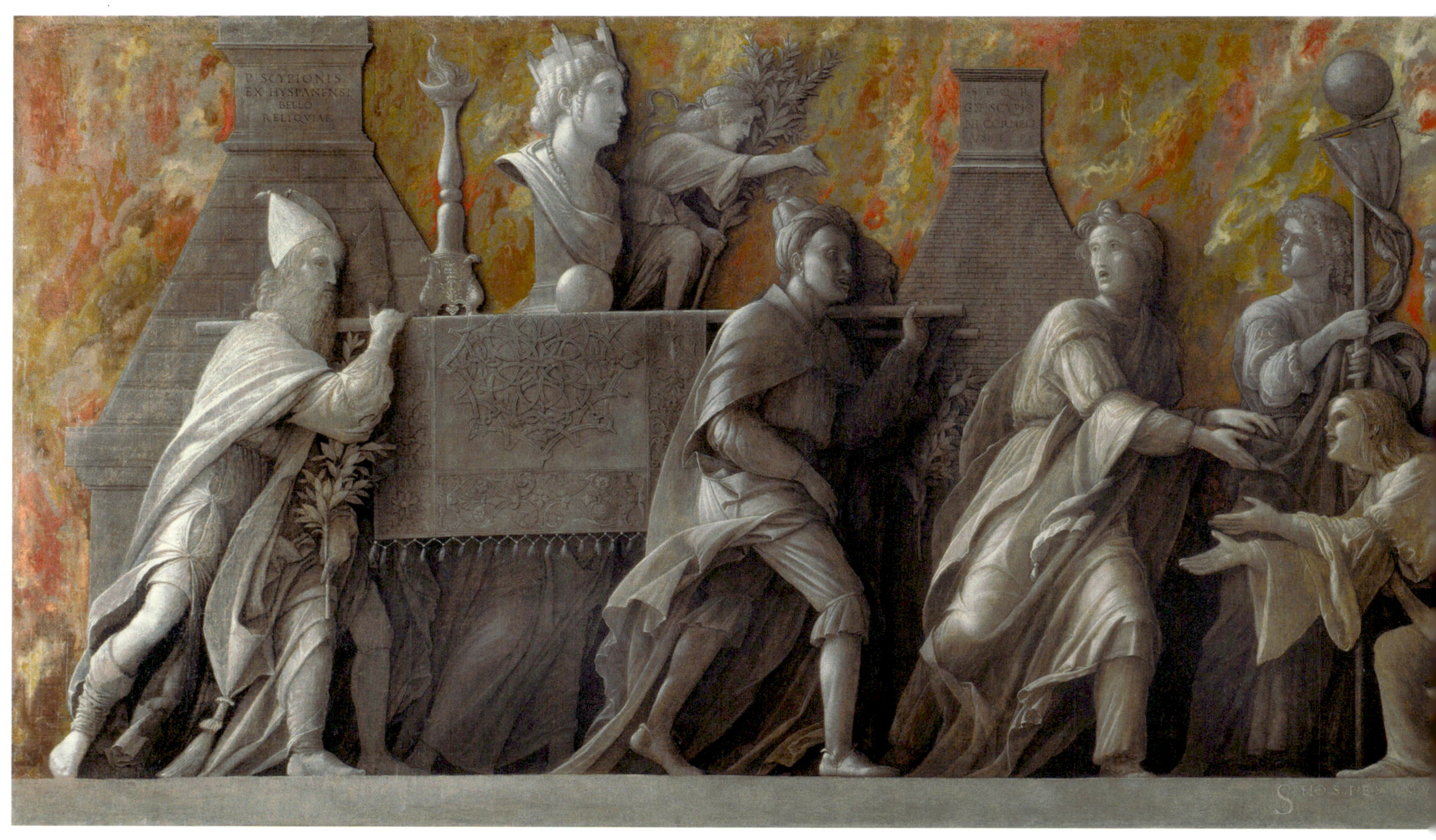

antiquity was Andrea Mantegna (1431–1506; pp. 40–41). For a palace belonging to the Cornaro family, Venetian patricians who claimed to have traced their Roman family tree all the way back to the 2nd century BC, he created an (unfinished) series of friezes in Padua in 1505, which deal with classical narratives, including the Cult of Cybele and the history of the family's ancient forefathers (fig. below). His paintings were intended to imitate an elaborate marble frieze. One can only wonder at how perfectly he succeeded in imitating marble and, at the same time, the perspective necessary for viewing the friezes from below. The graded shades of grey and the colourfully luminous background, as well as the sense of movement in the picture create the perfect illusion of sculpture that is almost alive. There is good reason that Mantegna's work came to inspire the British artist Bridget Riley (b. 1931) in her motion illusions (see pp. 100–103).

Over the centuries, grisaille repeatedly proved to be an excellent – and also a cost-effective – solution when it came to imitating sculptures and works of stucco. In the 18th century, the painter Jacob de Wit (1695–1754) of Amsterdam raised the technique to an exceptional quality, as his various pictures of putti always beg the question of whether one is looking at a work in two or three dimensions. The illusionistic

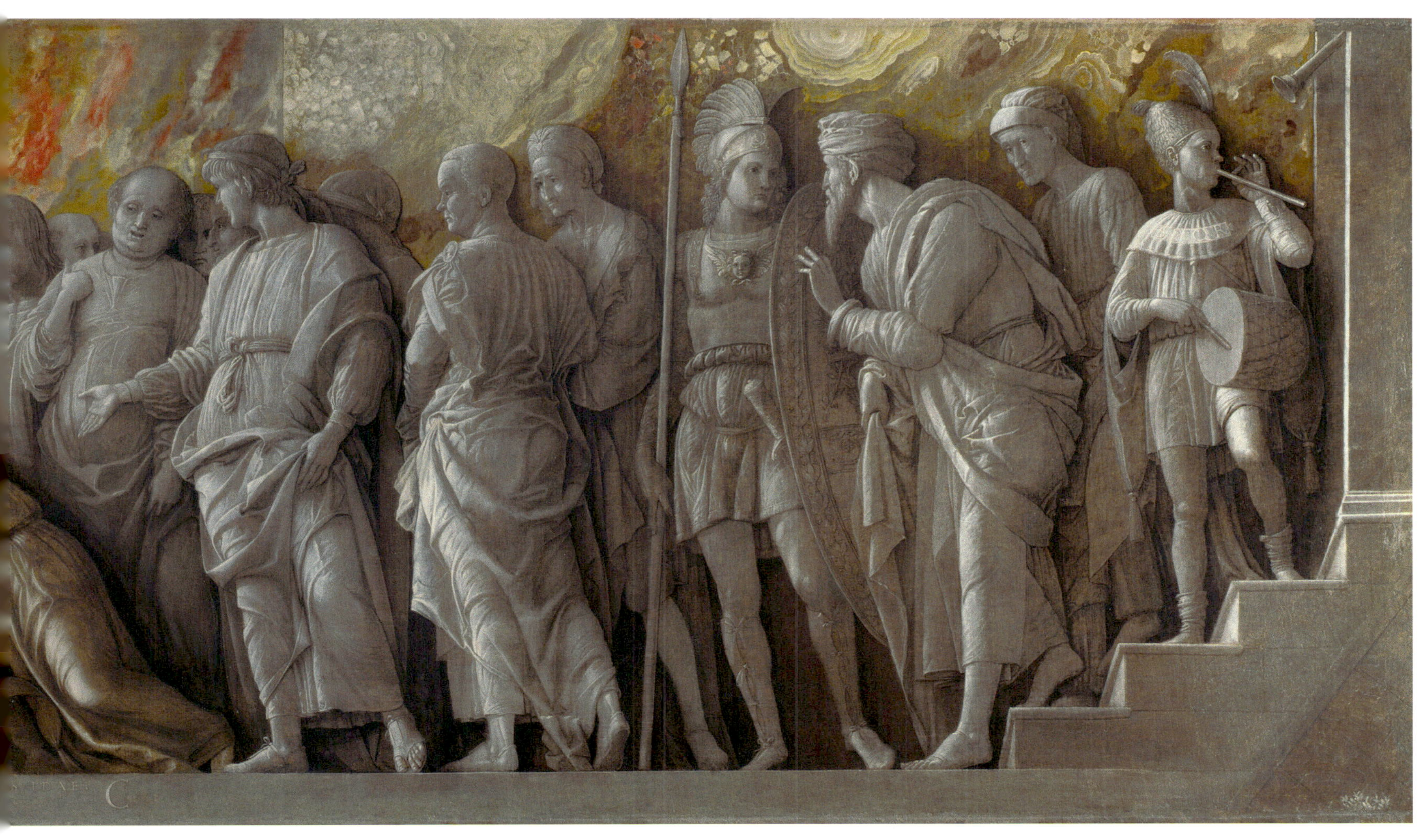

effect is intensified in photographic reproductions, which sometimes make it impossible to satisfactorily answer this question (fig. below).

At the start of the Renaissance, in the early 15th century, there were two centres of artistic production that drove its development: Italy and the Low Countries. In Italy, it was first Florence where artists such as Brunelleschi (1377–1446) and Masaccio (1401–1428) used linear perspective to create 'new spaces' for art. Here, emphasis was placed on narrative, which became more realistic and thus more credible through the use of spaces that seemed truer to life. In contrast, perspective held less importance for Netherlandish painters. They were, instead, famous for reproducing every minute detail in their pictures, for recreating a series of observations and, in so doing, creating a cosmos that combined to form a painting. Unlike the Italians, who conceived

▼ Jacob de Wit, *Three Putti Eating Grapes*, early 18th century

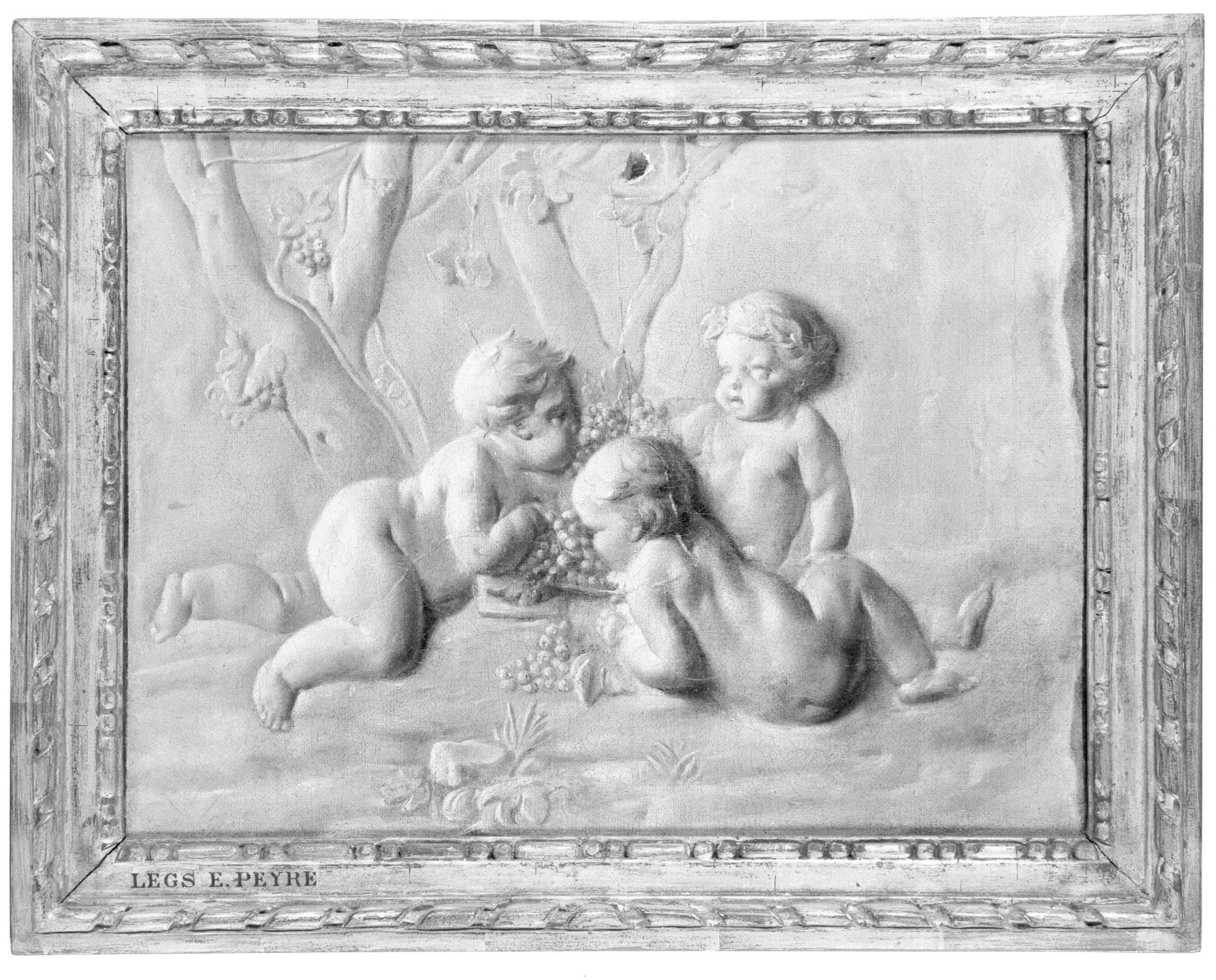

their paintings from large to small, artists in the Low Countries conceived their paintings from small to large, which at times leads to some early Netherlandish paintings appearing rather overly composed.

In the Low Countries, artists were more concerned with the precise observation and reproduction of things. One technique which played an important role in this process was oil painting, which although first developed in the 13th century was perfected at the beginning of the 15th century, especially by Jan van Eyck. In contrast to the opaque tempera paints that predominated in Italy, oil paints are applied through a process of glazing – i.e., in multiple layers. This allows the underlying layers to show through, which give the colours an unprecedented depth and brilliance as well as a tremendous luminosity to the pictures. The artists were in this way able to reproduce all kinds of surfaces, be they fabric, fur or metal, in a deceptively realistic manner. As a result of trade relations, works of art also gradually spread from North to South and vice versa, making oil painting famous in Italy, although it did not become as popular as in the North. It was mostly in Venice where oil painting had its greatest appeal.

There had been examples of still lifes and trompe l'œils as early as classical antiquity, but these passed into oblivion after the Fall of the Roman Empire. In the Christian Middle Ages, there were no still lifes; the Bible does not speak of objects, but of martyrs and saints, of rulers and kings. However, this attitude changed from the beginning of the 14th century as artists, through changes in philosophy and theology, began to rediscover nature and the visible world for themselves. The painted stories of saints were now furnished with the appropriate inventory of props, which in turn led to a certain liveliness and an increase in realism within the scenes. For example, in 1337, Taddeo Gaddi (c. 1290–1366) depicted a niche within the Baroncelli Chapel of Florence's Santa Croce, where wine carafes and a plate may be seen (fig. p. 58). Although this is not a painting in its own right and the depiction still seems somewhat awkward, a start had been made. What was missing was, on the one hand, the linear perspective of an artist like Brunelleschi to provide the correct representation of space and, on the other hand, the exact observation of things, as Netherlandish artists would later demonstrate. Yet even for the painters of the Low Countries, objects were still not yet important enough to merit being the sole subject of a painting.

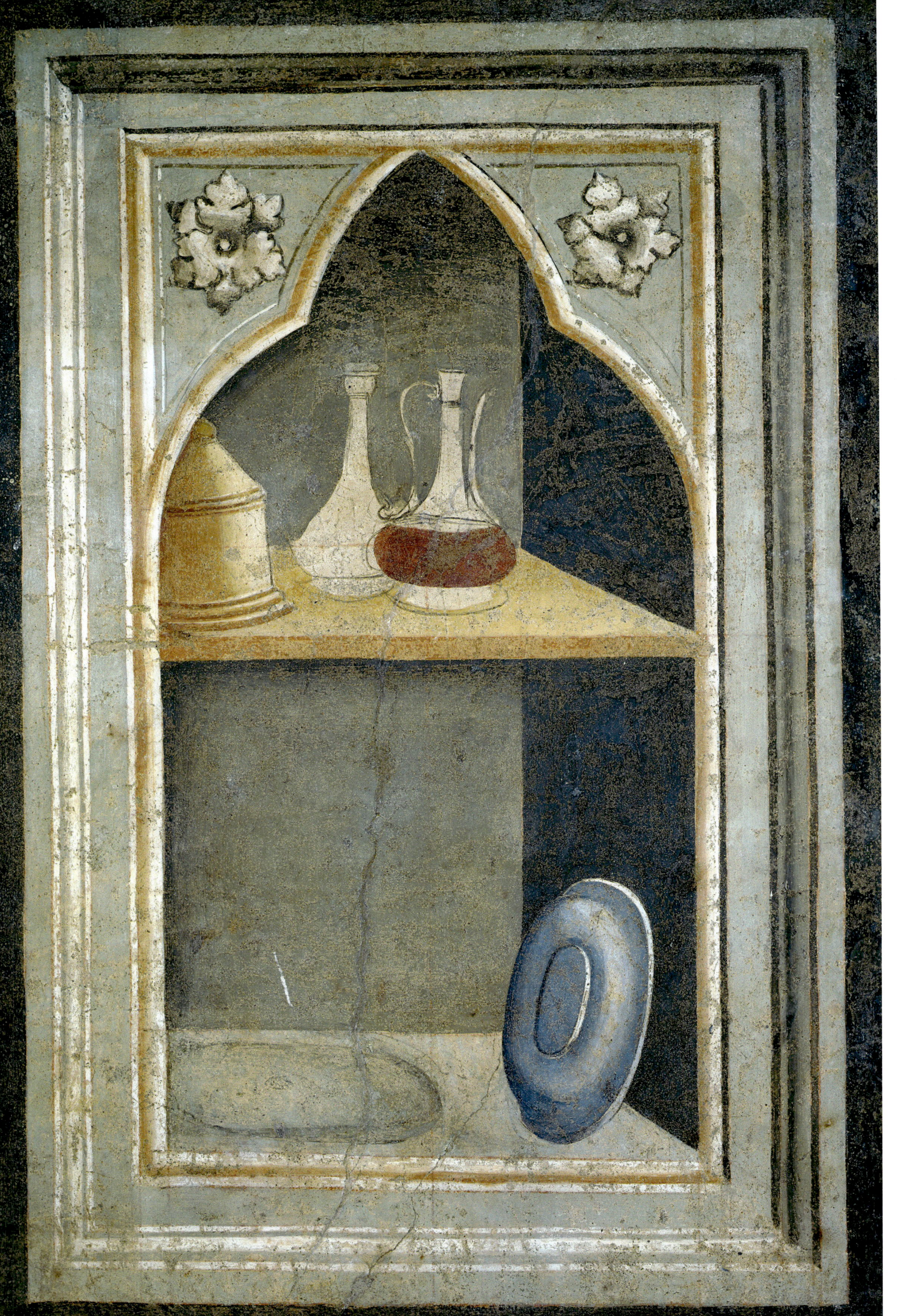

◀ Taddeo Gaddi, A painted niche in the Baroncelli Chapel, 1337

Nevertheless, the ground had at least been prepared for this, both in the South and in the North.

In this ebullient context, it is perhaps no coincidence that the first trompe l'œil and, at the same time, the first still life of the early modern era came, more or less, into being. The first artist who dared devote an entire picture to simple objects alone was the Venetian painter Jacopo de' Barbari (c. 1440–1516). He was not only very familiar with Italian painting and perspective, but also with artistic developments in the North, since he worked as court painter to the future Emperor Maximilian in Nuremberg and from 1503 as court painter to Frederick III of Saxony. He also knew Albrecht Dürer (1471–1528) from the latter's stays in Venice. Dürer began early on to draw and paint everything he saw. Whether animals, landscapes, urban views or simply a section of lawn, he put everything down to the smallest detail using his watercolours just as he saw them in nature. But even Dürer did not create a painting which featured only inanimate objects. It was Jacopo de' Barbari who first took this step. Yet it seems that opinions varied on the quality of de' Barbari's work, as Dürer wrote in a letter from Venice: "Anton Kolb would swear an oath that no better painter lives than Jacob. Others sneer at him, saying if he were good he would stay here [in Venice], and so forth."[11] Be that as it may, at least in this case, he was keener to experiment than his German and Italian peers and painted the first trompe l'œil of the early modern era in 1504 (see pp. 84–85).

With this minor work, de' Barbari revived a long-forgotten genre, but the great period of still life, and thus of trompe l'œil, would not begin until a hundred years later. There would always be painters who dealt with still life, but the perfect deception that stemmed from the seeming presence of the object depicted was much rarer. Such works were created in the 17th century by the Alsatian painter Sebastian Stoskopff (1597–1657), whose well-known still lifes, showing delicate glassware, he most probably painted with the help of a camera obscura, although this makes his pictures no less admirable. But Stoskopff succeeded in really deceiving the gaze with pictures of pictures, by appearing to paste prints to walls (fig. p. 61). The painting shown here features an etching of the *Triumph of Galatea*, based on a print made in 1644 after the painting of that name by Simon Vouet (1590–1649) from around

1642. Stoskopff attaches the 'etching' with twelve spots of red sealing wax to a dark wooden panel, as the corners of the paper appear to curl partially. One would like to take the sheet from the wall and study the print more closely. But both the paper and the print are neither paper nor print, even if the edges of the printing plate can be clearly seen in the supposedly soft surface of the paper. After all, everything is painted with oil, albeit so finely that one falls for the illusion. Once one has recognised that it is a trompe l'œil, once one has been '(dis)enchanted', the supposed artistic illusion becomes an examination of art itself, and the picture can be appreciated as an independent work and not only as a clever game of virtuosic talent.

▶ Sebastian Stoskopff, *Triumph of Galatea*, 1651

The still life and trompe l'œil would become an important branch of painting, especially in the Low Countries. Although they were accorded less respect than history paintings and portraiture within art theory, they were no less popular. In the Netherlands of the 17th century, there was a ban on altarpieces and other religious representations as a result of the Protestant theology of John Calvin. If the church had been one of the most important clients of art up to that point, this source of income disappeared for painters. This had an effect not only on their choice of motifs, but also on the art market in general. For now, painters were forced to find private patrons to commission work or buy their existing pictures. The open art market had its beginnings here. Still life played an important role in this, as painters were able to shine artistically while also incorporating spiritual, intellectual meaning into the objects depicted. The theme of the transience of all things earthly (vanitas), for example, was linked to Calvinist thought. Artists specialised in the subjects they had mastered in painting as well as what might sell well. This led to the development of various themes within still lifes with compositions featuring fruit, breakfast pieces, arms, hunting pieces, flowers and still lifes with any other objects that were at hand. And the art of the trompe l'œil, the deception of the senses, was an exemptional development within the genre.

One of the most successful artists in this field was the Dutch painter Samuel van Hoogstraten (1627–1678), who, after his training with Rembrandt in Amsterdam and several journeys through Europe, including a lengthy stay in London, ended up living in The Hague and his native Dordrecht (see pp. 86–87).

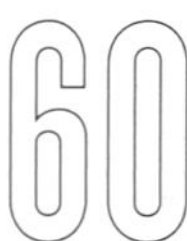

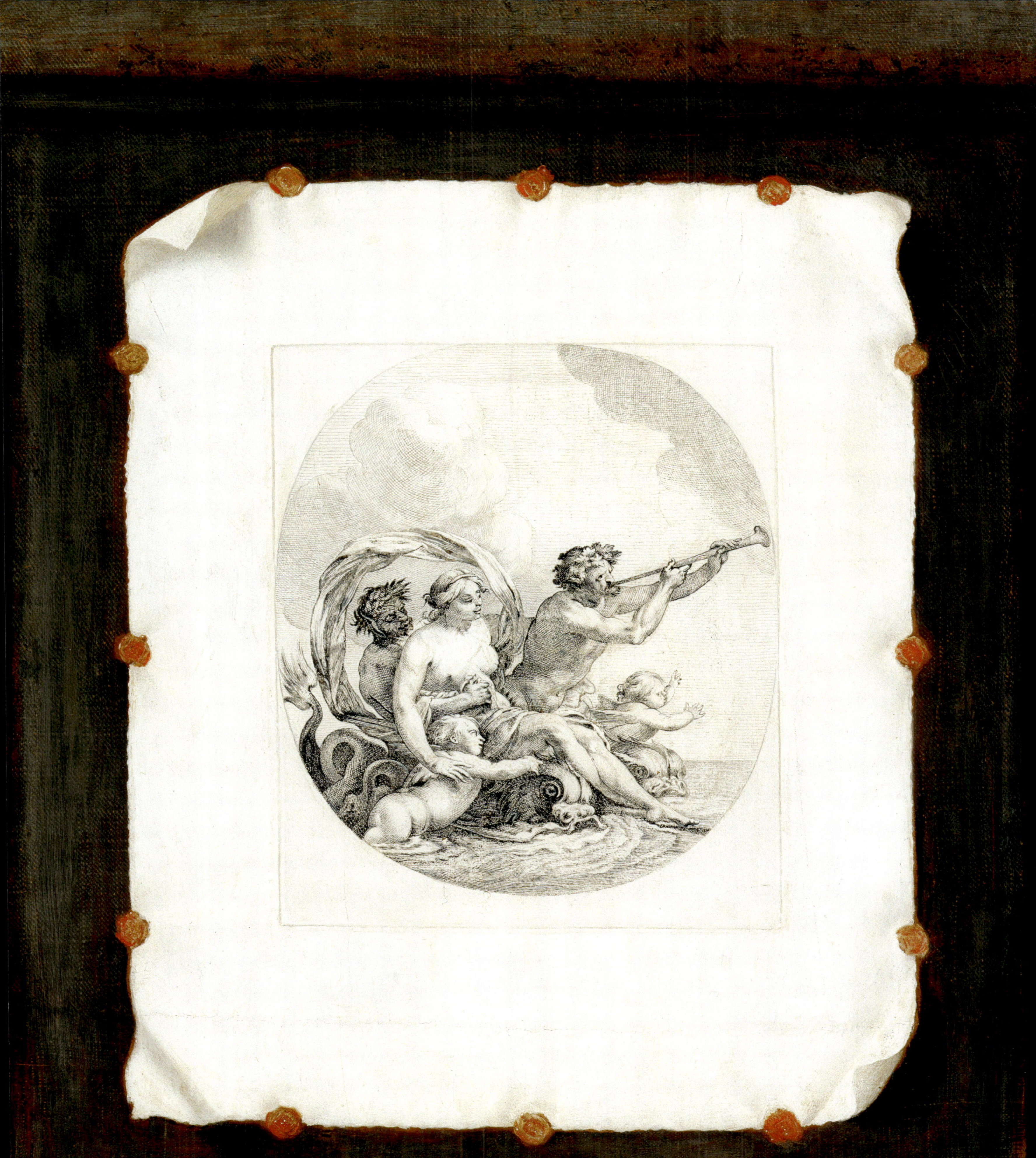

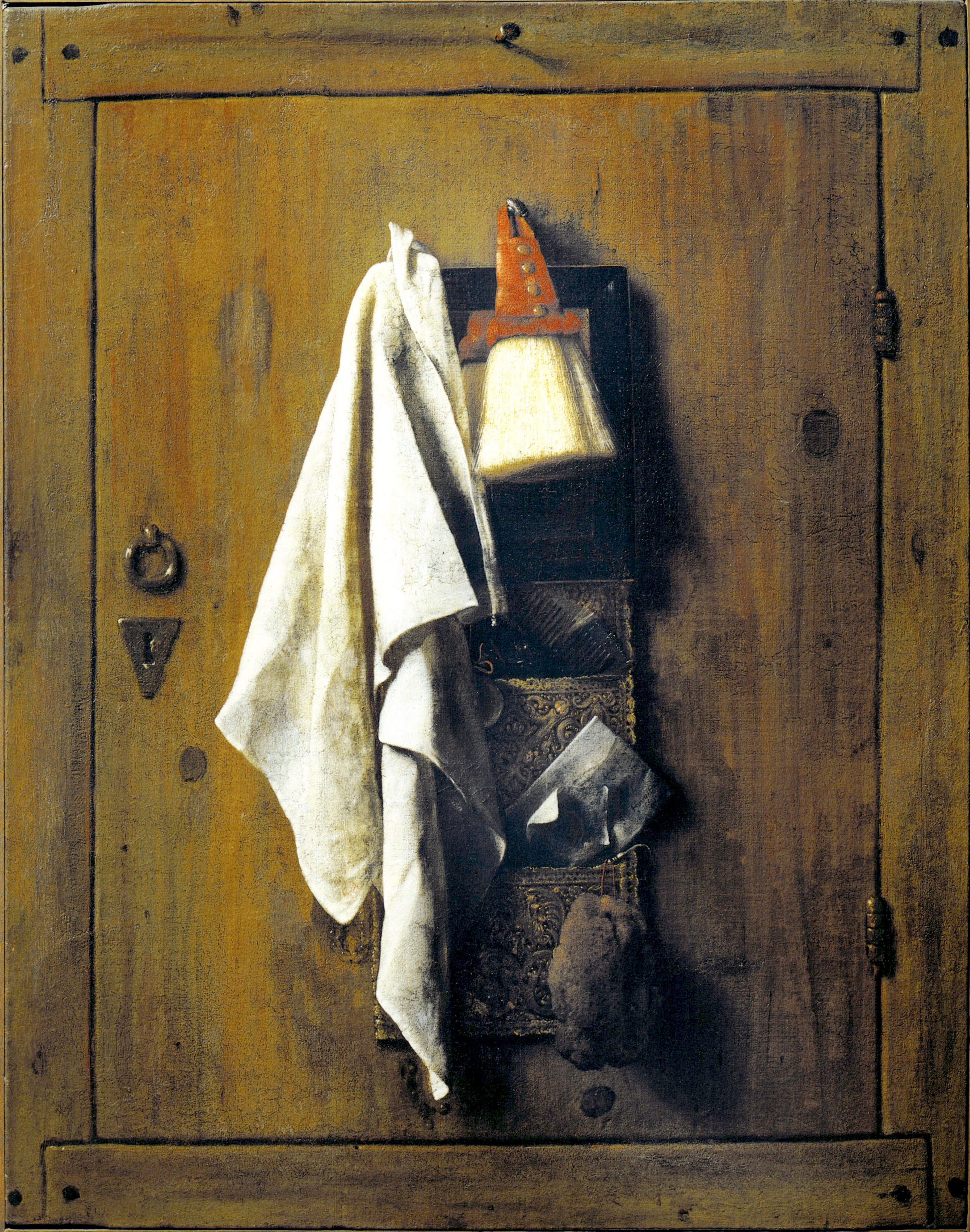

As fine and delightful as the objects in Hoogstraten's 'self-portrait' (fig. p. 86/87) may be, the objects in his painting of 1655 are as equally modest (fig. left). On the door of a wooden cupboard hangs a cloth, a leather belt bag with a brush, a comb and a few slips of paper. It is not too surprising that grooming articles were included here. Rather more surprising is the fact that the painter lends his full artistic attention to a cloth that does not seem particularly clean. The contemporary viewer would have been interested in his rich still life of a *Letter Rack* and would have approached it with great curiosity until they realised that they had fallen for the intended illusion. With this picture, it must have been exactly the other way around. The viewers would not have expected that an artist would pay so much attention to such a banal object and would consequently have first ignored the picture in the belief that it was a real cloth. This would have probably been quite a new experience. In which case, the work's subject would have transformed the image itself into reality, as it were - but only until the deception was discovered.

The near perfect illusion is also likely to have been the subject of the public's attention in the joint work of the Leiden painters Frans van Mieris (1635–1681) and Adriaen van der Spelt (c. 1630–1673) from 1658 (see pp. 88–90).

Another great master of baroque trompe l'œil painting was the Flemish painter Cornelis Norbertus Gysbrechts (c. 1610–after 1675), who, unlike his Dutch peers, did not have to expose himself to the forces of the open art market, but rather trained and lived in Catholic Flanders and from 1668 worked at the Danish royal court in Copenhagen for Frederick III and Christian V. Here, Gysbrechts created his most famous paintings, the most conspicuously inconspicuous of which became his most spectacular and radical work, the 'reversed picture' of 1670 (fig. p. 64 left). In fact, one sees nothing more than a framed picture from behind. The canvas in question is shown pulled over a wooden stretcher, which in turn is fixed by six nails to an outer frame. One can see part of the canvas edge, stray remains of paint left by the framer and a small piece of paper marked with the number "36" and affixed with sealing wax, which indicates a sale at auction. Perhaps the picture was actually presented there, standing on the floor, as is often the case during hangings and previews. The curious observer takes up

◂ Samuel van Hoogstraten, *Trompe l'Œil Still Life*, 1655

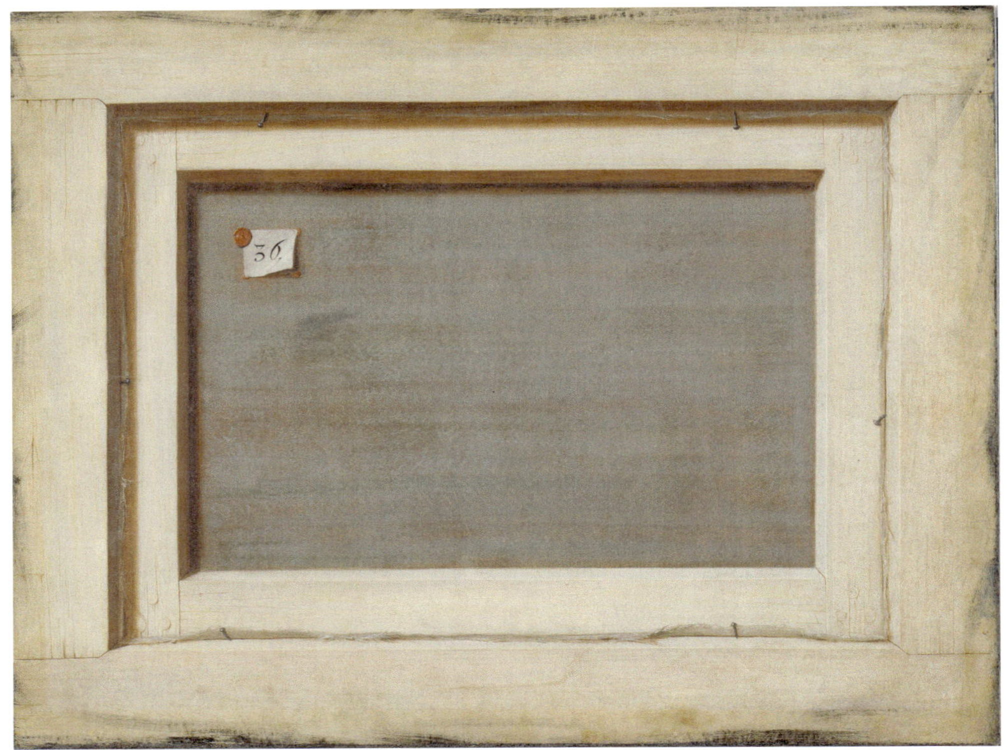

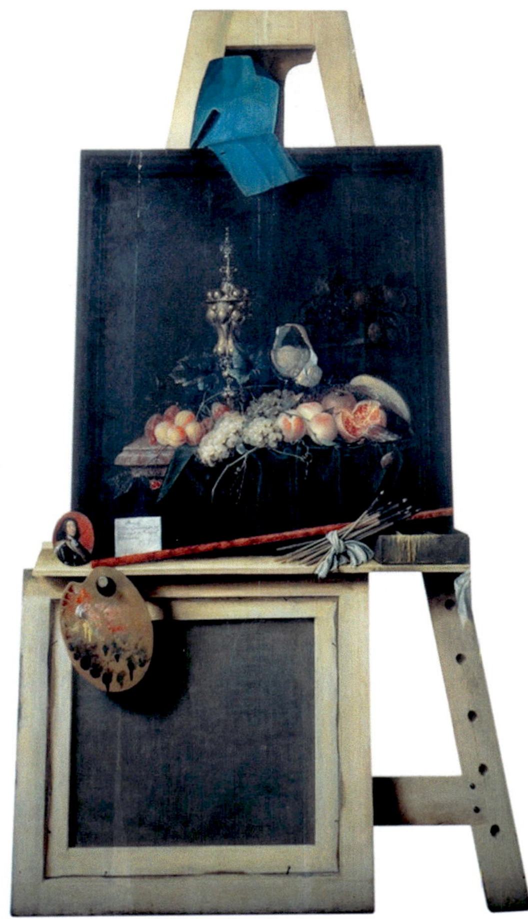

▲ **Left**
Cornelis Norbertus Gysbrechts, *The Reverse of a Framed Painting*, 1670
▲ **Right**
Cornelis Norbertus Gysbrechts, *Cut-Out Trompe l'Œil Easel with Fruit Piece*, 1670–1672

the picture to have a look at the front only to see the back again. The perfect illusion. It would be interesting to see the reverse side of the reverse side …

Gysbrechts was an expert in representing the tools of his trade. In another trompe l'œil from the same period (fig. above right), one is confronted by an easel with a perfectly executed still life, brushes, a palette, a cloth and another painting, which, leaning against a foot of the easel, has its back turned to us. This work, which is, in reality, only eight centimetres thick, was placed in the entrance hall of the present-day National Archives in Copenhagen following the move of the Royal Cabinet of Curiosities. It was brought together here with the pictureless picture, to the probably even greater amazement of the public.

In the course of time, new brilliant types of optical illusions were invented, such as pictures behind seemingly broken glass, an idea which enjoyed great popularity in the 18th century. Since it was at that time that the idea of protecting pictures behind glass was developed. The production of plate glass was improved and made cheaper during this period, so that it became customary to protect art works, especially

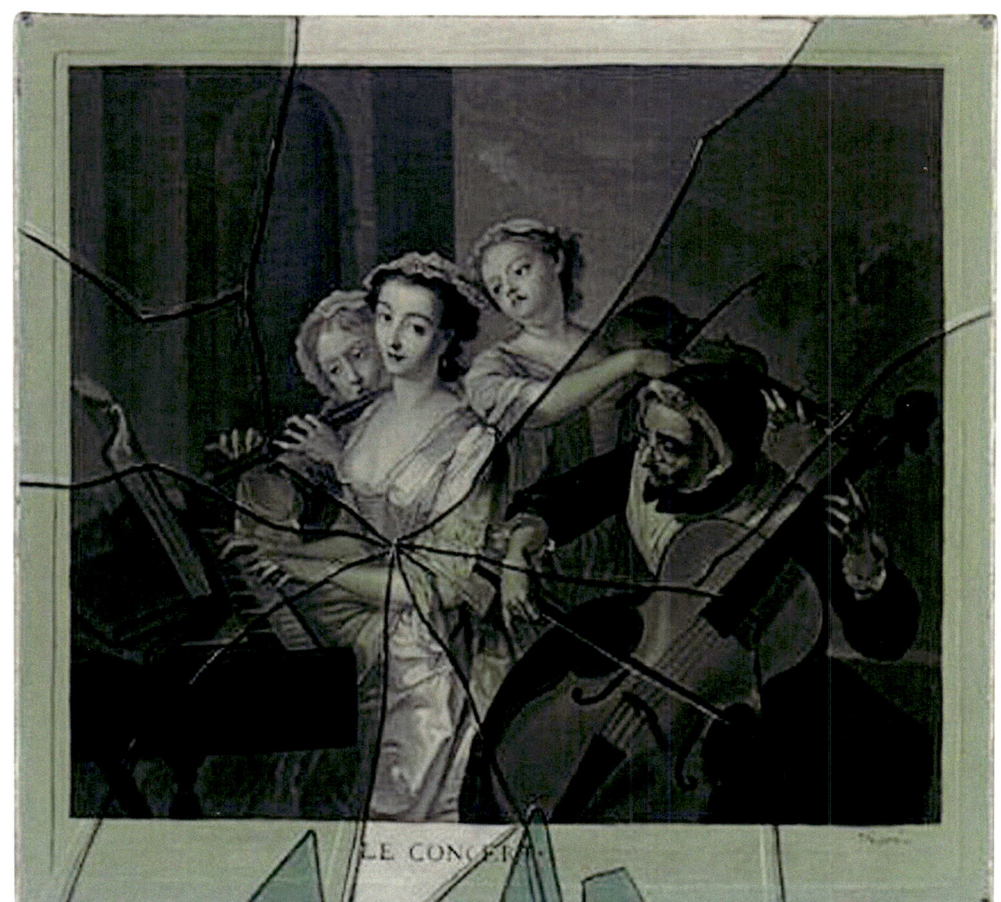

◀ François-Xavier Vispré, *The Concert*, c. 1760–1780

delicate graphic works, in this way. But, of course, one can also break glass. The French painter François-Xavier Vispré (c. 1730–c. 1790), who had lived in London from 1764, was a specialist in this. In his painting *The Concert*, he shows an etching behind a broken pane of glass (fig. above). Yet, here, everything is an illusion. The etching is not an etching, but a copy painted in oil by Vispré of a print by his colleague Philippe Mercier (1689–1760), and the broken glass consists also only of oil paint, which the artist has skilfully applied to the canvas. Vispré was very shrewd in his attempt to deceive: The picture is the usual size of a graphic work, the glass appears slightly greenish and the shards at the bottom of the picture, when framed, give the impression that they have become stuck in the actual frame. The shadows and the slight darkening of the glass fragments caught behind each other are extremely convincing. Perhaps Vispré also refers the broken glass to the print itself: It is well known that happiness is as fragile as glass. So, perhaps, the tips of the glass shards, which point to the heart of the pianist, are an indication of her lost happiness. In connection with such a trompe l'œil, an allegory of deception and the transience of love's happiness emerge.

Trompe l'Œil in the United States of America

In the USA of the 19th century, still lifes and especially trompe l'œil may not have been appreciated by critics, but they were well loved by the public. In the nascent country, people were in search of their own form of artistic expression and first looked to the traditions of Europe for inspiration. Still lifes were well suited to picking up current themes, since many of the objects represented came from the experience of the general public and were accessible directly, without the need for a great deal of knowledge in art history. At a time when trompe l'œil was taking something of an artistic break in Europe, it opened up new possibilities for artists in the United States. 'Making money' had always been an important subject in the United States and, unlike in Europe, artists also involved themselves directly in it. In the novel *The Rise of Silas Lapham* from 1885, the author William Dean Howells allows one character to rave, "there's no doubt but money is to the fore now. It is the romance, the poetry of our age. It's the thing that chiefly strikes the imagination."[12]

William Harnett (1848–1892) was the first of many trompe l'œil artists to take up the subject and paint dollar bills. This seems to reflect a certain obsession with money that was in the air. Many of these 'money painters', including Nicholas Alden Brooks (1840–1904), were visited by the police because their painted banknotes were so similar to genuine dollar bills that they were considered veritable counterfeits (fig. right). Sometimes trompe l'œils of banknotes had to be hung out of the reach of the public as viewers tried to detach the bills from the pictures' background. Accordingly, artists were advised to refrain from painting more notes. The artistic value of such works was, in any case, questionable and the threshold between art and genuine forgery actually seems extraordinarily low. Who knows how many talented painters have changed sides? The trompe l'œil would then, at the moment of realisation, no longer evoke the pleasant astonishment of having been taken in by the painter, but rather great irritation at having done so.

The aforementioned William Harnett was one of the most successful and productive painters within trompe l'œil, although he never saw any of his paintings in a museum during his lifetime, but rather exhibited

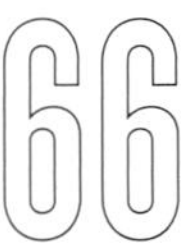

them in pubs, offices and shops. Although he and his entire genre were scorned by critics, Harnett was reasonably successful. His paintings were spread by means of chromolithography (multi-coloured lithography), which increased the public recognition of his work but took away from the magic of the trompe l'œil: "It no longer produces an illusion or, at least, not like a trompe l'œil in oil would, but rather retains everything that allows it to be identified as an oil painting", writes the French art historian Adrien Goetz.[13] In the original, however, it had indeed served to mislead (see pp. 92–93).

Harnett was one of several very talented and unconventional trompe l'œil painters in the USA at the end of the 19th century, amongst whom John Haberle (1856–1933) was probably one of the most humorous. One of his most famous works shows a small slate (fig. p. 69) as were hung in taverns so that the clientele could write down their orders with chalk on it. But the blackboard is already largely covered with childish scribbles, such as a grinning cat and other markings. The effect is startling. Maybe Haberle also wanted to avoid his audience actually jotting something down. He has done that himself; in spite of the blur of chalk, there is an offer on his own behalf to lend one of his paintings: "Painting 'A Bachelor's Drawer' is FOR RENT, Inquire of John Haberle Studio New Haven, Ct." The 'painting for rent' happens to be one of Haberle's most famous works: *A Bachelor's Drawer* (see pp. 93–95).

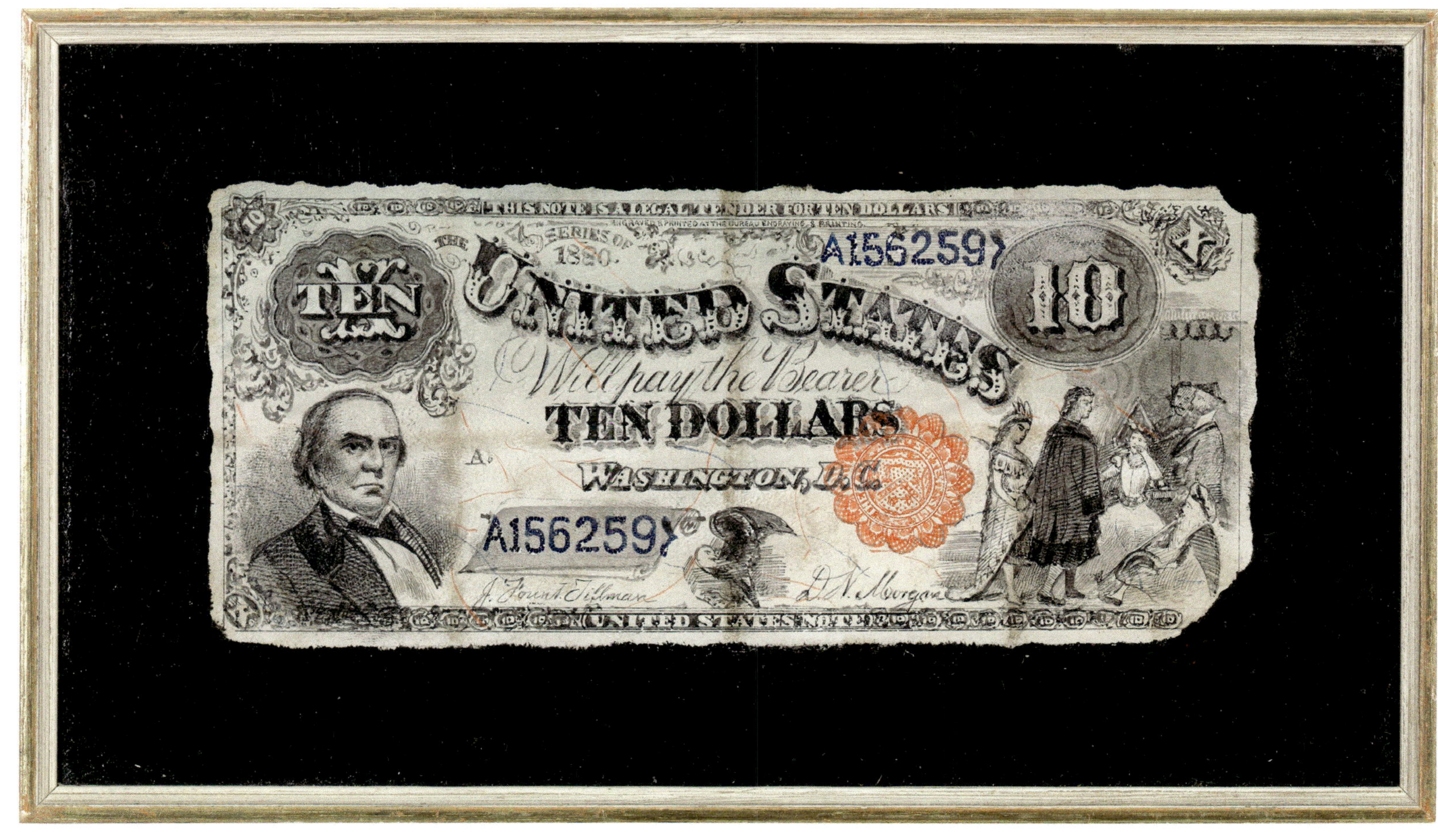

▼ Nicholas Alden Brooks, *A Ten Dollar Bill*, after 1893

As the interest in trompe l'œil had already diminished in Europe with the dawn of Romanticism, the star of the illusionists also faded in the USA with the rise of Impressionism. In the following decades, still life continued to play an important role in various artistic movements, but the art of optical illusion ceased for a long time to be in demand. With Surrealism, however, the painter's ability to depict things as realistically as possible was once again very popular. An outwardly clear pictorial language was necessary if one wanted to make one's audience believe something that is not - or does not appear to be - what it pretends to represent. One of the best-known artists in this field is probably René Magritte (1898-1967), who added to his famous picture of a pipe the written indication that it is not a pipe, but only oil on canvas which represents the image of such a pipe (fig. pp. 70/71). He thus simultaneously provides (at a single glance) a simple summary of illusionist art (see pp. 96-97).

In the 1928 painting *Attempting the Impossible*, Magritte can be seen painting a nude woman. Not yet completely finished, the artist realises that he is not creating a painting of a nude, but a real woman and thus a new reality that can even cast a shadow. It almost seems as if this picture is the antithesis to the pipe which is not a pipe. It would then effectively be the perfect painterly attempt to illude. To this, he said, "I am searching for the truth, but the truth remains a mystery".[14]

While René Magritte asks himself and his public fundamental questions about the picture itself and the essence of painting, and tried with his medium to find answers, the Dutch artist M. C. Escher (1898-1972) was preoccupied with perspective and its real and unreal possibilities. Escher's works, like those of Victor Vasarely (1906-1997), became, for a certain period, an indispensable part of pop culture. Obviously, the public liked - and likes - to be hoodwinked by such 'impossibilities' (figs. p. 77-78 and see pp. 98-99).

▸ John Haberle, *The Slate*, after 1895

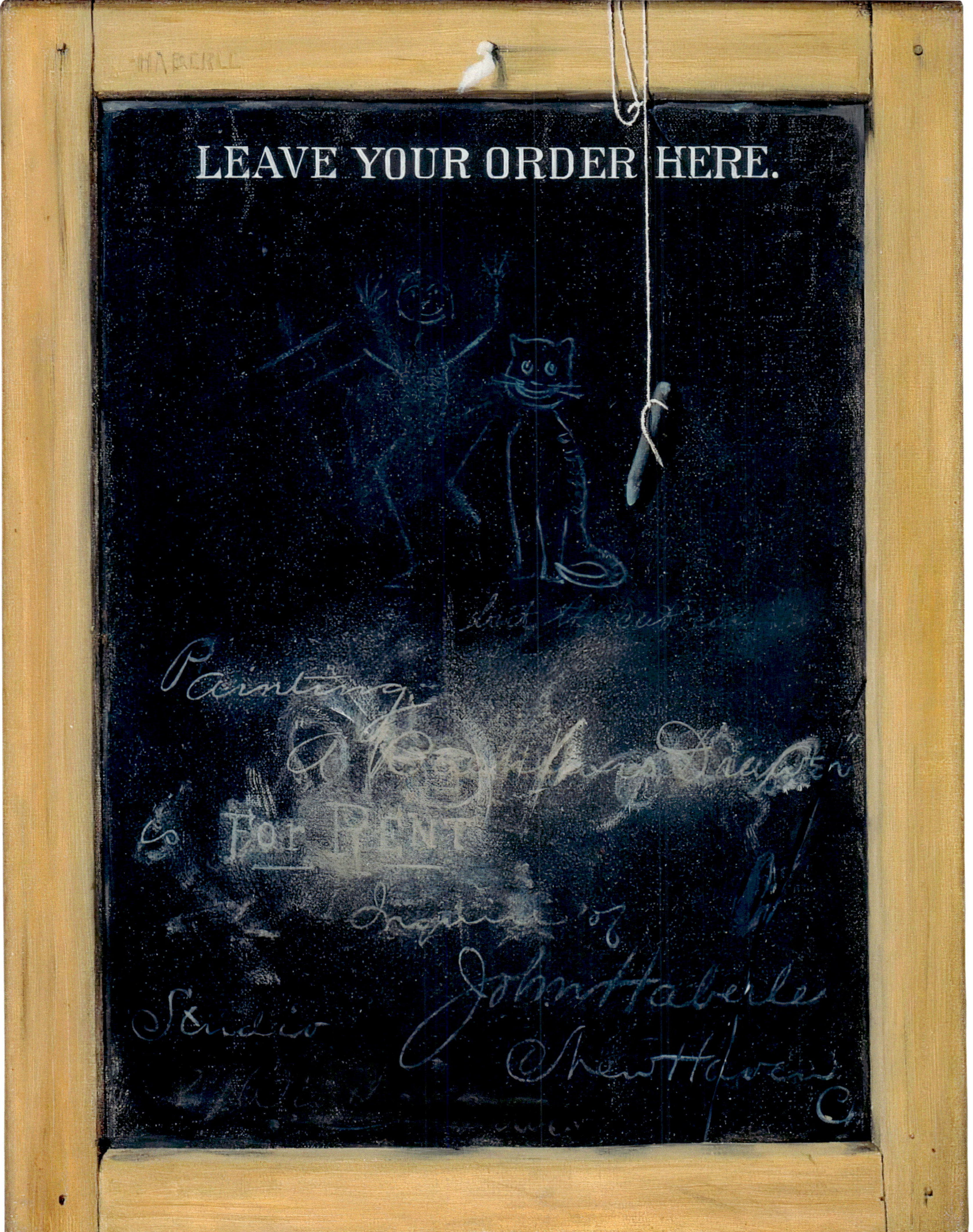
LEAVE YOUR ORDER HERE.
Painting
For RENT
Inquire of
John Haberle
Studio
New Haven

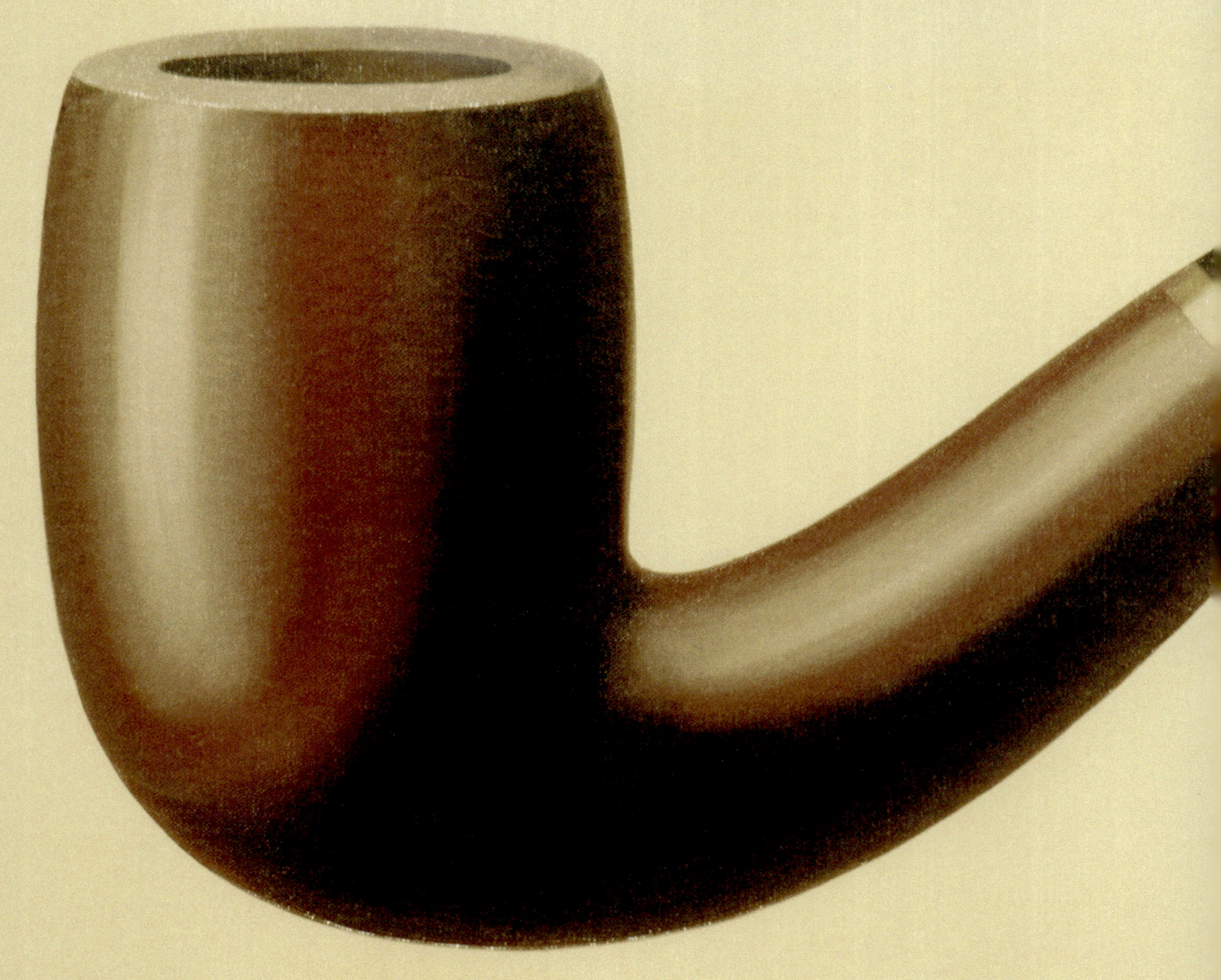
Ceci n'est pas

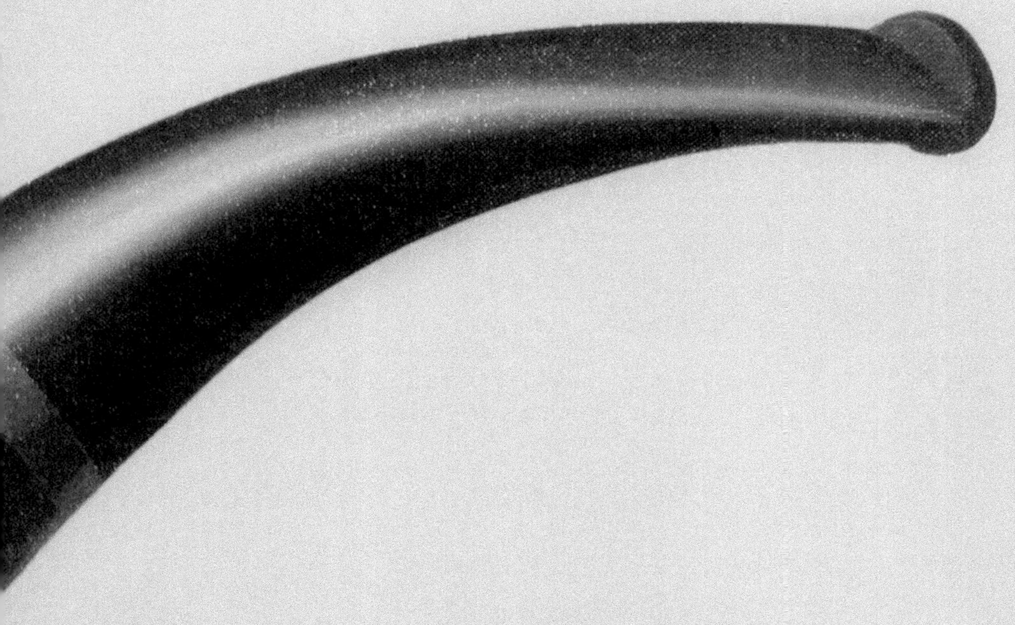

◄ René Magritte, *The Treachery of Images (This is Not a Pipe)*, 1929

Movement within the Picture

The illusionistic representation of movement in a picture is its own special case. Movement in a painting is, in itself, a contradiction, because painting is always at a standstill, just like photography. Even the imagery of film is made up of static snapshots of single moments that only evoke the illusion of movement through their rapid sequential projection, since the human eye is too lazy to perceive the individual frames as such. So what do painters do when they want to represent movement and dynamism? They make use of various illusions in which the viewer becomes 'co-author': The painter shows the body in question in a position that is obviously undergoing change, for example, a horse that is shown in a jump. Since we know what the normal course of such a movement is, we imagine the moment before the depicted pose and the moment after it. Through this sequence, we as viewer are inclined to accept a movement that is not actually visible.

The situation is different when it is a movement that does not change the form of the object depicted, as with a turning wheel. This problem is described by the Dutch painter Philips Angel (1618–1664) in his book *Praise of Painting*, published in 1642: "For whenever a cartwheel or a spinning-wheel is turned with great force one sees that, because of the rapid rotation, no spokes are really visible but only an uncertain shimmer. Although I have seen many pictures in which carriage wheels are depicted, I have never seen this imitated properly, but with each spoke drawn or painted in such a way that the carriage did not appear to move".[15] Diego Velázquez (1599–1660), painter to King Philip IV of Spain, solved this visual problem towards the end of his life, in his painting *The Spinners*, as an example to all (fig. right). The picture tells the story of Arachne's competition with Athena. In it, the painter shows a spinning wheel that appears to turn very quickly. He reduces the details of the wheel to such an extent that we can barely tell what it is. He relies on our visual experience. We know the effect of light falling on moving wheel spokes: They shimmer, and we can no longer recognise the individual spokes. And so, we conclude from this that such a wheel must be rotating very quickly. The illusion of movement and speed is thus created by means of light and visual reduction.

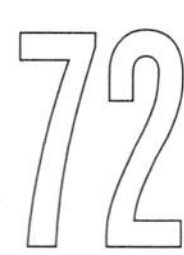

While the illusionistic representation of movement and speed was still the challenge faced by Velázquez, dynamism and speed themselves became the subjects of the Italian Futurists at the beginning of the 20th century. Their manifesto states, "We affirm that the beauty of the world has been enriched by a new form of beauty: the beauty of speed. A racing car [...] is more beautiful than the *Victory of Samothrace*."[16] But this applied not only to racing cars and trains, but apparently to dachshunds, as well, as can be seen in the painting *Dynamism of a Dog on a Leash* from 1912 (fig. p. 74). Here, Giacomo Balla (1871–1958) spreads out movement into its individual parts and reassembles them into a 'multiplicity of movement'. One can almost hear the clacking of the dachshund's claws on the pavement ...

However, this multiplicity of movement in the picture was certainly not as new as Giacomo Balla and the Futurists may have believed. As early as 1865, Wilhelm Busch (1832–1908) drew a series that anticipated the Futurists wonderfully. In the picture series *The Virtuoso* (fig. p. 75), he shows the furious playing of a pianist and the reaction of one of his fans. The pianist's fingers multiply from picture to picture (over fifty can

▼ Diego Velázquez, *The Spinners, or the Fable of Arachne*, 1655–1660

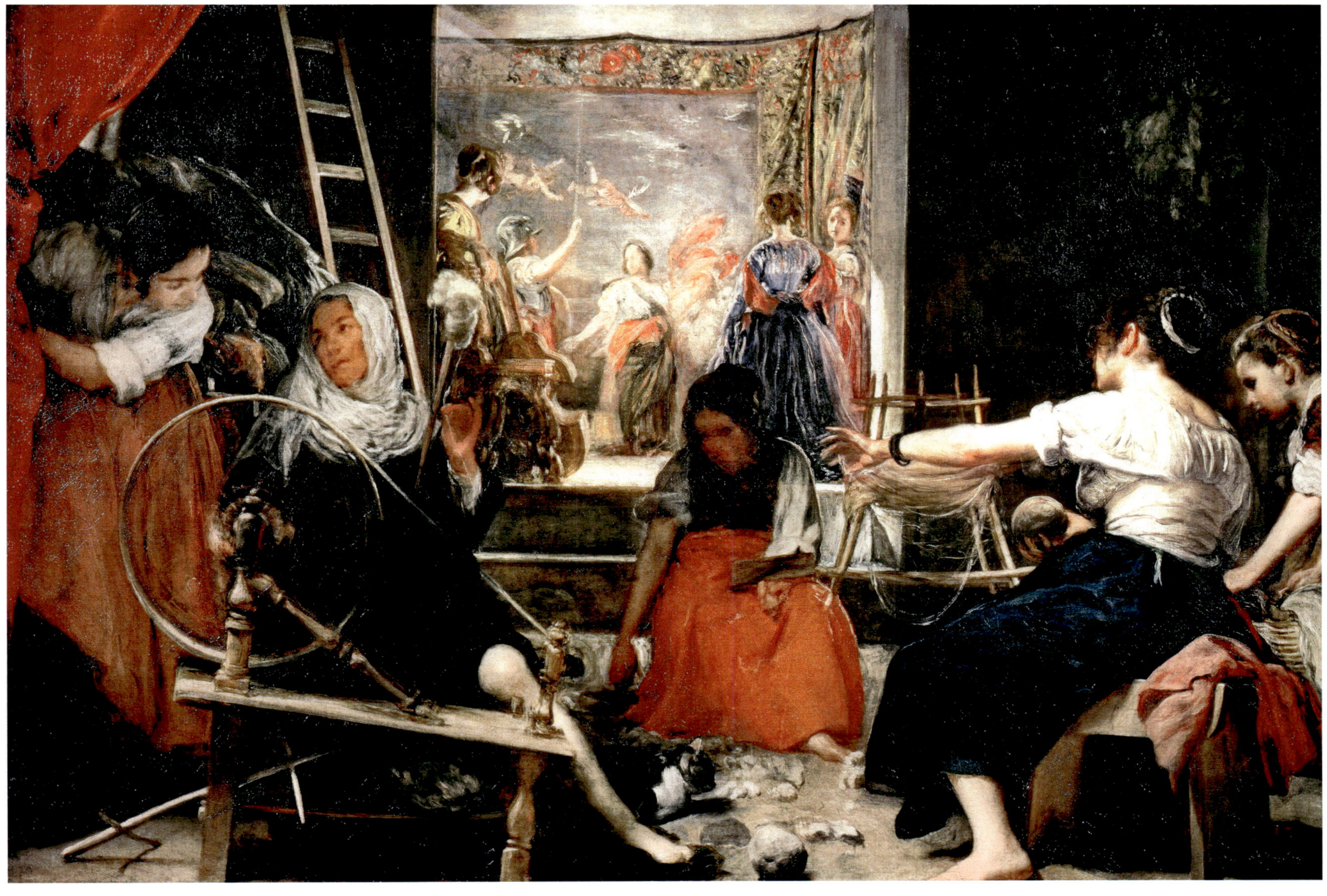

be seen in the "Finale furioso"), and the pianist himself seems to be lifted off his stool by the dynamism of his playing. Equally astonishing is the reaction of the enthusiastic listener, whose head in the final movement consists only of an eye and an ear. One virtually hears a wild piano sonata in the style of Franz Liszt (1811–1886), who was perhaps even the model for Busch's virtuoso. Wilhelm Busch is considered by many to be a godfather of comics because the very techniques that Busch invented here are still used today in comic strips to evoke the illusion of speed in what is actually a static medium.

British artist Bridget Riley also creates the illusion of movement in her paintings, but in a completely different way. Reduction is her technique of choice (see pp. 100–103). Comparable to Riley's images, the popular works of the Hungarian-French painter and graphic artist Victor Vasarely are equally as effective. Although the works of Vasarely and Riley appear somewhat similar, their respective backgrounds are different. Riley is inspired by her observations of nature, while Vasarely turned away from the figurative and towards the abstract early in his career. His art is based in part on the fundamentals of Bauhaus aesthetics and the colour experiments of the painter and art theoretician Josef Albers (1888–1976). When Vasarely came to Paris from Hungary in 1930, he worked as an advertising graphic designer, dealing with the question of how optical effects affect the viewer. He experimented with lines, patterns and structures as well as the effects that arise when

▶ Wilhelm Busch, *The Virtuoso*, 1865

▼ Giacomo Balla, *Dynamism of a Dog on a Leash*, 1912

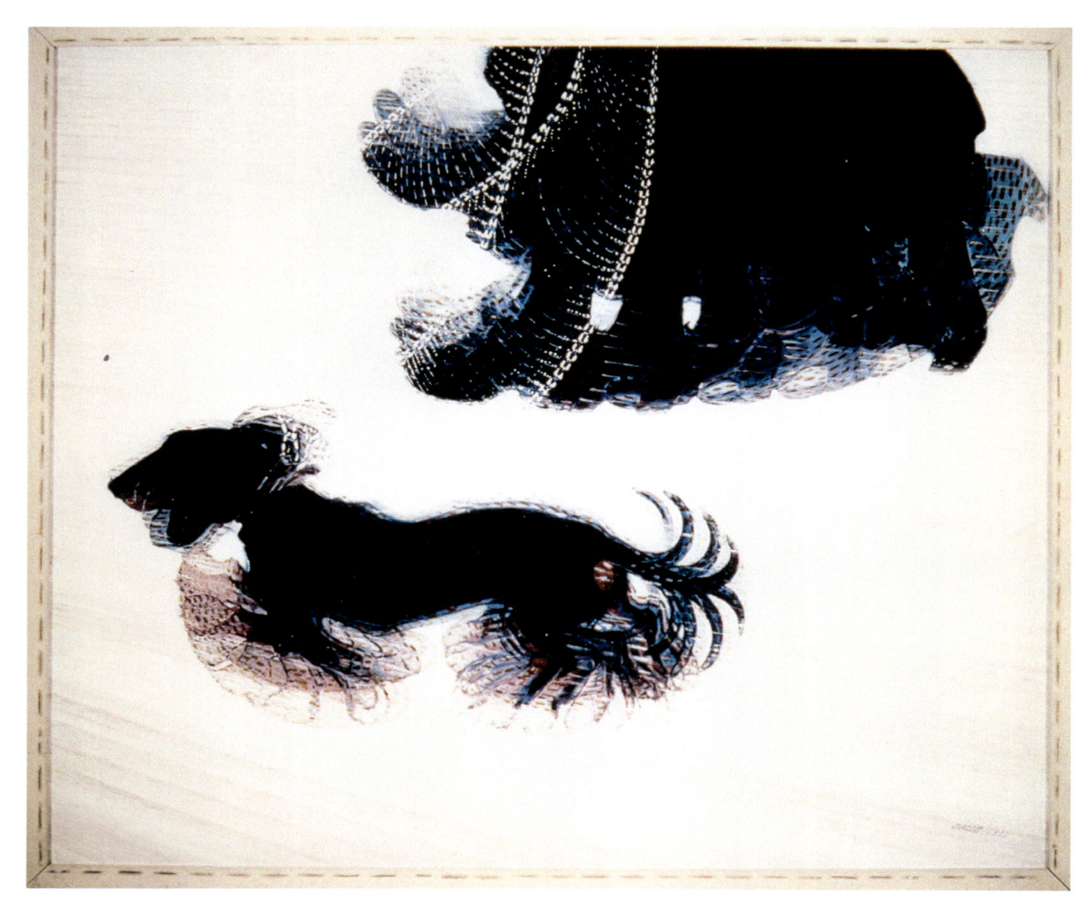

Der Virtuos.

Von **Wilhelm Busch**.

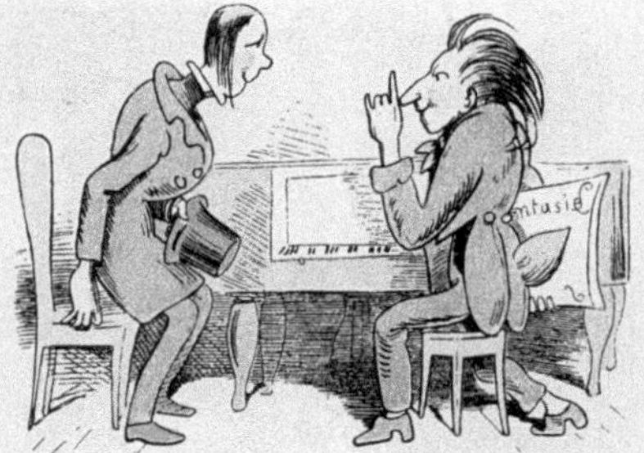

Silentium.

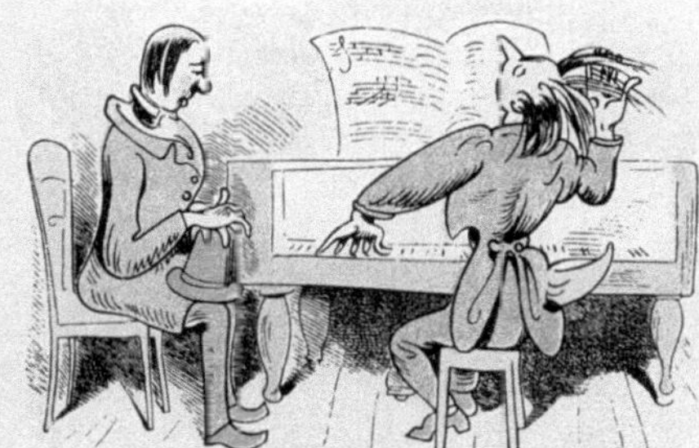

Introduzione.

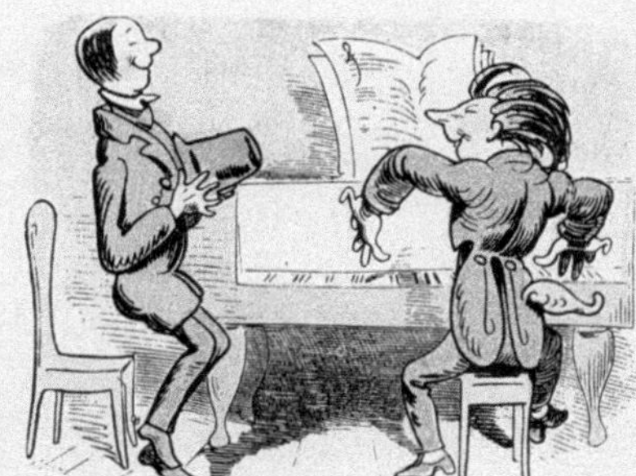

Scherzo.

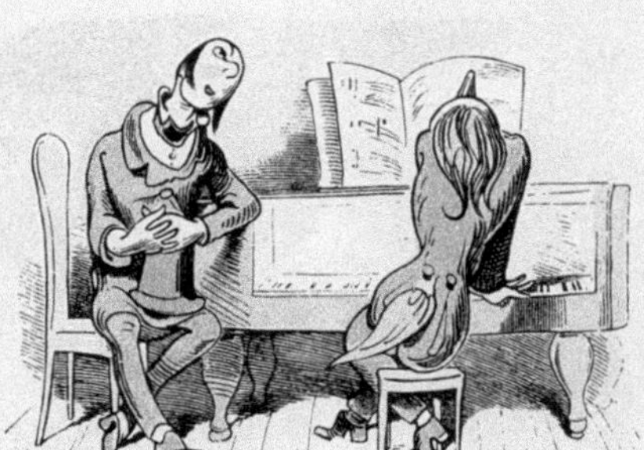

Adagio.

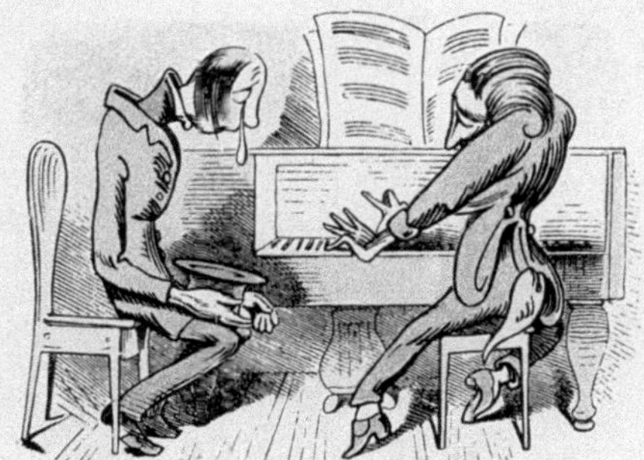

Adagio con sentimento.

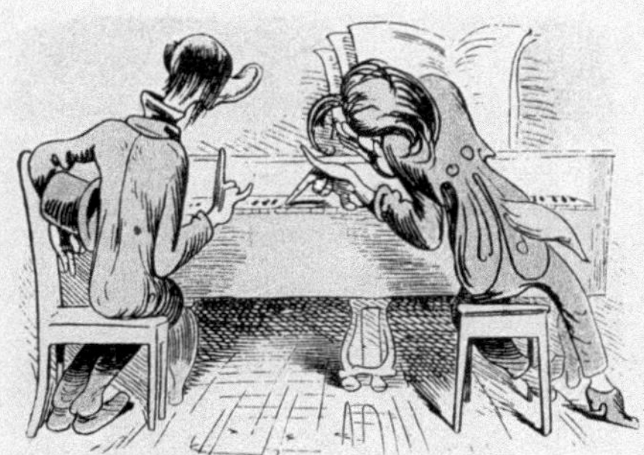

Piano.

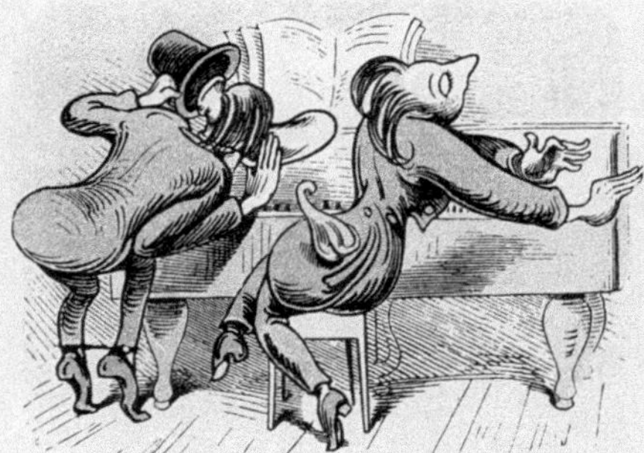

Smorzando.

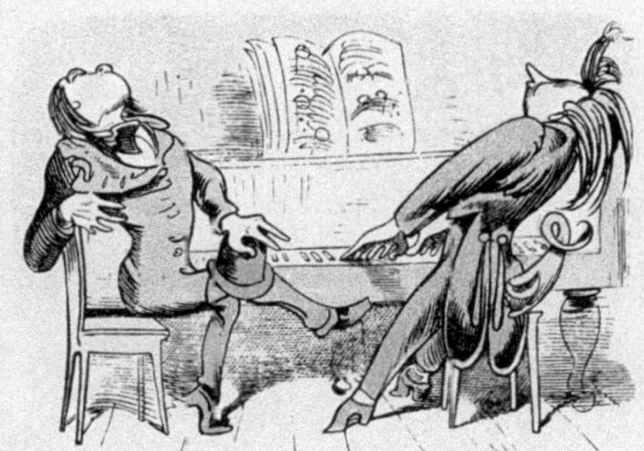

Maëstoso.

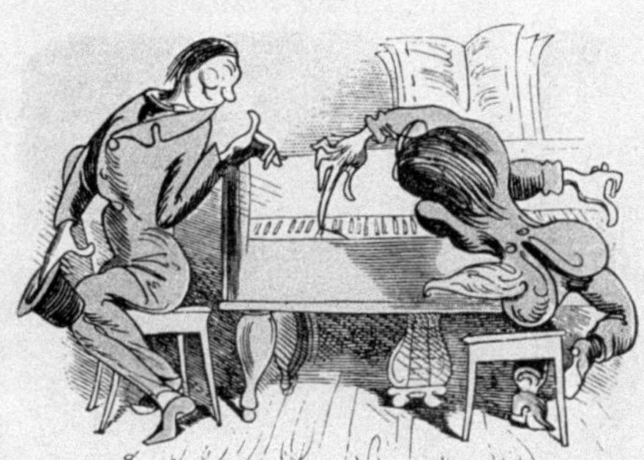

Capriccioso.

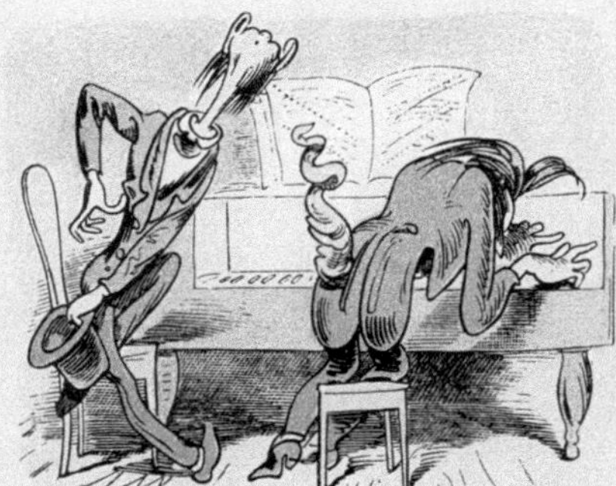

Passagio chromatico.

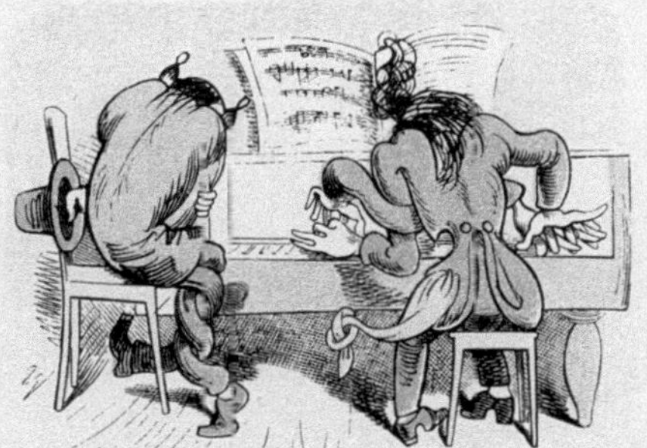

Fuga del diavolo.

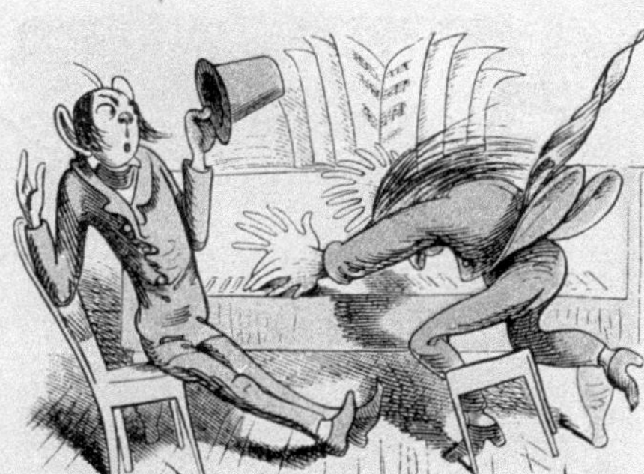

Forte vivace.

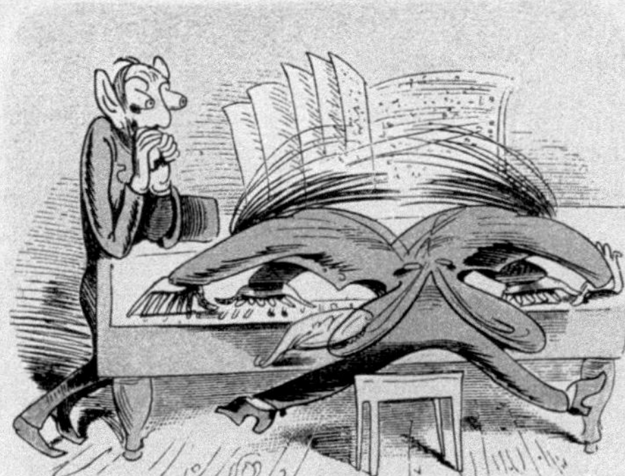

Fortissimo vivacissimo.

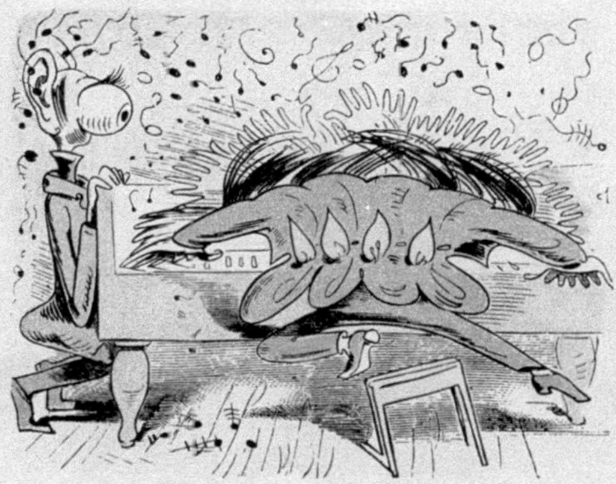

Finale furioso.

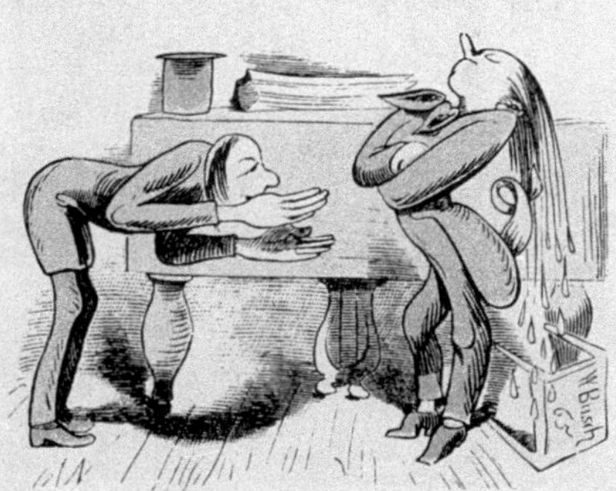

Bravo-Bravissimo.

Münchener Bilderbogen.
3. Auflage.

Manuldruck und Verlag von **Braun & Schneider** in München.

these are stretched or compressed. In his *Zebra* series (1932–1943; fig. p. 78), he succeeds not only in making the animals recognisable without outlines through the alternation of white and black, but also in suggesting volume and depth as well as movement and dynamism through the curve of the lines. All this, however, is only in the mind of the observer. His preoccupation with the processes of seeing and perceiving in relation to lines and surfaces became a central theme in Vasarely's work. He has this in common not only with Bridget Riley, but ultimately with the Dutch painters of the 17th century, who also wanted to explore the nature of seeing using the tools available to them, such as lenses, camera obscuras, telescopes and microscopes.

In the 1960s, Vasarely increasingly explored the possibilities of extending the two-dimensional pictorial space into that of the viewer. By compressing and stretching his recurring basic forms, which he began painting using vibrant colours, he succeeded in seemingly stretching his pictures into three-dimensional space (fig. right). Some appear to oscillate and pulsate. Vasarely's paintings and prints corresponded perfectly with the popular currents of the art of his time, in fashion and design. He also strove for creating work that could be both easily understood by the public and seen far and wide: "if the art product does not spill over the framework of the elite class of 'experts', art shall suffocate to death."[17] He succeeded to such an extent that after the immense popularity of his art in the 1970s the public seemed increasingly sated. His works could be seen not only in museums and poster galleries, but also on the street: Vasarely created the new logo for the Renault car company, a seemingly three-dimensional rhombus, in 1972, the same year he created the logo for the Olympic Games in Munich. Both Victor Vasarely and Bridget Riley are usually considered to be part of the op art – or optical art – movement in which optical effects are achieved through the use of abstract forms and patterns, and which led Josef Albers to the corrective suggestion that all art is indeed optical: "To distinguish any art as optical is just as meaningless as to call some music acoustical or some sculpture haptic".[18]

At the end of this chapter on the painterly attempts at deception, a picture by the American painter Mark Tansey (b. 1949) should be mentioned that encapsulates various aspects of the art of optical illusion: *The Innocent Eye Test* from 1981 (fig. pp. 80/81). As if in a historical photograph from the 19th century, we see several men who appear to be scientists together with a cow, which gazes at a painting of further bovines. The painting the cow is looking at is again a kind of optical illusion, since the original is by the Dutch painter Paulus Potter (1625–1654), who painted the first life-size painting of a bull and a cow with *The Bull* in 1647. In it, he depicted the minutest details, down to the very flies that buzz around the bull. Tansey's work seems to show

▼ Victor Vasarely, *Feny*, 1973

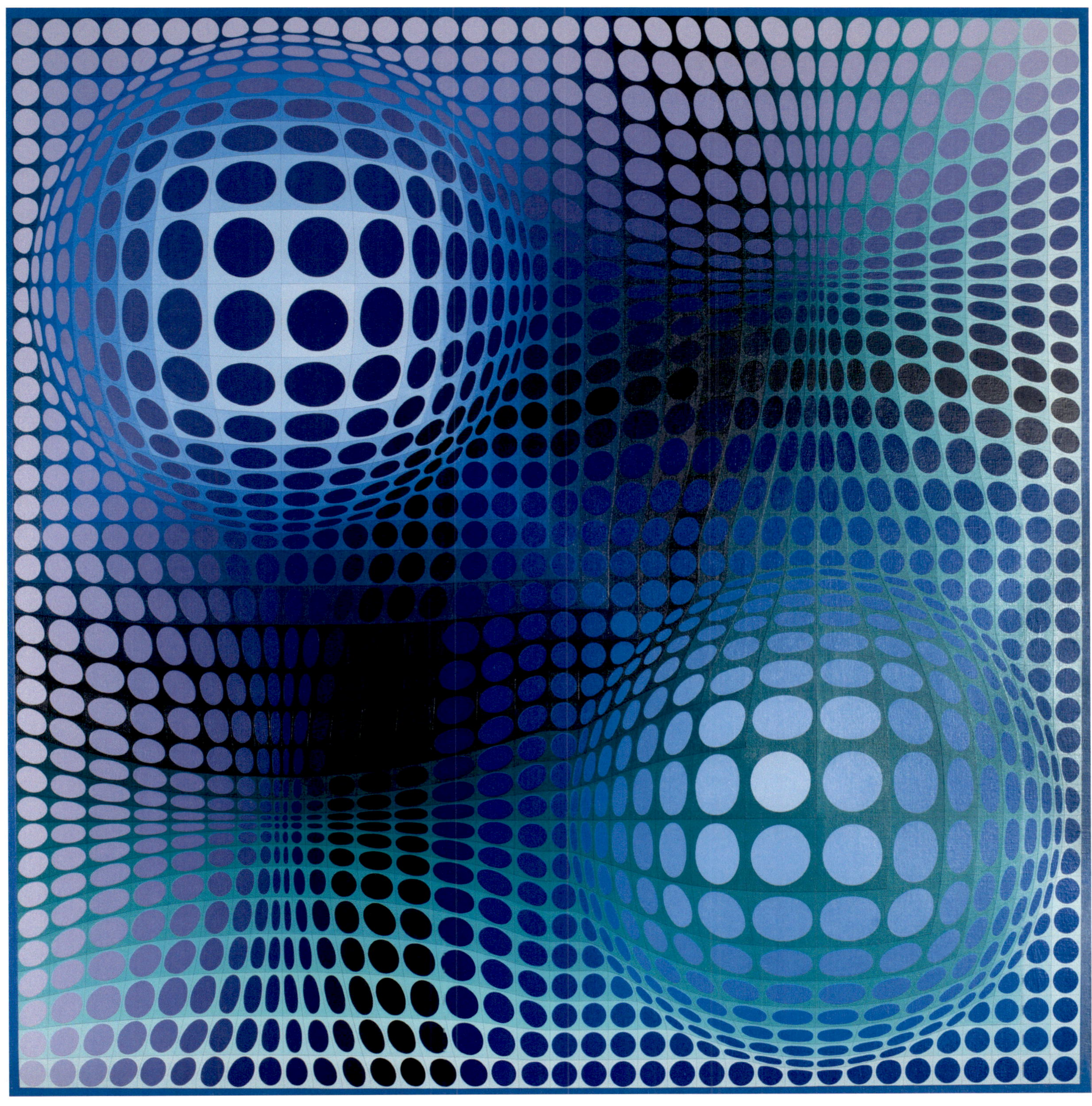

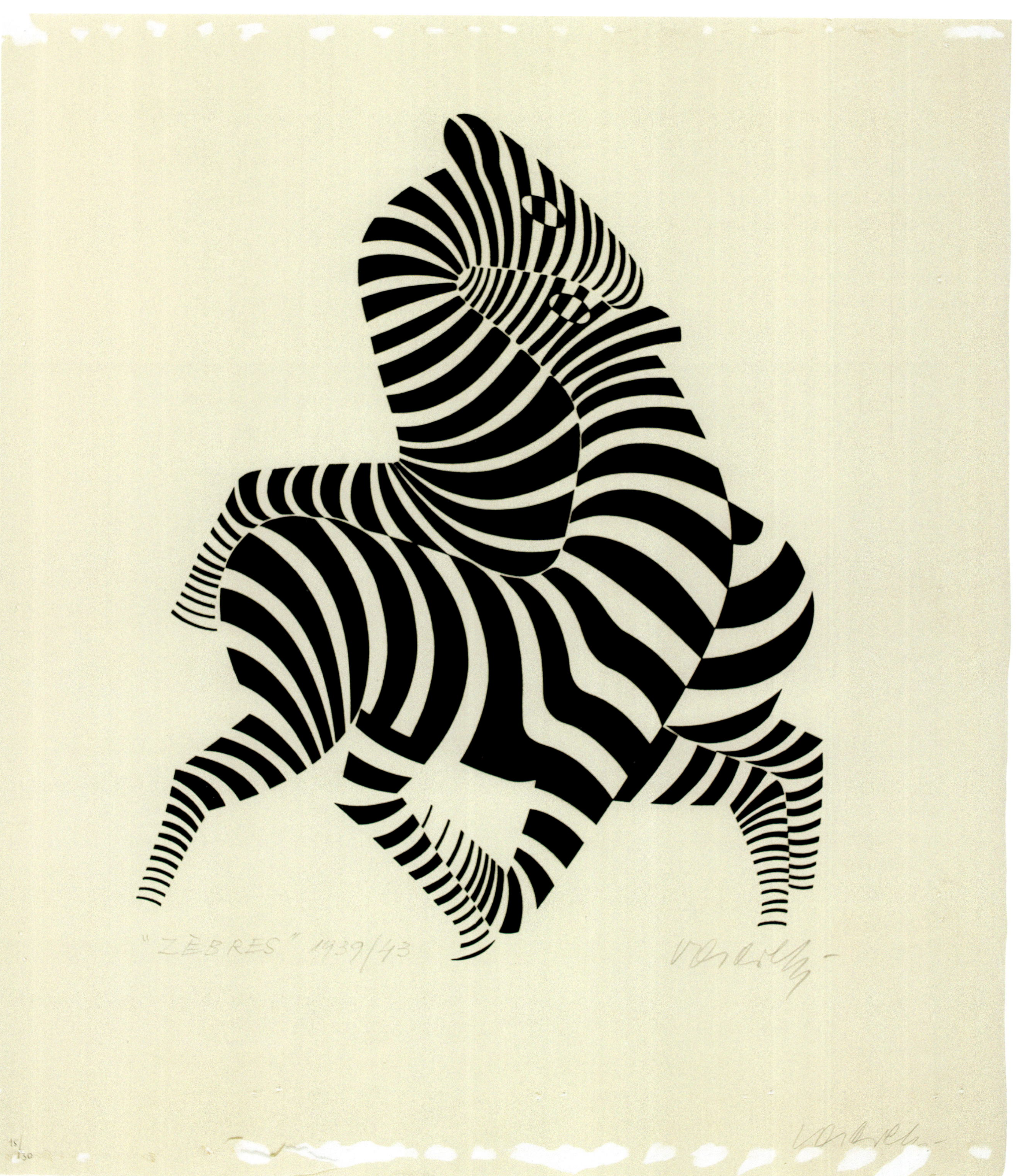
"ZÈBRES" 1939/43

a kind of experimental test to determine whether an animal's innocent eye can be deceived by painting. Tansey alludes to the primordial competition, which itself used optical illusions, between the ancient painters Parrhasius and Zeuxis in which animals also became jurors (see pp. 8–9). The question arises as to how the 'scientists' might even judge the reaction of the cow, or what reaction is expected at all. Can the cow distinguish between reality and art? Perhaps she turns right to take a closer look at the *Haystack* by Claude Monet (1840–1926) hanging nearby. Tansey's painting – with its use of black and white making it reminiscent of historical photographs – could almost be regarded as a document of such an experiment into the perception of man and beast.

◀ Victor Vasarely, *Zèbres* (*Zebras*), 1939/1943

▶ **Overleaf**

Mark Tansey, *The Innocent Eye Test*, 1981
Oil on canvas, 198,1 x 304,8 cm

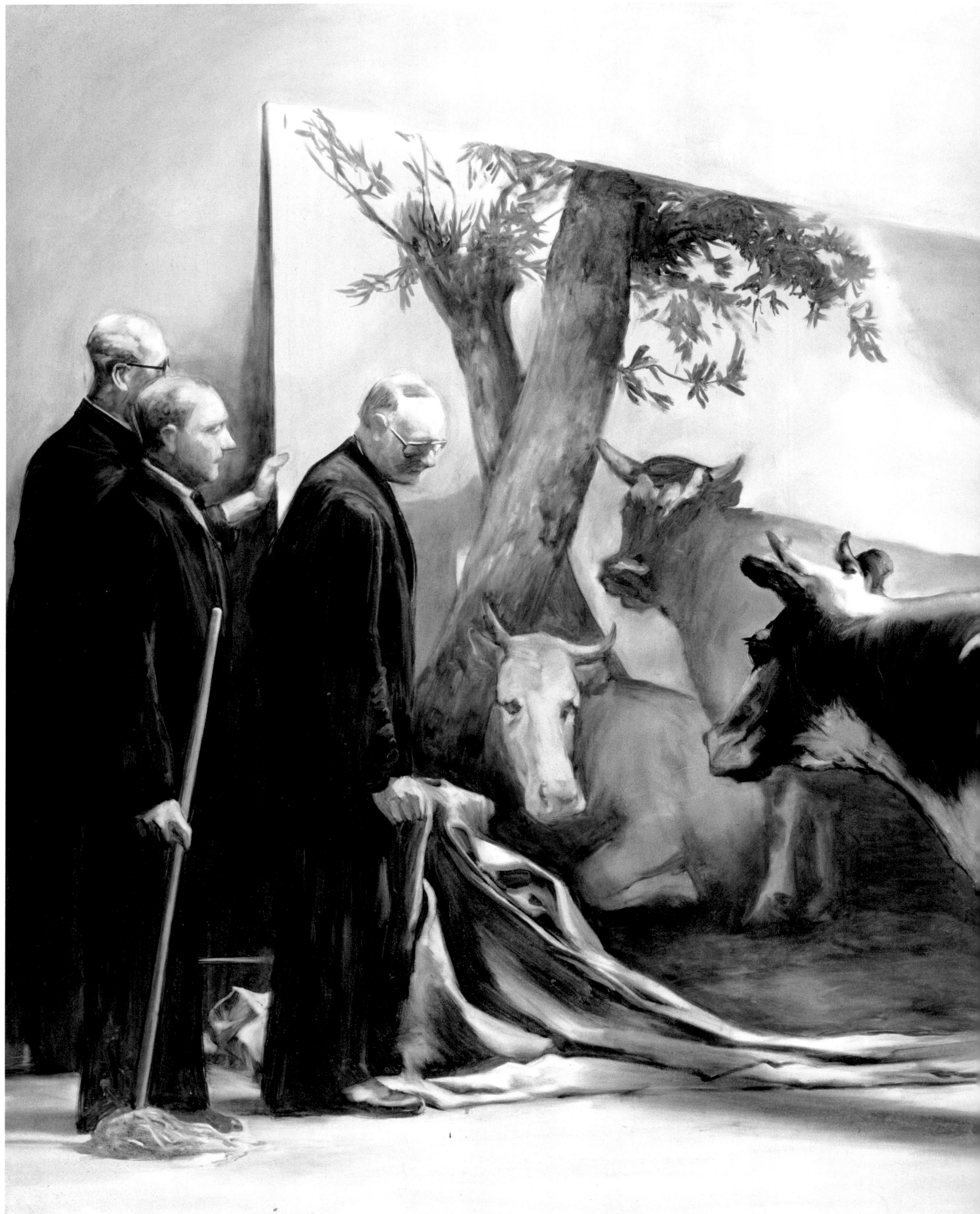

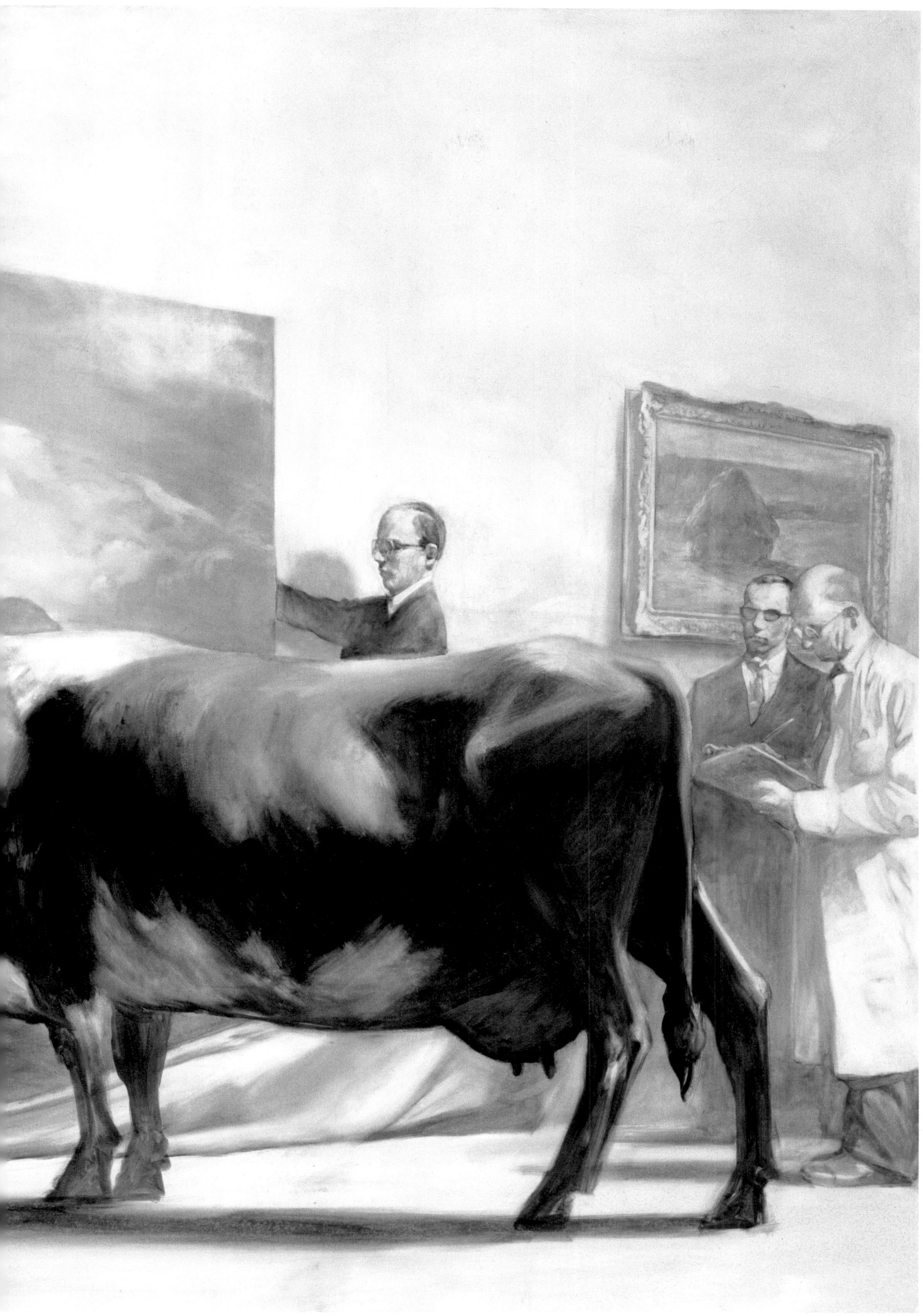

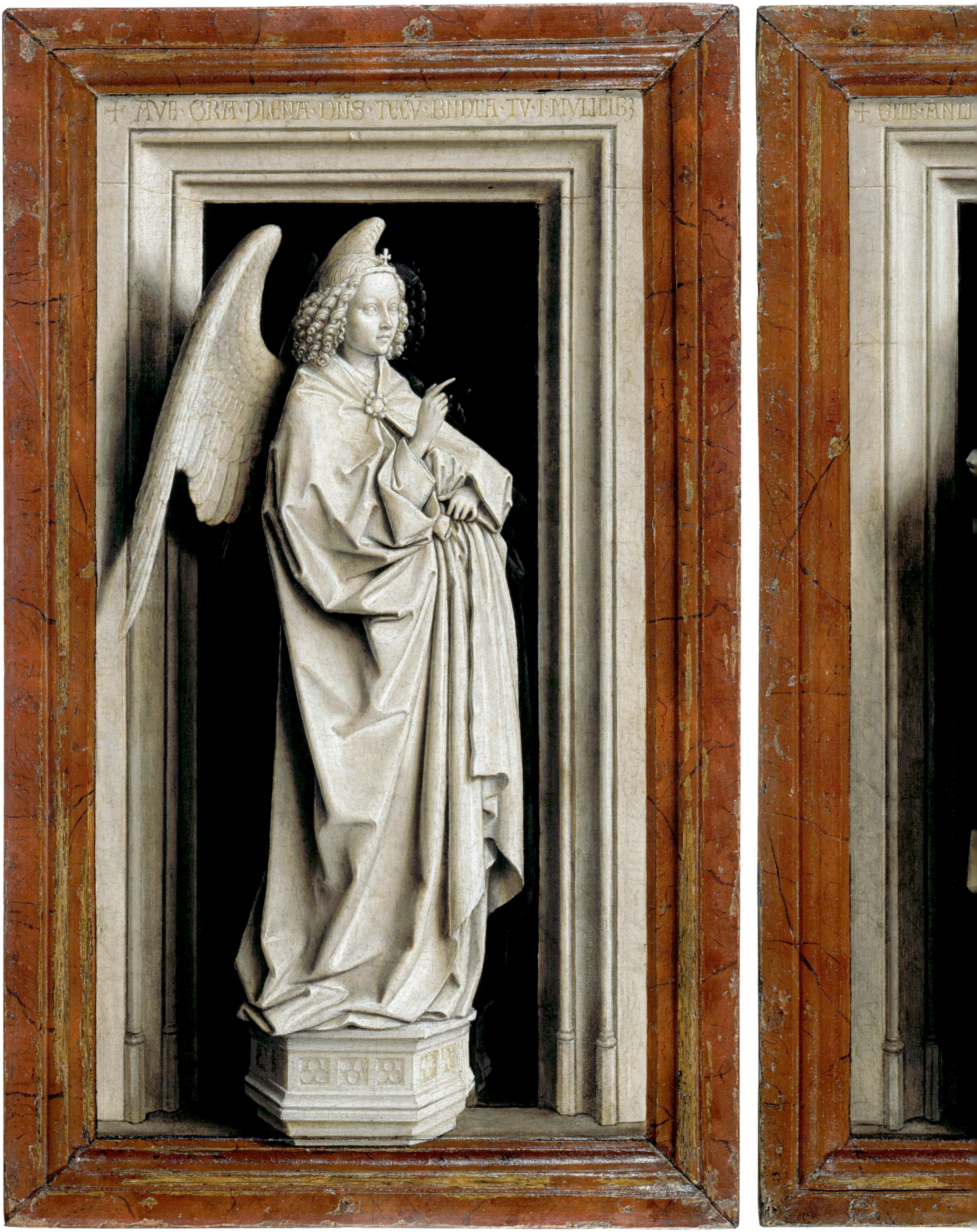

✝ AVE · GRA · PLENA · DNS · TECV · BNDCA · TV · I · MVLIEIB

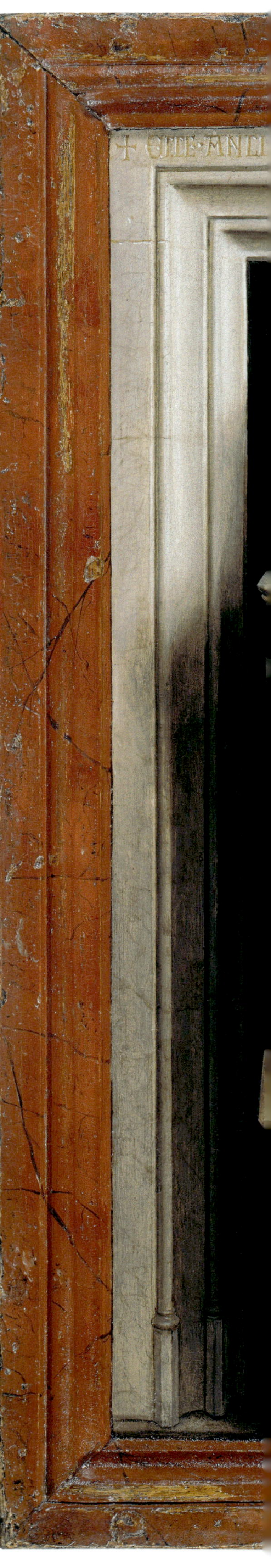

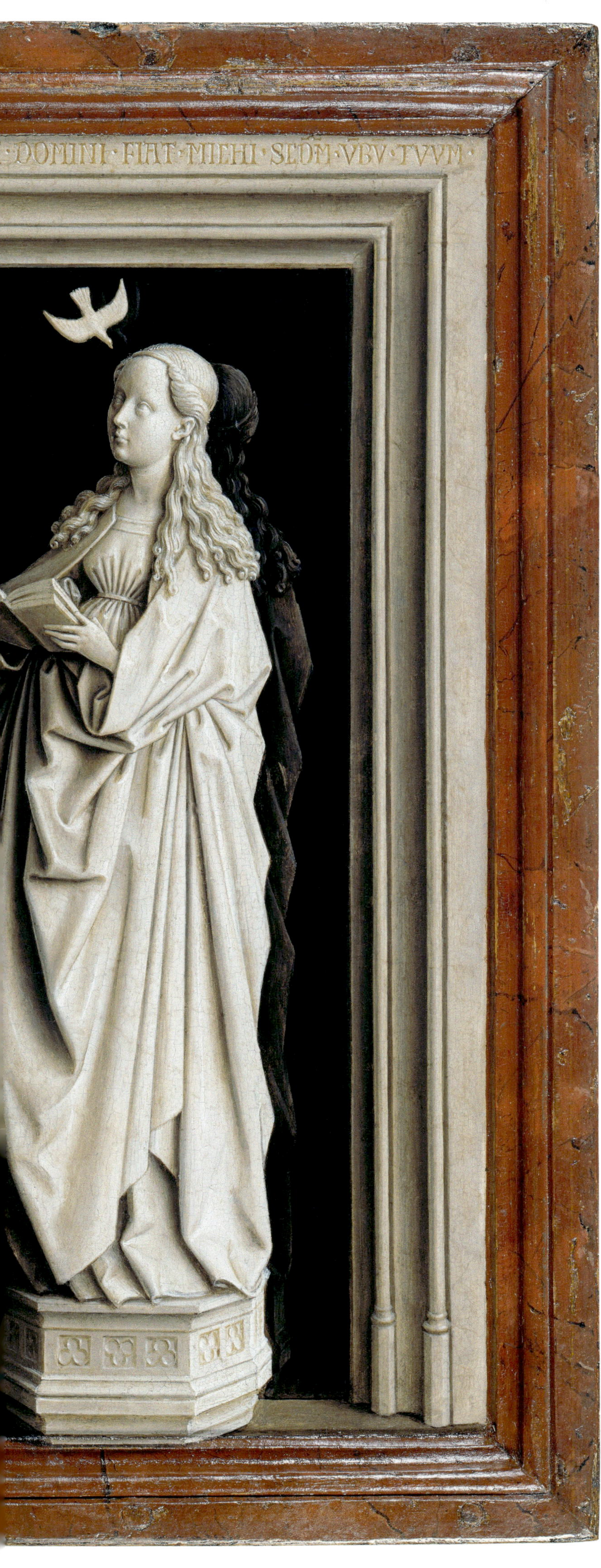

Jan van Eyck

The Annunciation, c. 1433 – 1435

Oil on panel, diptych: 38.8 × 23.2 cm (left wing), 39 × 24 cm (right wing)
Museo Nacional Thyssen-Bornemisza, Madrid

In the 14th century, winged altarpieces became popular both for church and private devotional use, which, with their shutters open on Sundays and feast days, provided the faithful with a glimpse into the world of the saints. On the other days, they remained shut and only the outer wings could be seen. In order to lend these religious works a costly air even when closed, the exteriors were sometimes embellished with grisaille figures, which, when skilfully executed, seemed convincingly like real sculptures. With the *Ghent Altarpiece* in the St Bavo Cathedral in Ghent, completed in 1432, which Jan van Eyck (c. 1390 – 1441) created with his brother Hubert (c. 1385 – 1426), Jan gives an impressive display of his mastery, which is even more convincing on a smaller scale. This small diptych shows the scene of the Annunciation with the Archangel Gabriel and the Virgin Mary as two statuettes, each standing in a niche. More accurately, they seem to be placed before their niches, since the plinths upon which they stand appear to protrude beyond the edge. The reflections of the figurines can be seen in the background – also a reference to the aforementioned 'paragone', since this reflection in the painting manages to portray both the front and back of the statuettes simultaneously, something that sculpture could not manage (see p. 54). Through Van Eyck's delicately executed style of painting and the shadows cast by one of Gabriel's wings on the frame, for example, the flat oil figures appear quite tangible to the observer.

Jacopo de' Barbari
Dead Partridge with Gauntlets and Crossbow Bolt, 1504

Oil on limewood, 52 × 42.5 cm
Alte Pinakothek, Munich

On a wooden wall panel hang a dead partridge and a pair of iron gauntlets held together by a crossbow bolt. In the lower right, a piece of paper folded twice is 'affixed', possessing a double meaning. For one, it contains the signature of de' Barbari (c. 1440–1516) as well as his emblem, the caduceus of Hermes, and the year of the work's creation: 1504. This indicates that de' Barbari regarded this painting as an independent work of art and wished it seen as such. The piece of paper, also known as a 'cartellino', became a recurring motif in the tradition of trompe l'œil painting, because it is so excellently suited to misleading the public. The 'cartellino', like the other objects, was painted on wood, but it is not the wood which we see before us. De' Barbari deceives us with a painted wooden wall that seems all the more realistic because he even depicts the wear that the panels have supposedly suffered. Today, it is assumed that the painting was part of the decoration intended for a trophy room, which is probably why de' Barbari also faked the surface of the wooden wall. Imagine a hunting party returning to this room and catching a glimpse of the gauntlets and hunting trophy, the partridge, hanging on the wall. Perhaps these hunters would also like to read what is written on the little note of paper. As they approach, however, they soon realise that these items are not real objects at all, that they have fallen for the painter's deception. If one imagines the fresh colours of the picture at the time of its creation and the, probably none too bright, lighting that would have existed in the room, de' Barbari may well have succeeded in creating the perfect illusion. The sense of surprise was likely as great as it had been for those present during the unveiling of Masaccio's *Holy Trinity* fresco almost a century earlier (see pp. 38–39). All the more so since the viewers of de' Barbari's painting were witnessing something completely unusual, since this was the first trompe l'œil painting since antiquity. In fact, it was also the first autonomous still life since classical times. With this picture, de' Barbari founded two extremely successful genres of painting. This trompe l'œil pretends that what one sees actually does exist at the moment of seeing – but only up to the moment of realising that it is a deception. So it is a very contemporary kind of art, indeed.

There are no religious references in de' Barbari's painting; the picture shows only what it shows. However, as is common in still lifes, it is quite possible that the painter inserted symbolic meaning into the work beyond the effects used to deceive. This could be related to his use of the partridge, for the following reason. The ancient painter, sculptor and inventor Daedalus, who, amongst other things, created the Labyrinth which held the Minotaur, had a nephew named Perdix, who was also his best pupil. Perdix came up with such important inventions as the saw, the potter's wheel and a pair of compasses, a tool essential for painting. Daedalus became so jealous of his nephew's talents that he threw him from a high ledge. The goddess Athena, however, saved the nephew by turning him into a partridge, allowing him to fly away – the bird's scientific name remains *Perdix perdix*. Perhaps with this picture, de' Barbari poses the question of the relationship between art and power, symbolised here by the gauntlets and the crossbow arrow. What the partridge shot down from its flight actually means in this context, however, can no longer be clarified definitively.

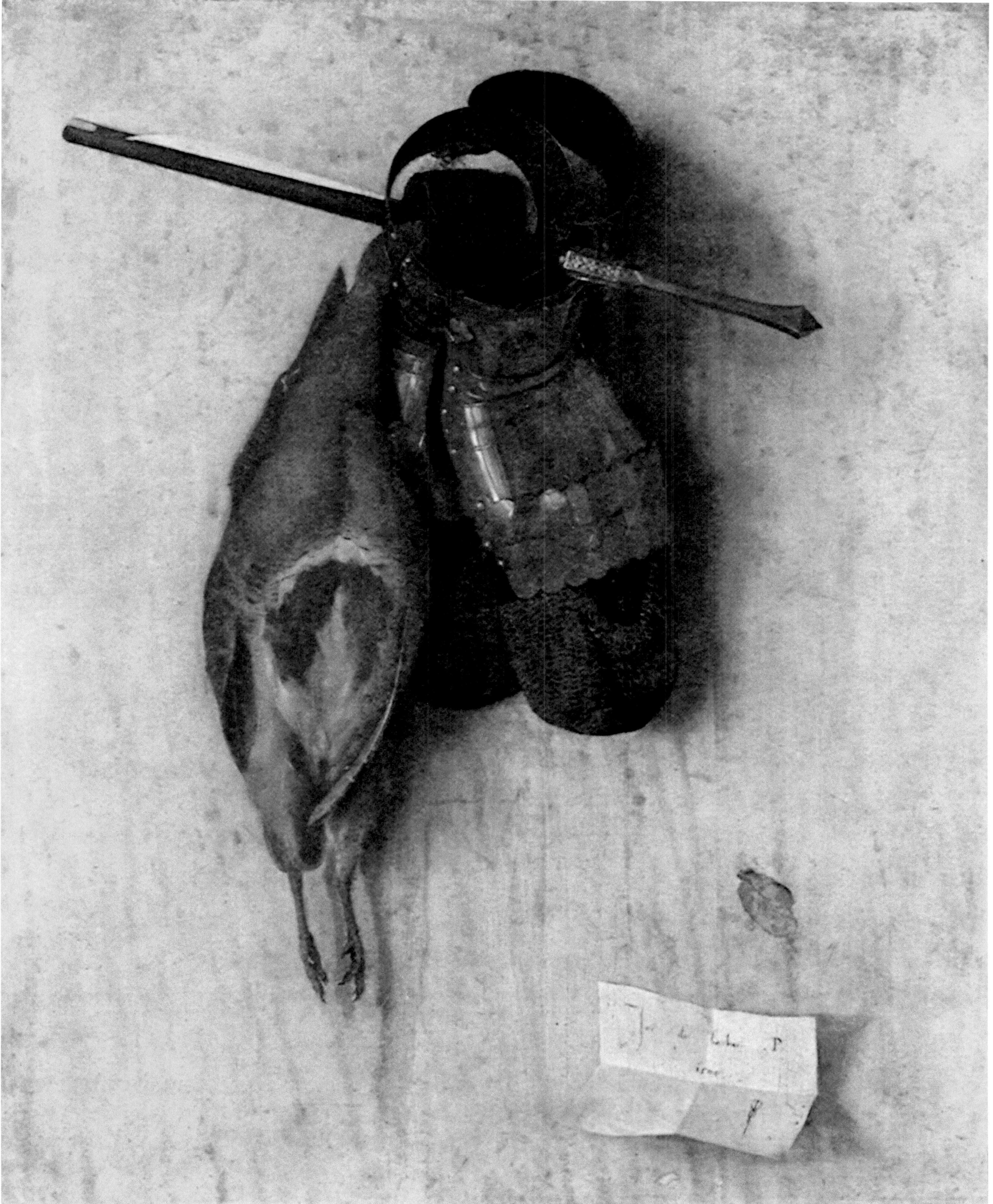

Samuel van Hoogstraten

Letter Rack, 1666/1678

Oil on canvas, 63 × 79 cm
Staatliche Kunsthalle Karlsruhe

Samuel van Hoogstraten (1627–1678) shows in his trompe l'œil, painted around 1670, not only a perfect optical illusion, but also a self-portrait, which emerges from proverbial wisdom. Tell me what you have, and I will tell you who you are. The many, varied objects on this letter rack describe him and his interests and undertakings. For example, the quill and the pen-knife refer to his occupation as an author, which he additionally underlines with the two small books, two tragedies written by him. In addition, Van Hoogstraten seems to have attached great importance to his appearance, as indicated by the comb and razor. However, the comb also stands for orderly thinking – and this is most likely the more important meaning for Van Hoogstraten. Additionally, a portrait medallion of the Habsburg Emperor Ferdinand III may be seen, which Van Hoogstraten received in 1652 in recognition of his great skill in painting. In the corresponding letter, he is compared with his peers of antiquity Zeuxis and Parrhasius (see pp. 8–9). Van Hoogstraten was thus a man of many talents. The painter pays tribute to the writer, but the painter still takes centre stage here – not only because of the honour he received from the emperor, but also because of the painting itself. The careful examination of these many individual details however almost leads one to forget the fact that the painting itself is the most important endorsement of the painter and reference to his profession. The small pamphlet on the left indicates the actual theme of the work. It is the *Principles of Philosophy* (*Principia philosophiæ*) of René Descartes, published in 1644, in which deception is treated as a central concept. This text and the trompe l'œil of the painting demonstrate Van Hoogstraten's concept of art. For him, painting – and in particular still life painting – is ultimately based on illusion and deception.

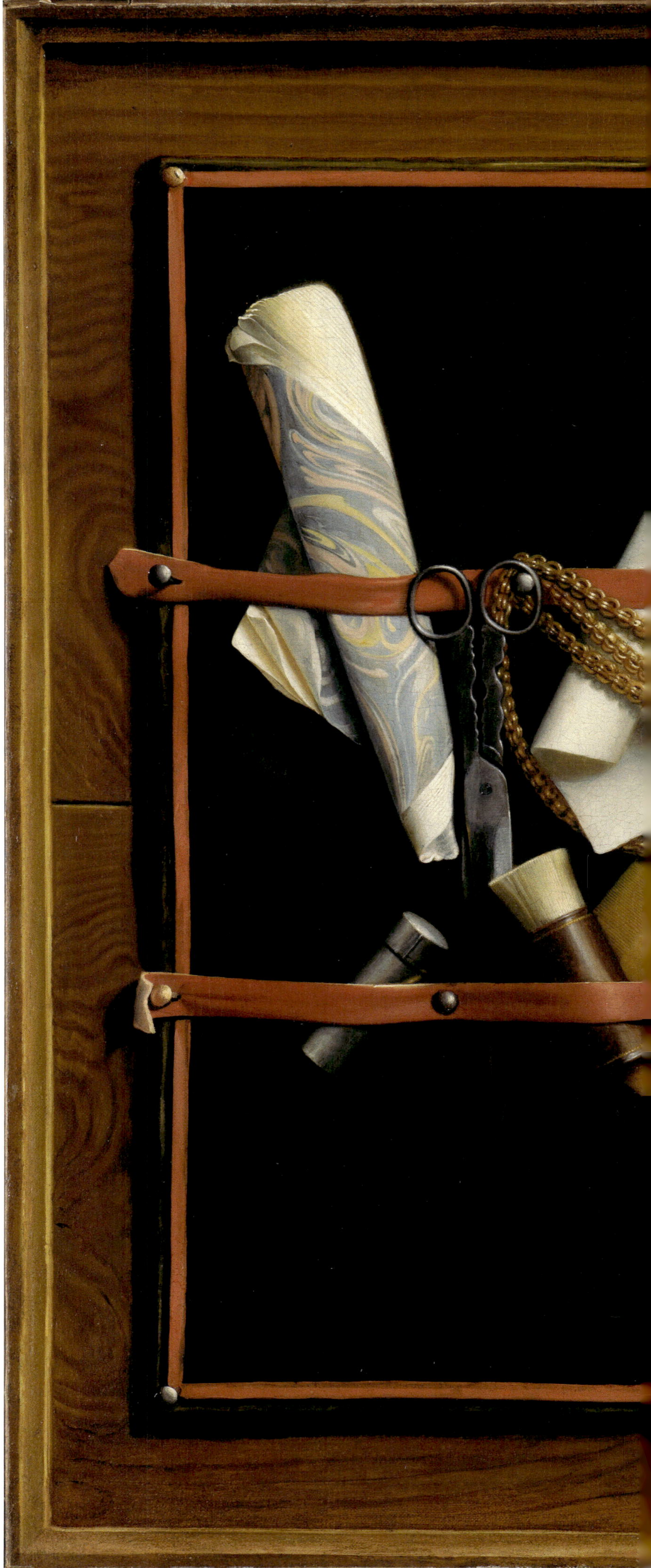

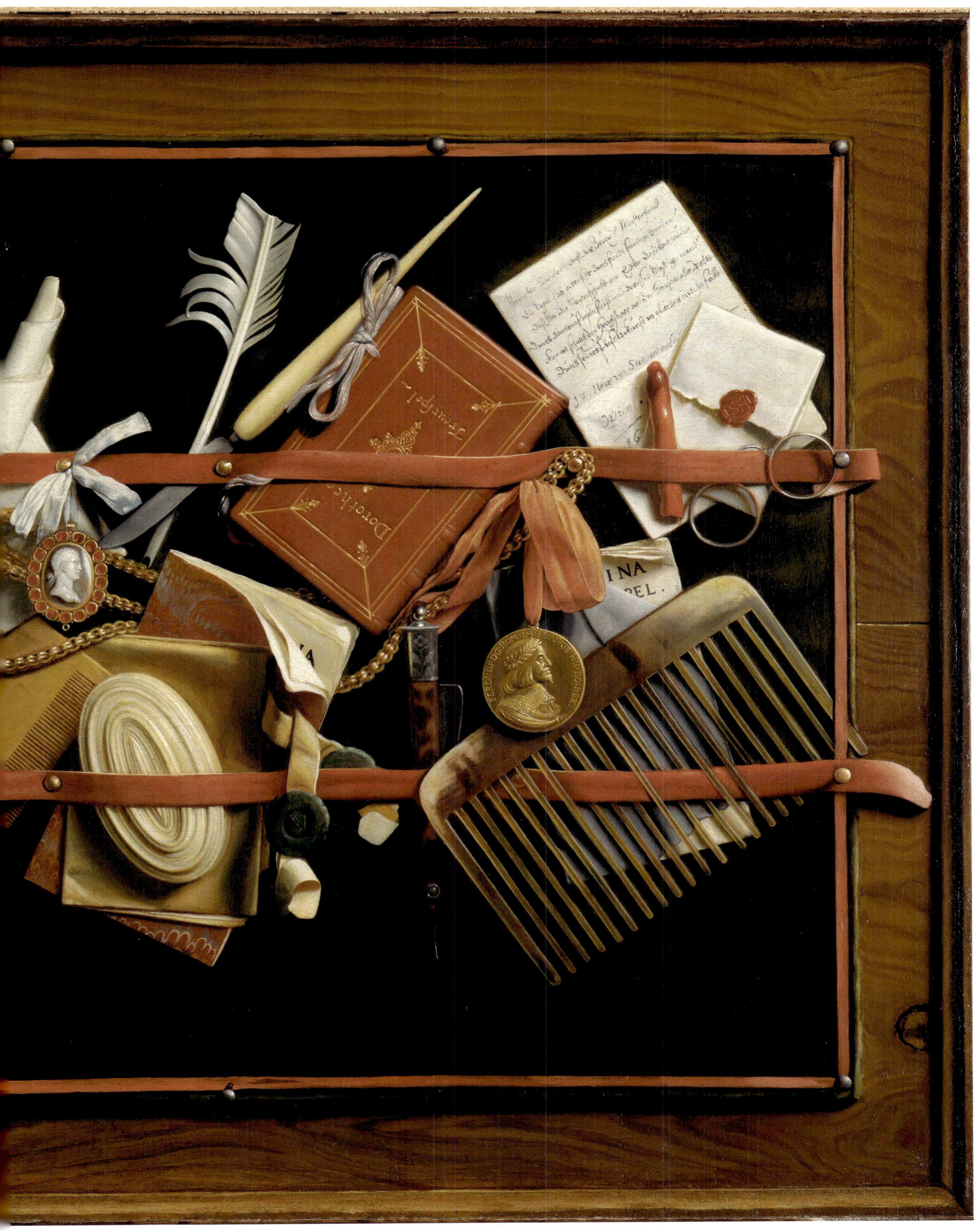
Treurspel.
I NA
PEL.

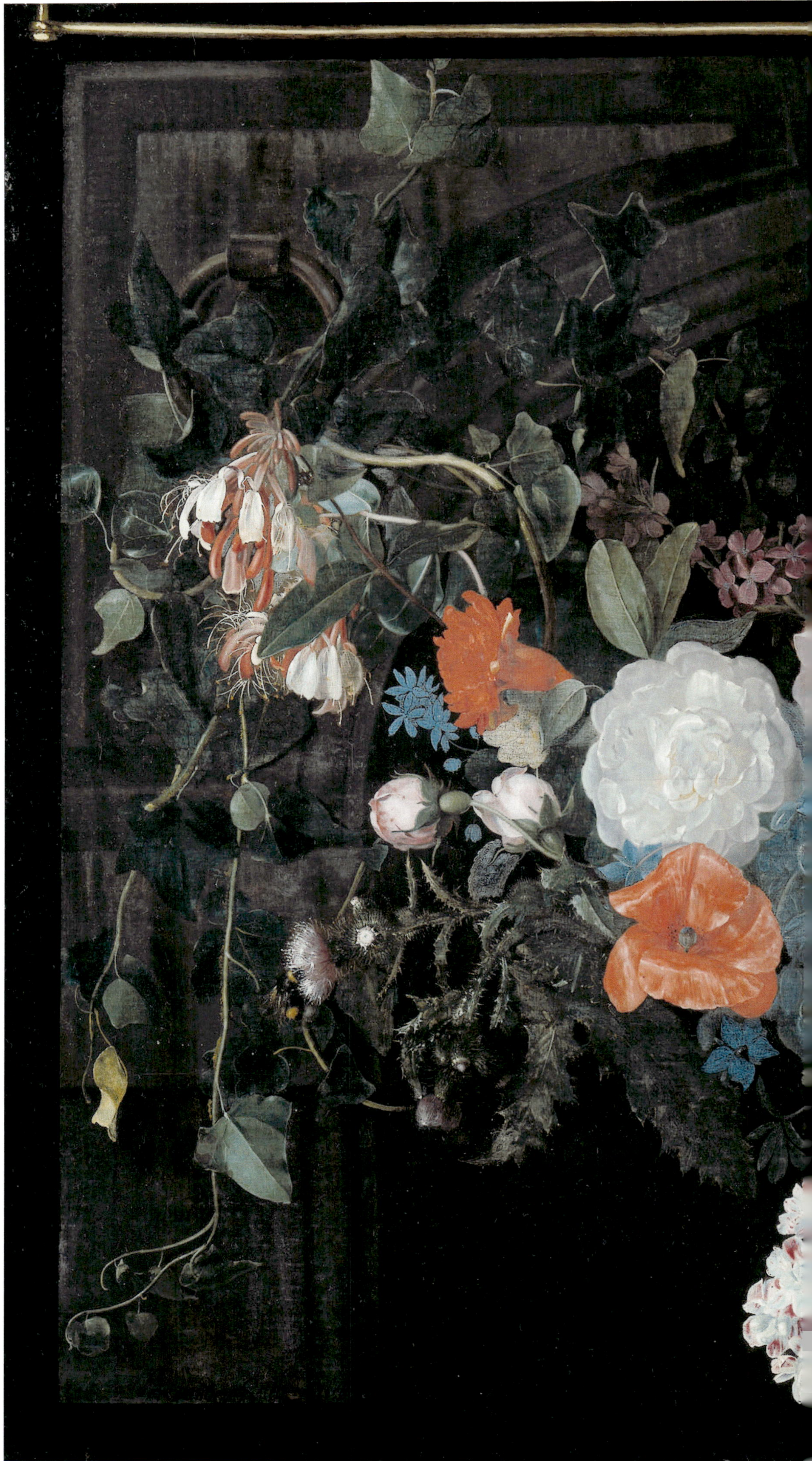

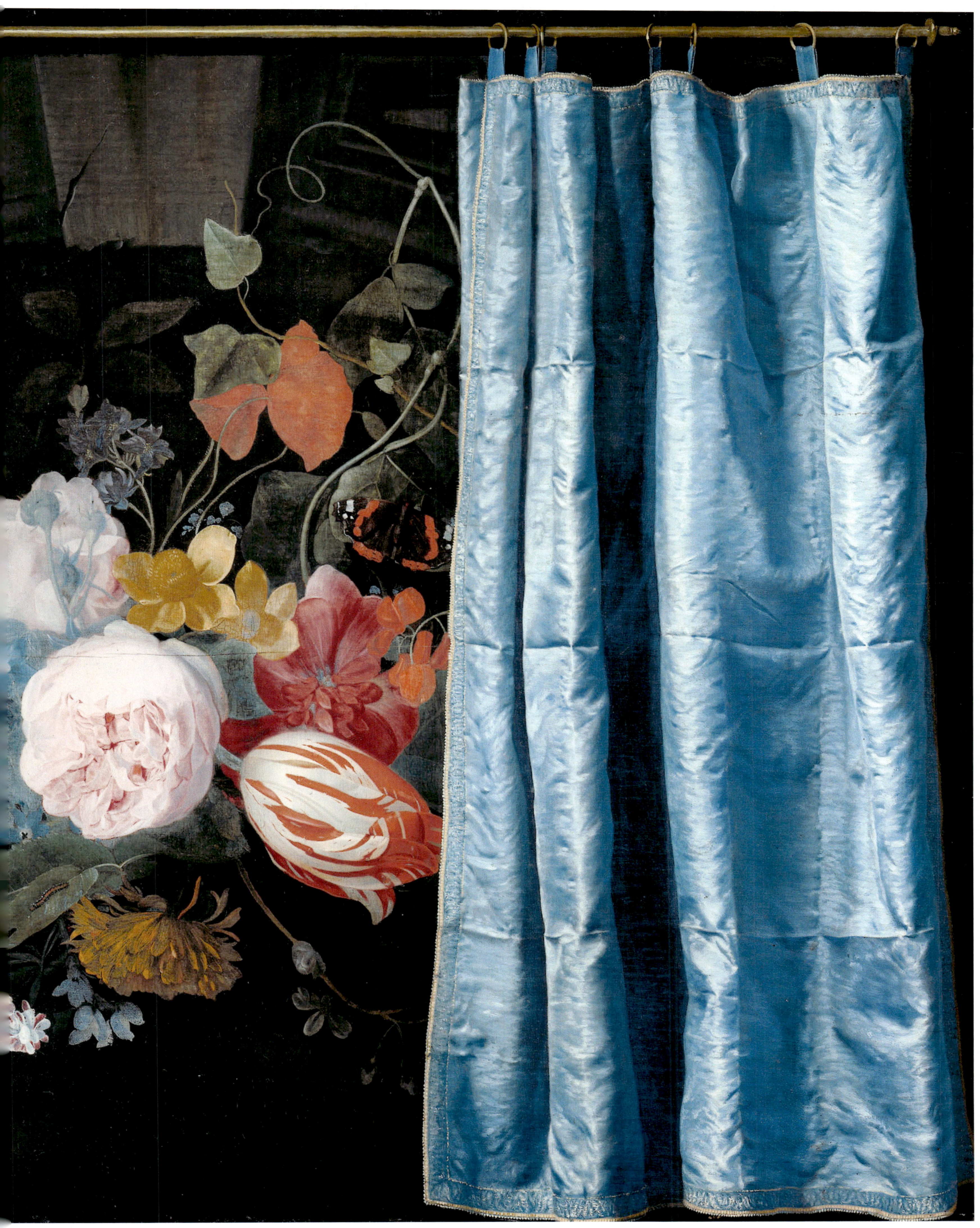

Adriaen van der Spelt and Frans van Mieris

Still Life with a Flower Garland and a Curtain, 1658

Oil on panel, 46.5 × 63.9 cm
Art Institute Chicago,
Wirt D. Walker Fund
◀ **Previous spread**

The public might well have been taken in by the almost perfect illusion created by the joint work of the Leiden painters Frans van Mieris (1635 – 1681) and Adriaen van der Spelt (c. 1630 – 1673) from 1658. Together they created one of the most convincing trompe l'œil paintings of their day. And this was accomplished with a very clever trick: Floral still lifes were in great demand in the middle of the 17th century as trading in flower bulbs – especially the bulbs of tulips – had led to a boom on the Amsterdam Stock Exchange and finally, in 1637, to the first market crash in history. Even after this speculative bubble burst, trading continued. Floral still lifes were very popular and were also used as a kind of elaborate catalogue, amongst other things, to give customers an idea of which flowers bloom from which bulbs or seeds. Characteristic for this is the fact that in paintings, like the one presented here, flowers are shown together that do not bloom at the same time. In addition, the floral still lifes were part of a traditional 'competition' in the creation of beauty between art and nature.

Van der Spelt painted the fragrant flowers, which were not intended as an illusion, in contrast to the almost tangible silk curtain of his colleague Van Mieris, which covers part of the floral picture. This would not have been completely out of place; curtains hung before pictures were often used to protect against dust and light. Van Mieris plays with this custom and tricks his audience into believing they see such a protective curtain. The drapery is painted so realistically that, for a moment, one could think it real. This, in turn, was a speciality of the painters from the birthplace of Rembrandt (1606 – 1669), Leiden, who became known as 'Leiden Fijnschilders' (fine painters). The artists who succeeded Gerrit Dou (1613 – 1675) were concerned with meticulously naturalistic painting, with an almost enamel-like surface treatment in which one can no longer distinguish the brushstrokes. And certainly, the two painters with their drapery also make reference to the famous competition between the painters of antiquity, Zeuxis and Parrhasius, in which a deceptively real painted curtain was the decisive factor in affirming the victor (see pp. 8 – 9).

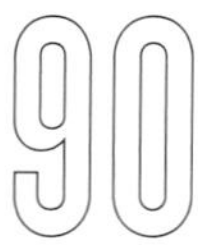

Jan van der Vaardt
Violin and Bow,
c. 1700

Oil on panel, 97.1 × 78.1 cm
Chatsworth House Trust

Just as Cornelis Norbertus Gysbrechts found fame in Denmark, his Amsterdam colleague Jan van der Vaardt (c. 1650 –1727) moved to London in 1674 to paint portraits, landscapes, still lifes and a now very famous trompe l'œil of a violin. The painting was produced around 1723 for Devonshire House, the London townhouse of the Cavendish family – since the 16th century, one of England's most influential (and wealthiest) families, the Dukes of Devonshire. The house in Piccadilly was destroyed by fire in 1733, but the painting was saved and taken to their country house Chatsworth House. Here, becoming the most popular item in an art collection, as large as it is exquisite, the painting found its ideal place on one of two doors. When the first door is opened, the violin along with its bow may be seen on the second, apparently hanging from a metal peg. The setting is perfect: The picture, with its painted wood, is set into the actual door panel, the lighting conditions are ideal and one has the feeling that one could take the instrument down from its metal peg, which, to stage the 'fake' violin even more subtly, is a very real metal knob.

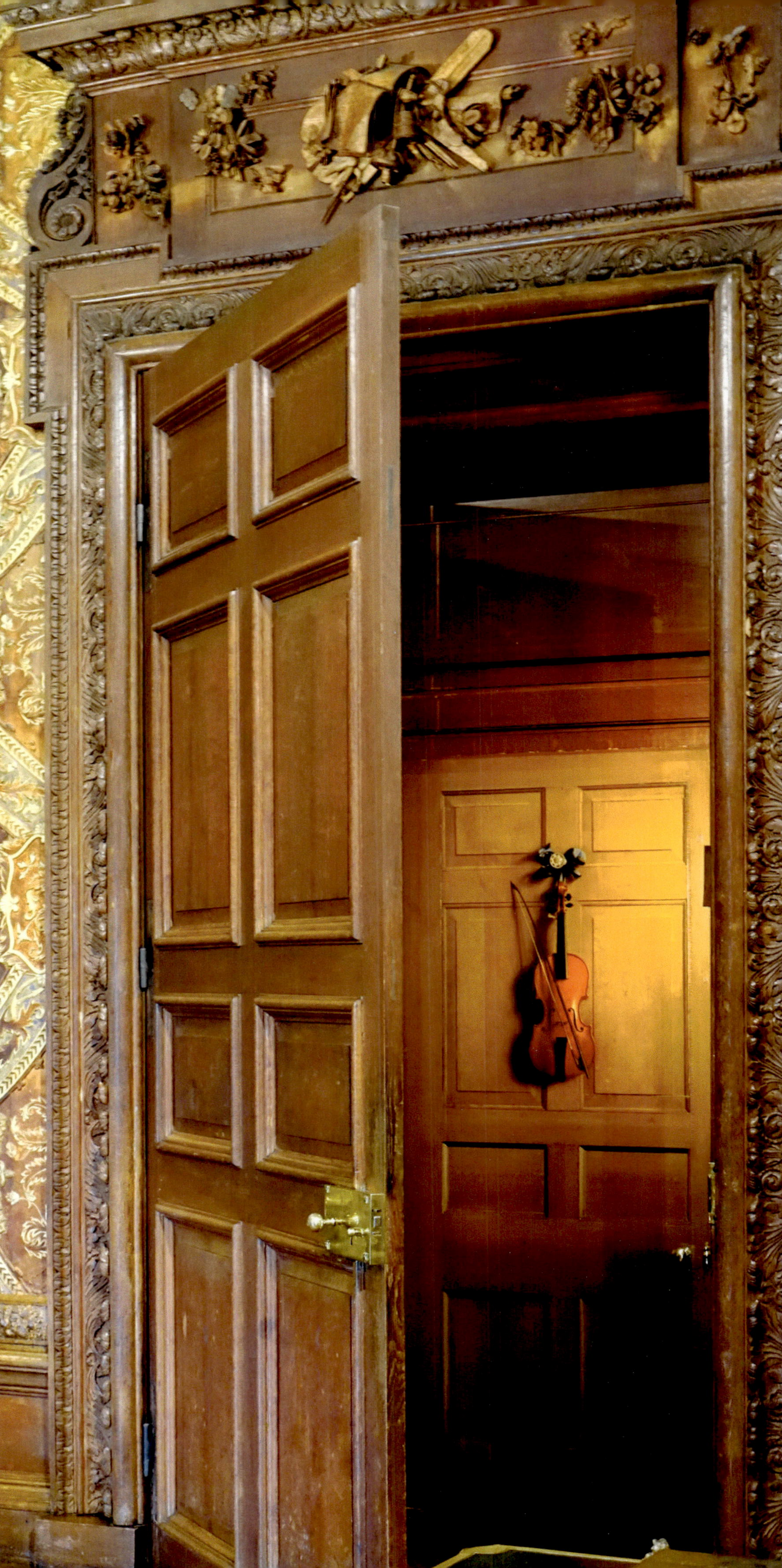

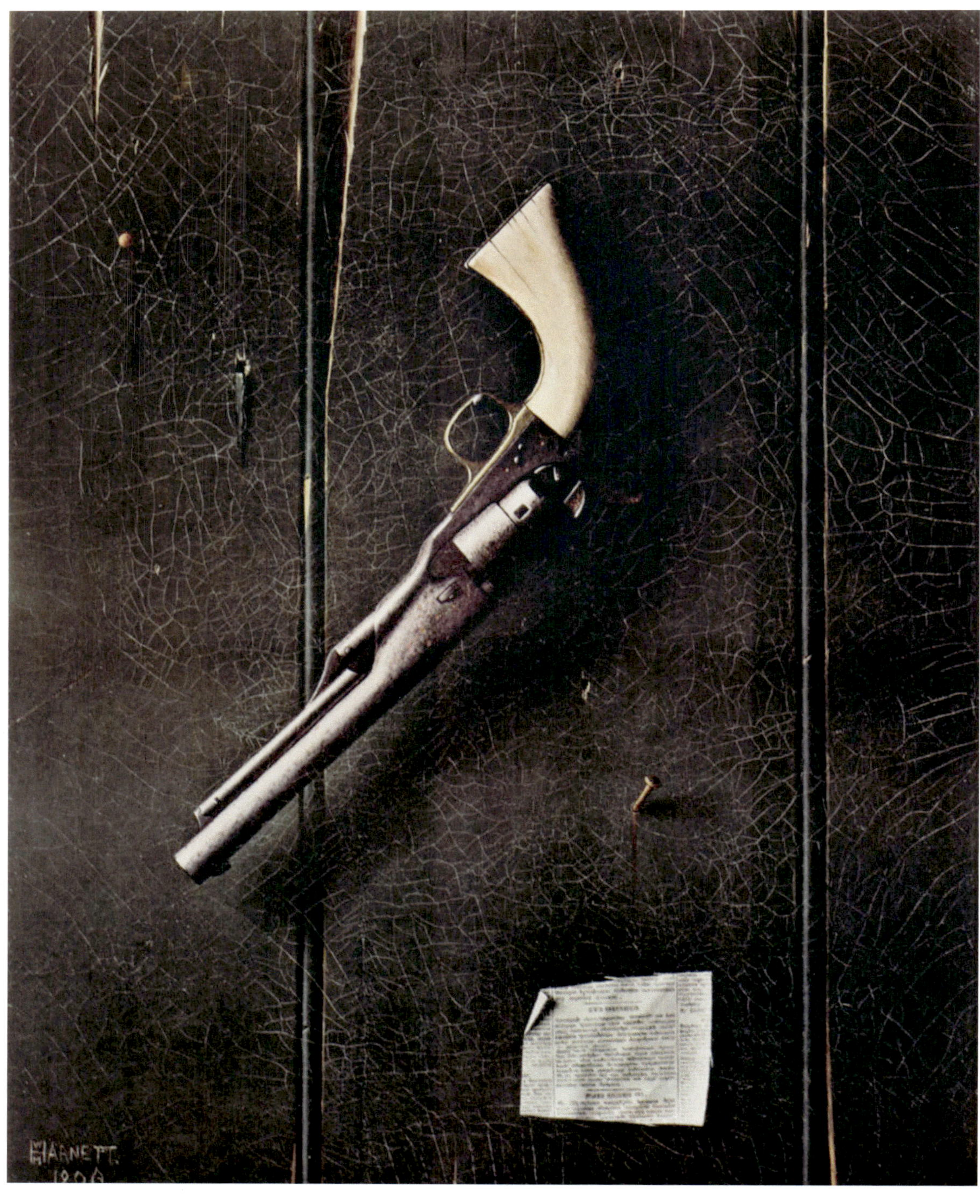

William Harnett
The Faithful Colt, 1890

Oil on canvas, 57.2 × 47 cm
Wadsworth Atheneum Museum of Art, Hartford, Connecticut
The Ella Gallup Sumner and Mary Catlin Sumner Collection Fund, 1935,236

◀ **Facing page**

John Haberle
A Bachelor's Drawer, 1890–1894

Oil on canvas, 50.8 × 91.4 cm
The Metropolitan Museum of Art, New York
Purchase, Henry R. Luce Gift, 1970

▶ **Overleaf**

In 1935, the gallery owner Edith Halpert noticed *The Faithful Colt* by William Harnett (1848–1892) in the shop window of a New York jeweller's and was thrilled. She saw a model of the 1860 .44 calibre army revolver, which had been manufactured over a hundred thousand times by the end of the century and had been used by Union soldiers during the American Civil War. It was also known as "the gun that won the Civil War and tamed the Wild West". The nickel-plated revolver with an ivory grip hangs with its trigger guard from a nail driven into a rather shabby-looking wall. There is no doubt that it is Harnett's own firearm, and apparent from the signs of wear, there is equally little doubt that it has been hard used. But when and for what purpose? At the Battle of Gettysburg? For personal use? Anything is possible, and thanks to Harnett's illusionistic abilities, one feels the urge to take the Colt off the wall and examine it more closely. Perhaps the newspaper clipping that seems to be pasted below will tell us more. But no. Harnett had the quirk of painting such clippings so that they remain ineligible.

It is therefore left to the imagination of the observer. Everything seems possible; nothing is certain – after all, this is a trompe l'œil. Even without this information, Edith Halpert was elated and found sponsors to purchase the painting for the Wadsworth Atheneum in Hartford, Connecticut. In doing so, she rescued William Harnett from oblivion and, in an exhibition in 1939, turned him into one of the best-known still life and trompe l'œil painters in the United States. A potent sponsor had also been found quickly for funding – Colt's Patent Fire Arms Manufacturing Company has its headquarters in Hartford.

A Bachelor's Drawer by John Haberle (1856–1933) is a very humorous, Americanly modern version of the 17th-century Dutch letter rack. Haberle collects all sorts of references to himself and his work in this drawer, just as the Dutch painters had done before him. Banknotes, a pipe, concert and theatre tickets, a penknife, matches, photographs of dancers and a pin-up photo. All this looks very much like the life of a bachelor, if it were not for the photograph of a baby and a small booklet of baby names. Perhaps the objects do not refer to a bachelor after all, but to a husband's sentimental reminiscences of the carefree times before marriage.

However the picture is intended, it is clear from the newspaper cuttings and the small tintype with his likeness to the lower right that the work is mainly about Haberle and his art. In the newspaper clippings, one can read about painted banknotes that seem all too real. Such dollar bills actually brought the artist a visit from the police. On another piece of paper, a headline can be deciphered which refers to a duped cat ("It fooled the cat"). Here, Haberle refers to one of his early trompe l'œil paintings, *Grandma's Hearthstone* (1890), which allegedly deceived a cat so that it curled up in front of the painted fireplace. Perhaps the artist was thinking of the forefathers of trompe l'œil, Zeuxis and Parrhasius, and the birds that pecked at the painted grapes (see pp. 8–9). And perhaps this painting is also meant to recall Samuel van Hoogstraten's tongue-in-cheek letter rack of 1658 (see pp. 86–87). A comb may even be spotted in Haberle's 'self-portrait', as in the one by his Dutch predecessor. Whether it also stands here as a symbol for orderly thinking is anyone's guess.

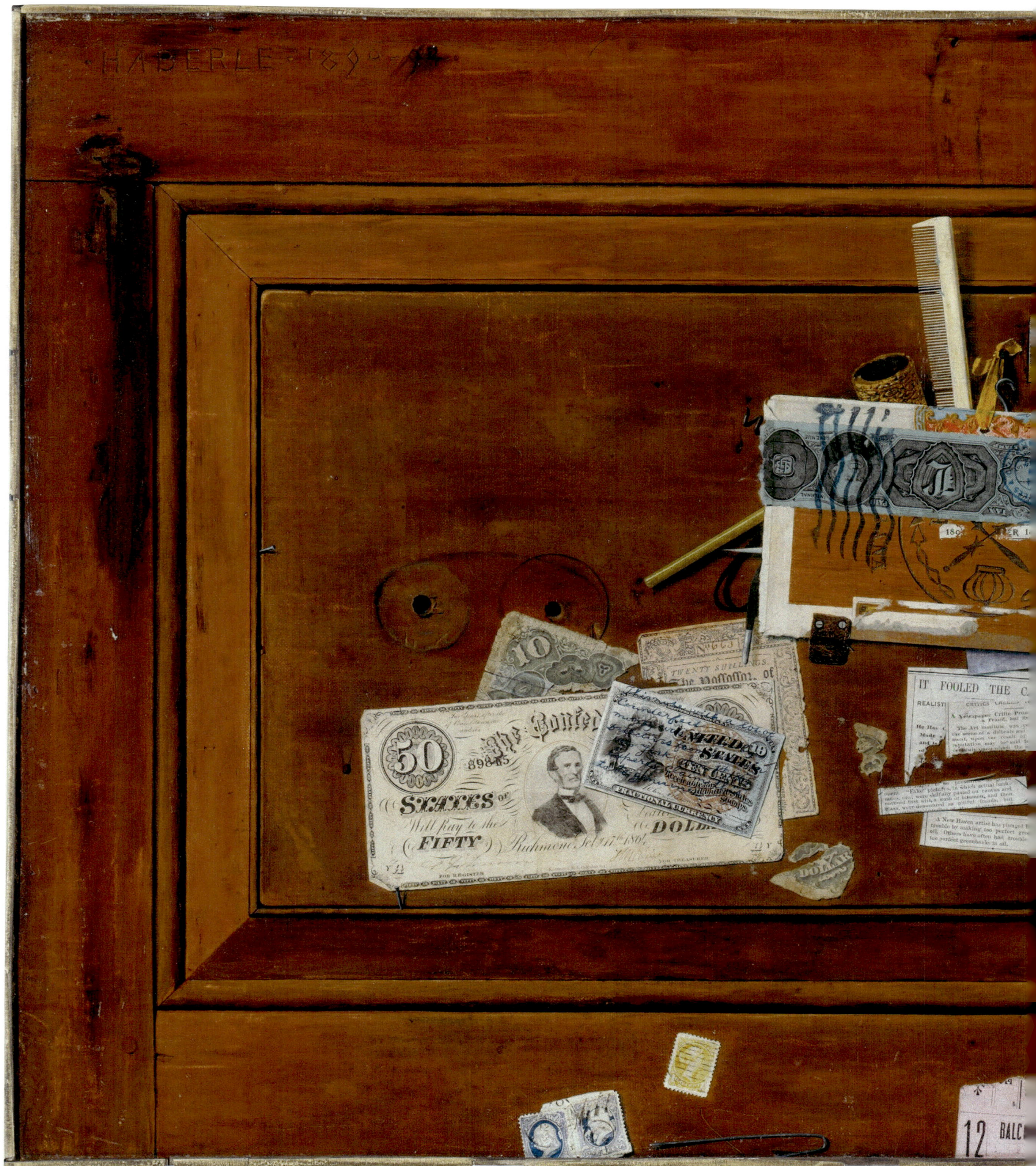
50
STATES
FIFTY
TWENTY SHILLINGS
FRACTIONAL CURRENCY
IT FOOLED THE C
12

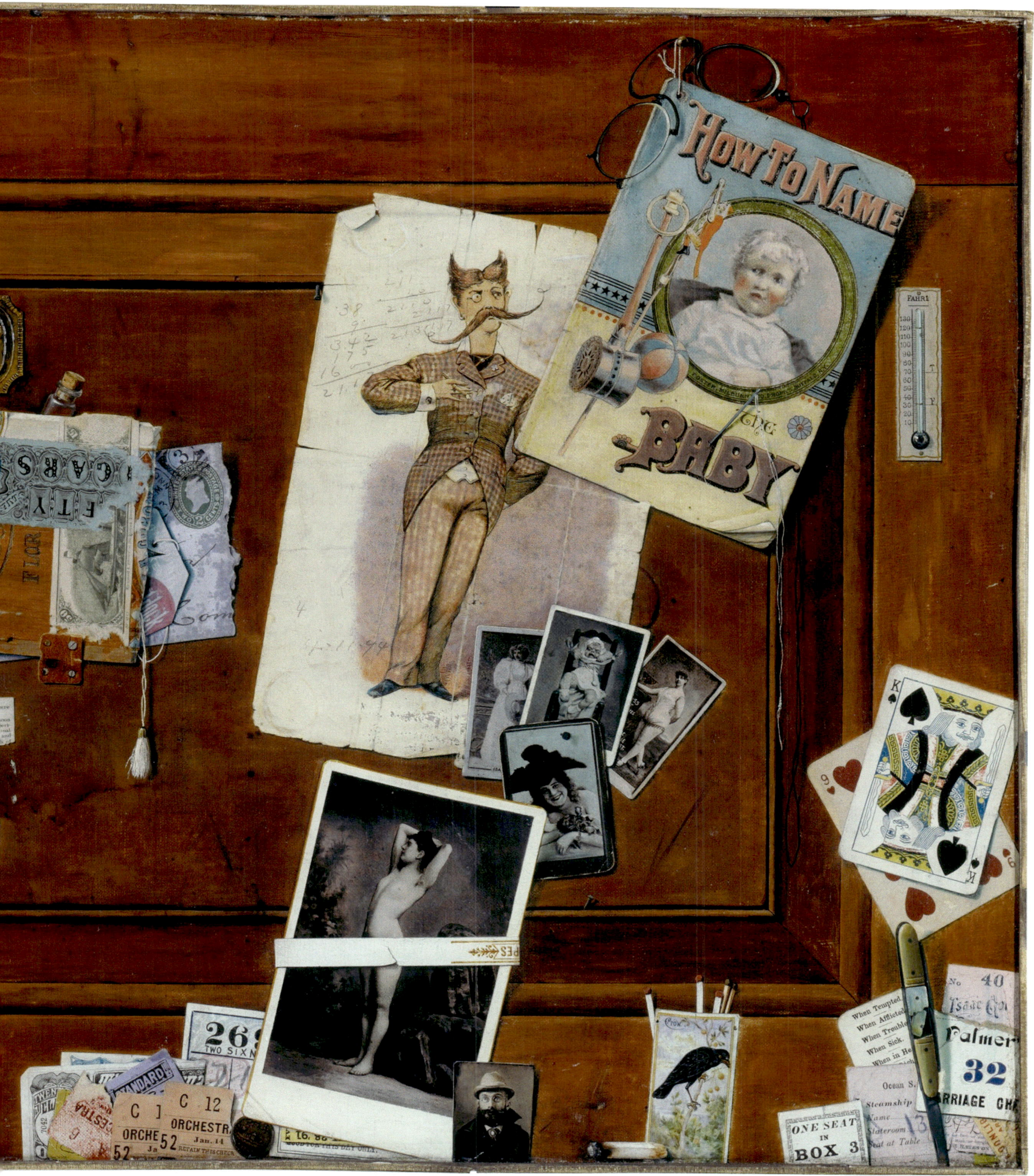
HOW TO NAME
THE
BABY
FAHR
ONE SEAT
IN
BOX 3
ORCHESTRA
STANDARD
TWO SIXN
Palmer
32
ARRIAGE CH
No 40
Steamship
Ocean S.
When Tempted
When Afflicted
When Sick

René Magritte

The Palace from Curtains, III, 1928–1929

Oil on canvas, 81.2 × 166.4 cm
The Museum of Modern Art, New York
The Sidney and Harriet Janis Collection

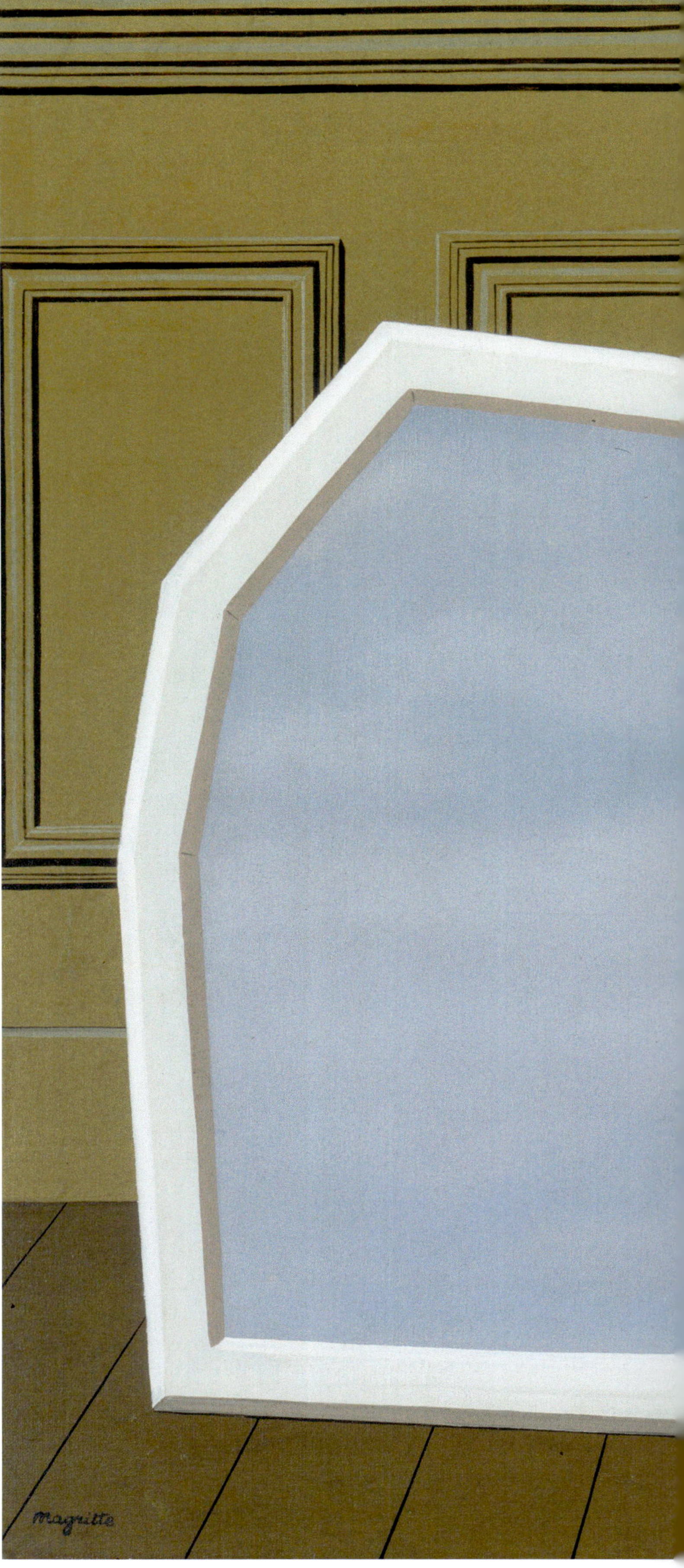

The Belgian artist René Magritte (1898–1967) saw himself more as a thinker than a painter – a thinker who used images. He himself said, "I don't believe in ideas. If I had any, my paintings would be symbolic, but they aren't. They're simply thoughts that become visible."[19] Magritte was continuously preoccupied with the relationship between things and the system of naming them, and how they are represented, as well as with the question of what is reality and what is illusion. In the painting *The Palace from Curtains, III* from 1928–1929, two heptagonal pictures stand on the floor, leaning against a wood-panelled wall. One shows a painted sky, while the other shows the French word for sky: "ciel". The painting demonstrates Magritte's way of thinking very precisely. He assumes that no one knows exactly what constitutes the world really, so we have to use our powers of imagination to create a picture of it.

Magritte has painted a realistically seeming sky in the left-hand picture within the picture, just as he imagined it at that moment or as he actually saw it. So it is a real or a fictitious sky, which does not really matter, because it is still, despite everything, just a likeness of the sky. What is more, each observer also has a different idea of the sky, so Magritte paints the word "ciel" in the right-hand picture within the picture so that everyone can imagine their own sky. The image of it is thus created in the mind of the observer and, in this way, may be closer to the real sky than the image Magritte himself has painted it. In the pictures Magritte creates and the thoughts he has, the acts of thinking, seeing and imagining are brought into ever new constellations and connections so that one can always look anew at one's own relationship to pictures and art itself.

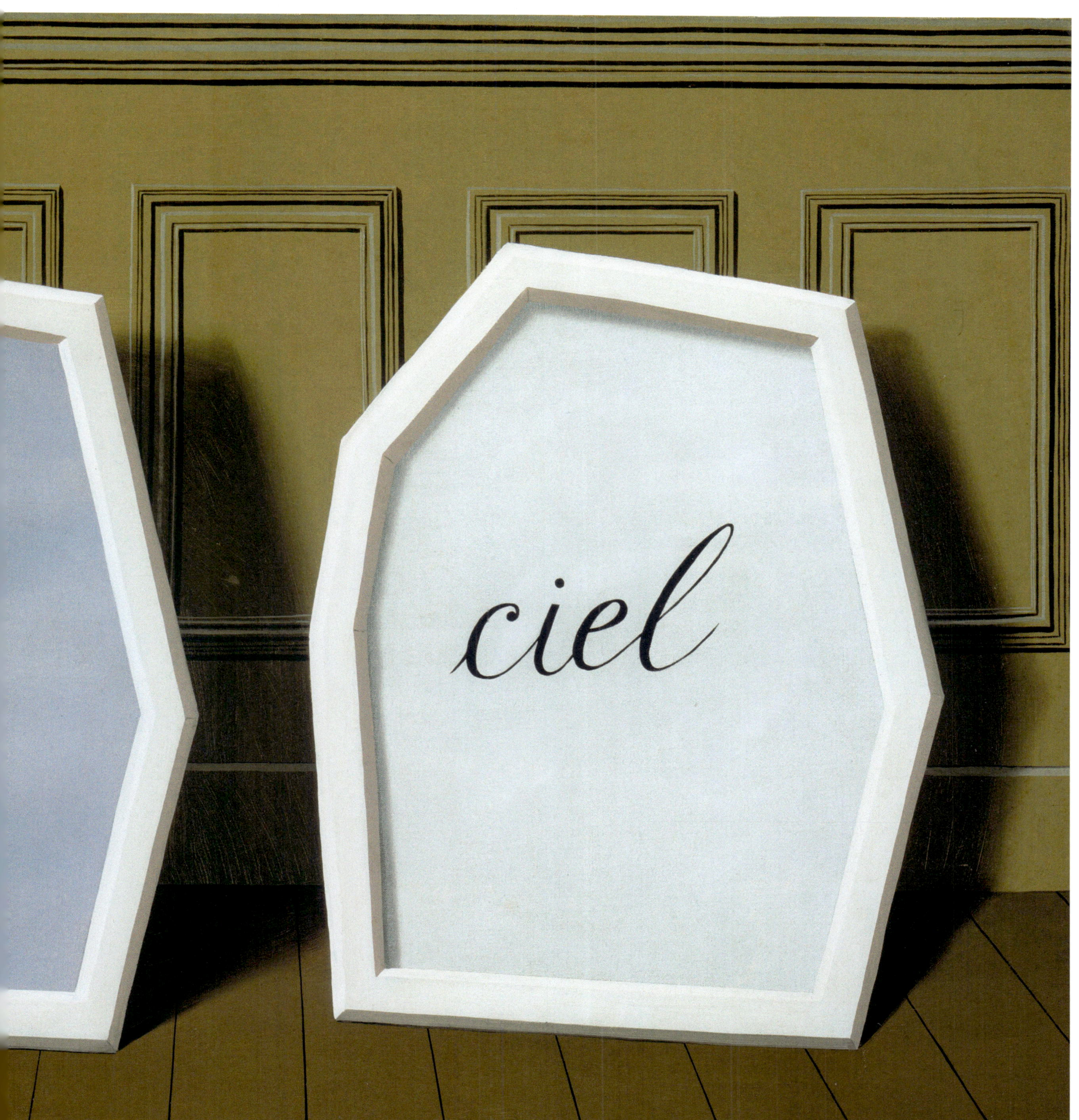
ciel

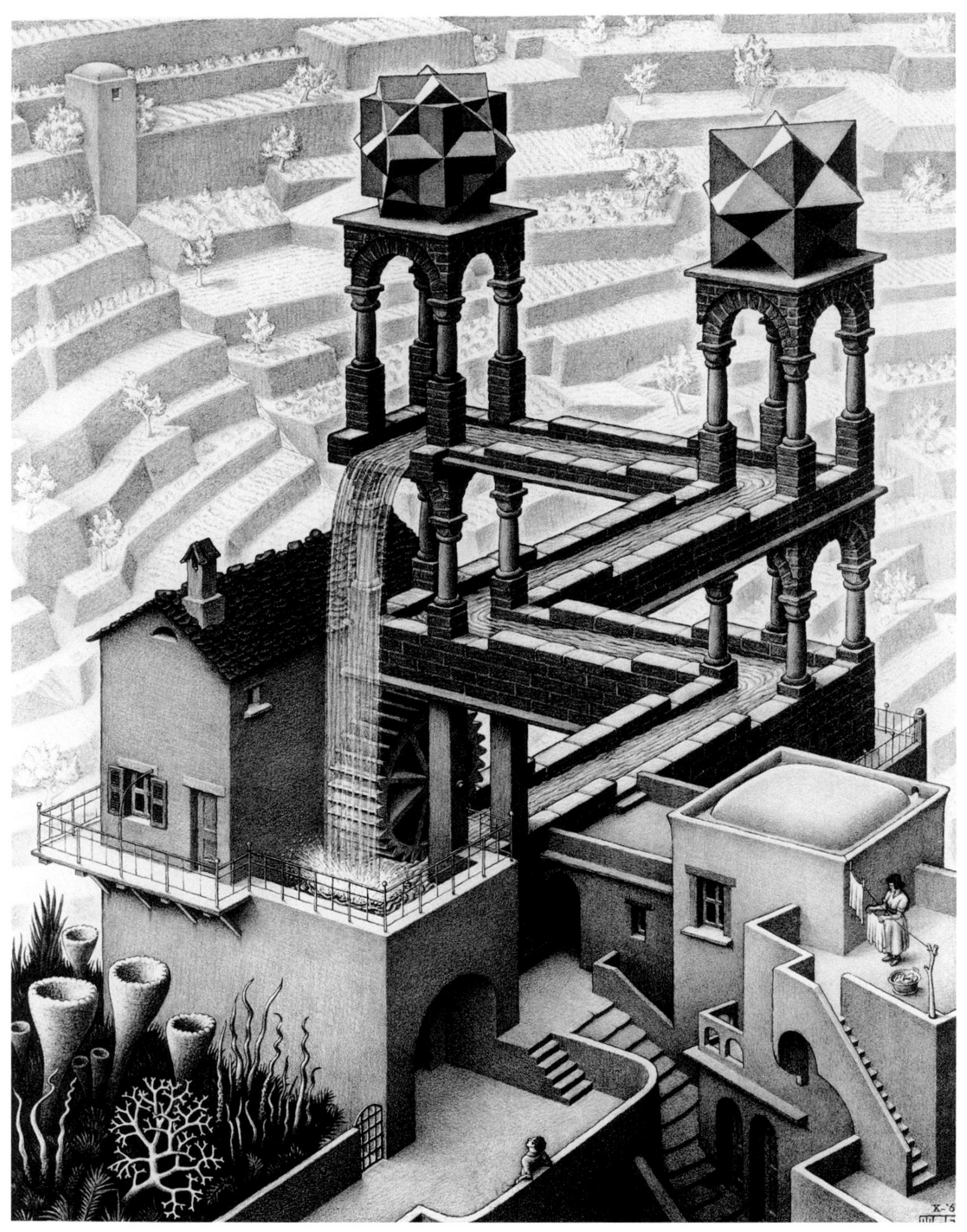

M. C. Escher

Waterfall, 1961

Lithograph, 38 × 30 cm

The art of M. C. Escher (1898–1972) is a special case in the realm of illusionist art. In his pictures, he applies the rules of perspective yet achieves completely illusory structures. At first glance, everything seems logical. One can follow each element and see how it leads to the next, and yet still, one is led astray. At the beginning of his art, Escher dealt with patterns and how they constantly shift and change. An important inspiration was the Moorish patterns he had seen at the Alhambra in Granada. What did not satisfy him, however, for all his fascination, was the lack of figurative depictions in the abstract art of Islam. In the patterns created by Escher, it is precisely figures, such as fish and birds, that transform from one to the other, almost unnoticed, before our eyes. Studying the different figures at the beginning and the end, one has to concentrate considerably not to miss the fluent optical transition.

The situation is different in his perspectival constructions, as in one of his most famous lithographs, *Waterfall* from 1961. We see a watermill set before a terraced slope, plus the seemingly relaxed miller and his wife, who is busy hanging up the laundry. The miller is observing his wonderful construction, which has allowed him to provide unlimited power for his mill, for he is obviously in possession of a perpetual motion machine which, once activated, will continue to run forever – with the minor limitation, noticed by the artist himself, that the water lost through evaporation would, now and then, have to be replenished. It is a closed circuit: The water falls onto the mill wheel and runs through a system of canals back to the point where it falls onto the mill wheel, only to return through the system of canals … But the whole thing cannot work because the transitions, though perfect when seen individually, do not fit together as a whole. If one takes a closer look at the construction, one gets stuck at every corner, because it seems so clear and yet looks so unclear. The whole is obviously greater than the sum of its parts. Escher's fascinating picture is based on the so-called Penrose triangle (fig. below). Here, three four-sided beams each meet at right angles, and while each meeting appears correct in itself, seen as a whole, they do not. Escher used this principle three times in his waterfall construction, to the complete confusion of his audience. Interestingly enough, the mathematician Roger Penrose (b. 1931) was himself inspired by Escher's early work in devising his triangle, which then, in turn, inspired the artist to create his picture – an astonishing cycle that seems to be repeated in the painting itself.

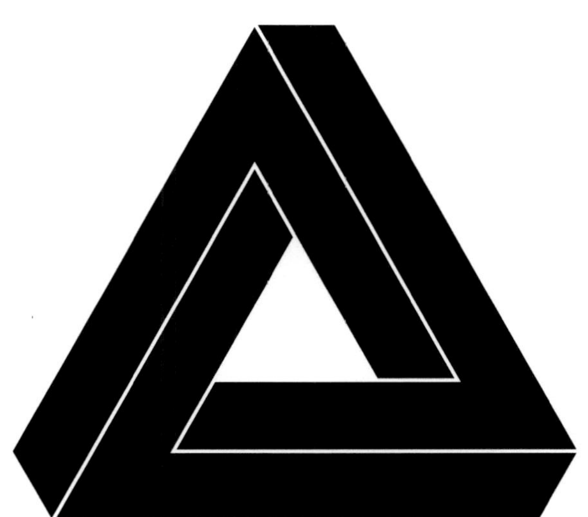

Bridget Riley

Blaze 1, 1962

Emulsion on hardboard,
109.2 × 109.2 cm
National Galleries of Scotland,
Edinburgh
▶ **Facing page**

Streak 2, 1979

Acrylic on canvas,
113.7 × 251.5 cm
Monsoon Art Collection,
London
▶ **Overleaf**

In the 1960s, the British painter Bridget Riley (b. 1931) began to create her own illusions of movement. But it was not the movement one might think one sees when looking at the spinning wheel in Diego Velázquez's canvas *The Spinners* (fig. p. 73), for example, or the blurred movement in a photograph. Riley works with abstract art, which at first seems somewhat contradictory if one considers that her inspiration comes from painters such as the pointillist Georges Seurat (1859–1891) or Andrea Mantegna (see pp. 40–41). Riley's movements arise in the mind, triggered by lines, dots, zigzag patterns or waves, which she applies to the canvas with meticulous precision. Through slight changes, curvatures, displacements and refractions, through compressing or by spreading out the elements and an almost infinite repetition of these factors, the works begin to appear to move. In structure and effect, her paintings are reminiscent of the minimal music of such a composer as Philip Glass (b. 1937), in which rhythm, movement and emotion are similarly created through constant repetition with the slightest variations.

What is astonishing about Riley's abstract art is her inspiration – besides the aforementioned artists – from nature: "I draw from nature, I work with nature, although in completely new terms. For me nature is not landscape, but the dynamism of visual forces – an event rather than an appearance."[20] Along with Seurat and Mantegna, Jackson Pollock (1912–1956) provides another model for her work. This is as surprising as it is comprehensible. Amazing, when one compares the apparent chaos of Pollock's paintings with Riley's meticulous works, and understandable because both artists have the same concept of 'open space'. As with Pollock, Riley's paintings are, as it were, also without beginning or end, without centre or perspective. They present themselves as a segment from an infinite continuum. Visiting an exhibition with Riley's works can be exhausting – one looks at the paintings and they start to shimmer. They appear to be set in motion, stasis becomes kinesis. And just as in classic trompe l'œil, these paintings are also only completed by the viewers – and their minimal movements. Regarding this, Bridget Riley says, "So like your own looking, it moves. It doesn't move. It's absolutely still. But you, by looking, you move it."[21]

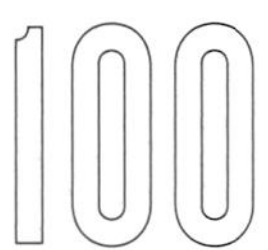

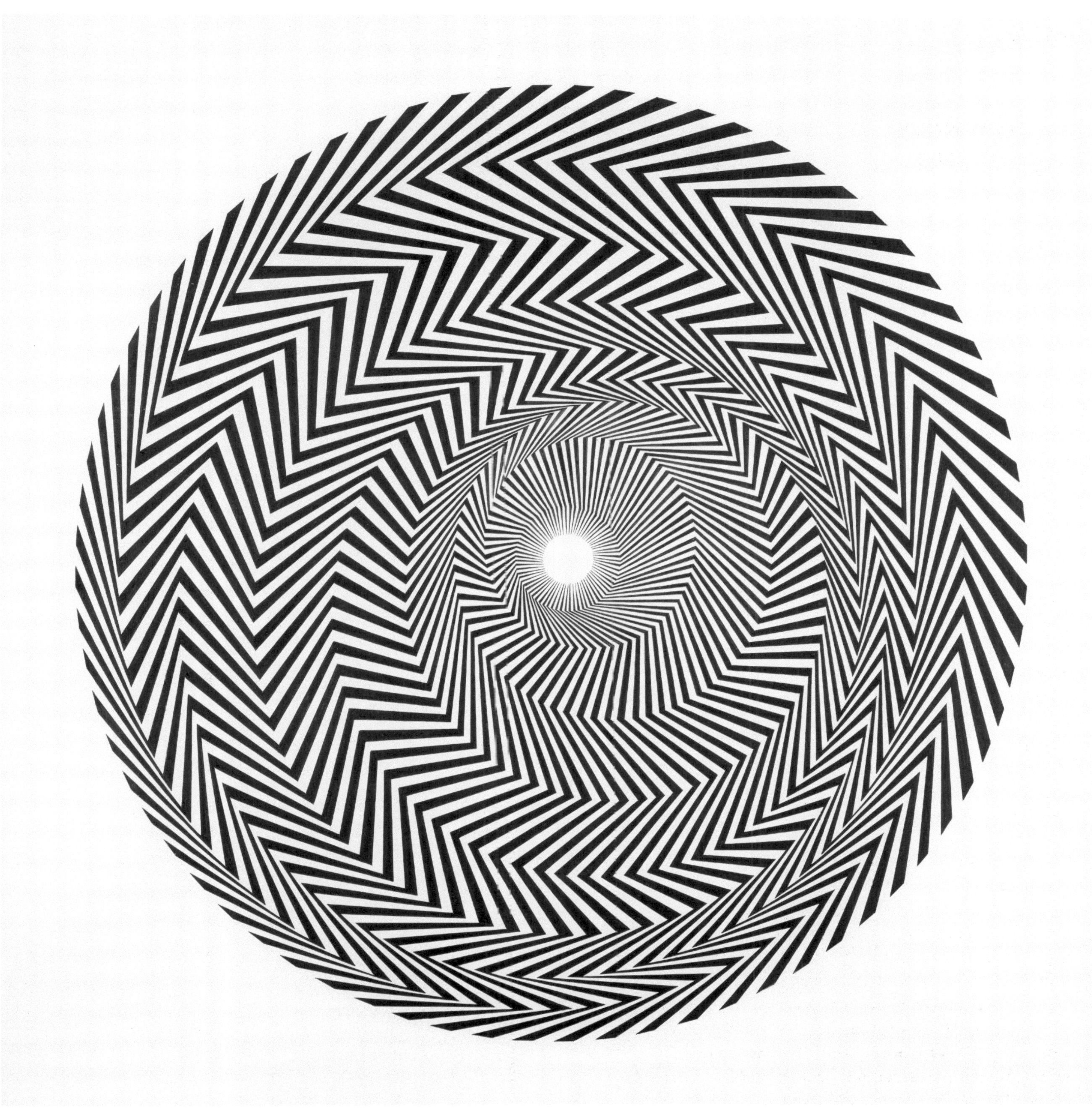

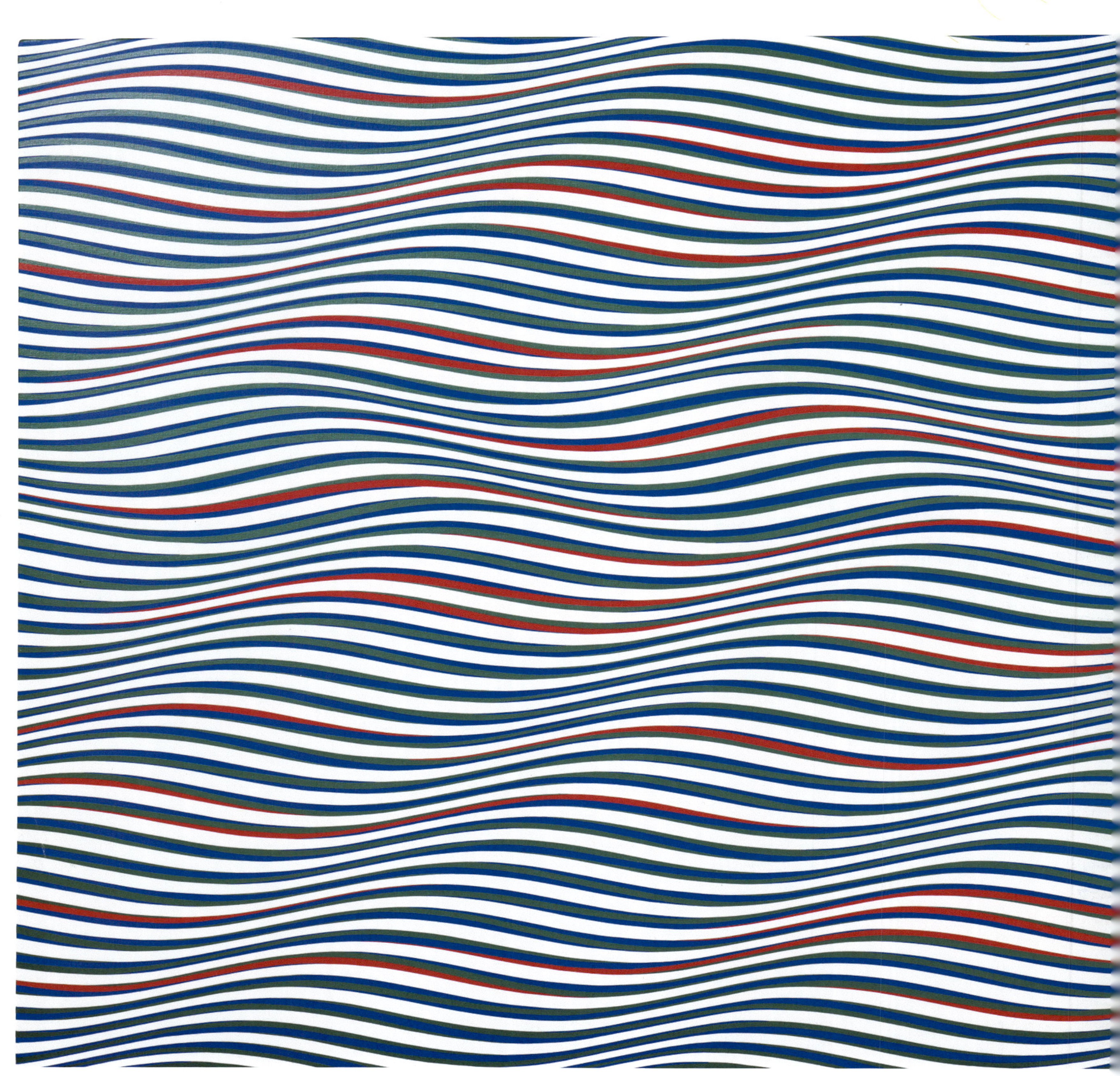

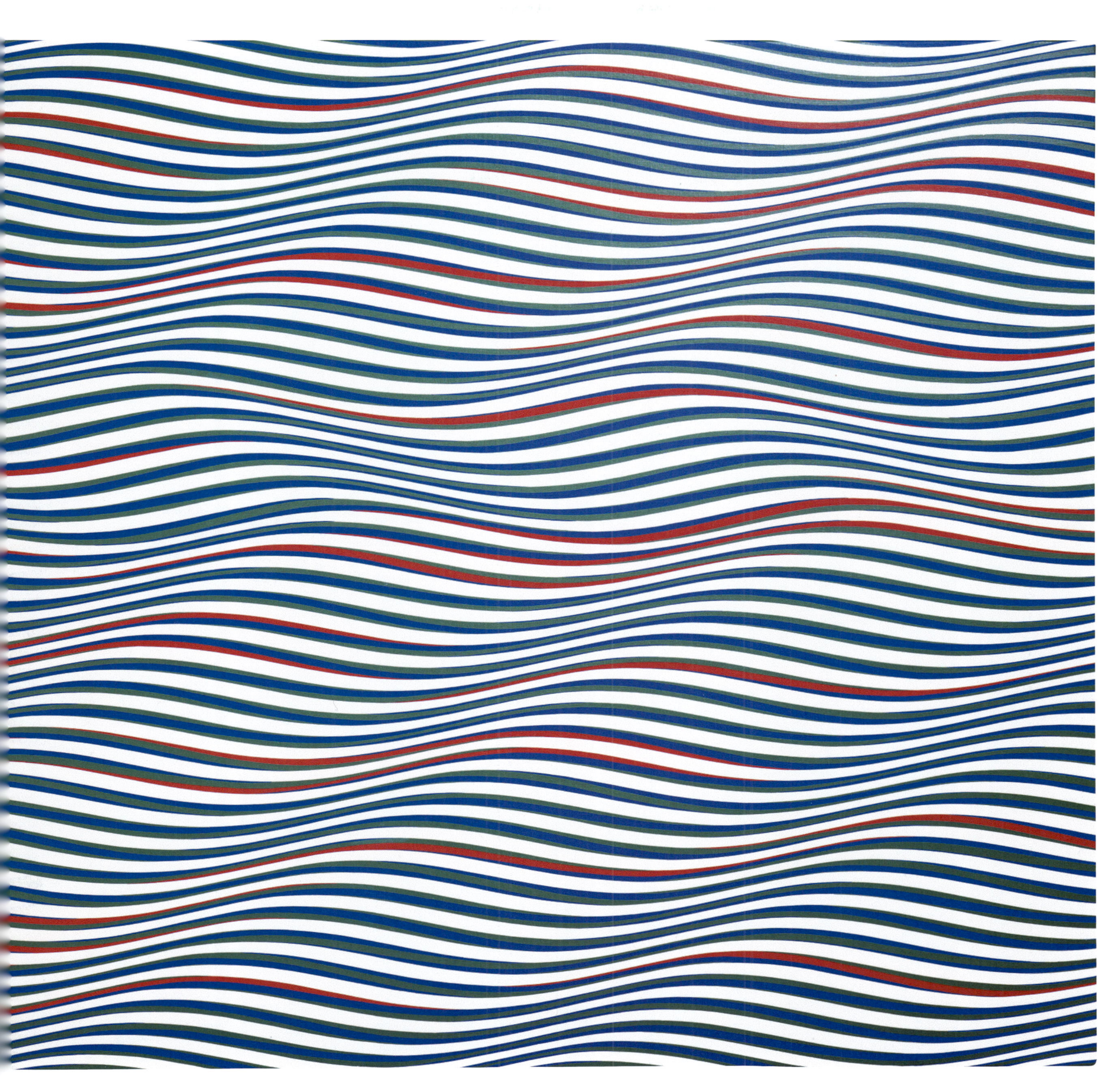

PHOTOGRAPHY

Automated Drawing

The invention of photography can be seen as a provisional end point to the development of naturalistic painting. Since the end of the Middle Ages, painting has attempted to draw closer and mimic nature as accurately as possible. Brunelleschi's linear perspective was a significant step in this direction, as was the use of oil paint. Many painters also used the technical means available to them in their time, be it concave mirrors, lenses, the camera lucida or the camera obscura. In regard to the physics of optics, these artists were well equipped. In the mastery of their craft, too, many artists made considerable contributions. For others, however, this was not enough; they wanted the image they saw projected by their lenses to be transferred automatically to the paper. There were two kinds of innovators who invented photography for their own purposes: those who could actually paint and wanted to use the possibilities of the camera obscura to inject their work with a certain amount of rationalism, like Louis Daguerre (1787–1851), and those who drew less well and wished the image that the camera obscura provided them to be transferred as accurately as possible to paper. The latter group included William Henry Fox Talbot (1800–1877). Disappointed by the quality of the sketches he made during his honeymoon, he came up with the idea of leaving the art of drawing entirely to the sun and chemistry. Both Daguerre and Talbot were extremely successful with their respective methods, the daguerreotype and the negative-positive photographic process, and both would have a lasting influence on art. And by using a machine to capture something exactly, 'true to life' as it were, they also seemed to hold out the promise that what one sees in a photograph must have been exactly the same in reality at the time it was taken.

The Credibility of Photography

This credibility was long one of photography's greatest assets and it has still not been completely disregarded. Yet, even one of the first daguerreotypes from 1838 fails to live up to this 'promise' (fig. below). It shows a street in Paris, the Boulevard du Temple, swept empty except for a shoeshine boy and his customer. The picture was celebrated for its 'objective', detailed representation. But it is far from 'truthfully' depicting the street. The people seem to have completely disappeared from Paris and the colours with them. Nevertheless, a well-disposed observer might say that it did indeed look like this. Of course, Daguerre's intention was not to deceive the viewer; the passers-by on this busy street were not captured by the daguerreotype simply because of its long

▼ Louis Daguerre, *Boulevard du Temple*, 1838

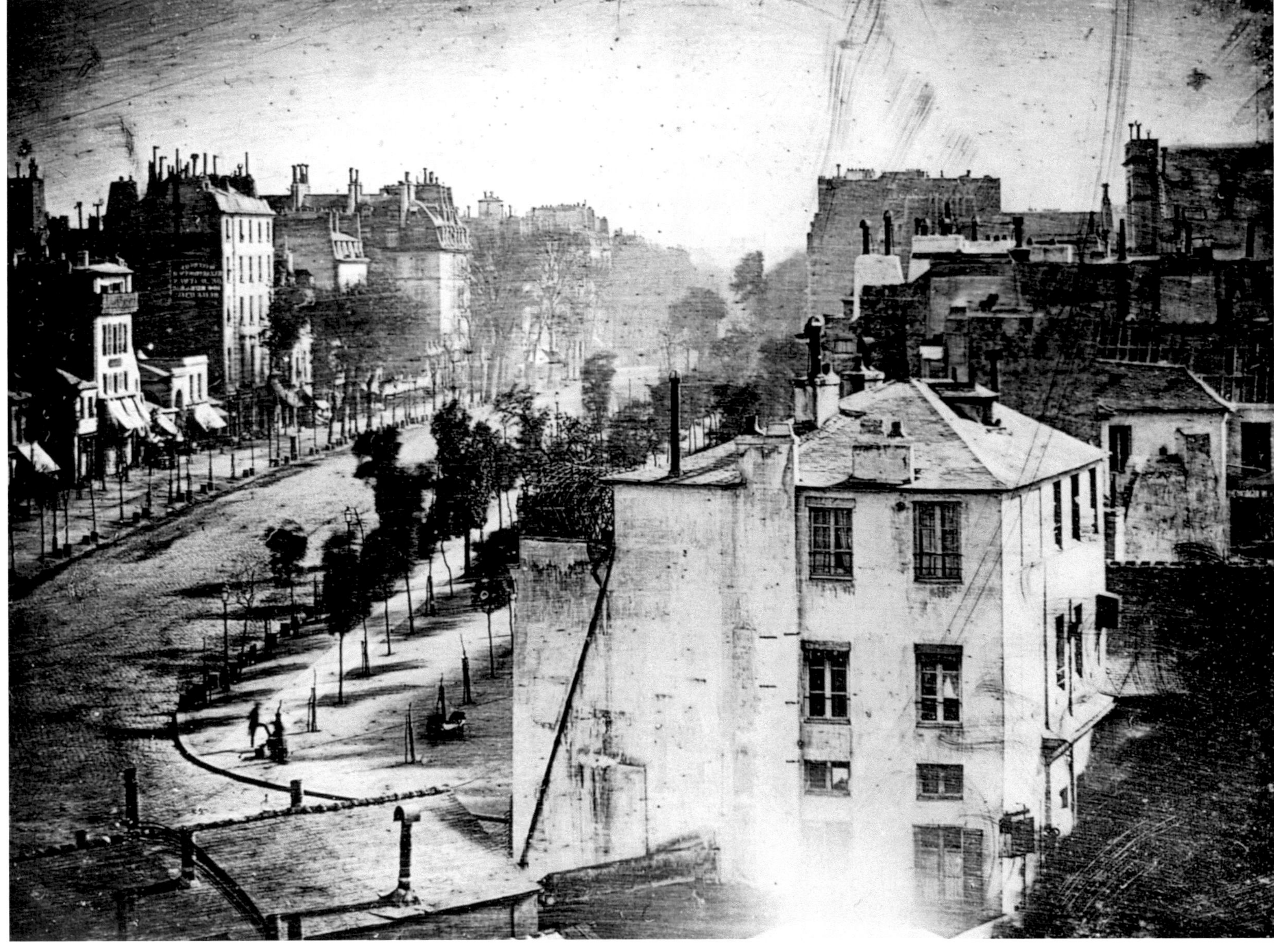

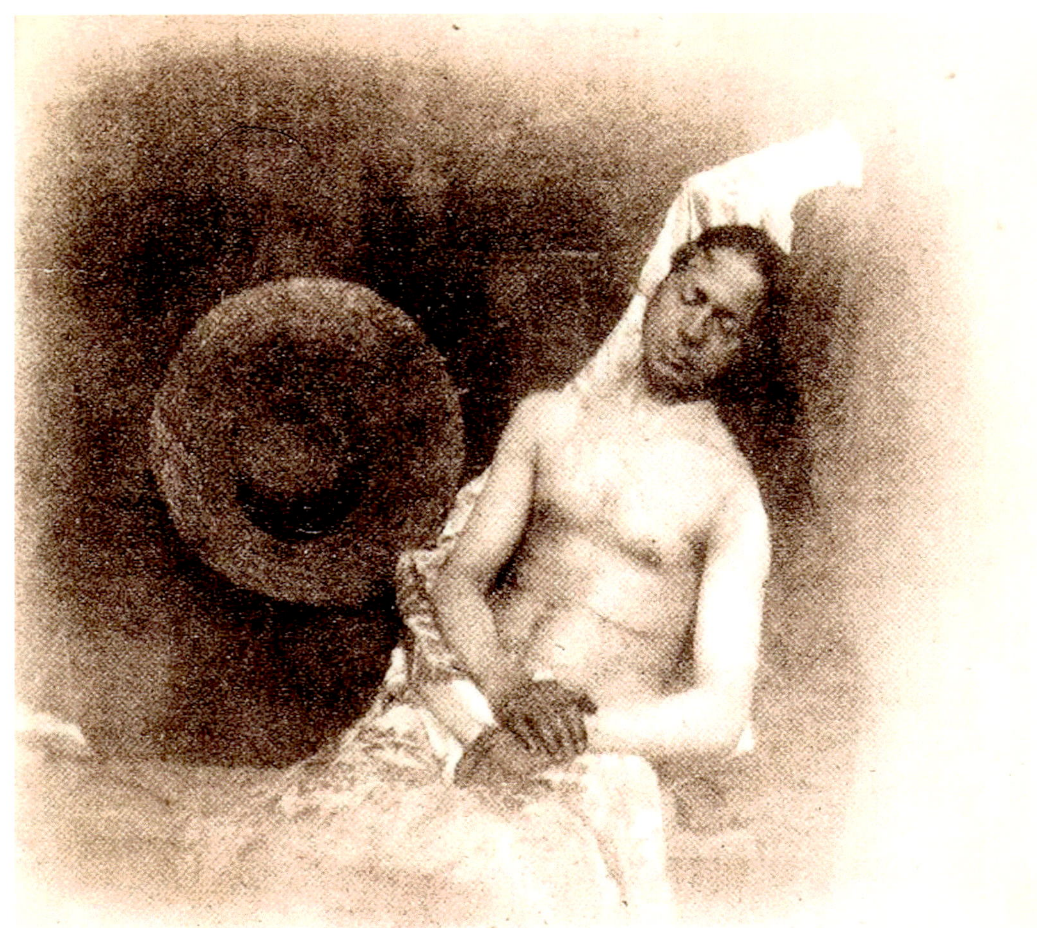

◀ Hippolyte Bayard,
Self-Portrait as a Drowned Man, 1840

exposure time, and colours could not yet be reproduced. But this ambivalence in how photography was received and the credibility ascribed to it run like a common thread through its history, right up to the present day. Even if Hippolyte Bayard (1801–1887), who we count amongst the pioneers of photography, very early on – and with a rather derisive humour – undermined this very credibility with his 1840 *Self-Portrait as a Drowned Man* (fig. above). However, he was not trying to criticise the credibility of photography, but rather that of the French State. The picture was a bitter commentary on the preferential treatment given to Daguerre and his invention. On the back of the picture, the photographer wrote, "The government, which had been far too generous to Monsieur Daguerre, has said it can do nothing for Monsieur Bayard, and the poor wretch has drowned himself." This was despite the fact that Bayard had gone so far as to organise an exhibition of thirty of his photographs using his own technique two months previous to the announcement of Daguerre's process – incidentally the first photography exhibition in history.

In 1925, the German-born art historian Rudolf Arnheim wrote in his essay "The Soul in the Silver Layer", "Photography is first and foremost the faithful reflection of reality".[22] But the belief that photography is completely objective, or even neutral, in showing what it shows, simply because it is accomplished by means of a machine, has meanwhile somewhat weakened. Because of the many factors that play a role in the creation of a photograph, this much-praised objectivity is, in truth, hardly possible: the choice of subject, angle of view, choice of lens, exposure time, sharpness, aperture and so on influence every photograph. The American photographer Roger Ballen (b. 1950) sums up the appropriate scepticism in the following sentence: "A photo is an abstraction of reality that should not be confused with reality."[23]

War and Illusion

Of course, photography is also susceptible to manipulation, be it during the taking of the picture or while developing the image. Famous examples of such manipulations can already be found early on. When the British photographer Roger Fenton (1819–1869) was commissioned to document the Crimean War in 1855, he did so with the proviso of England's Prince Albert that he was not to photograph the dead, but to show the heroism of British troops rather than the negative side of war. In order to achieve this, and at the same time emphasise his own bravery, Fenton photographed not only the officers and the camps, but also the *Valley of the Shadow of Death* (fig. below left), a road strewn with cannonballs. Today we know that Fenton probably deposited the cannonballs there himself to demonstrate the dangerous nature of his

▼ Left
Roger Fenton,
Valley of the Shadow of Death, 1855
▼ Right
Alexander Gardner,
Home of a Rebel Sharpshooter, 1863

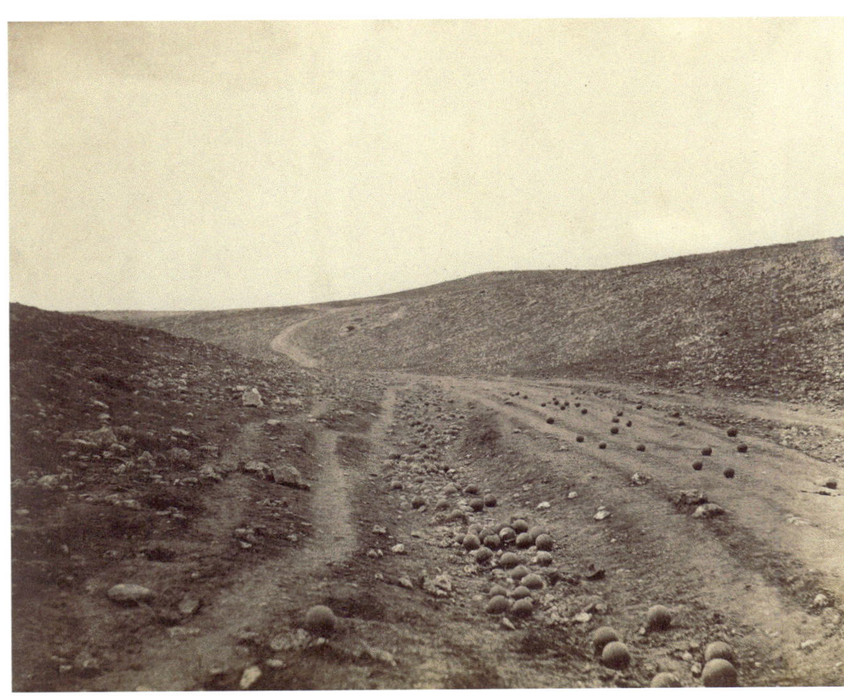

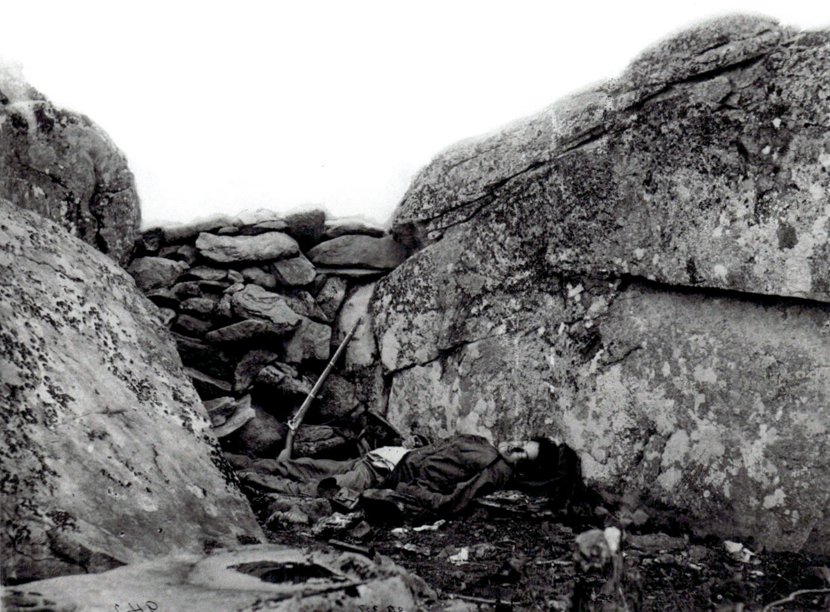

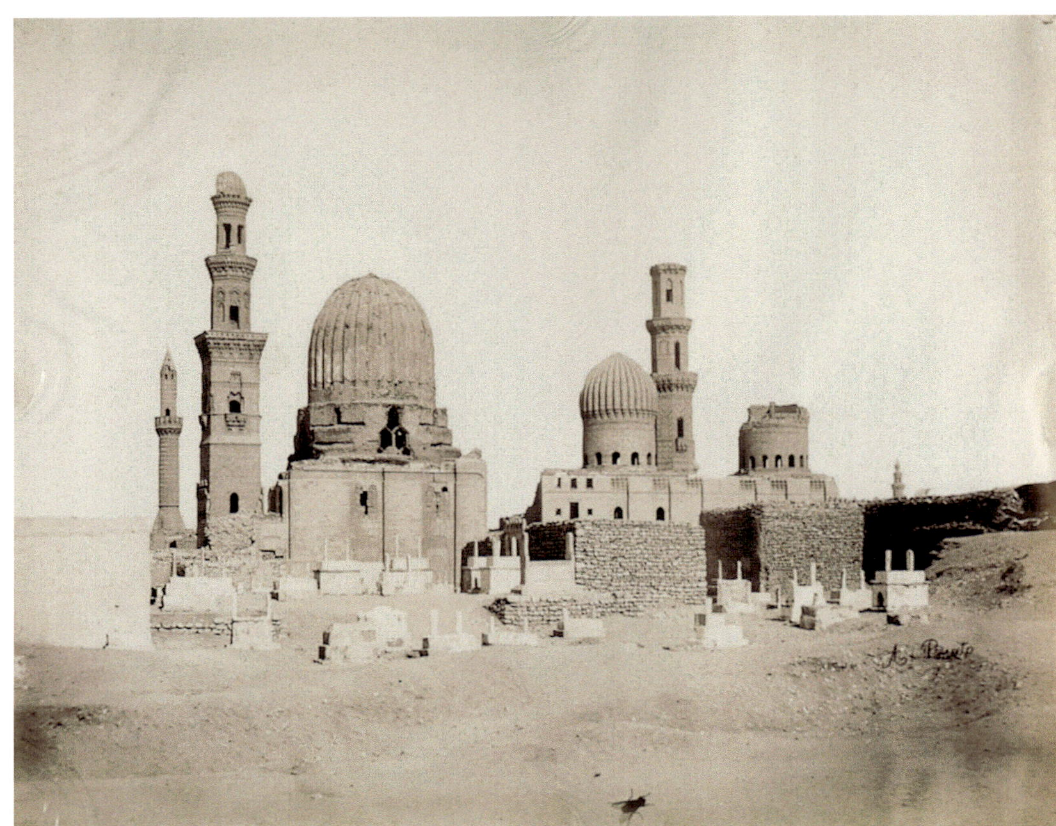

◀ Antonio Beato,
Mameluk Tombs with Fly, c. 1870

mission. The American photographer Alexander Gardner (1821–1882) went one step further in his *Photographic Sketch Book of the War* of 1865/1866 (fig. p. 107 right). Like Fenton, the necessary long exposure times prevented Gardner from photographing combat operations, so he concerned himself instead with their aftermath. For this purpose, he draped corpses in such a way as to maximise their dramatic effect. For Gardner there was as little disgrace in doing this as there was for Fenton, since it aided him in bringing the horrors of war closer to his audience.

In photography there is no trompe l'œil as there is in painting, per se. Seldom is such trompe l'œil successful, and when it is, it happens by chance, as in Antonio Beato's (1835–1906) photograph *Mameluk Tombs with Fly* (c. 1870; fig. above). Of course, this was not a planned photograph of a fly in front of these graves. The fly was lost within the bellows of the camera and ended up being recorded as a photogram on the collodion plate – an error in the image that could have been retouched. But as an artistically educated person, who apparently also had a sense of humour, Beato carried on processing this photograph with the fly in it and so, without having planned it, created a classic of trompe l'œil, illusionist art: the fly on the picture with which Giotto is said to have fooled his teacher Cimabue at the end of the 13th century (see p. 12).

Illusion in photography works on a different level than it does in painting. In contrast to classic, painted trompe l'œil, photography, while providing perfect reproductions, never pretends that what you see in the picture is present at that very moment. In contrast to painting, there is no effect intending to amaze that plays with the supposed three-dimensionality of the image. The illusion of photography is based on its aforementioned credibility, which has so far been almost unshakably attributed to it, that what one sees in a photograph must also have happened like that at a certain point in time in a certain place.

Painted Photography

As can be seen from the photographs mentioned thus far, the documentary integrity of the photographic image was, from the start, not the case. For a long time this was due not least to the technical constraints but also the tradition of photography asserting itself as an independent art form and not simply something that emulates painting. In fact, in the 1960s, photorealistic painting did exactly the opposite when painting ended up imitating photography. Here, too, technical limitation played a role: the limited possibilities of enlarging colour photography. Artists such as Chuck Close (b. 1940; see pp. 126–127) and Richard Estes (b. 1932) did not use people or landscapes as models for their paintings, but rather photographs of these motifs, which they then painted. They allowed their gaze to wander over the photographs and then interpreted them.

In the 1970s, using a virtuoso painting technique like Chuck Close, but with strong colours and smooth brushwork, Richard Estes also created paintings that look like giant photographs (fig. pp. 110/111), with one important difference: Photographs, especially coloured ones, could not be produced in this quality and size at this time. Photorealist painters like Estes, however, used photographs as models, because, as the painter put it, photography provides him with "the best pointers to the theme I want to paint."[24] And these were above all scenes from urban life and thus a glimpse of the 'American Way of Life' of the time. In photorealism, unlike in photography, the picture is carried less by the actual subject and more by the image produced by one or more photographs of a scene. Photorealistic paintings are thus more pictures of images of

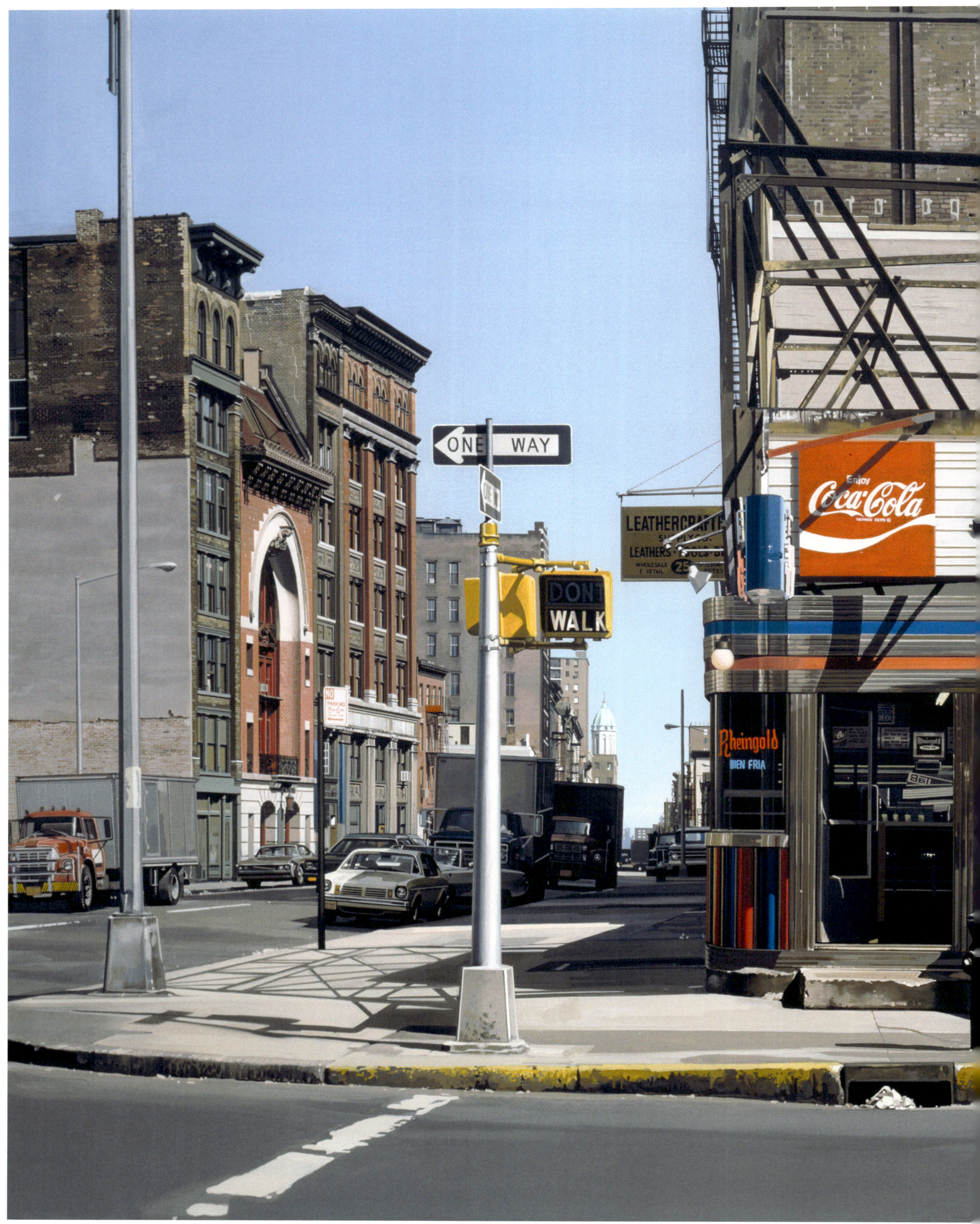
ONE WAY
DONT
WALK
Enjoy
Coca-Cola
Rheingold
BIEN FRIA

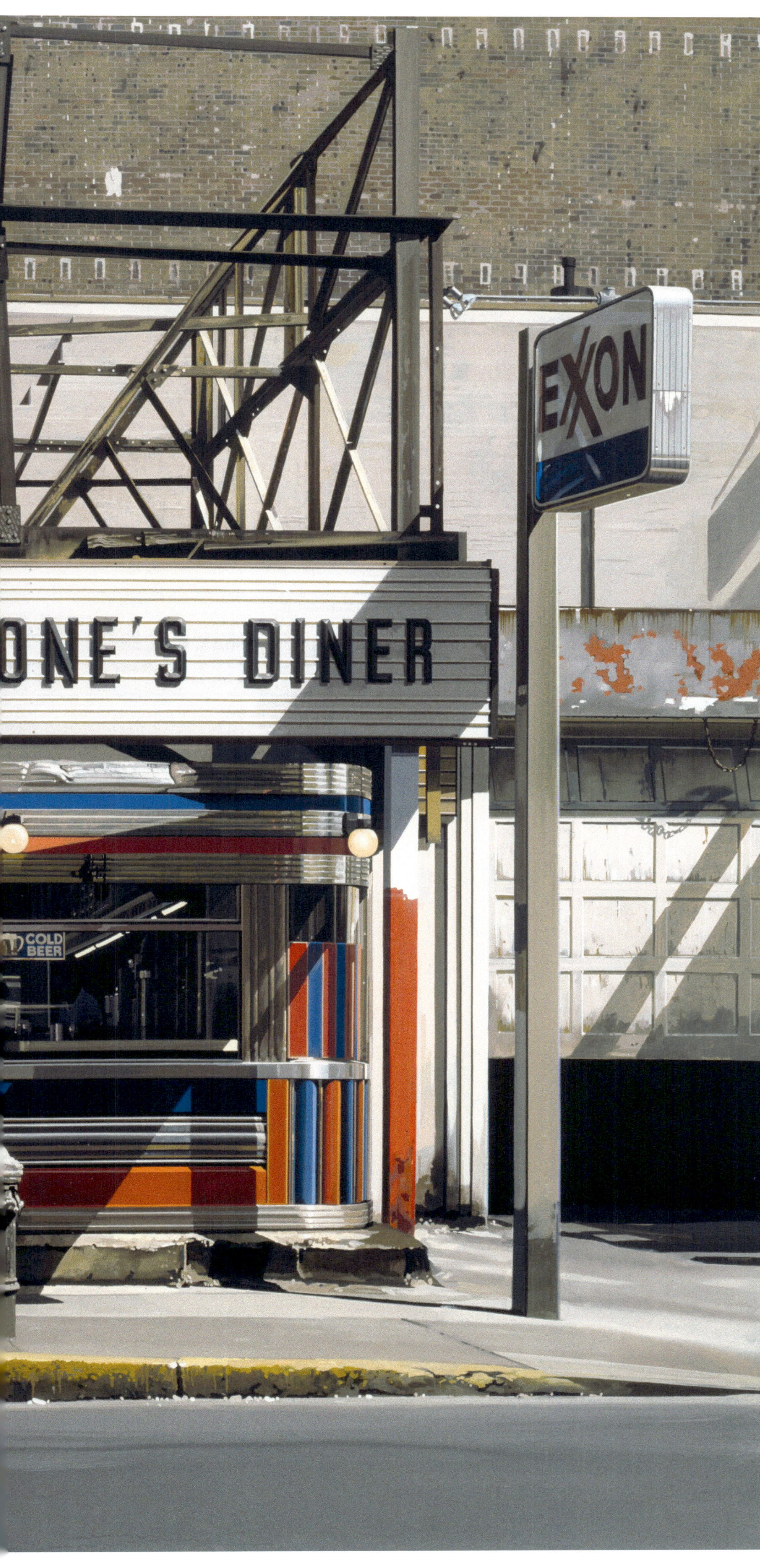

◀ Richard Estes, *Jone's Diner*, 1979

reality and in this sense a further step away from it. Through meticulousness, a brilliant painting technique and the almost dissecting gaze taken in the act of representing reality, a certain coolness is produced, and an indefinite uneasiness in the mind of the observer emerges. What one sees appears, at the same time, real and yet somehow slightly alien. One looks upon a surface with smooth brushstrokes and a subject matter that seems interchangeable, which can thus perhaps be understood as a critique on the attitude to life of this time. Richard Estes was at least aware of this clean, smooth surface, which can lead to emotional detachment, because he writes, "I really try to make things look dirty, but it's interesting because even in a photograph it doesn't look as dirty as it really is."[25] As a contemporary observer, one finds oneself thinking about the effort that was made at the time for something that could be photographed today so easily and printed in a similar size or larger. Photorealism is an example of an art form that is an expression of its time. But even today, more and more people paint in styles that are figurative and hyperrealistic – perhaps as an antithesis to digital photography, which at times seems even colder.

The Emancipation of Photography

With photorealism, artists attempted to use photography for their purposes in painting, an approach which had been common in both histories. So far, however, the 'transfer' has not been very consistent and nothing being near deceptively real has been produced. The borders between photography and painting seemed blurred, even if photorealistic painting usually evokes a different feeling in the viewer than does the photograph itself, a fact that is due perhaps to the different way that each technique is conceived: In painting, the image is composed and constructed from nothing, so to speak, whereas in photography it is seen as a finished image, cut out of the continuum of space and time, as it were.

And two important differences remained: the restricted size of photographic prints possible at the time and the fact that the painter may construct their picture just as they wish, with all possible precision and meticulousness, whereas the photographer could only reproduce what they saw in front of them. This changed fundamentally, and with lasting repercussions, with the invention and perfection of digital photography and the almost infinite possibilities provided by digital picture manipulation. The advent of digital technology meant that photography was able to emancipate itself from 'simple reproduction' and create its own reality. But despite everything, the majority of photographers still need a photographed subject matter as their source material. Just as sketches are a preparatory stage for the finished image in painting, for many 'illusions' in (now mostly) digital photography this preliminary step consists of individual shots that are combined and merged in different ways to form a unified image.

Infinite Space

Andreas Gursky (b. 1955) is a pioneer, one of the most successful and influential contemporary photographers (see pp. 128 – 131). He claims that "with the current digital possibilities, there is no longer a difference between photography and painting".[26] Looking at his pictures, one is inclined to agree with him. As one can see from Gursky's photographs – or perhaps it would be appropriate to say photographic paintings – photography is increasingly emancipating itself in the Digital Age from the single image created with the release of the shutter. Using Photoshop and similar image editing software, the photographer can draw on old photographic tropes and compose completely new and seemingly impossible worlds in the style of M. C. Escher (1898 – 1972; see pp. 98 – 99).

Erik Johansson (b. 1985) is a master at this: a place in which the world is turned on its head (fig. p. 114 above), a lake that breaks into mirror shards on its banks, a house in the country and a giant pair of scissors that seems to have gone wild, cutting everything to ribbons, or a man who rolls out an asphalt road like a huge carpet (fig. p. 114 below). These are motifs and images by the Swedish photographer and 'retouching artist' in which he succeeds in making the impossible look completely normal. The trick is that Johansson has actually photographed everything that can be seen. Even when photography was still a hobby for him, the fact that a photo was already completed with the click of the shutter release was not enough for him as an enthusiastic draughtsman. For Johansson, the first 'click' is only the trigger for many further clicks and ultimately also the trigger for his compositions, which are compiled from this multitude of clicks. "So it's more about capturing

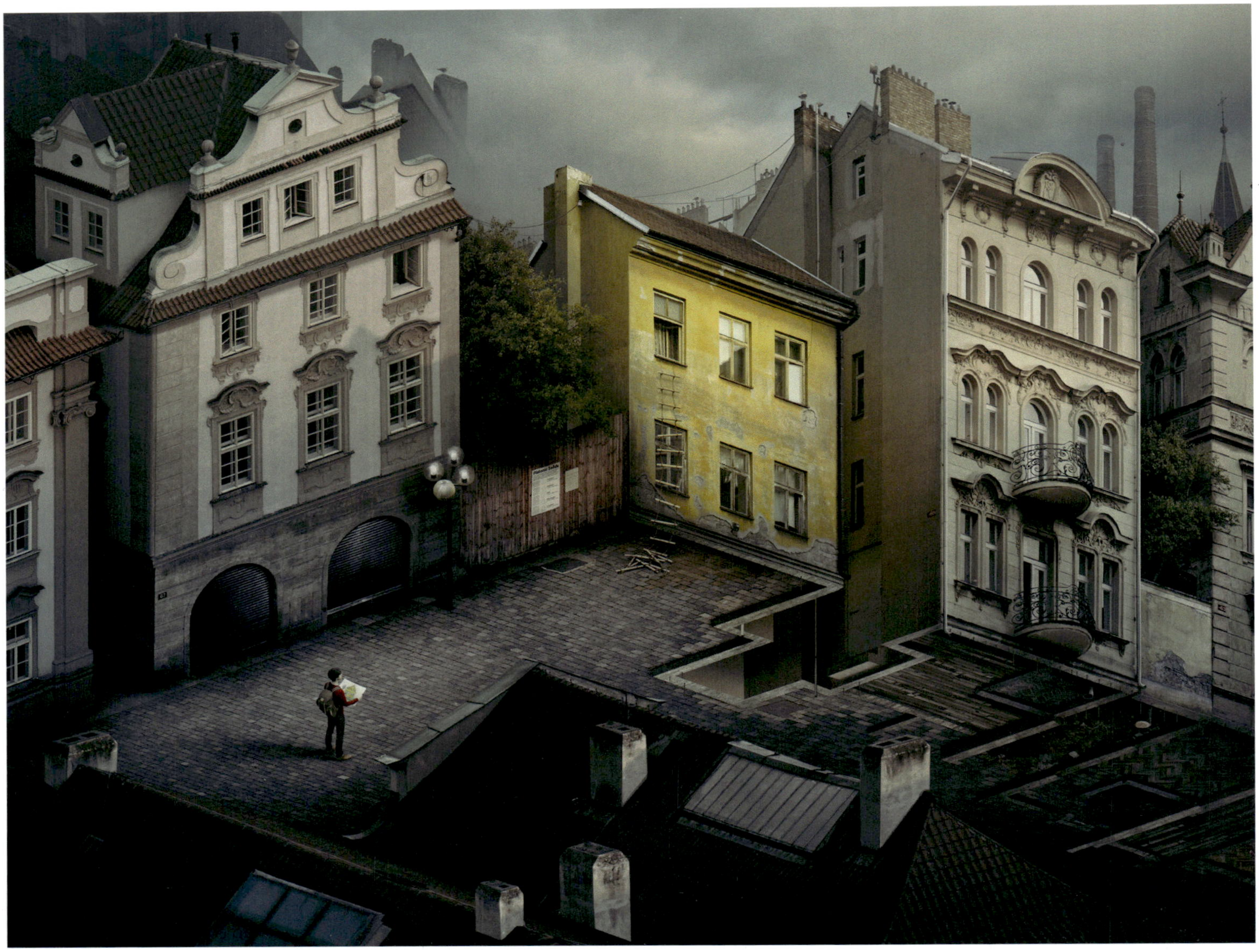

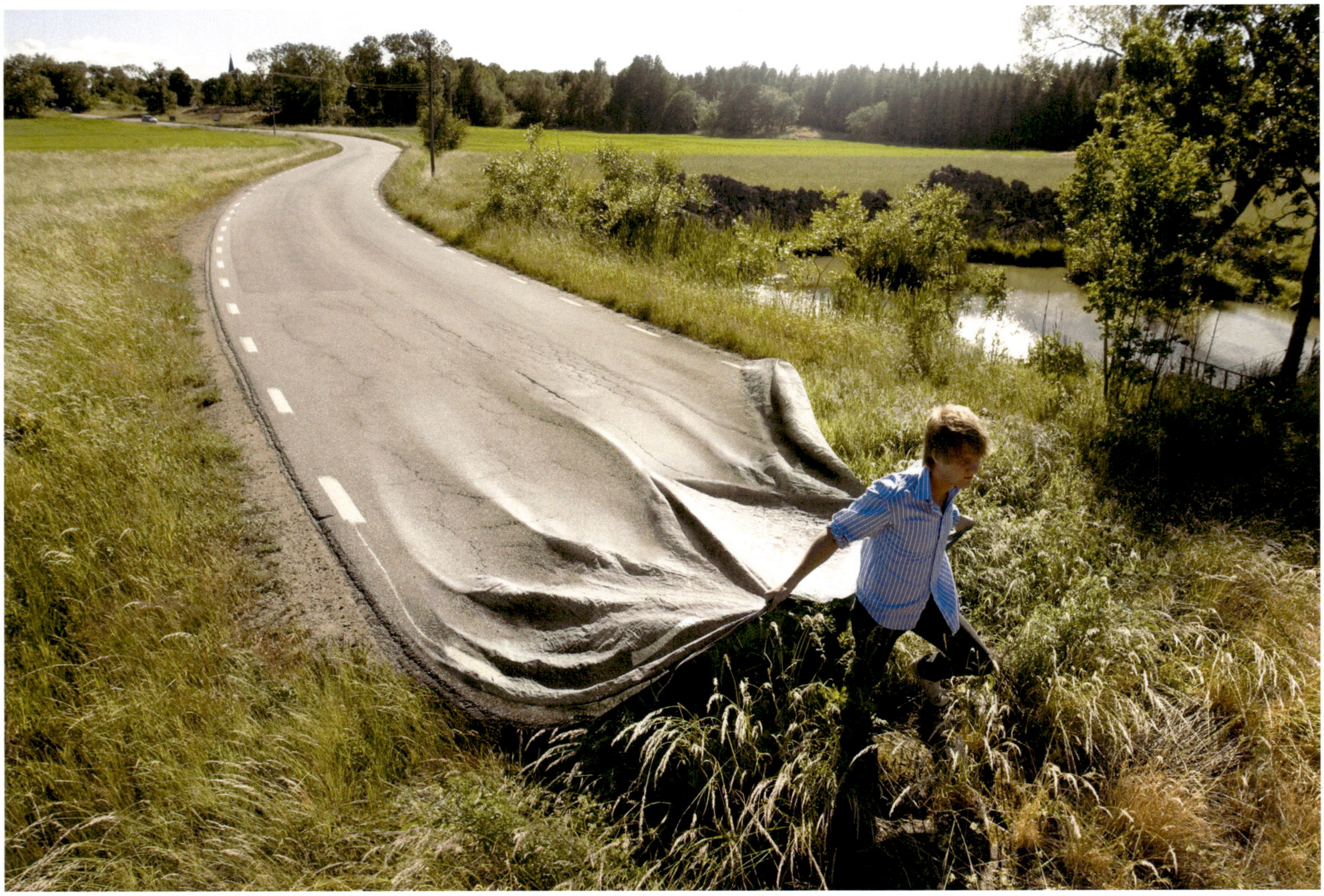

an idea than about capturing a moment really."[27] He picks up where other photographers leave off. As a "photorealistic surrealist", as he calls himself, he wants to create images that the viewer cannot easily consume. Instead, it is necessary to take time and think about how the artist managed to create them. Much like Gursky, Johansson realises his ideas, and those of his advertising clients, by using photography with all its digital recording and editing possibilities, just like a painter uses his brushes and paints. "All the tools are out there, and the only thing that limits us is our imagination."[28]

◀ Erik Johansson, *Under the Corner*, 2017

◀ Erik Johansson, *Go Your Own Road*, 2008

▶ **Overleaf**

Thomas Demand, *Control Room*, 2011

Collected Time

As amazingly illusory as the surreal moments in Johansson's pictures are, their believability and the confusion that this ultimately gives rise to play a relatively minor role. This is not the case when it comes to the American photographer Pelle Cass (b. 1954). Here, the short – and sometimes not so short – moment of doubting whether what one is looking at might not after all be real, plays an essential role (see pp. 132–135).

The 'illusions' of Thomas Demand (b. 1964) work differently than most others in this chapter, not only because they are still produced as analogue, film photographs. His pictures show rooms, one or other of which strike us as strangely familiar. The observer looks at the pictures and suddenly something sparks in their brain, and they remember the context from which they know this or that space. The pictures are historically, politically or socially important, or at least known from the media; but they are deserted. Nobody is to be seen, and the spaces are very clean, almost sterile, like after the excessive cleaning of a crime scene. Apart from the spaces, there is nothing else available to us but our memory, which begins to sort these places according to the events with which we associate them. And yet, when we look at them, there remains a feeling of 'artificiality'. The spaces depicted are not real, but life-size, detailed replicas, illusions made of cardboard and paper, sterile in their artificiality, but deceptively real all the same. Demand's rooms are copies of copies of rooms in which something happened that was significant enough for them to appear in the media: the Geneva hotel bathroom, in whose bathtub the former Minister-President of

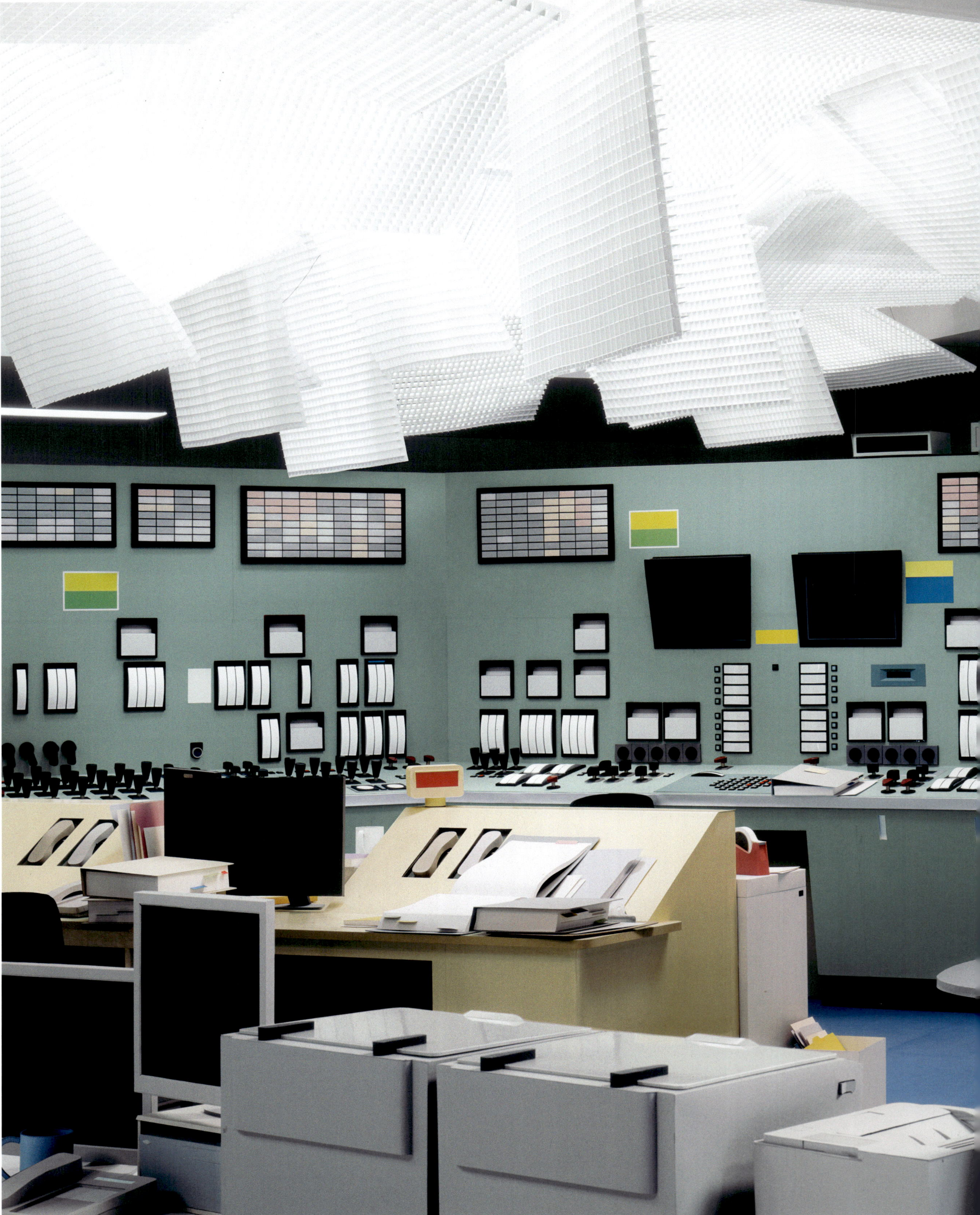

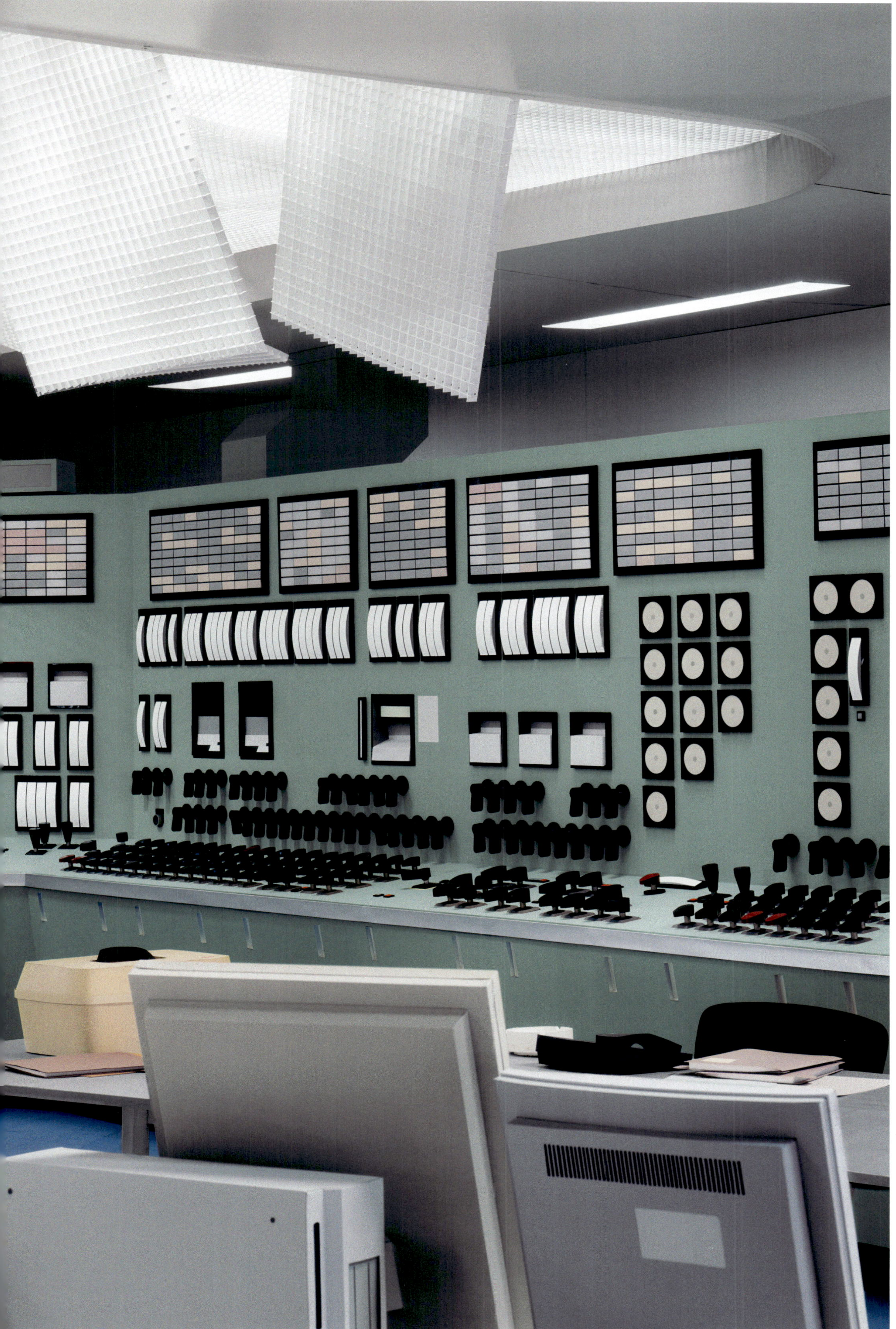

Schleswig-Holstein Uwe Barschel was found dead in 1987, the Berlin headquarters of East Germany's secret police, ravaged by protestors in 1990, and the control room of the nuclear power plant in Fukushima, Japan, shortly after the earthquake and tsunami in March 2011 (fig. pp. 116/117). Demand's photographs are an examination of media and memory, reproduction and reality, as well as a challenge to the viewer's memory to line up their view of things with that of history, and to pick apart what results from the process. Demand explains, "The photograph gives you the information you need to see exactly what it is, and then it falls apart before your very eyes."[29] Thus the illusion falls apart in just the same way as the re-constructed room fell apart long before, since Demand destroys his constructions after he has photographed them. The photograph is the real work of art, and it lives from the near perfect illusion.

▼ Georges Rousse, *Darmstadt*, 2015

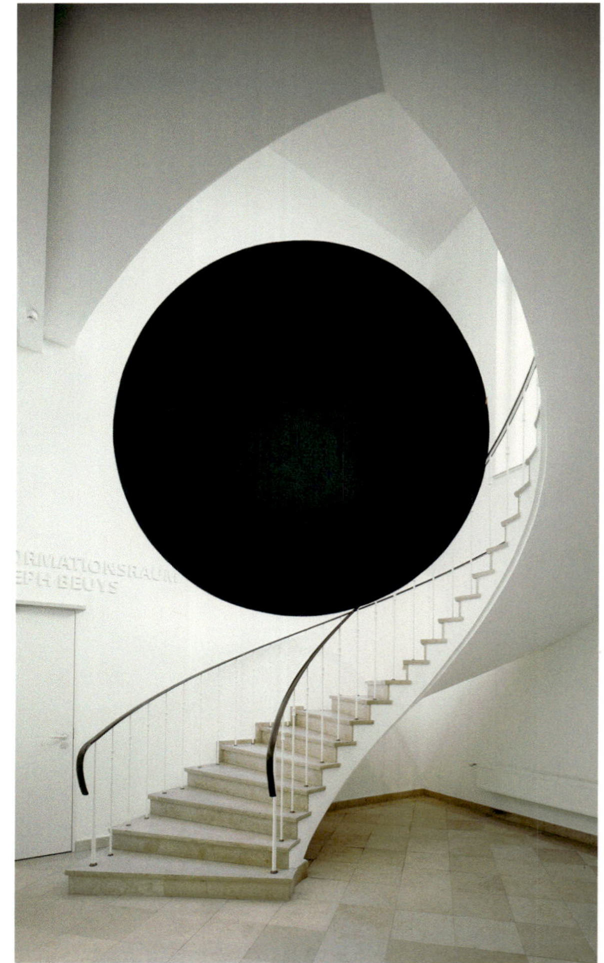

Photography as the Perfection of Painting

The two artists George Rousse (b. 1947) and Felice Varini (b. 1952) have a completely different approach to photography, painting and illusion itself. As mentioned earlier, photography can be seen as the perfection of naturalistic painting, a view which can be applied to both artists in a very particular way. Though their art can be seen and experienced in real life, in analogue space, in something of an act of 'on-site reception' – and it is a completely different experience, one that only works from a specific viewpoint – through photography, it becomes perfect and, ultimately, also visible to a larger audience.

What happens in George Rousse's artwork is similarly complex to what happens in that of Felice Varini (see pp. 136–137). It is easily visible in the photographs but simultaneously difficult to understand. In Rousse's pictures, painting and photography develop a symbiosis with the physical space, apparently creating a layer between space and the observer (fig. right). In the centuries since Brunelleschi, Masaccio and Alberti, artists have attempted to evoke the illusion of three-dimensional space on a two-dimensional surface, until George Rousse turned this around to suggest the illusion of two-dimensionality in three-dimensional space. The confusion this causes in the minds of viewers, unaccustomed as they are to this reversal, can perhaps be compared to the amazement experienced by the contemporaries of the first Renaissance artists in Florence when they saw with astonishment works of linear-perspective on church walls. In these works, the gaze is drawn from the painted surface into the apparent depth beyond, what Leon Battista Alberti described as looking through a window (see pp. 18–19). This is not the case with George Rousse. Although our gaze penetrates into the depth of space, it is held back by a field of colour that seems to float in that very space. The viewer sees a picture that seems to have completely detached itself from the architectural context of the space shown. Rousse invents an imaginary space, a new layer within space that is only visible and existent when he photographs it or when one stands exactly where the camera is positioned

For the Chinese artist Liu Bolin (b. 1973), the 'collaboration' between painting and photography plays an essential role. Without photography, an important element in his art would be missing, because it unites the various 'disciplines' of his art (see pp. 138–139).

The Ukrainian graphic designer Alexey Kondakov (b. 1984) brings photography and painting together in a unique and very distinctive way. And this is done with a perfection that makes it hardly possible to distinguish between the two merged art forms. While looking at the painting *Bacchus on the Throne* by the Dutch painter Caesar van Everdingen (1616–1678), Kondakov realised that, in their needs, the gods of ancient mythology were not so unlike us today. Like us, they seem to enjoy being sociable, having a drink and being entertained. Kondakov wondered what the painting would look like today and transplanted the group from their canvas to a bus stop, which he had photographed in his hometown of Kiev (fig. p. 120). He posted the picture online and was surprised by the overwhelming response it received, like all his subsequent pictures. He appropriately titled his series *The Daily Life of Gods*. Kondakov is by no means the only – or even the first – artist to take figures from historical paintings and to confront them with our present world, but he achieves a different quality through a thorough mastery of Photoshop. By relocating these figures in scenarios from today, he gives them a new environment in which they may be perceived differently and are given a new identity and story. The various characters become modernised, and one can identify with them very differently than when they are in their historic context. Kondakov brings the gods down to earth and humanises them in the process. It is helpful, of course, that the behaviour of the gods of the ancient world is already quite human, as is well known from Ovid's *Metamorphoses*, for example. Additionally, the painted figures have a naturalness about them that makes them look almost as if they had been photographed. When one considers the conclusions drawn by British painter David Hockney (b. 1937), who demonstrates in his book *Secret Knowledge* how many painters in history created their figures with the help of lenses and various other optical devices such as the camera lucida and the camera obscura, Kondakov's new compositions indeed seem to be proof for his thesis. In 2016 Kondakov spent some time as an artist in residence in Naples to create another series. The environment made for even more harmonious results, as one has the feeling that the baroque and rather picturesque cityscapes and building façades fit still better to the

▼ Alexey Kondakov, *Osokorki Station*, 2014

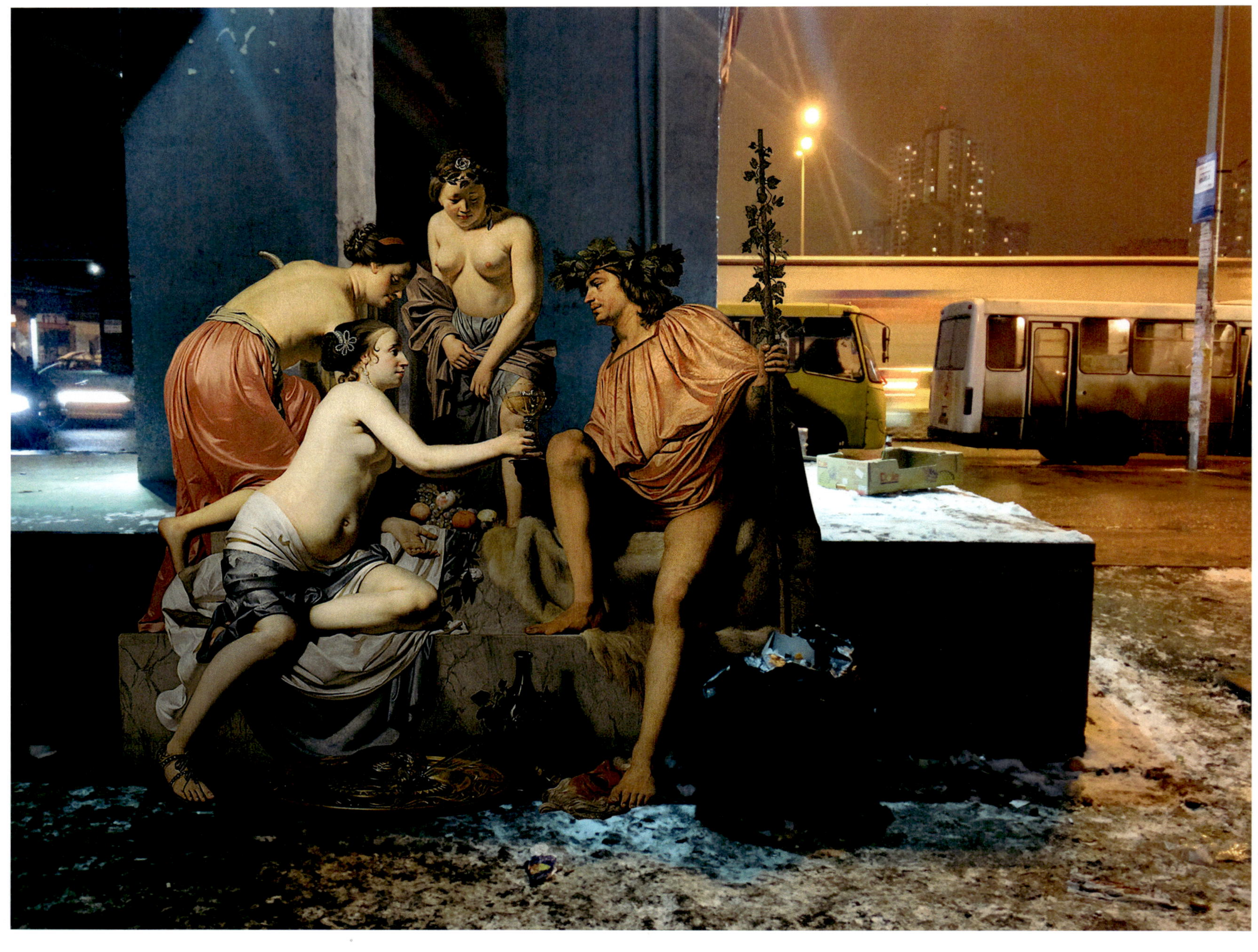

figures. Kondakov used paintings from Francesco Hayez, William Bouguereau and Caravaggio, and transfers the figures to balconies, courtyards and pizzerias.

Photography as Classical Trompe l'Œil

Traditionally one photographs places, landscapes and buildings in order to show them and thereby show that one was there and that one did indeed see this thing or that. However, in May 2016, in Paris – in the Cour Napoléon of the Louvre, to be precise – one could photograph something that was not there. At least it would have seemed not to have been there. The photographer and street artist JR (b. 1983), who caused a sensation with his giant portraits glued to streets, buildings, bridges, trains, slums and favelas the world over, made the iconic pyramid of the Chinese-American architect I. M. Pei (1917–2019) disappear for a while. That thing which many Parisians have wanted most to see, ever since the structure of the Louvre's new main entrance opened in 1989, became true, at least for a month – and at least when the courtyard was viewed from a particular vantage point. At the Louvre's invitation, JR created a giant trompe l'œil by photographing the parts of the museum's Sully Wing normally covered by the pyramid when looking towards the east of the courtyard. He then pasted the black-and-white pictures onto the nearly 700 glass surfaces of the pyramid and thus made it disappear. The effect was astounding, also – or perhaps precisely – because, although the building wing was photographed in black and white, it was still possible to create the impression that no pyramid stood on this site. With this trompe l'œil, a distinctive and popular background for infinitely many selfies disappeared at the same time. This was also the artist's intention, who quite rightly criticises the fact that people taking selfies are focused more on lionising themselves by positioning themselves in front of some famous background, than on showing the very object of attraction before which they stand. "Hundreds of tourists take selfies with the pyramid everyday, so I wanted to make it harder for them. I want them to actively look for it and talk to each other while moving around to find the best spot to take the picture."[30] With this installation, for a short time, they had the opportunity to do just that.

▶ JR, *The Secret of the Great Pyramid*, 2019

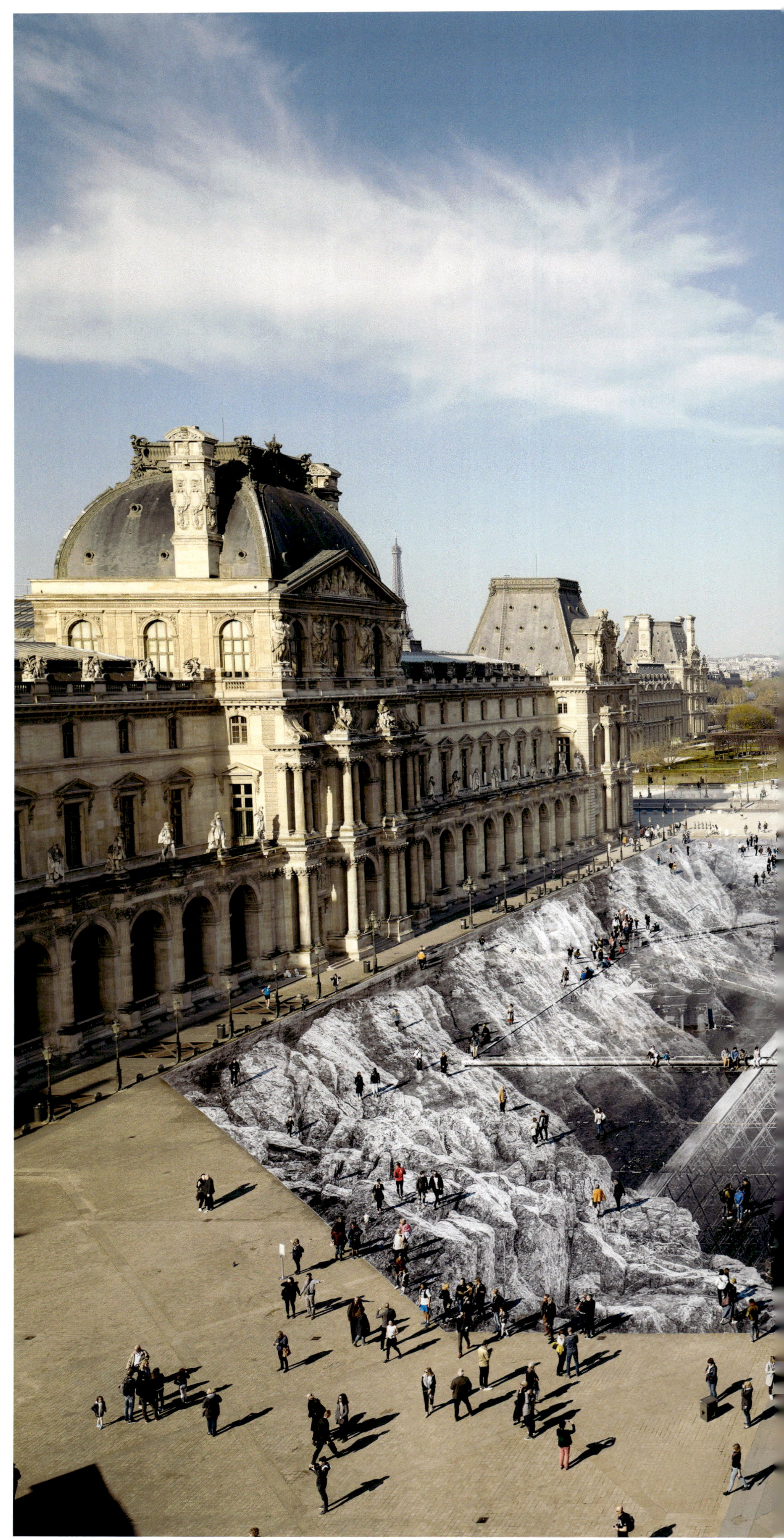

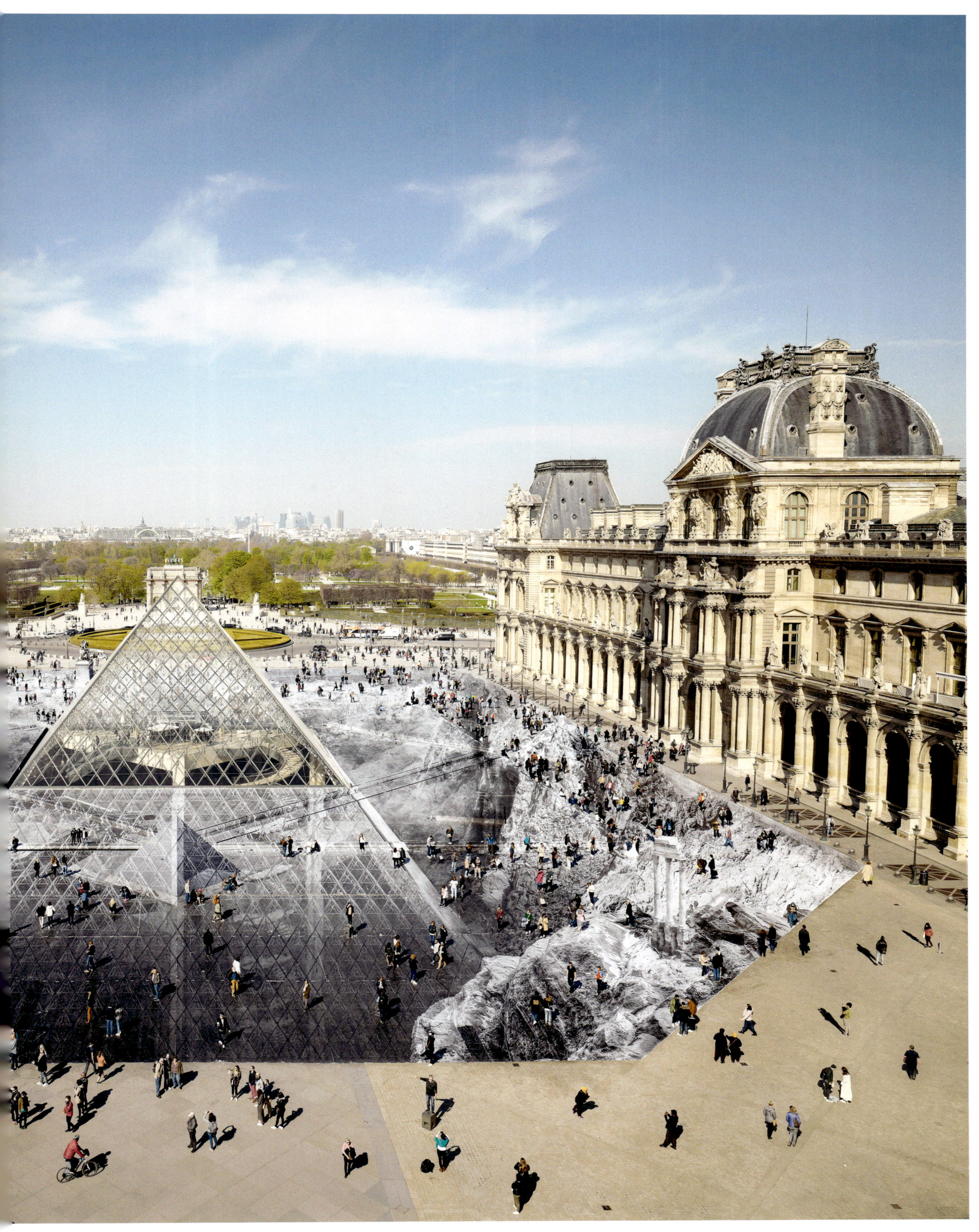

Three years later, JR 'resurrected' the pyramid in the truest sense of the word. In his installation *The Secret of the Great Pyramid* (fig. pp. 122/123), created in 2019 for the structure's thirtieth anniversary, he uncovered the foundations of the pyramid (which the Louvre had said have been buried for millennia). In his largest work to date, over 1,600 square metres in size, JR created an almost classical anamorphosis – a representation in distorted perspective – that was conceived from a point on the top floor of the Sully Wing and also broadcast from there on screens for the duration of the installation. In four days, 400 volunteers assembled the 2,000 paper strips that made up the work of art. And within a day, it was destroyed again. JR had intended for the installation to be short-lived. He said, "The images, like life, are ephemeral. Once pasted, the art piece lives on its own. The sun dries the light glue and with every step, people tear pieces of the fragile paper. The process is all about participation of volunteers, visitors, and souvenir catchers. This project is also about presence and absence, about reality and memories, about impermanence."[31] For the Louvre, however, the main point was the pyramid, which has long been controversial. JR's artwork was intended to show that even after thirty years the pyramid still has the power to inspire artists.

Digital image manipulation and production technology continues to progress, tirelessly and with ever increasing speed. As in computer games and animated films, photographing individual components in real life will often no longer be necessary. Moreover, digital manipulation is no longer being used only for artificially created fantasy worlds but has also began penetrating into the 'real' world of images. Thanks to artificial intelligence, it is now possible to create portraits that look completely realistic and make all the attempts at deception and illusion that art has made so far seem amateurish (fig. right).[32]

▶ Computer-generated faces, 2018

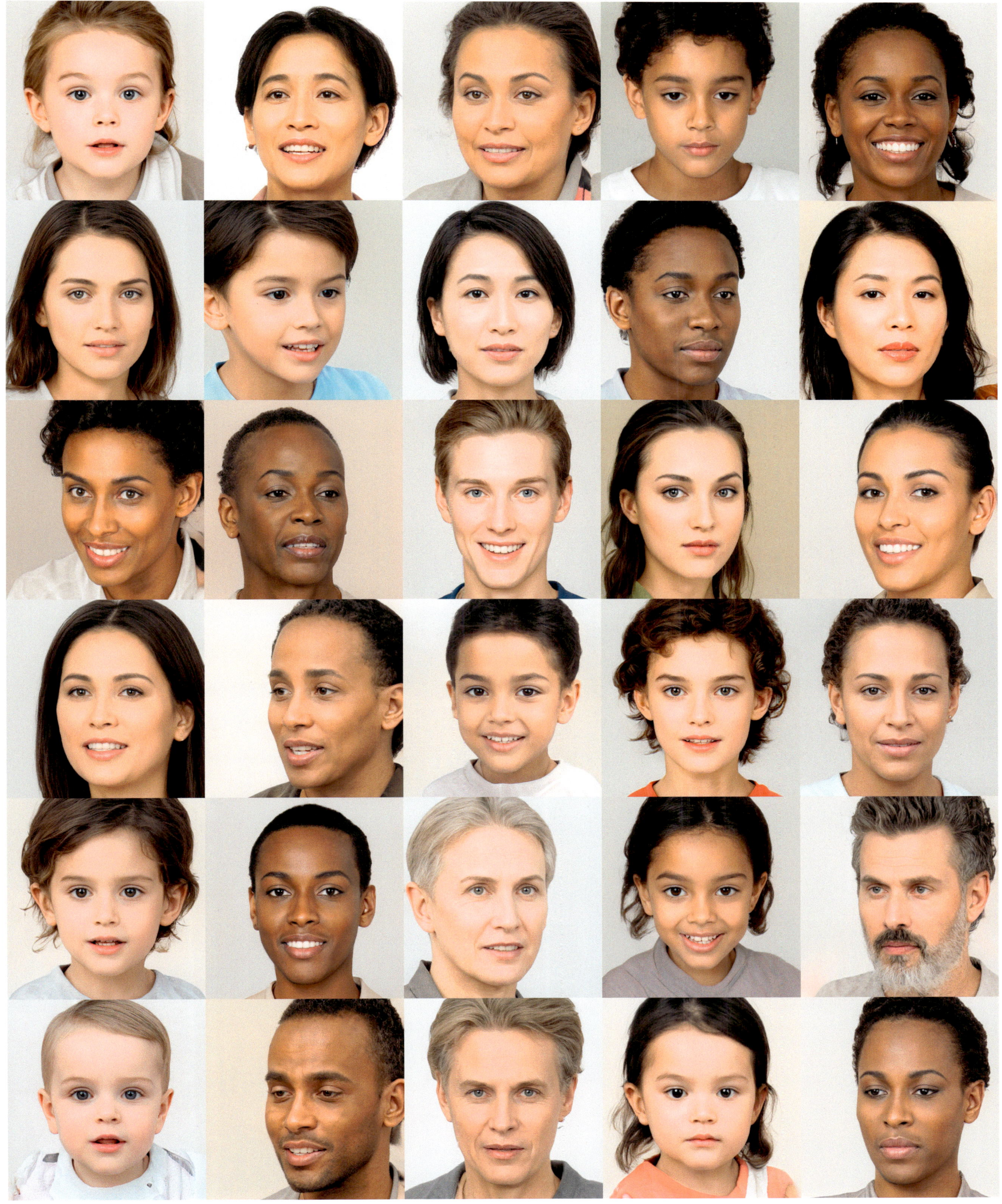

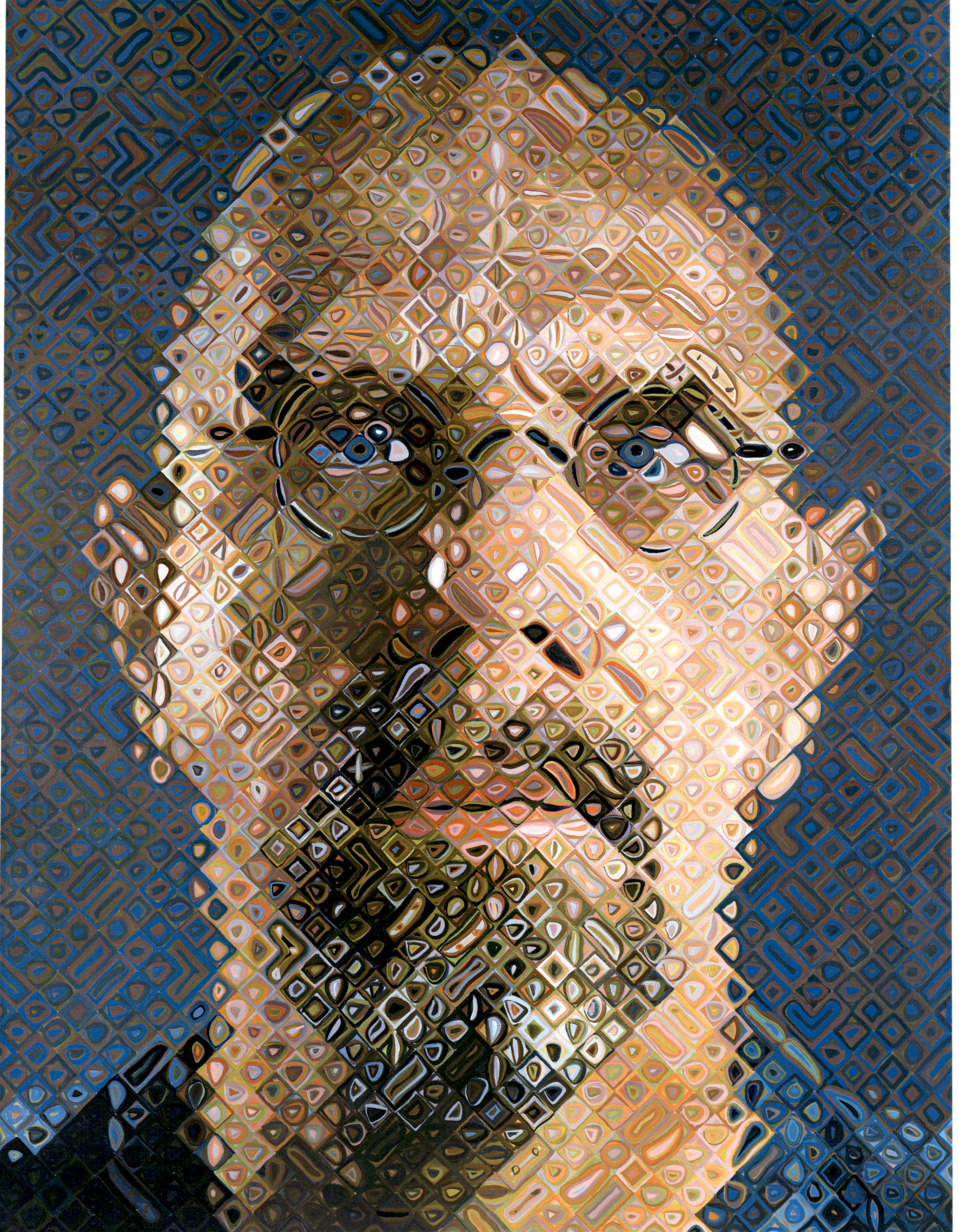

Chuck Close

Self-Portrait, 2000–2001

Oil on canvas, 275.6 × 213.4 cm
San Francisco Museum of Modern Art

Chuck Close (b. 1940) helped establish photorealism with the black-and-white portraits he painted from photographs of friends at the end of the 1960s. At first glance, *Phil* looks like a black-and-white photograph in the style of Richard Avedon (1923–2004) – particularly if only seen as a small illustration in a book. However, the work measures 2.74 × 2.13 metres, and this size lends it a completely different dynamic. The painting was not created in a portrait session with the composer Philip Glass (b. 1937), but from a photograph that Close enlarged to the final dimensions using the traditional grid method. It is thus an image of an image, a painting that imitates a photograph. With this first series of portraits, from which this work is taken, Close plays with the credibility and faithfulness to reality of photography while at the same time elevating it as a subject worthy of art by turning a photograph into a huge work on canvas. Close thereby recognises photography as an art form. Simultaneously, he puts it in its place by painting something of such a museum-worthy size, paired with a richness of detail, that it lays bare the technical limitations of photography, at least of that time. It is playing a game with artistic techniques, in which painting (still) enjoys priority. In the 1980s, Thomas Ruff (b. 1958) shot a series of portraits, which were printed in a similar size, but with a completely different effect, despite the comparable formats. The sheer size and rigorous precision of Close's paintings, which make no effort to compensate for the blurriness of the photograph, give rise to a certain sense of alienation. The viewer is confronted with a larger-than-life reality that can only arise through the artificiality of painting. Close's portraits are not primarily concerned with the depicted persons, but rather with representation itself. "There is a relationship between a likeness of someone and artificiality. [...] That's why I've never liked being labeled a Realist. I'm just as interested in the artificial as in the real, and above all in the tension between the two".[33] Close continues to experiment, and his later works produce results in which the use of a pattern of grids makes them ever more abstract. And here, too, there is again a game of illusion and artificiality: Usually, one recognises more the closer one gets to a painting. With Close, it is the other way around: The further away one moves, the more precisely the face can be recognised.

Andreas Gursky

Beelitz, 2007

C-Print, 307 × 219 × 6.2 cm,
Düsseldorf

▶ **Facing page**

Amazon, 2016

Inkjet-Print, 207 × 407 × 6.2 cm,
Gagosian, New York

▶ **Overleaf**

Andreas Gursky's photographs are not examples of classical trompe l'œils, but rather perfectly executed illusions, the effect of which is once again based on the credibility given to photography. In a certain sense, the process of creating his pictures parallels the large cluster of themes dealt with by Gursky (b. 1955) in his photographs: modern mass society and its associated phenomena, such as mass production and products, intensive farming and industrial livestock production, mass sporting and political events, as well as mass leisure events. An asparagus field in Beelitz stretches to the horizon (fig. right), a Formula One race track in Bahrain becomes a seemingly endless mirage across the desert, the three-storey Westfalenhalle in Dortmund is sampled and transformed into an 18-storey techno temple for the city's annual Mayday rave and Amazon's warehouse appears, roughly, as one would imagine it (fig. pp. 130/131).

In his pictures, Gursky plays with the traditional trust placed in photography, which has always been regarded as proof of a concrete situation. What the camera eye saw must have happened as shown or must have thus existed in that moment. This is only conditionally true, however, for Gursky, who says, "Any claims on the truth in [my] pictures are only to be answered in the sense that a particular event did in fact happen and did take place in the here and now."[34]

But his images also relate to the fact that the viewer may equally assume that it is not entirely unlikely that, in our time of 'never-ending' growth, the factories, fields and cities in his pictures could actually be as gigantic as Gursky shows them. This uncertainty creeps into some of his photographs. The best example of this is the picture *Amazon* from 2016. To be sure, Gursky shows reality, but stretches it spatially until it reaches a size that barely seems realistic. The manipulations are so perfect, so subtle and suggestive that, at first, they do not stand out – especially if the viewer is ignorant of the reality. The starting point is the real situation, but the image itself is an artistic realisation of it, or in Gursky's words, "The picture is not true, but it is truthful."[35] The special quality of his pictures is the combination of distance and detail. "My pictures are always composed from two positions. Viewed from extremely close up, they are legible down to the smallest detail. From a distance, they turn into mega-signs."[36] His pictures actually need their large scale since the ambivalence between proximity and distance can ultimately only be discerned properly when confronted with the large format of his pictures in exhibitions.

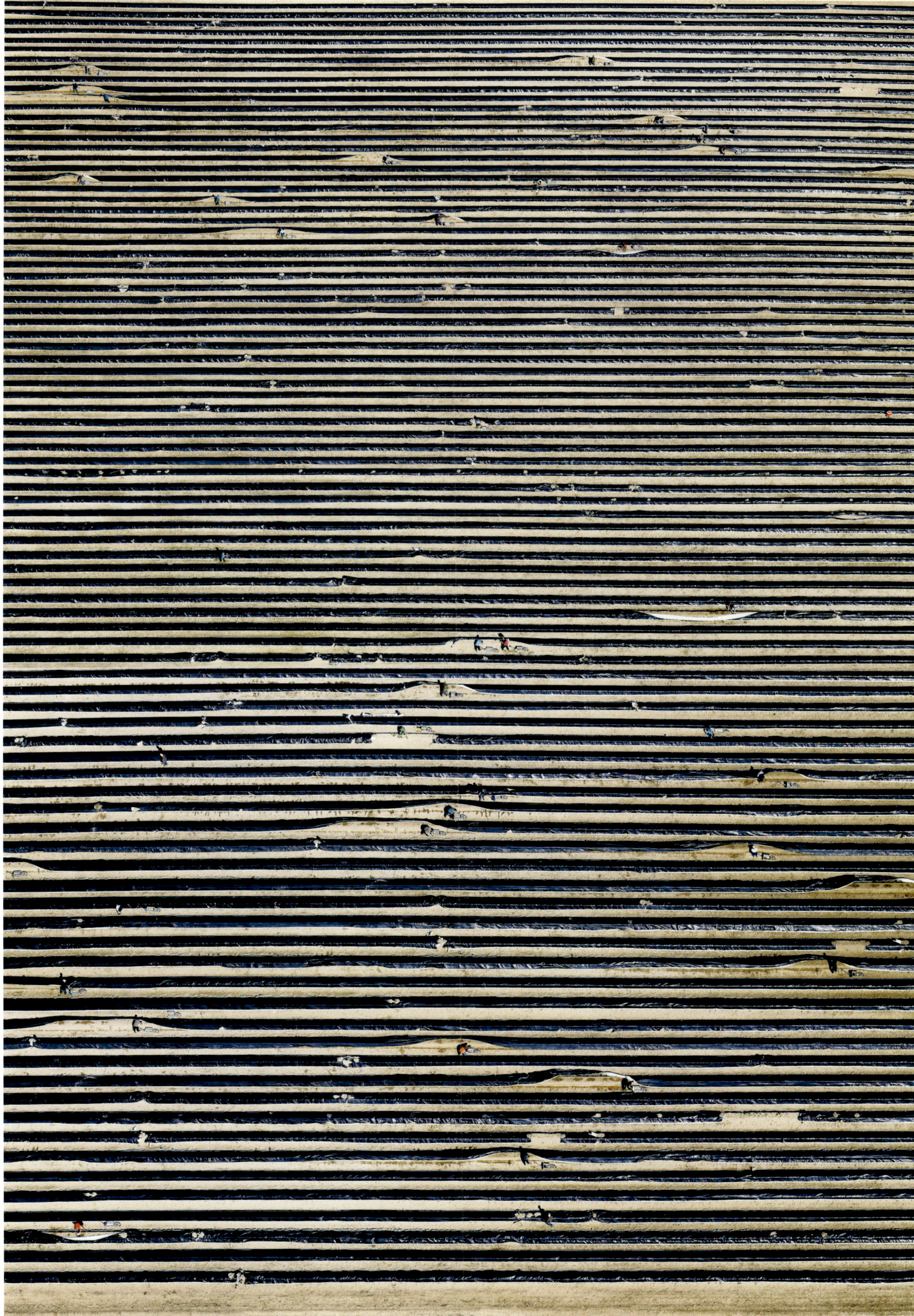

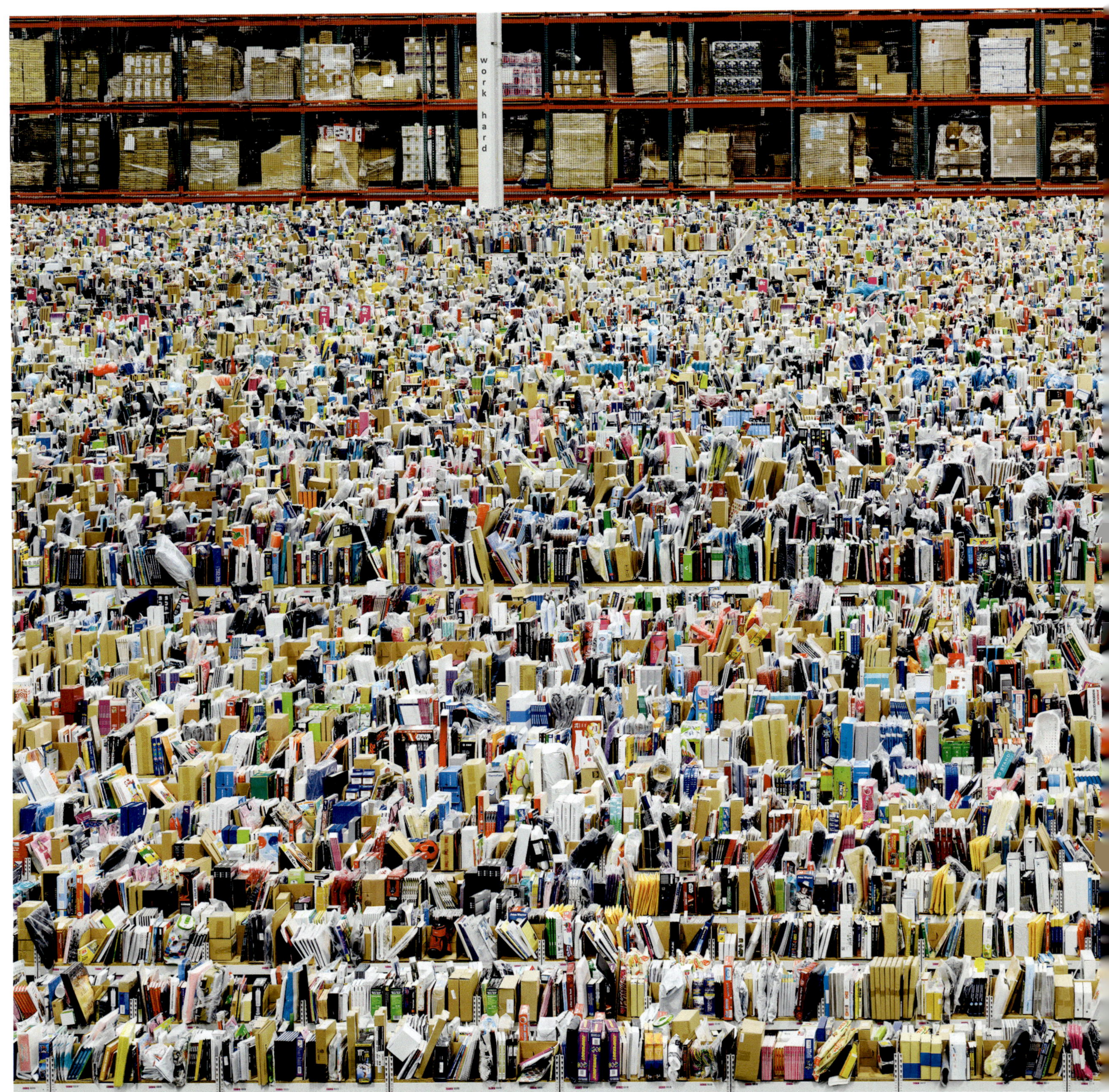
work hard

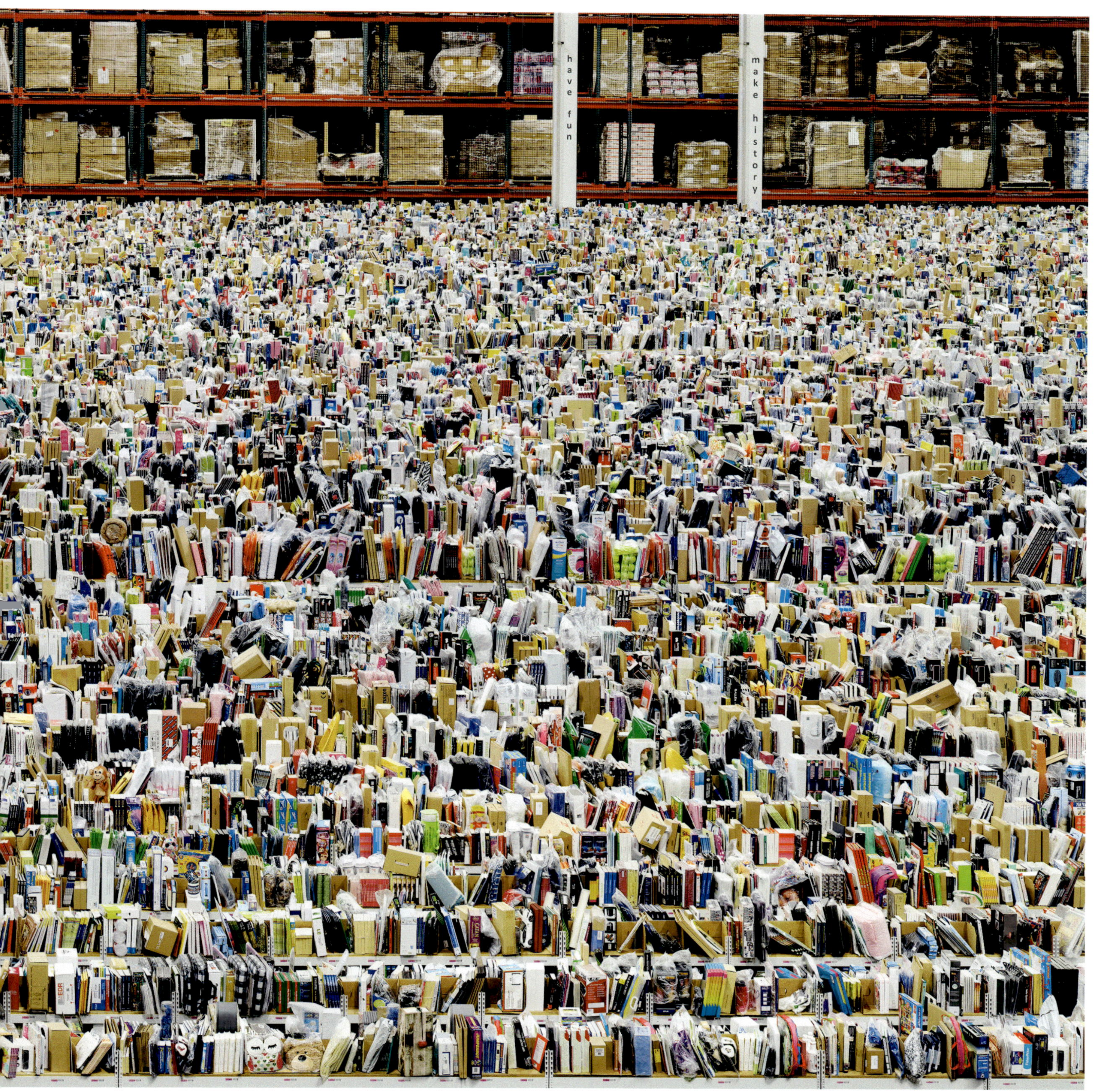
have fun
make history

Pelle Cass

New Pavement on Congress Street II, 2017

Digital photography, Photoshop

▶ **Facing page**

Football Game, Harvard, 2017

▶ **Overleaf**

In the photographs of Pelle Cass (b. 1954), doubt always plays a part: whether almost all the people on this street really did wear blue shirts (fig. right), whether they and their shadows really walked so symmetrically or whether the many football players, perhaps in the course of attempting some strange world record, were indeed all on this playing field (fig. pp. 134/135). This effect arises because, as with Gursky, what one sees in the photographs actually happened: "My work looks real because it is real", says the artist, "It all happened just as you see it, just not at the same time."[37] This is the essence of the thing: "the purpose of time is to keep everything from happening at once",[38] American science fiction author Ray Cummings wrote in 1922. But Cass intervenes and lets everything, it would seem, happen at the same time. He photographs a certain place, very often over a particular period of time, and then superimposes these images digitally over each other. Then he selects what will remain in place and what will once again disappear. Because of this process, he calls his photographs "still time-lapse". Cass does not change anything else; he does not move any figures or add anything he did not photograph within the given period. He has a few fixed rules, of which this is the most important. Another rule he has established for his work is rather charming: twins always remain in the picture, because, he reasons, the viewer will be convinced that he must have manipulated them. In principle, however, he only makes one decision: what stays in and what is left out. In a similar way, when one observes a particular place for a while, one later remembers some people but not others. But everyone remembered was really there. That is why many of his works seem so confusing yet deceptively real. Cass's works are vaguely reminiscent of those of Andreas Gursky. But whereas Andreas Gursky primarily 'expands' space, Cass expands time, and captures many moments that nobody would be particularly interested in – or even notice. Thus, these seemingly unimportant moments also occur in his pictures, and they can still be seen long after they actually happened. Even today, the French photographic legend Henri Cartier-Bresson (1908–2004) continues to shape photography with his principle of the "decisive moment". Pelle Cass decided to go in exactly the opposite direction, and he photographs any number of 'undecisive moments', creating his pictures in this way.

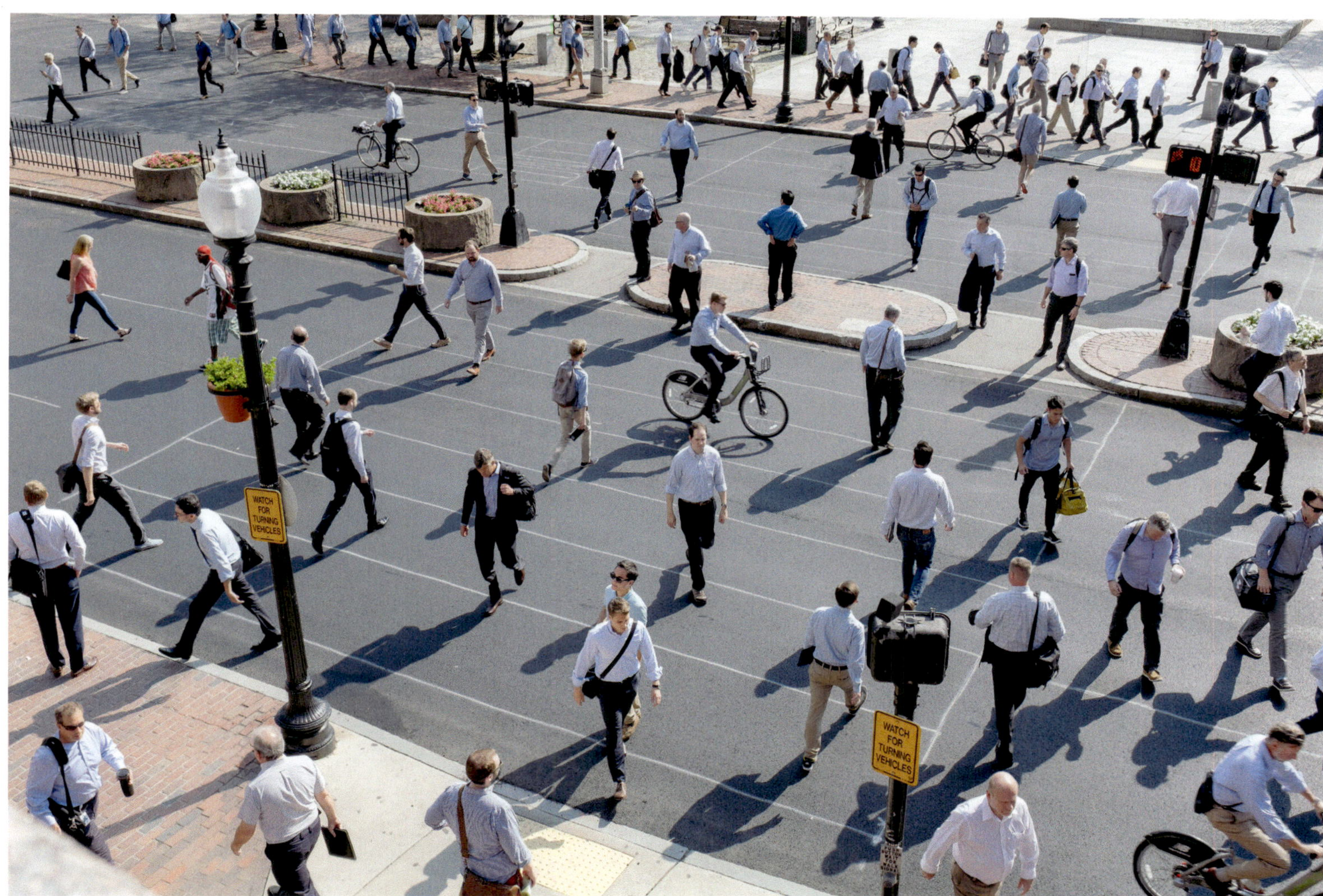
WATCH FOR TURNING VEHICLES
WATCH FOR TURNING VEHICLES

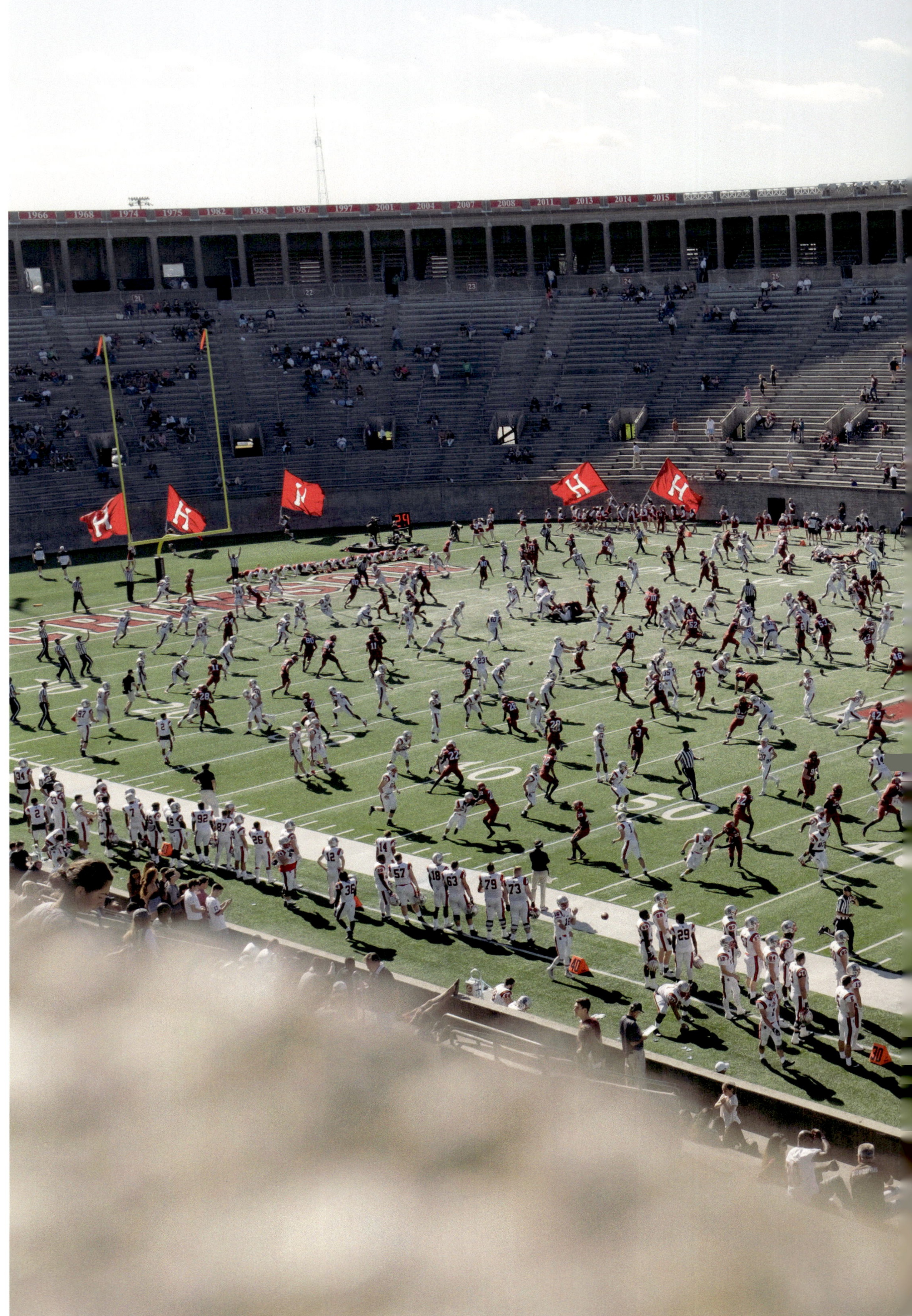

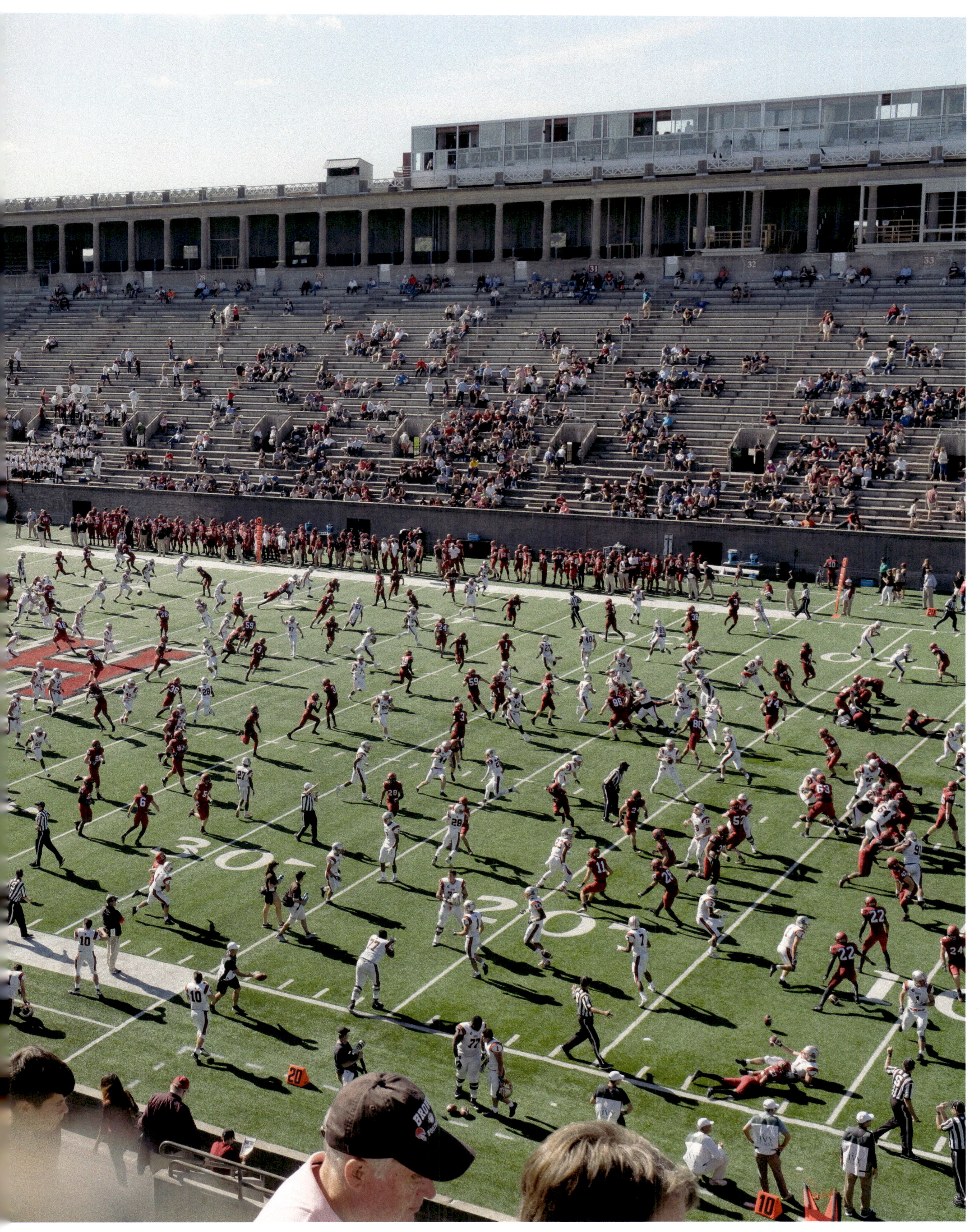

Felice Varini

Trois ellipses ouvertes en désordre,
Hasselt, 2014

White colour on 99 buildings

Felice Varini (b. 1952) creates his pictures in three-dimensional space (and in the resulting photographs). There, the many individual elements of his artworks, which at first do not seem to have any relation to each other, appear randomly scattered. "My field of action is architectural space and everything that constitutes such space. These spaces are and remain the original media for my painting."[39] Varini works with geometric forms and bold colours, so that one can easily recognise his works within the architectural, at times confusing, context upon which he fixes his art. However, this only fully works from a single point, the one from which Varini conceived his geometric figures. The work is distributed in space so that one's own singular point begins to wander. The viewer shapes the work by moving through the architectural space, connecting the parts they see on walls, windows, doors and posts with each other and with the space. When the viewer reaches the point from which Varini started, the fragments scattered throughout the architectural space resolve themselves wonderfully into the figure that the artist had in mind from the very beginning. The result is a curious transformation of the space. It becomes a two-dimensional canvas for Varini's shapes, which now seem to float as if upon tulle. Painting and architecture are drawn together through photography and result in images that astonish the viewer.

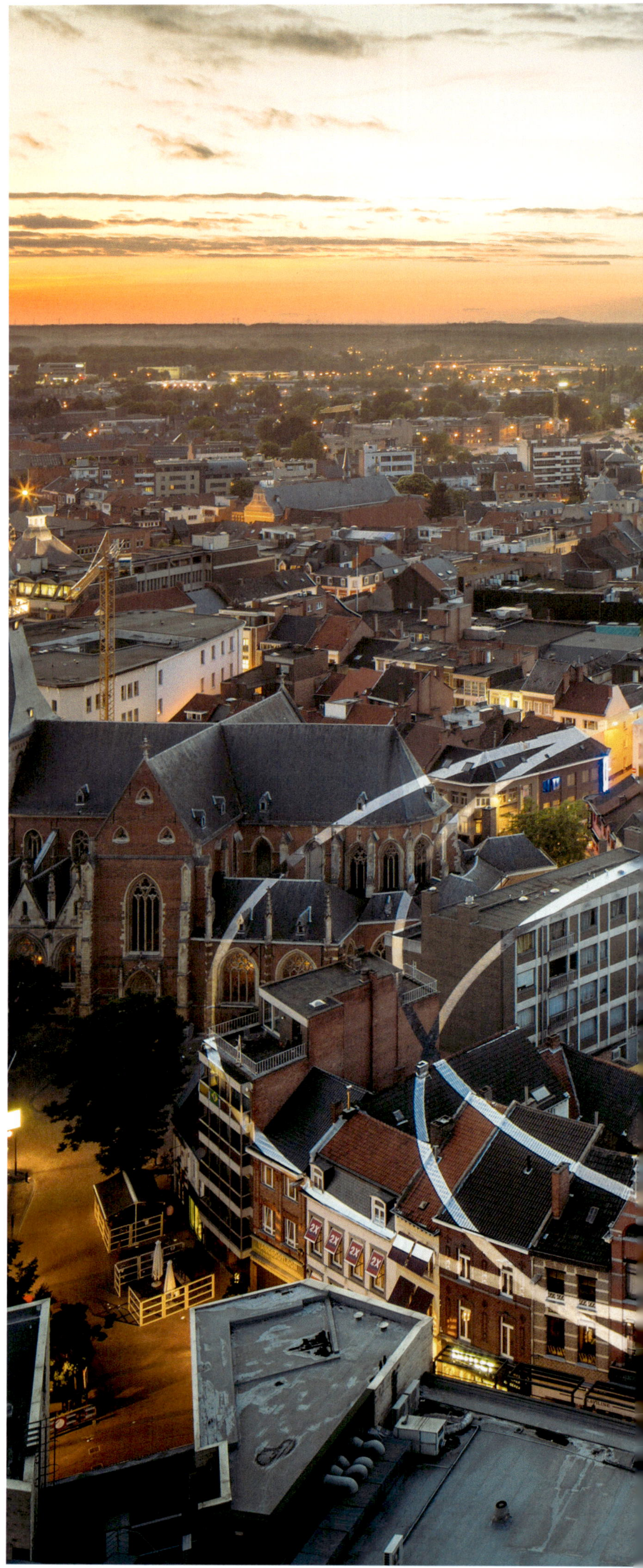

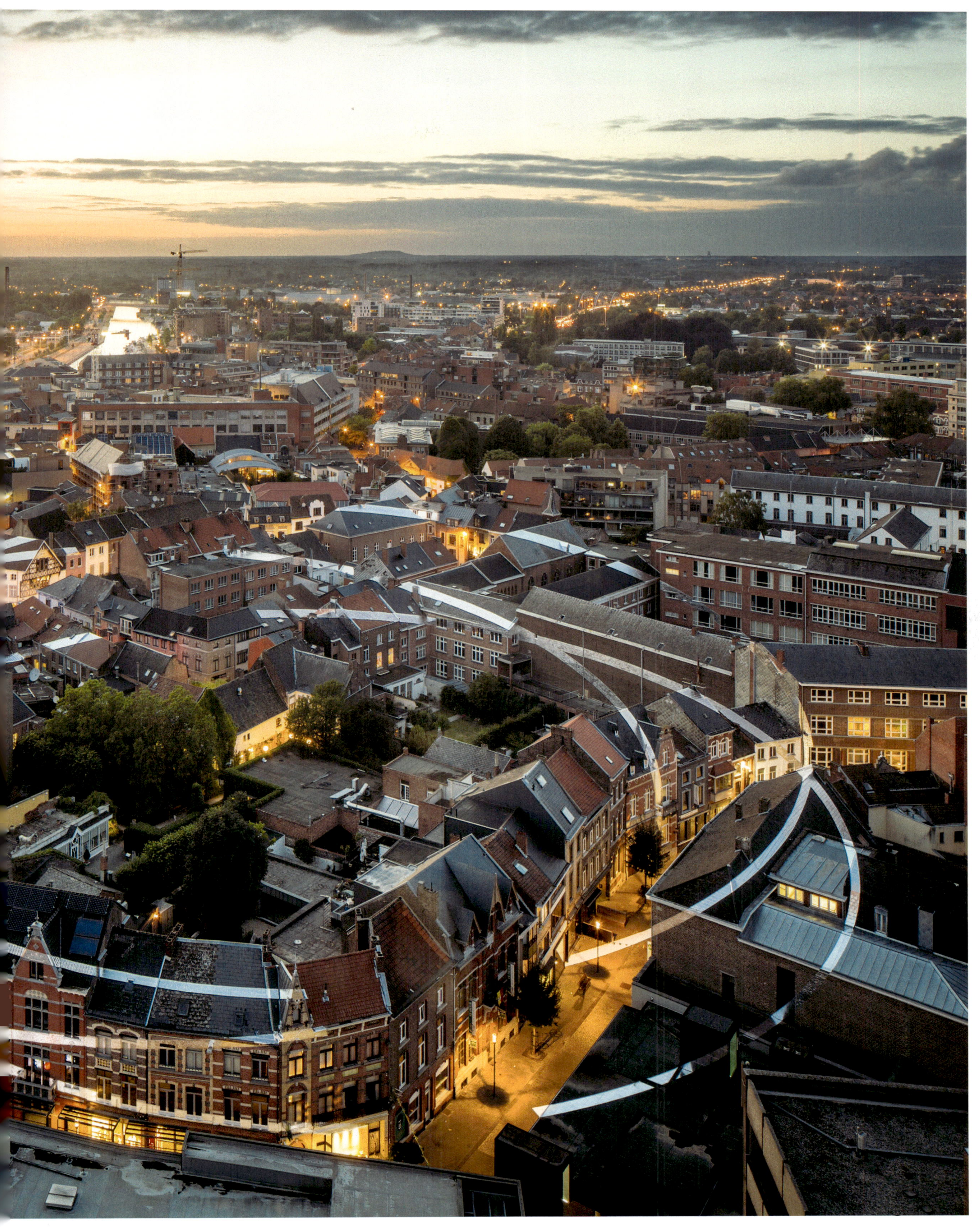

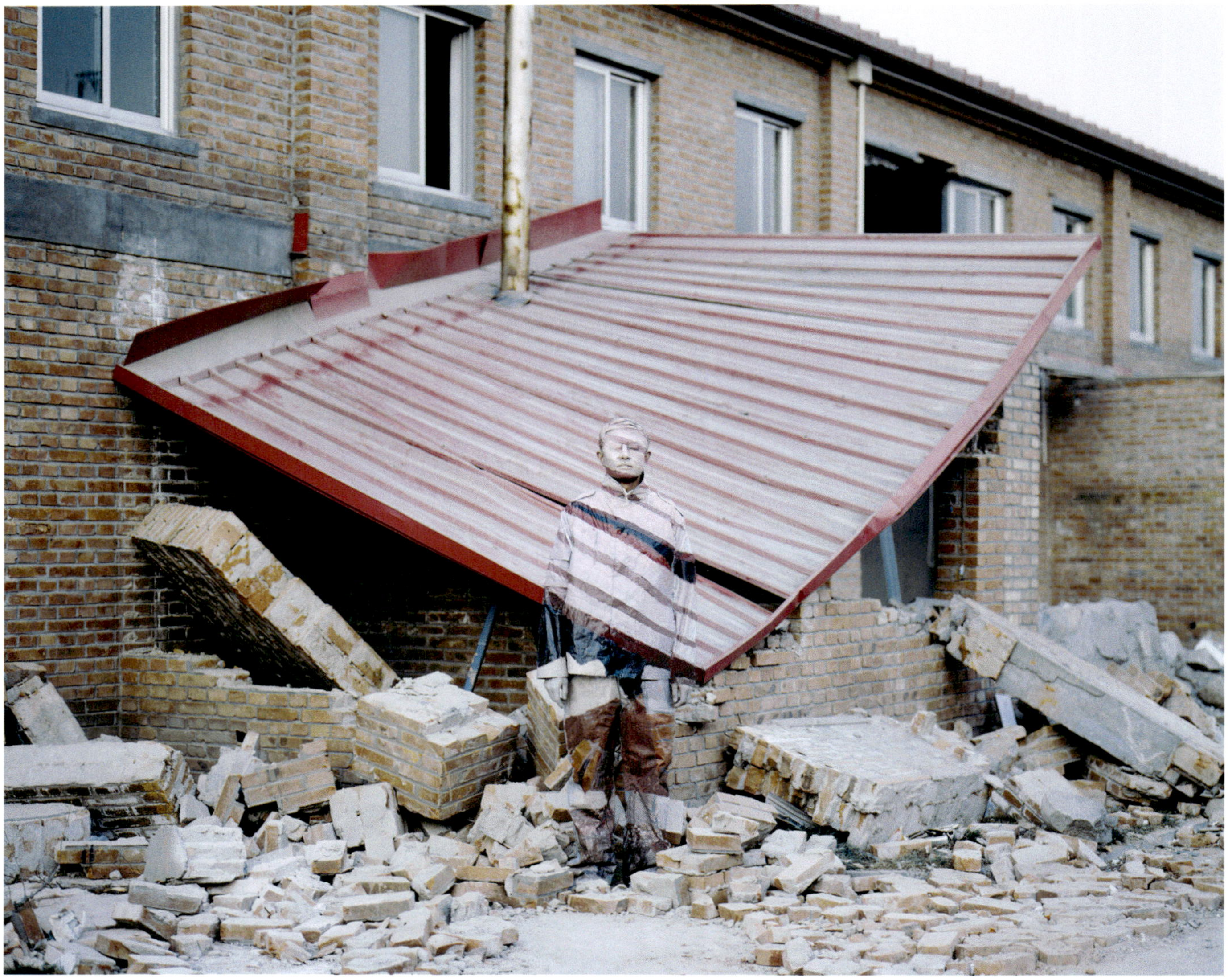

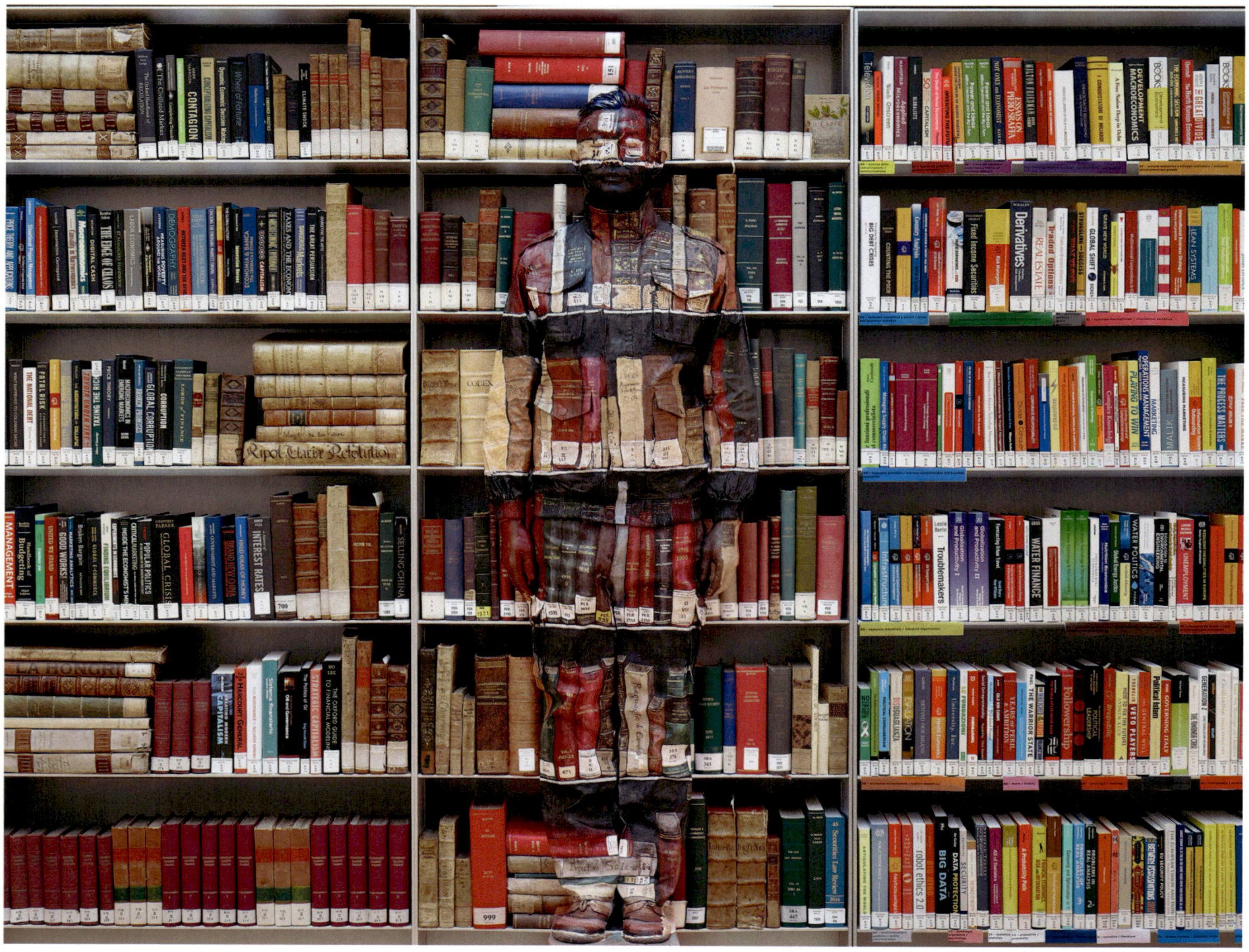

Liu Bolin

Hiding In The City, Suojia Village No. 2, 2006

Archival Pigment Print, 126 × 160 cm

◀ **Facing page, above and below**

The fascinating art of the Chinese artist Liu Bolin (b. 1973) has a serious and rather tragic origin story. In his homeland, he worked as a sculptor and created a scandal with numerous caricatures. The individual and their autonomy are his subjects, a subject that does not necessarily arouse enthusiasm and is often perceived as an act of criticism by Chinese officials. In response, his studio in Beijing was destroyed in 2005. This led to a radical change in his art and his medium of choice: He disappeared – which would seem to have been what the regime had wanted. However, Liu only disappeared into his art, and he did so almost perfectly. He initiated his series *Hiding in the City* by assuming the colours of each respective background, much like a chameleon, and is thus almost impossible to spot. He staged his own disappearance. With his combination of sculpture, body painting and photography, Liu managed to vanish so well that he became internationally visible – which is hardly likely to have been the objective of those who destroyed his studio. The backgrounds against which Liu Bolin disappears usually have a symbolic meaning, such as election posters, industrial buildings, China's national flag or Mao's Mausoleum. Yet, Liu's art can only reach perfection through photography. His work ultimately requires the two-dimensionality and frontal view of the camera in order to function perfectly. The viewer needs time to distinguish the camouflaged figure from the structures of each background. In reality, even a tiny shift from the focal point is enough to dissolve the illusion. Liu's message is clear: Even the greatest egalitarianism and the compartmentalisation and subordination of the individual within the masses cannot, ultimately, extinguish the individual. Even if it sometimes takes longer to be recognised – when his figure is found, it appears all the more vividly. Liu's art of deception is like mimesis within nature; the individual protects itself by adopting or imitating the colours and forms of its habitat in order to avoid being discovered by its predators. By publicly disseminating his mimesis through photography and digital media, Liu is symbolically mocking state surveillance.

SCULPTURE

Humanity's Other Image

"Noble simplicity and sedate grandeur" is a dictum used by the archaeologist Johann Joachim Winckelmann (1717–1768) to describe the dignity of ancient statues, which – carved in pure marble or cast in fine bronze – show the idealised bodies of the gods and of myth. Our image of antiquity has been lastingly influenced by Winckelmann and his bon mot – and it is wrong. Antiquity was far from being as lacking in colour as is often imagined. The mistake lies not only with Winkelmann, but also in the perception of antiquity within Renaissance art theory. In fact, antiquity was colourful; the temples were painted, and the gods and warriors were covered in pigment. Even then, artists wanted to present a picture of the heroes and gods that was as true to life as possible, however one may interpret the idea of gods being 'true to life'. The ancient statues, which were later uncovered in the Middle Ages and increasingly in the Renaissance, had over the centuries largely lost their colour. In addition, Winckelmann was studying Roman copies of the original Greek sculptures and thus became a victim of their own misinterpretations. But the bare marble matched the image of the world of antiquity which had been popularly formed. The written word painted a different picture, however, with plenty of references in ancient texts to the colourfulness of their sculptures. In Euripides's tragedy *Hypsipyle*, for example, we read, "Look – run your eyes up towards the sky and take a look at the painted reliefs on the pediment" (fig. right).[40] The pediment figures had to be clearly and precisely recognisable because, though placed high up, they told the

▶ *Paris*, archer from the west pediment of the Temple of Aphaia on Aegina, c. 480 BC, colour reconstruction

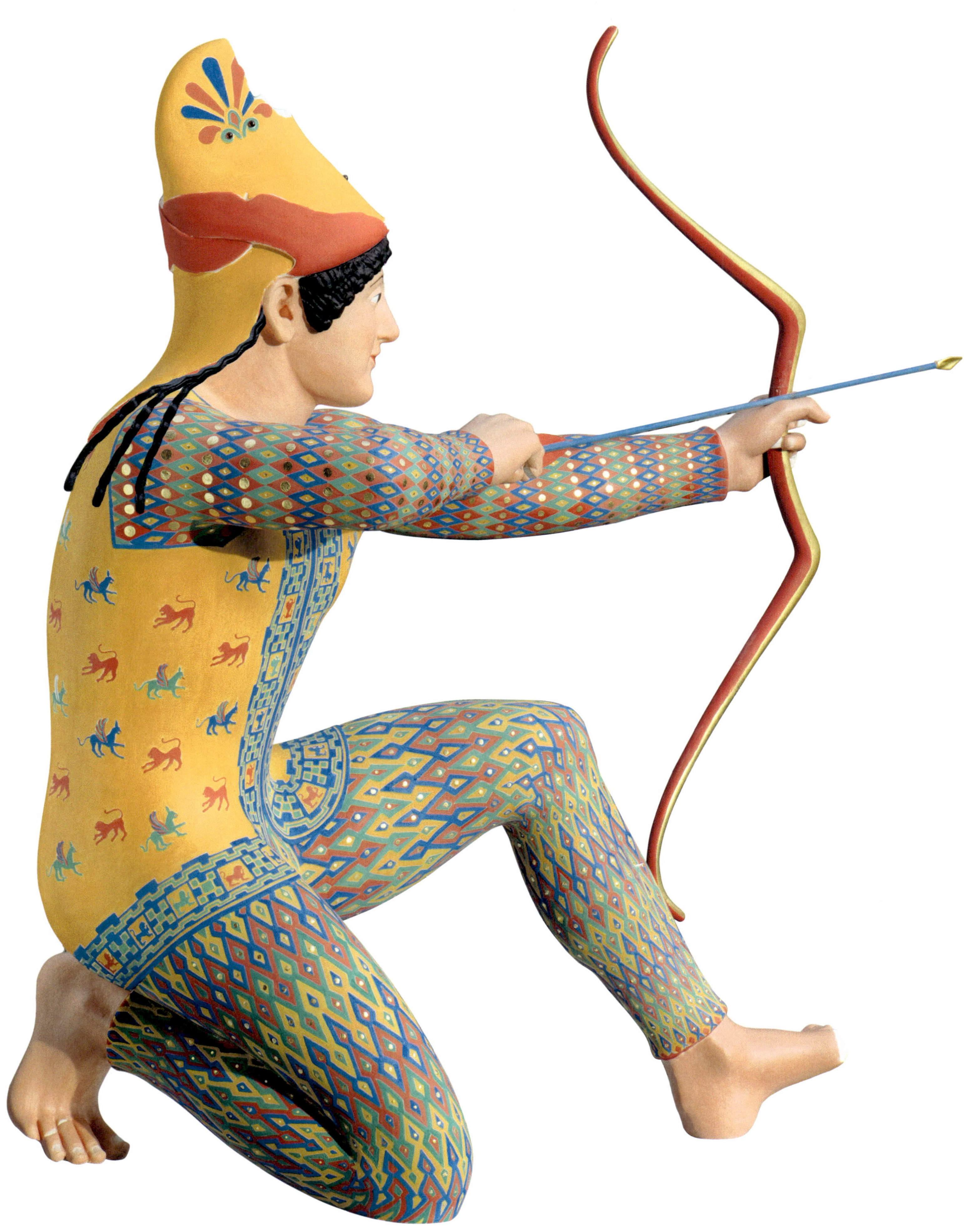

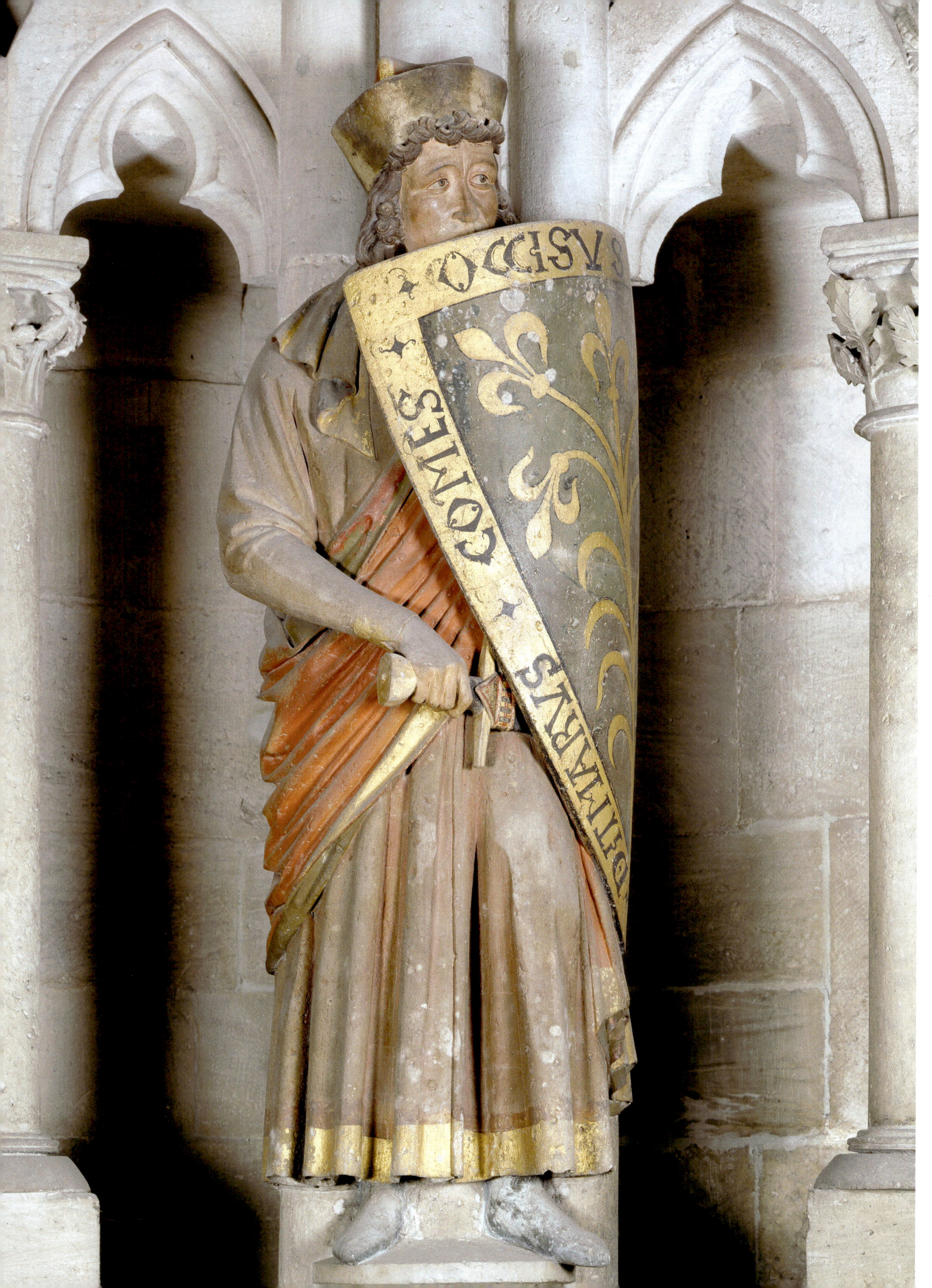
OCCISVS
COMES
DITMARVS

◀ Naumburg Master, *Count Dietmar*, c. 1250

stories of gods and heroes, after all. Today, the use of ultraviolet light and other modern investigation techniques have aided in proving and reconstructing the original colouring of many ancient sculptures. Unpainted figures may even have originally constituted a major flaw, as can be read in Helen's lament in the tragedy by Euripides bearing her name: "My life and fortunes are a monstrosity,/ Partly because of Hera, partly because of my beauty./ If only I could shed my beauty and assume an uglier aspect/ The way you would wipe color off a statue."[41]

As in painting, where the best painter was considered the one who could paint the most realistically, so in sculpture, the illusion of being true to life was equally important. By the Middle Ages, however, this had not played a role for centuries. At that time, people wanted to distance themselves from the all too carnal here and now and turn their attention to the hereafter. For a long time, things remained the same, but a change in approach to both sculpture and wood carving came, as in painting, in the 13th century. In terms of cathedral building, sculpture had been presented with new tasks, which usually had little to do with illusionistic realism. One artist who took exception to this was the so-called Naumburg Master, who around 1250 created, with his donor portraits in the choir of Naumburg Cathedral, probably the most extraordinary and realistic figures of his time (fig. left). If one disregards the fact that the portrayed personalities lived around two centuries before the sculptures were created, one could speak of an astonishingly portrait-like resemblance. The Naumburg Master probably had the necessary models from which to work, but what he made of them was highly unusual. Through the postures, facial expressions and gestures of the figures alone, as well as in their visual relationship to each other, he tells an exciting story of betrayal and murder – and he does so in a church chancel. And of course, the figures were painted in colour, as can still be seen today.

The illusionistic design was of decisive importance for engendering piety amongst the people. The more realistic and true-to-life a religious figure like Christ as a child (fig. p. 144) or on the cross was, the more direct was its contact to the faithful and the more intense the effect. Especially in depictions of the Passion of Christ, the

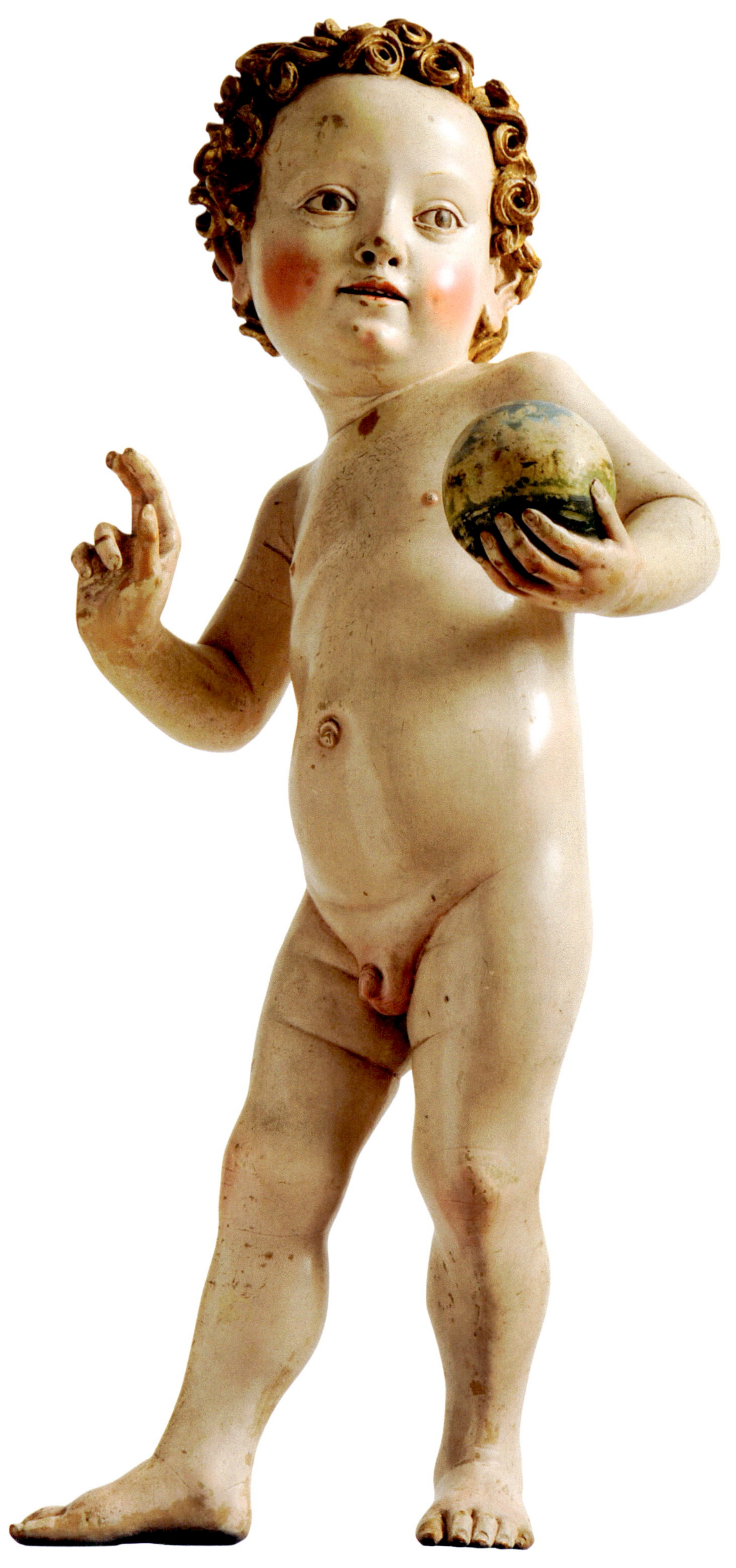

'compassio' (i.e., sympathy) was an important aspect. And for this, the figures had to appear correspondingly lifelike.

While images of the Christ Child were usually on the cute side, those of his Passion were often much starker. In Mystery and Passion Plays, the intention was to show the Saviour 'made flesh'. For this purpose, all the stops were pulled out, from the painting to the use of glass eyes, to real hair and blood (see p. 159).

That works with religious content can still function today and trigger vehement 'compassio' can be seen in the example of the sculpture *La nona ora*, which the Italian artist Maurizio Cattelan (b. 1960) created in 1999 (fig. pp. 146/147). It shows Pope John Paul II on a red carpet; struck down by a meteorite, he lies on the ground, supported by his ferula. The title, "The Ninth Hour", refers to the hour in which Christ died on the cross. In a classic hyperrealistic manner, the pope is depicted absolutely true to life. The convincing work and the 'compassio' awakened by it led two Polish members of parliament to roll away the meteorite and set the Pope on his feet at an exhibition in 2000 at the Zachęta National Gallery of Art in Warsaw, and to sack the museum director. It would seem that religious zeal has hardly diminished over the centuries.

Painting the figures of Saints and Christ, be it as a child or suffering in the Passion, was immensely important. It is not without reason that the artists who painted and gilded the figures were often better paid than their carving peers, although this may also have had something to do with the higher cost of the pigments.

Painted sculptures and busts were of great importance during the Renaissance, even if the theoretical discussion about painted or unpainted sculptures was by now well underway. Many artists were convinced that sculptures had to remain 'pure' – i.e., unpainted – because of the discovery of sculptures dating from antiquity in which the colours had faded, and which were most often Roman copies of Greek originals. The sculptor's idea and the purity of form should be the focus of attention. In these 'vanguard' circles, the process of painting sculpture was considered more a craft than an art. Despite this debate, painted terracotta sculptures, which were coated with colourful glazes, were still popular, especially in Italy, and particularly as portraits (fig. p. 148). And also with religious

◀ Gregor Erhart and Hans Holbein the Elder, *The Christ Child,* c. 1500
▶ **Overleaf**
Maurizio Cattelan,
La nona ora (*The Ninth Hour*), 1999

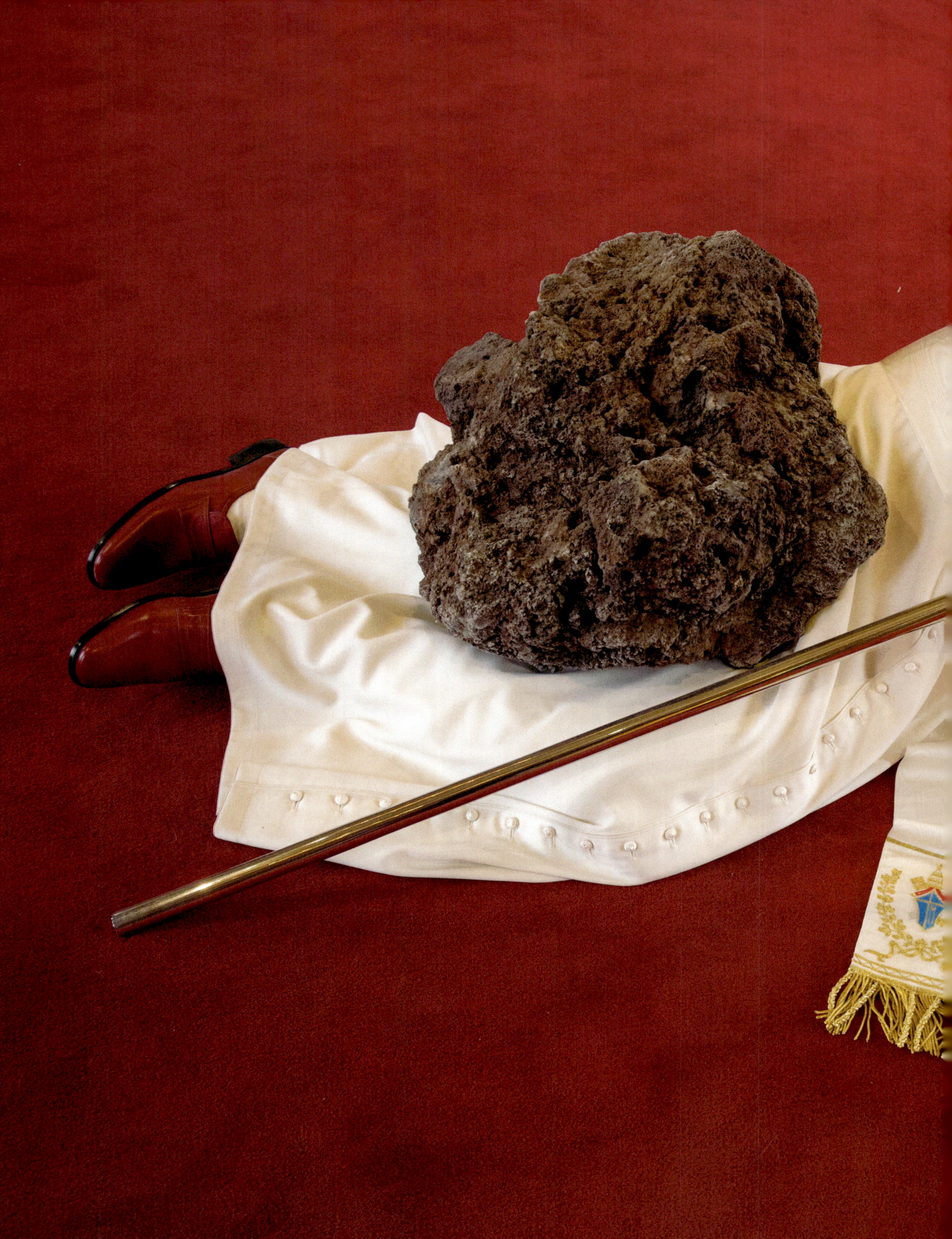

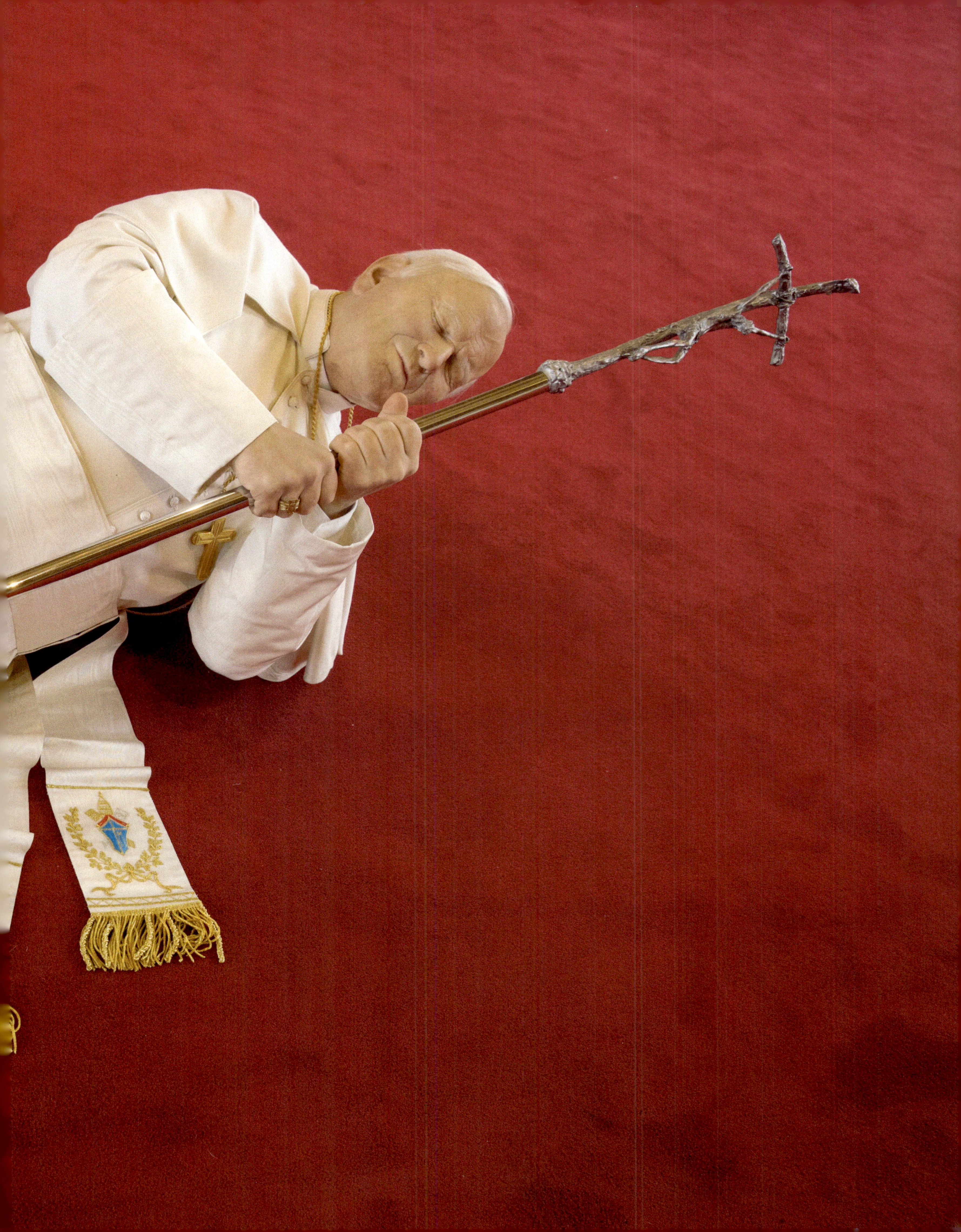

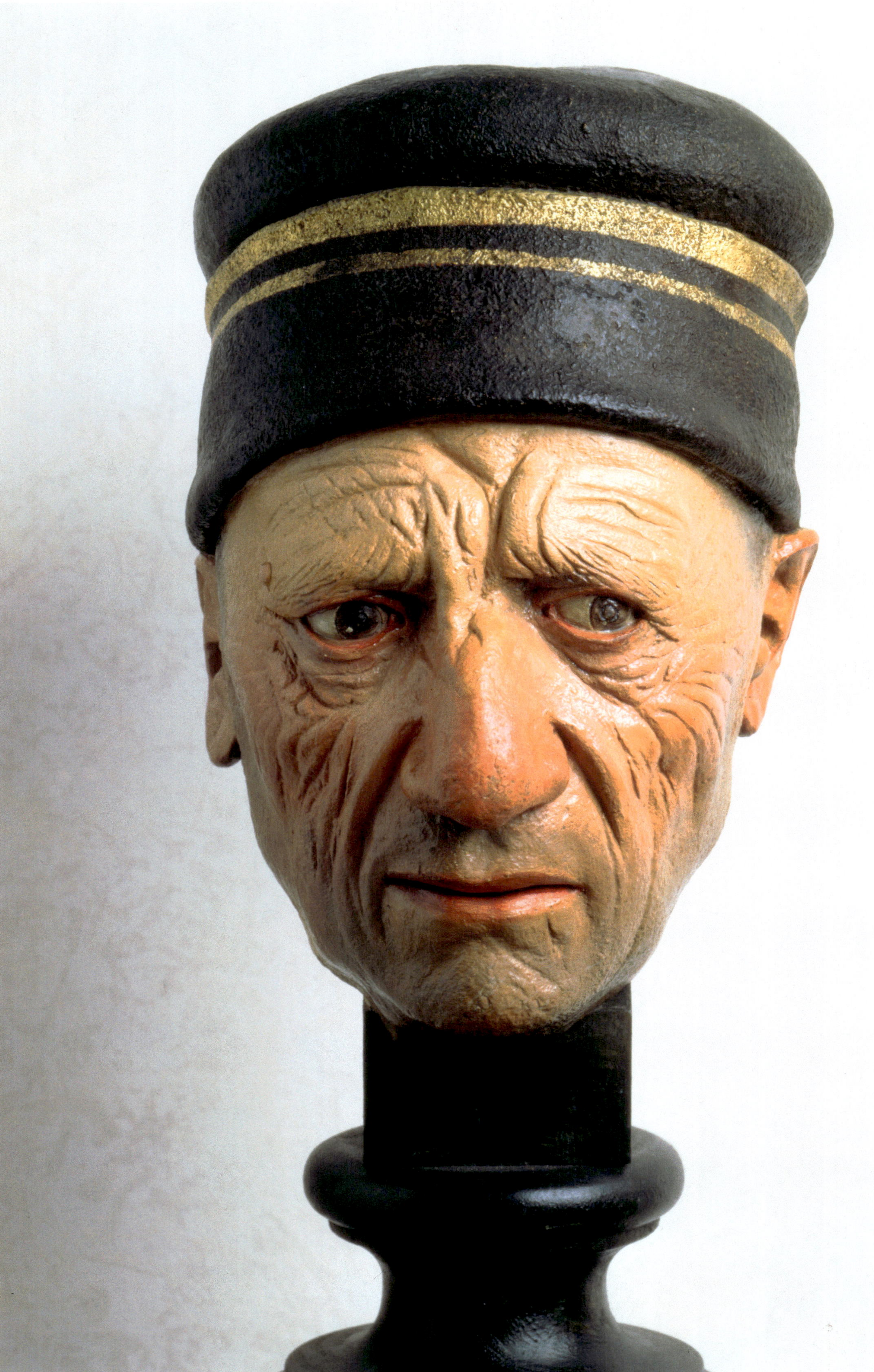

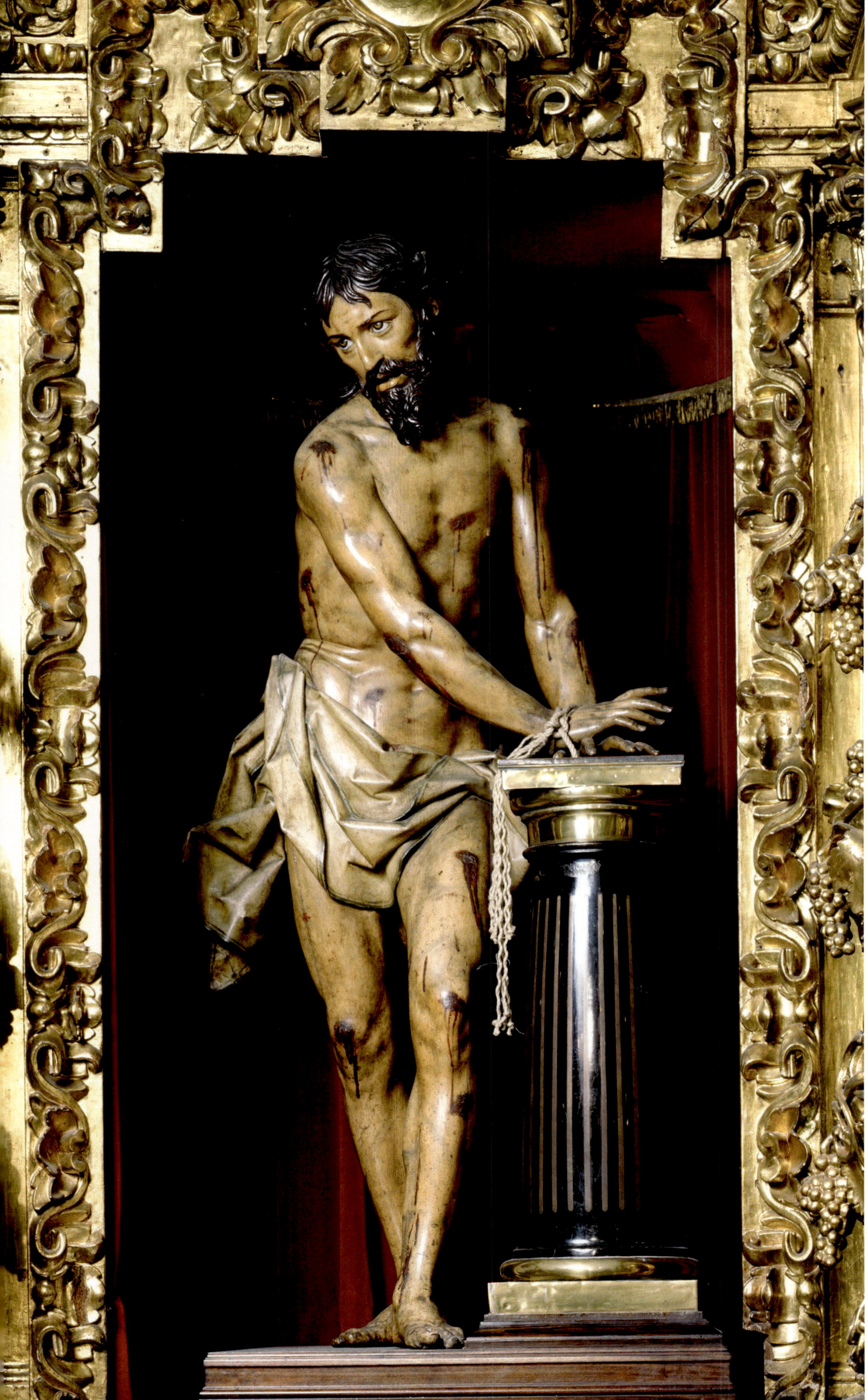

◄ Guido Mazzoni, *Head of an Old Man*, c. 1480/1485
◄ Gregorio Fernández, *Christ at the Column*, 1619

pieces, importance was given to verism, those depictions, as realistic as possible, of an ultimately idealised truth. The life of Christ tells of God become man, who may be shown 'true to life' with only great difficulty. Violence and suffering, however, are human and comprehensible and therefore also poignant. But such a powerful emotional impact is very rarely achieved with white marble. Artificial eyes alone, made of glass, create a connection between sculpture and observer that is hard to ignore. Especially in the Catholic south of Germany, as well as in Italy and Spain, such representations were very popular.

With the Renaissance, Spain underwent a somewhat different development than the great centres of art, Italy and the Netherlands. Here sculpture moved in a more 'realistic' direction. Since the 16th century, polychrome sculptures have been created in which the incarnation of Jesus is not only shown to the public with every artistic means available, using glass eyes, ivory teeth, real hair and perfectly lifelike painting, but one may say that the public has been confronted with it. No idealised aesthetics based on antiquity, nor overly exalted figures, these representations are made instead as realistically as possible in order to establish a closeness with humanity in its suffering and so to evoke candid, palpable feelings. One of the masters in this was Gregorio Fernández (1576–1636) of Valladolid, whose figures of Christ still impress today (fig. p. 149).

What polyester and silicone are for contemporary sculpture, wax was in the 17th and 18th centuries. It was highly valued for its ability to create illusionistic effigies. In an encyclopaedia of the arts and sciences published in 1747, it was noted that wax portraits were preferable to paintings because they conveyed such vividness that the only thing they needed to be truly alive was the ability to speak. This assessment can be understood from the profile portrait that Antoine Benoist (1632–1717) sculpted of Louis XIV around 1705 (fig. right). Unlike the many representative paintings of the Sun King, the vitality here is almost frightening. Everything, up to the beard stubble, is reproduced in the most painstaking manner. It is very likely that Benoist actually modelled the profile directly from the the monarch's head in order to achieve such realism. It is far from the official painted portraits by, for example, Hyacinthe Rigaud (1659–1743). As

▶ Antoine Benoist, *Louis XIV*, c. 1705

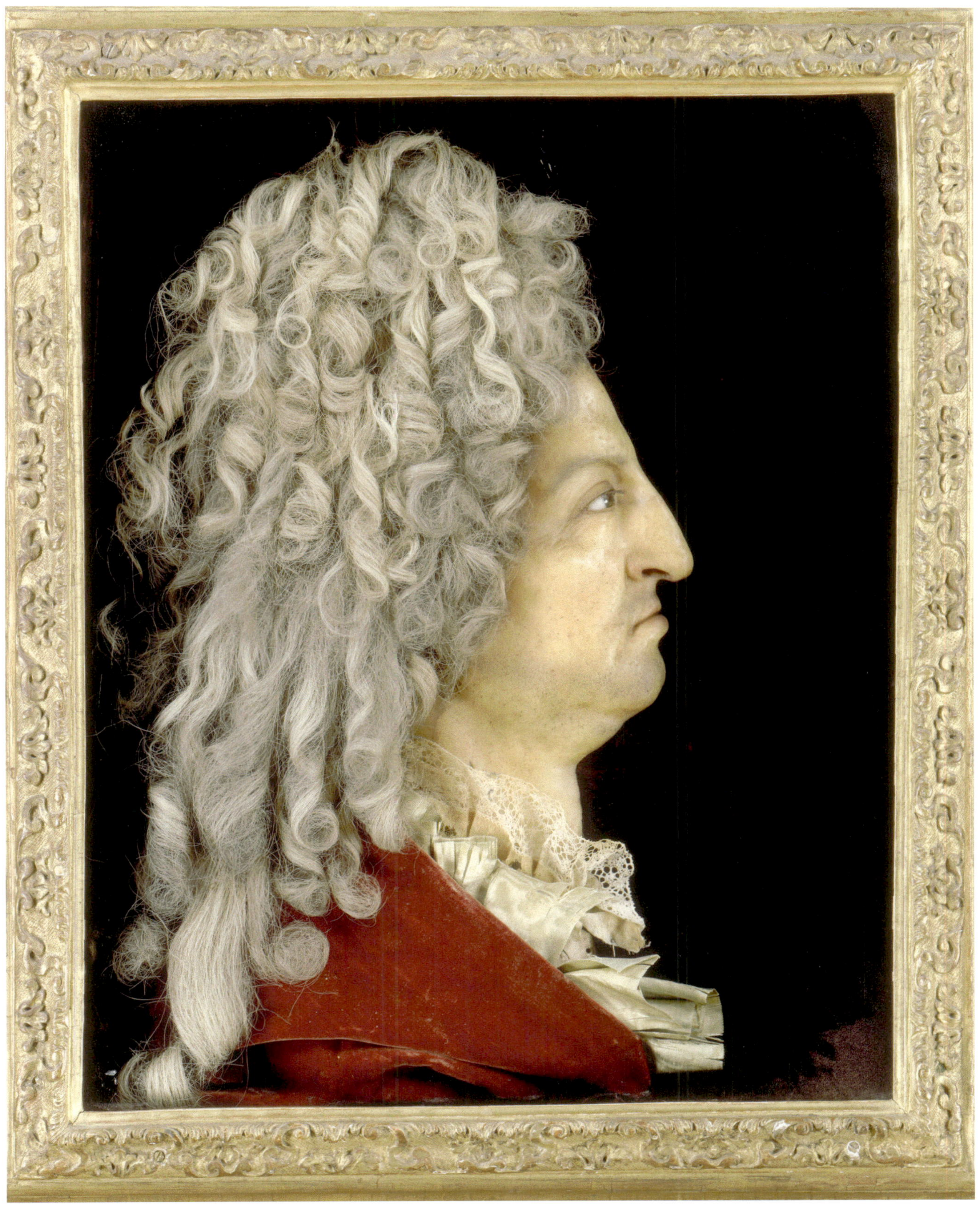

early as 1668, Benoist was granted the privilege by the king to sculpt portraits in wax of members of the court at Versailles. He created a total of forty-three portraits, which the artist was eventually allowed to exhibit throughout France. It was the first time that large sections of the population gained an insight into life at court. The success was so great, and the portraits were apparently so convincing, that the Duke of York, later King James II of England, invited Benoist to London in 1684 to do the same. After Benoist's death, over ninety wax portraits were listed in an inventory, of which the portrait of Louis XIV is the only one to have survived. Nevertheless, the idea of the waxworks, which started here, has survived.

With the end of the Baroque and its pompous style, the time of artful wax portraits also ended. The times changed. The extreme, perhaps disturbing for us today, closeness to life of this type of portraiture stood in contrast to the distanced embodiment of virtue and idealism preferred by classicism. The art of wax itself did not die out, however, but found application in panopticons and wax museums. It was especially in demand during the French Revolution (1789–1799). During this time many prominent figures, such as Marie-Antoinette and Louis XVI, but also revolutionaries like Danton and Robespierre, were beheaded by the guillotine. The heads were put on lances and publicly displayed. However, as they decayed quickly, they were replaced by wax heads made from the death masks and these were later exhibited in the Museum of the Revolution. A reconstruction of Robespierre's head shows what this might have looked like (fig. right). Making the wax heads was the responsibility of the talented wax sculptor Marie Grosholtz (1761–1850), who may have lost some customers to the guillotine as a result of the Revolution but was still able to put her skills to good use. She became known as Madame Tussaud and her cabinet of wax figures, founded in 1835 in London's Baker Street, still enjoys great popularity today.

For the art world of classicism, however, the wax figures were not artful enough. One was to look again to the Renaissance and thus to bare marble as well as brownish-golden shimmering bronze. With these materials, more noble artistic goals, such as the rebirth of antiquity and its virtues, as well as the expression of forms and

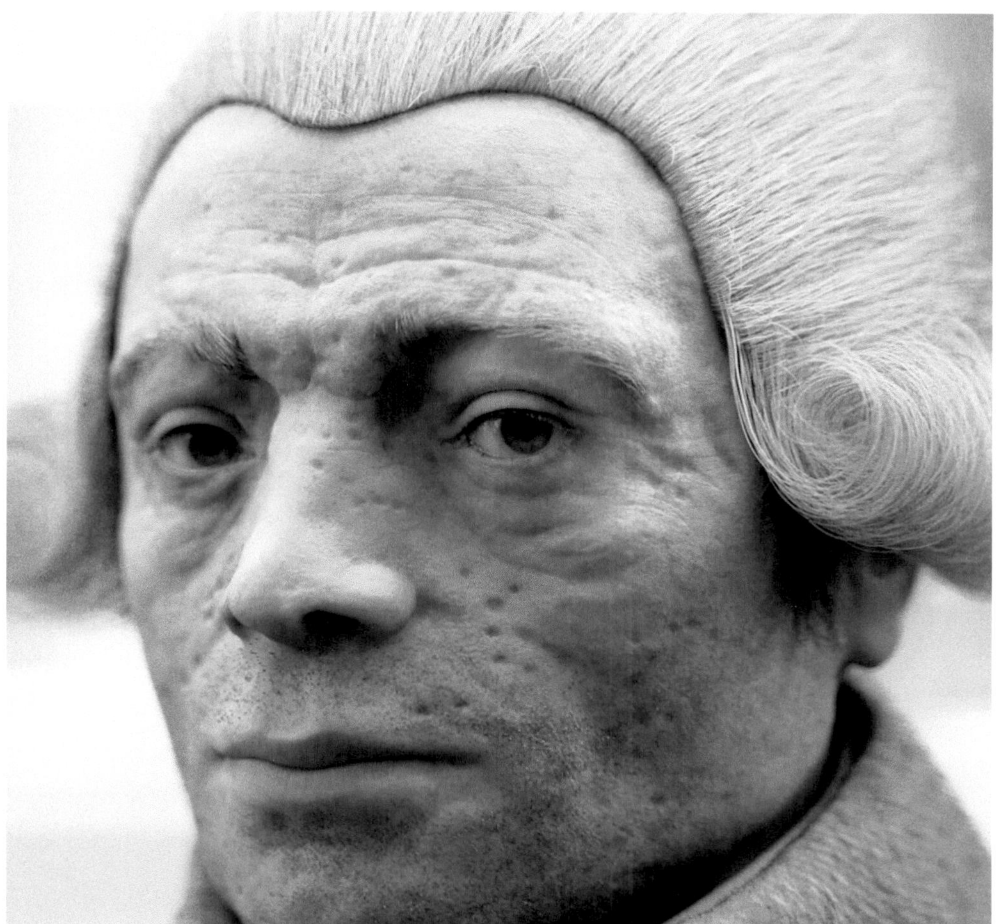

◀ Philippe Froesch,
Maximilien de Robespierre, 2013

ideas, could be achieved more suitably. Veristic, realistic or even illusionistic sculptures were no longer in demand. Those who wanted to see realistic or illusionist art could look at paintings by artist of the Salon or simply go to the waxworks. In the following decades, art moved increasingly further away from illusionism. It was less about the 'what' and more about the 'how'. In fact, illusionist sculpture only revived in the 1970s with the works of Duane Hanson (1925–1996) and John DeAndrea (b. 1941). And it did so only as an antithesis, as a reaction to the abstract formalism that predominated after the Second World War, especially in the USA (see pp. 160–161).

The sculptures of John DeAndrea are completely different from Hanson's work, despite a similar style (fig. pp. 154/155). They are completely devoid of social or sociological references, history, biography or social criticism. They stand in space almost like the statues of antiquity. In contrast to these, however, they are not ideal images of goddesses or heroes, but of real people with all their blemishes. This is why one is somewhat disoriented when first encountering them; the border between reality and illusion seems to be completely suspended for a moment. DeAndrea's figures stand, sit or lie and make no eye contact with the viewer, who, in turn, sometimes feels embarrassed, because at first one does not want to get too close to them, does not want to disturb their space, until one is quite sure that it is really only an illusion of reality. It is the character of the models themselves that gives the figures their power and effect. Perhaps it is also this awareness that they are not fantasy figures that tends to make the viewer handle them with greater respect and care. It may also be the absence of aloofness that the figures radiate. DeAndrea's figures, despite their often barely concealed nudity, never have anything suggestively erotic or

▼ John DeAndrea, *Linda*, 1983

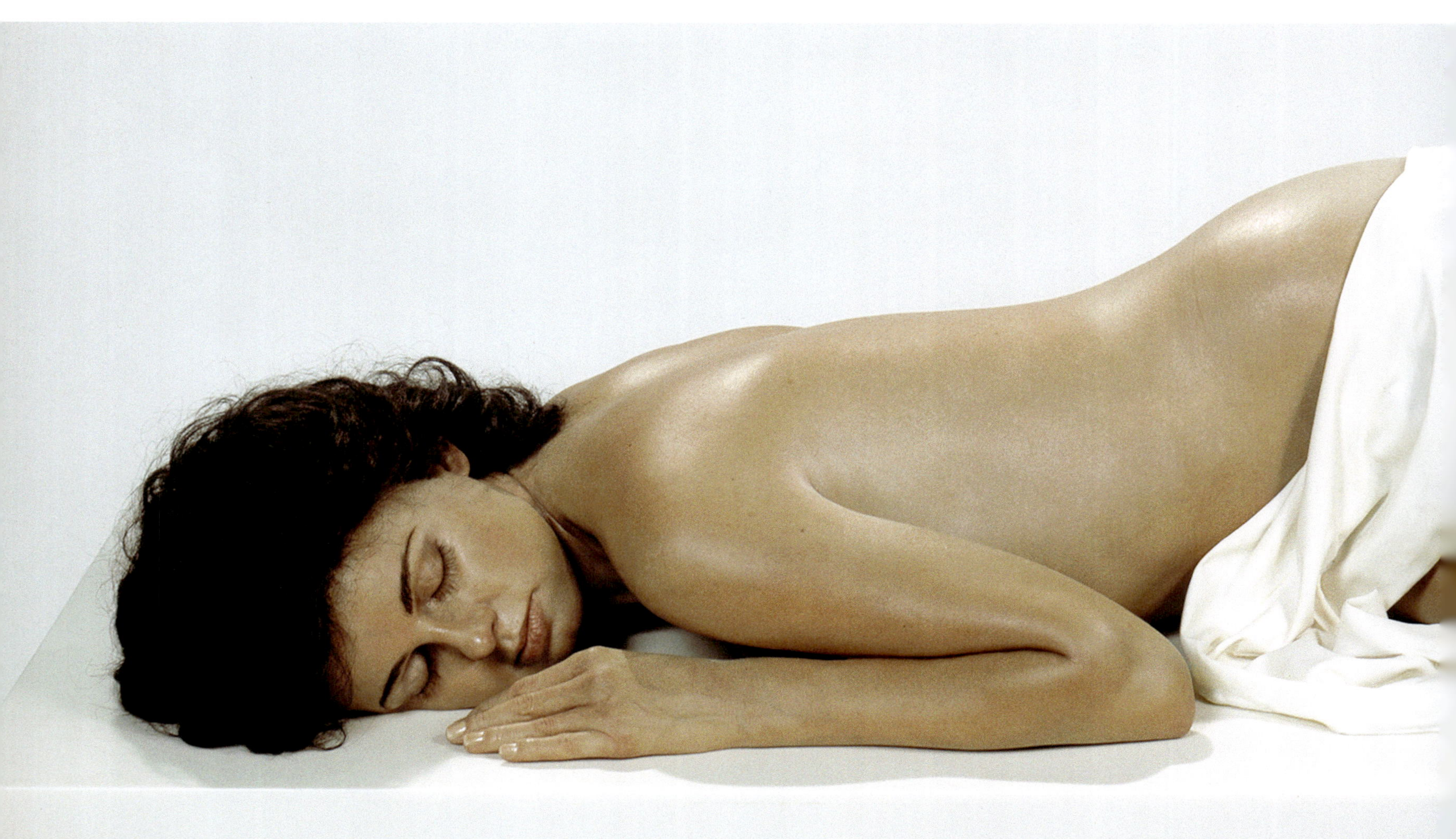

provocative about them. Rather, they possess a tender vulnerability or even a self-evident serenity. They occupy their space without comment, calm and serene, and this gives viewers a freedom to think whatever they want.

Realistic sculpture is often confronted with the criticism that, put simply, it only depicts reality because the abstraction from and distance to life, as found in a painting for example, is missing. The works of Ron Mueck (b. 1958) cannot be accused of this. They show beings that look very realistic but are clearly not. The term hyperrealism, the exaggeration of reality, which is used for works by Duane Hanson and John DeAndrea, is only first fully justified in Ron Mueck's sculptures (see pp. 162–165).

In contrast to Hanson and DeAndrea, Mueck's sculptures are not direct casts – How could they be with these dimensions? – but freely-made sculptures that are formed in silicone, and then hair is applied and they are painted with great attention to detail. The Australian artist Patricia Piccinini (b. 1965) takes a similar approach to

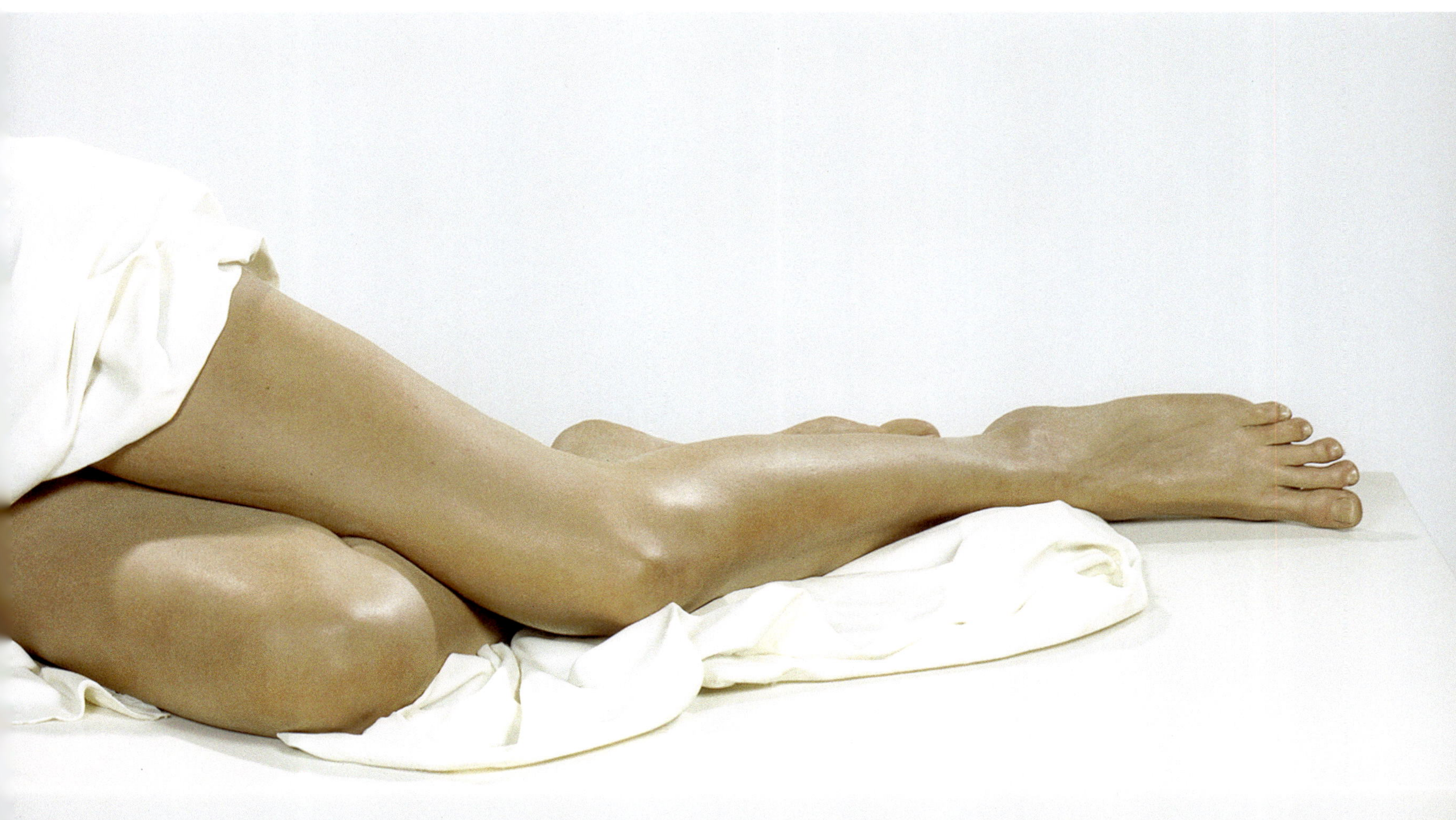

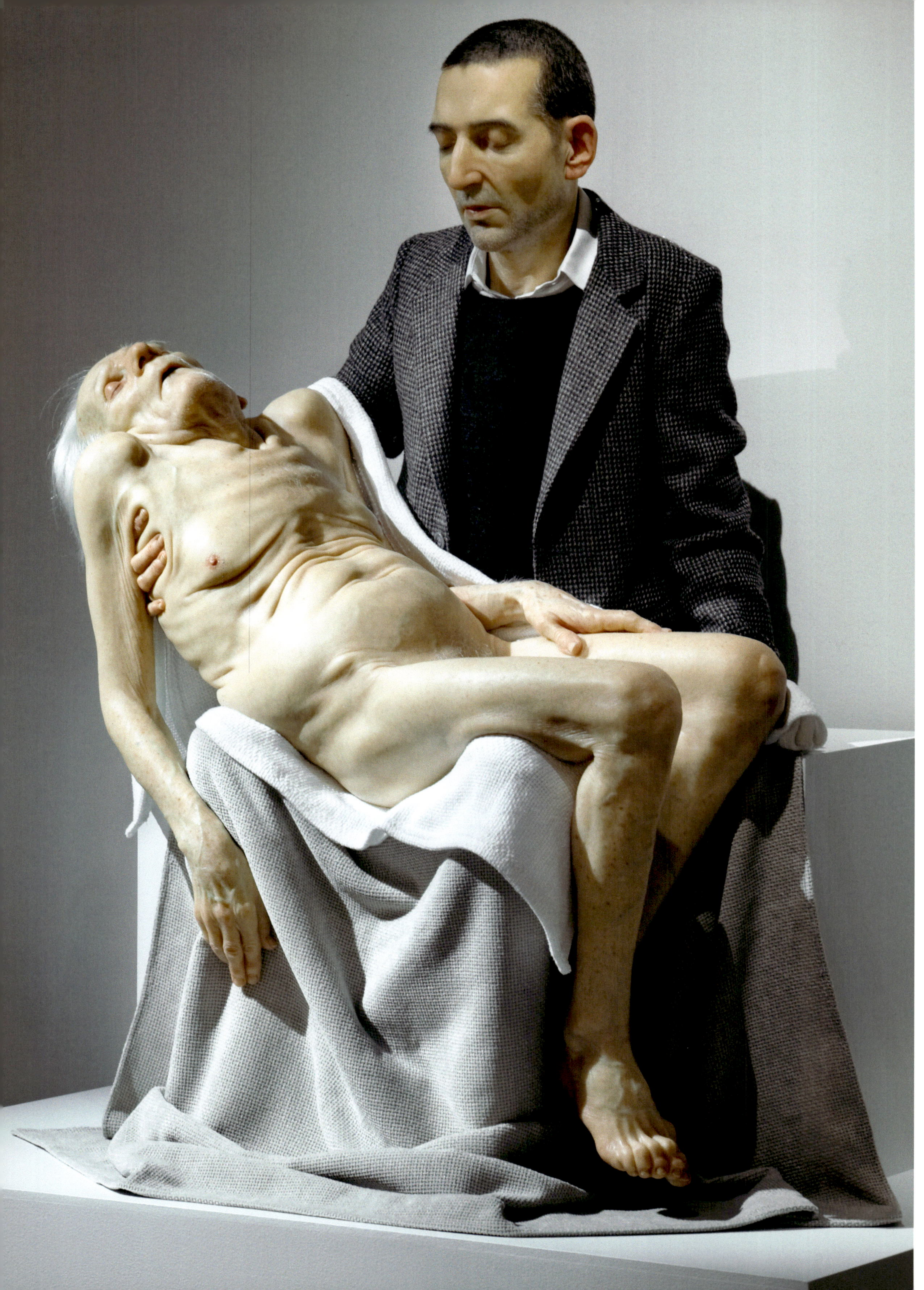

◀ Sam Jinks, *Still Life (Pietà)*, 2007

her work. But these are the only similarities between Ron Mueck's large and small figures and Patricia Piccinini's surreal creatures (see pp. 166–167).

The Australian sculptor Sam Jinks (b. 1973) worked with Patricia Piccinini for a while before devoting himself to his own artistic career. His extremely subtle sculptures give observers the opportunity to engage with life, suffering and death in a way that is rarely done, or required, in everyday life. Sam Jinks uses classic motifs, such as the Pietà, to communicate with the audience (fig. left). His figures are significantly smaller than real people, but not so small either that one can avoid them and elude their effect. On the contrary, his choice of size intensifies and concentrates the confrontation with the figures and their very human worries and emotions which Jinks depicts. For someone who has had experiences with death, his figures express compassion and give observers the feeling that they are not alone in their fate. If one has had no experience with death, Jinks manages to give the viewers an idea of it, which despite all the suffering does not seem hopeless. The reactions at an exhibition of his *Pietà* in Benalla, Australia, in 2008 are significant: "Some people cried when they saw the work and others were speechless. Everyone was impressed and spent long, quiet moments coming to terms with the sculpture and the response which it involuntarily created."[42]

The British artist couple Tim Noble (b. 1966) and Sue Webster (b. 1967) deal with death in a way completely different from the artists of so-called hyperrealism. Their sculptures often consist of the figures of dead animals or all kinds of rubbish which, artfully arranged, are then magically brought to life with a targeted beam of light. Their work *The Masterpiece* from 2014 (fig. p. 158) consists of casts of a range of animals such as rats, frogs and snakes set in silver. The light casts a shadow on the gallery wall and this shadow miraculously shows the profile of the two artists. It is the perfect illusion: creating life (so to speak) from death. But this 'life' only exists as long as light falls on the dead. This is where Plato's allegory of the cave comes to the viewer's mind, which – in short – explains that the shadows that we see of life, when turned away from reality, do not show life as it actually is. Even though it may often seem so from the limited perspective of the viewer. The difference between Plato's cave and the artwork of Noble and Webster is that here one sees not only the shadow, but also the objects casting the shadow as well as the light source itself. But here, too, it is ultimately not clear what the truth is: is it the dead silver animals, is it the shadow, is it the light, or is the truth only the context, the relationship and the relation of all these components together? Be that as it may, for everyone, here as in Plato, the truth is a very personal thing and often only a beautiful illusion.

▼ Tim Noble and Sue Webster, *The Masterpiece*, 2014

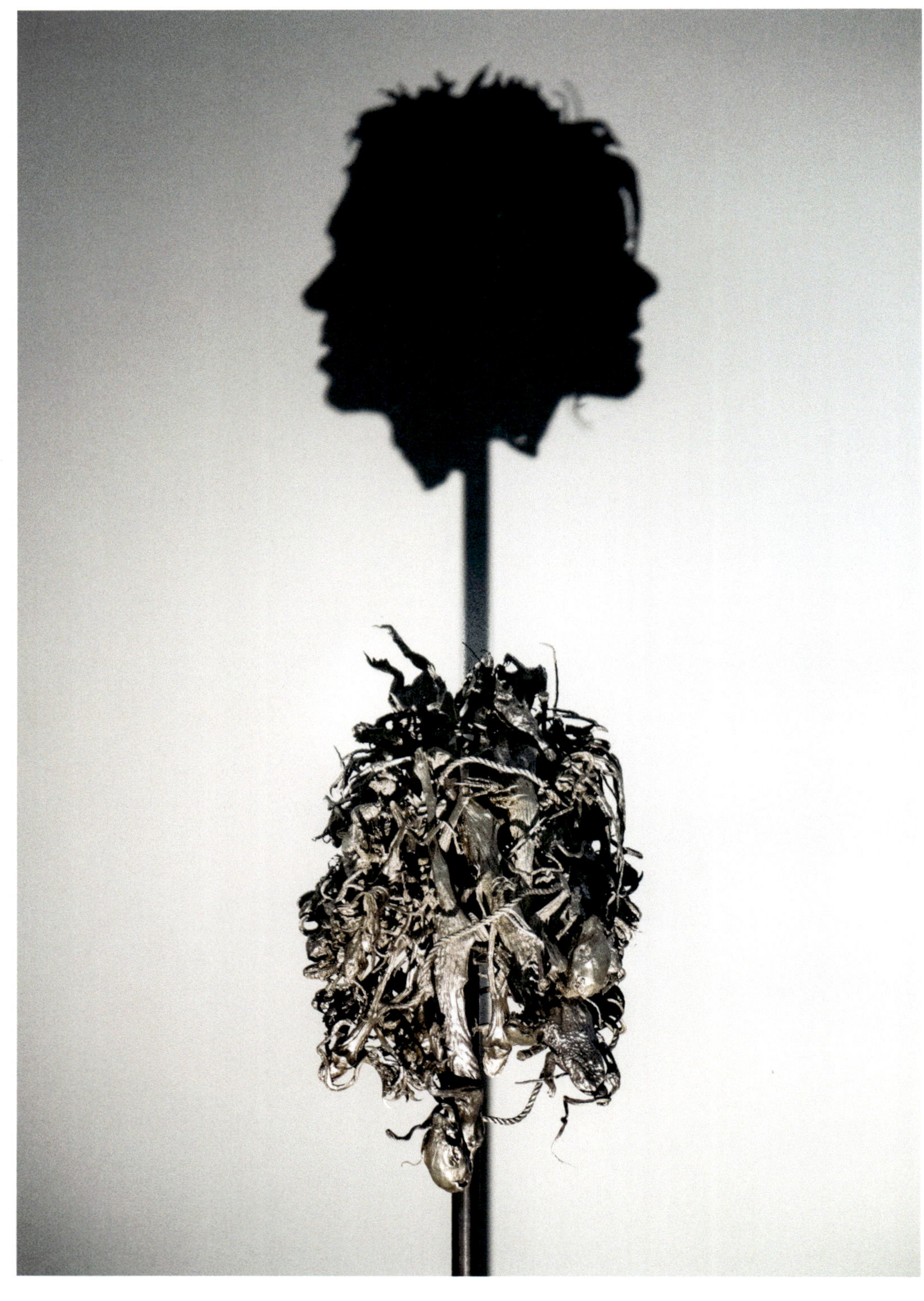

Anonymous

Miracle Man, c. 1500

Painted wood, length 180 cm
Church of St Nicholas, Döbeln

An extremely impressive and dramatic example of the illusionistic representation of Christ is the so-called *Miracle Man*, sculpted in Saxony around 1500. It is a 1.8-metre-tall figure, which was very likely conceived and modelled after real life or, in this case, after real death. A hollow gaze, waxy, pale skin with bluish shades and a head, shoulders and arms streaked with blood, the blood on the front of the head is painted, while on the back, real (animal) hair was used; the sculptor had even thought to use real hair for the beard. The blood seems to run from the wounds left by the actual crown of thorns that the figure had worn during the Passion Play for which it was conceived.

To push realism to the point of perfect illusion, the *Miracle Man* had articulated joints. Arms, legs, head and torso are connected by metal hinges, which in turn are covered by leather in the colour of the pallid corpse. Relying on such a figure and real actors, one could perform each station of Christ's Passion in an realistic fashion to the extreme: from the Flagellation to the Crucifixion to the Descent from the Cross, in a 'theatrum sacrum' nearly brought to life. The climax of this gritty spectacle of piety, so close to realty, would have been the final lance thrust by Longinus which would have initiated an actual flow of blood. Inside the hollow torso of the *Miracle Man* was a receptacle, probably sealed with wax, perhaps a bladder, which allowed real animal blood to gush from the wound at Christ's side. The effect must have been intense and very direct, as would have been the deceptive illusion of the Son of God 'made flesh'.

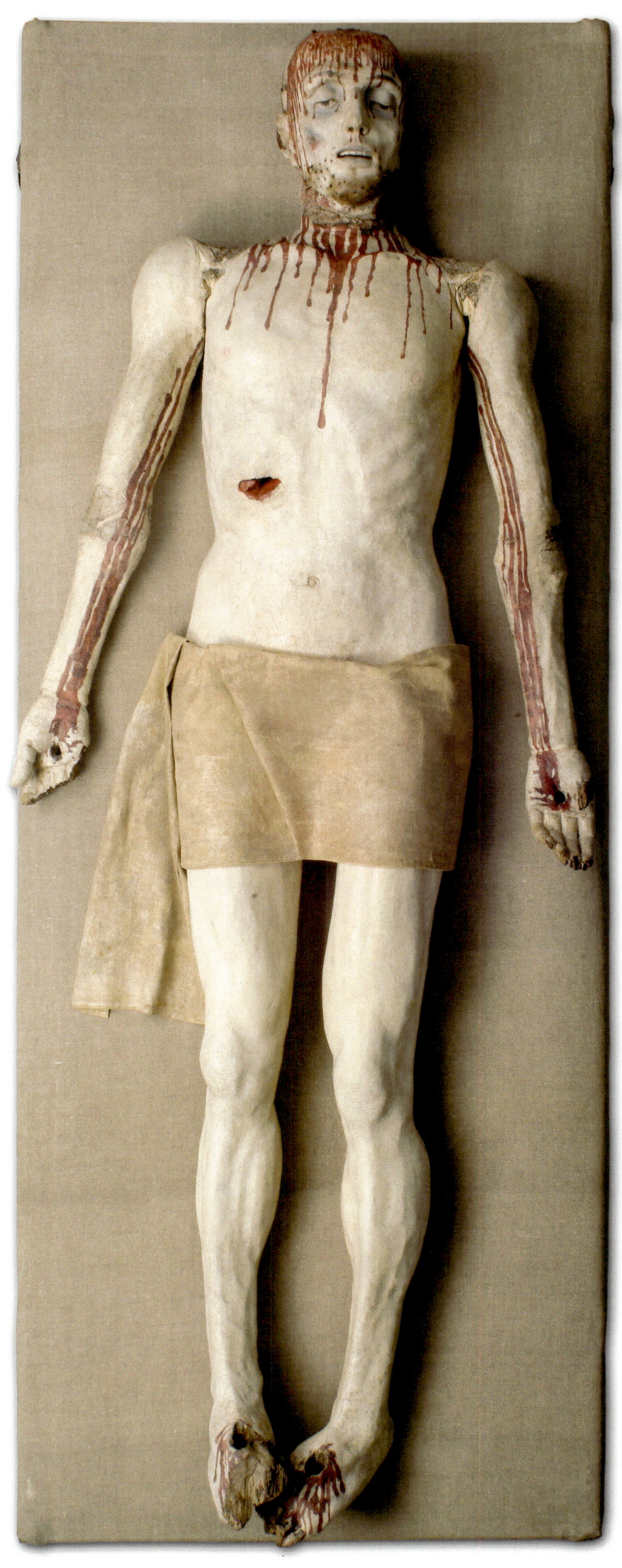

Duane Hanson

Man on a Bench, 1977

Vinyl, polychromed in oil,
accessories, life-size
Saatchi Gallery, London

Unlike in painting, 'normal', everyday people were never – or very rarely – considered a subject suitable for sculpture: people who have done nothing particularly special, who simply go about their day, doing their work or enjoying their holiday. Why would they? What should interest the artist in such cases? The American sculptor Duane Hanson (1925–1996), however, understood the point of interest. He recognised the fact that it is the average people themselves that most matter. House painters, tourists, tradesmen, women shopping for groceries or people on a park bench. These are the figures that Hanson began to portray and exhibit in the 1970s, in all their banality, all their normality but also, in all their dignity, extremely realistic and very closely observed. Hanson's figures are, through and through, everday Americans of the late 20th century. What he shows is the American way of life. The sculptures were so novel in their verisimilitude that during exhibitions they were often taken to be real people and spoken to. Hanson achieved this illusion by making moulds of real people and casting them in polyester (later in bronze for conservational reasons), painting them as he saw fit, as sculpture painters have done throughout the centuries – but even more meticulously and convincingly. In addition, real hair was applied, real clothing and all the attributes and accessories that belong to his characters.

By moving people from their environment to a museum or gallery space, he liberates them from their anonymity and gives them a voice. Although the figures are modelled on real people, Hanson does not intend them to be 'waxworks'. His aim is to sympathise with them, to see them eye-to-eye and engage with their situation and environment. Although their environment is only very rudimentary: a few tools of the trade, a gadget or something to pass the time. The figures thus remain active in their own world and do not enter into the reality of the audience. One sees the people with their at times empty, at times sad looks, and one begins to compare oneself with them, to relate to them, emotionally, socially – in whatever mood or from whatever position the observer may react to the work of art.

What is most touching is the dejection and the vulnerability that Hanson's figures exhibit. 'Tired', 'bored', 'frustrated' and 'exhausted' are adjectives that go through the viewer's mind. "My work deals with people who lead lives of quiet desperation. I show the empty-headedness, the fatigue, aging, frustration", says the artist.[43] A visit to a Hanson exhibition can be rather depressing. The melancholy and loneliness of the figures are clearly noticeable, just as every pore and every wrinkle is visible. Even his couples give off this sense of loneliness, perhaps even more so than the single figures. Hanson's 'people' seem as if they were captured in a moment of their own unknown story, trapped by it. We become witnesses to the quiet drama of their lives.

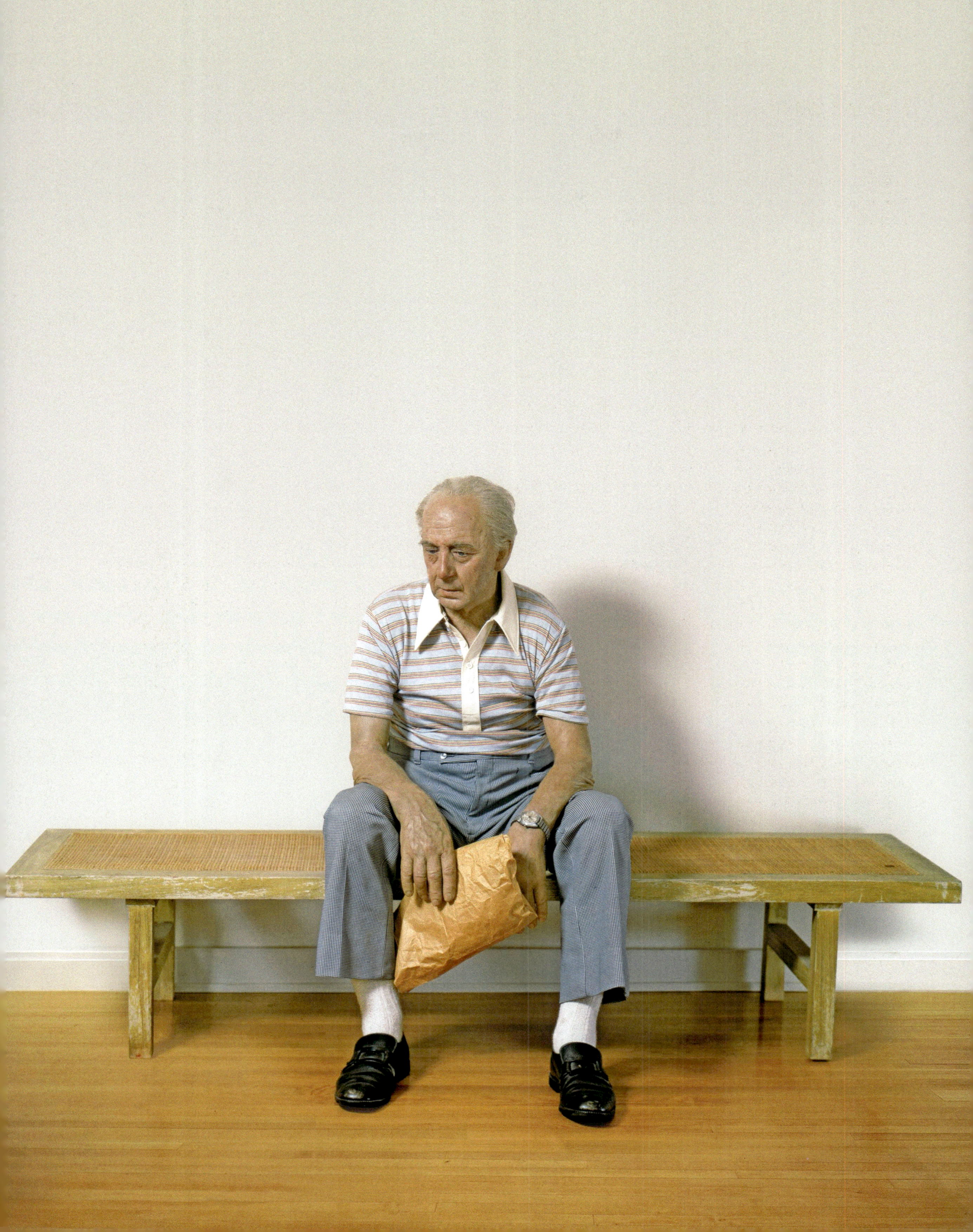

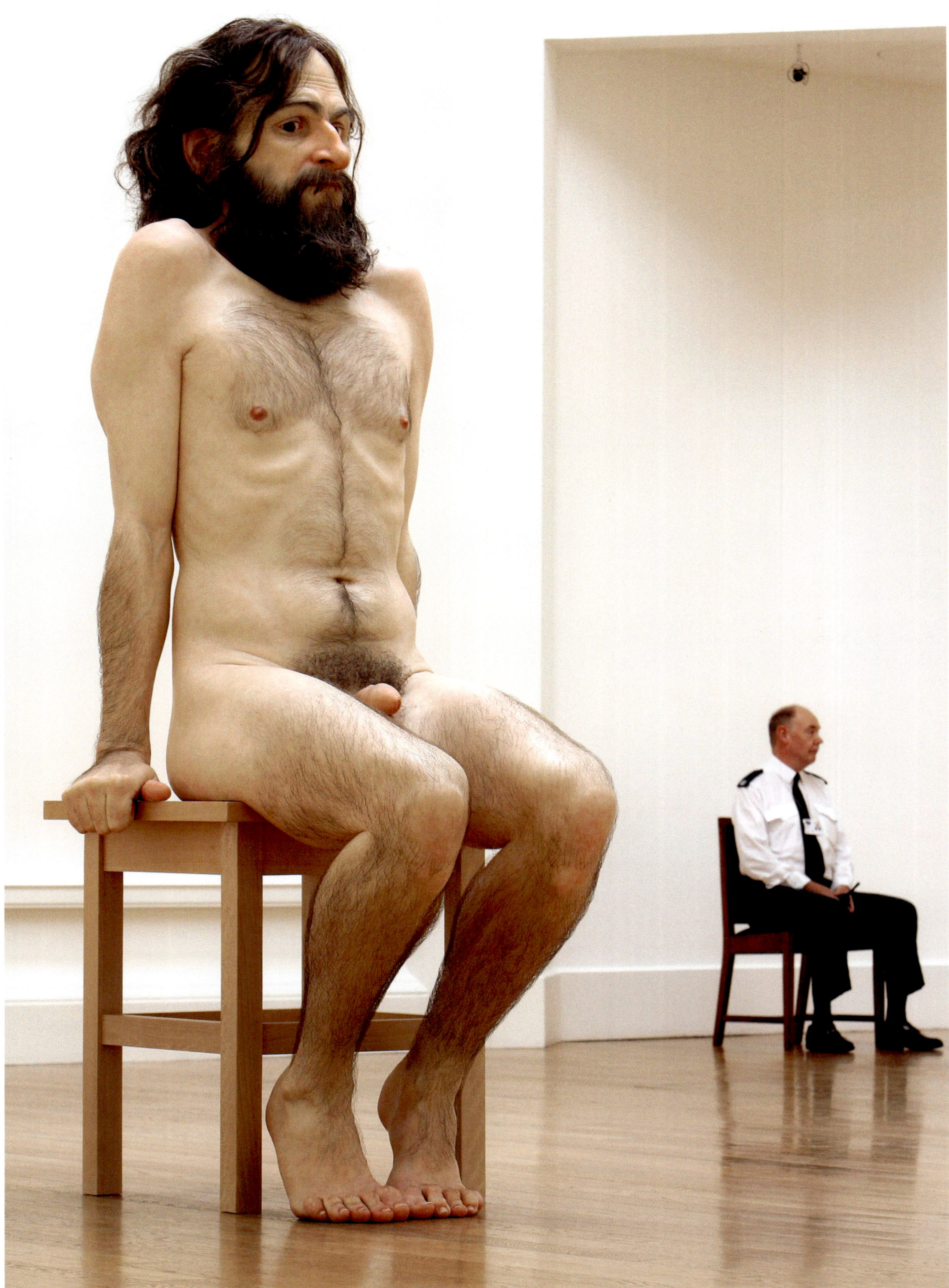

Ron Mueck

Wild Man, 2005

Mixed media, 285 × 162 × 108 cm
McClelland Sculpture Park and Gallery, Langwarrin / National Galleries of Scotland and Tate
◀ **Facing page**

In bed, 2005

Mixed media, 162 × 650 × 395 cm
Queensland Art Gallery | Gallery of Modern Art, Brisbane
Installation view, Fondation Cartier, Paris
▶ **Overleaf**

With a painting, however lifelike or realistic it may be, it is much easier for the observer to abstract it than a life-size figure standing in front of them – or larger-than-life, or much smaller, as with the sculptures of Ron Mueck (b. 1958). These abnormal sizes especially do not let us go, making their effect greater, they seem more threatening or more touching. This is the case because, despite the strangeness, the vague possibility troubles us that such a being could really exist. A contradiction arises between the eye and the mind. All this happens in fractions of a second. We know what it is we are looking at and the setting in which we find ourselves, and yet, the illusion still works. And that ultimately provokes the greatest fascination and represents the greatest art.

Normally the sense of touch enables us to test the reality of something. The warmth and moisture of skin, the hair, the hardness or softness, all of this is denied to us as well-behaved exhibition visitors. We are reduced exclusively to sight, while remaining aware of how often this solitary sense gives us incorrect information. If we can only see, who will tell us then whether our perceptions are accurate reflections of reality – and if so, of which reality?

Through their largeness, or their smallness, Mueck's figures exist in a dimension of their own. By no means does one consider them to be beings from another world; for that, their visible emotions are all too similar to ours. The change in size is a form of abstraction that intensifies our engagement with the sculpture. The figures are not portraits of people, but of states of mind. Unlike Duane Hanson (1925–1996) and John DeAndrea (b. 1941), Mueck's figures often make eye contact with us. And no matter how unreal the proportions may be, it affects us (see pp. 153–155, 160–161). In this way, we can observe the figures and come so close to them as is rarely possible with real humans. This closeness strengthens our engagement with what the artist presents to us. The utterly perfect technique plays a subordinate role, specifically because of its perfection. Mueck has said that "Although I spend a lot of time on the surface, it's the life inside I want to capture."[44] And he succeeds in this in a unique way. Whether he creates giants or Lilliputians, what really grabs us is their emotional state. And this becomes clearly recognizable through the change in dimensions as if under a magnifying glass. Mueck's themes are birth, death and everything in between.

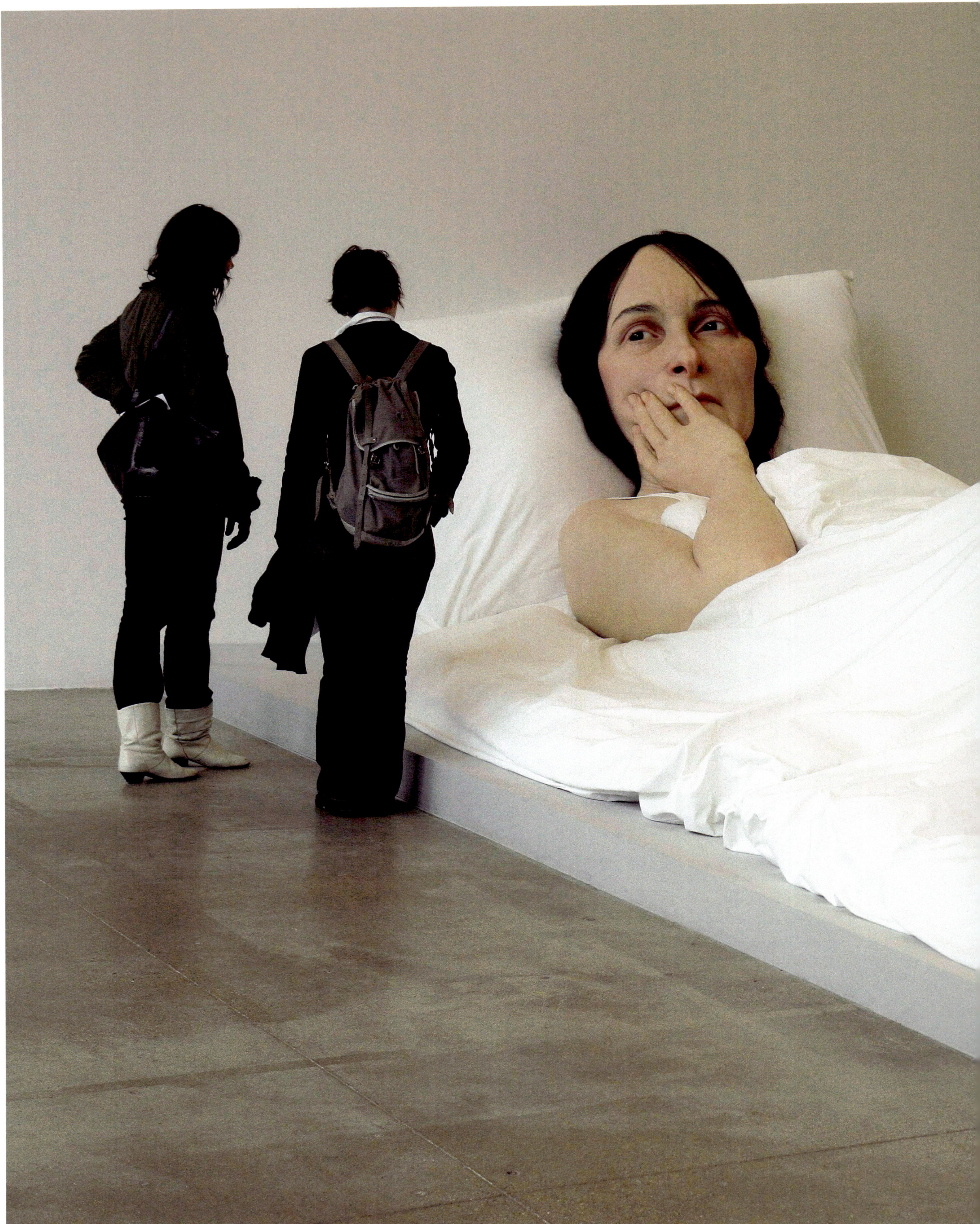

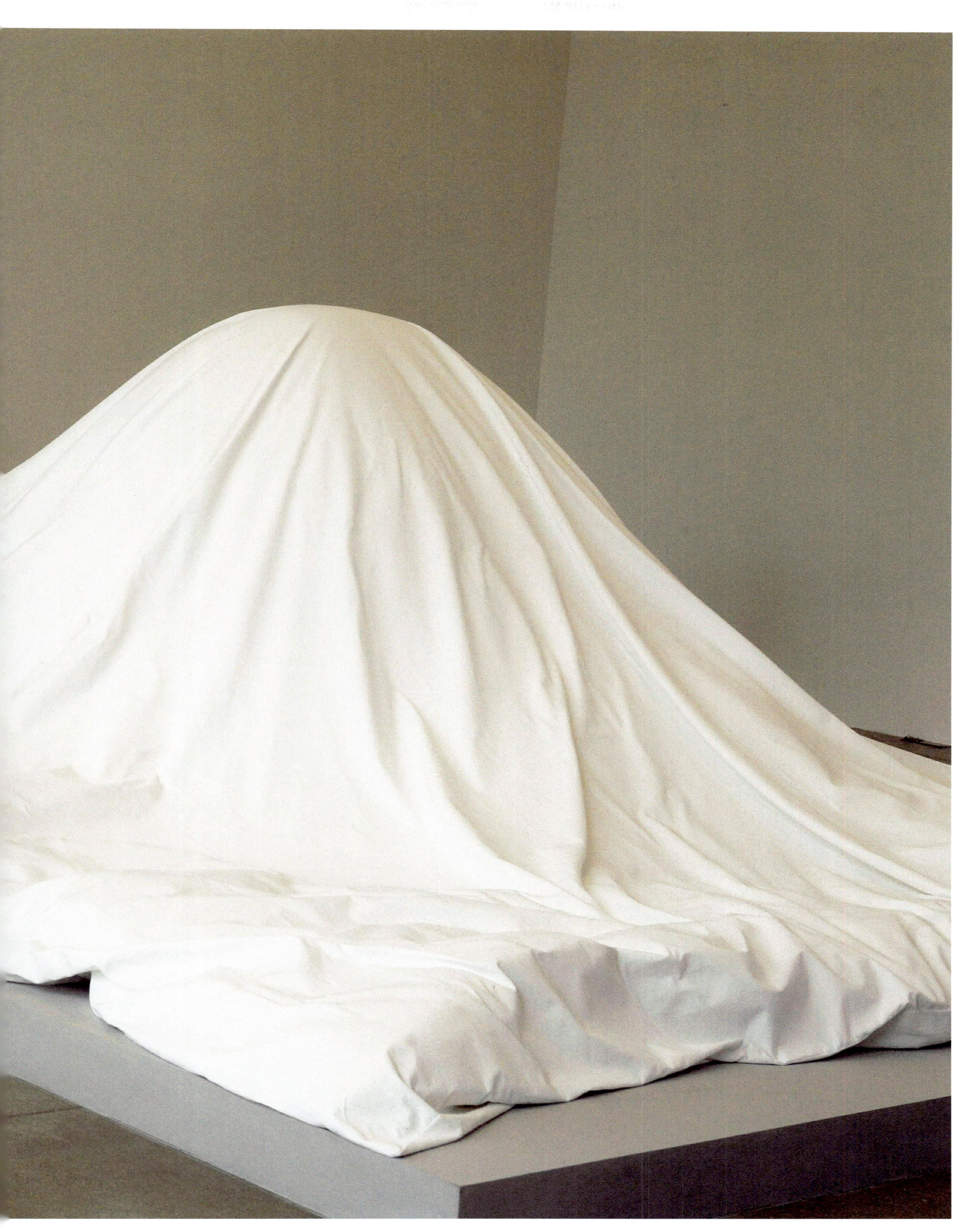

Patricia Piccinini
The Bond, 2016

Silicone, fibreglass, human hair, clothing, 162 × 56 × 50 cm

The sculptures of Patricia Piccinini (b. 1965) really seem to come from another world. Perhaps the words of the biologist J. B. S. Haldane (1892–1964) are true of her work: "the universe is not only queerer than we suppose, but queerer than we can suppose".[45] Piccinini's work wrestles with developments in science, nature and technology, as well as with the possibilities of genetic engineering. Many of her figures are composite beings which at first seem absurd or surreal. After further thought, however, they may not be as odd as one might hope. In times in which human ears grow from the backs of mice, many things seem feasible. Even a creature like in *The Bond*, whose cuteness is irresistible despite its strange physiognomy – "The back is essentially the sole of a running shoe"[46] – at least for the mother. The emotional bond between mother and child, between beings in general, is a central theme and a point of constant fascination for the artist. To this end, Piccinini's sculptures question the mechanisms of scientific progress, something that is now often financed by large corporations whose developments are not committed to the general public but to their shareholders. Piccinini's figures are hybrids that do not yet exist. However, the possibilities of their realisation might just be under investigation right now in various laboratories. In this sense, "This crossing of an animal with a shoe doesn't seems so surreal. But it is", Piccinini explains.[47]

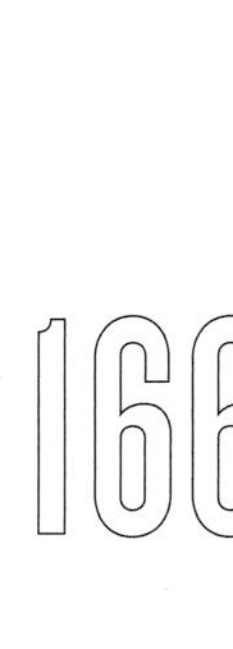

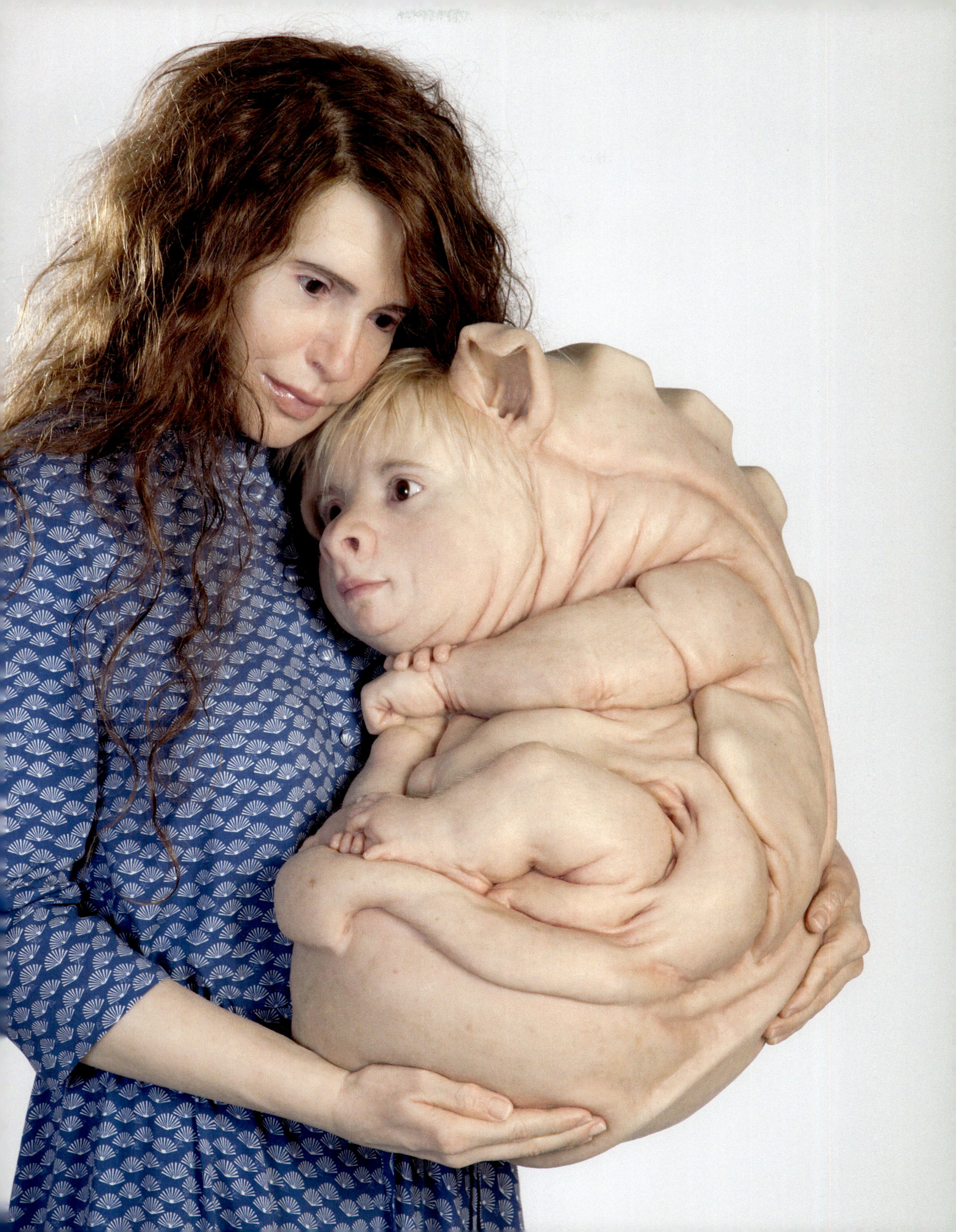

STREET ART

The World Around Us

Street Art is a very young variation in art, even as it makes use of traditional forms like painting and sculpture, as well as photography. The only thing that unites all branches of street art, however, is the fact that it takes place, as the name implies, in the street, on building walls and in other open spaces, visible to all and consumable by all. The best-known form of street art is graffiti, usually tags or pictures most often created with spray paint on walls. Its beginnings go back to the early 1970s in New York City, when young people began to discover the street and especially subway cars as their canvas. Here, as with the French impressionists of the 19th century, a well-known technical development exerted an enormous influence on the development of the art form. Whereas for the impressionists it was tubes of oil paint that made it easier for artists such as Claude Monet (1840–1926) and Auguste Renoir (1841–1919) to paint outdoors in nature, *en plein air*, for the New York artists, it was the aerosol spray can invented by the Norwegian chemical engineer Erik Rotheim in 1926 which enabled them to work over large surfaces and, most importantly, quickly. They had to be fast, because regardless of how artistic their works were at times, they were also usually illegal.

Artists like Lee (Lee Quiñones, b. 1960), Blade (Steven Ogburn, b. 1957), who decorated over 5,000 trains between 1972 and 1984, and Lakes (Richard Mirando, b. 1961) sprayed their large pictorial tags – short artist signatures – with artistic skill onto subway cars (fig. right). The cars of the New York City Subway were especially popular because, once painted with a tag, the train would move through the city as a

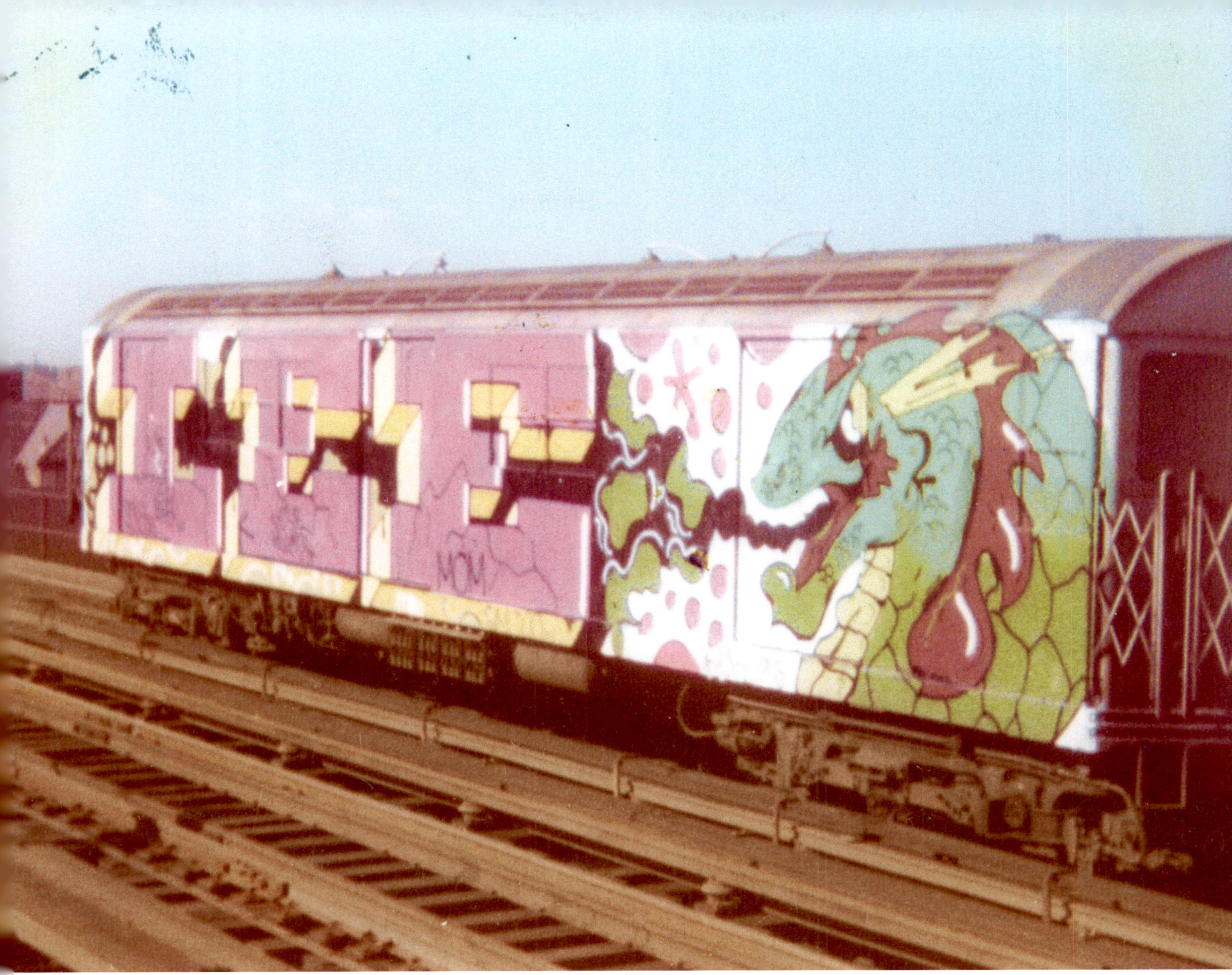

travelling gallery until the next cleaning and could be seen by everyone. Thus, street artists conquered a completely new terrain. For the majority of young artists, it became a way to express themselves, find self-affirmation and make themselves 'heard' in a metropolis like New York. In addition, for many, it was an alternative to gangs and violence. Because the tags on trains could also be seen by other artists, ever newer styles quickly developed as graffiti artists challenged and inspired each other. Graffiti spread rapidly around the globe.

▲ Lee Quiñones, *Year of the Dragon*, 1979

The Swiss artist Harald Naegeli (b. 1939) was one of the first graffiti artists in Europe. He became known as the 'Sprayer of Zurich' and sprayed over four hundred figures on the walls of his hometown which also earned him a nine-month prison sentence in 1984. Graffiti art gained even greater fame through painters like Keith Haring (1958–1990) and Jean-Michel Basquiat (1960–1988), who made it from the New York graffiti scene into the world of established art and became stars. Movies such as *Style Wars* (1983) and the book *Subway Art* (1984), with photographs of painted trains, were seen and sold all over the world and helped this new art form spread rapidly.

However, all this had little to do with illusionist art. That first began in Paris in the early 1980s with the French graffiti artist Xavier Prou, better known as Blek le Rat (b. 1951), who had been inspired by the New York artists. He was fascinated by them but did not want to copy them. He also did not want to spray tags because he felt they would not match with the architecture of Paris. Blek came up with his own technique that proved groundbreaking: He used so-called 'pochoir' (French for 'stencil').

▼ Blek le Rat, *Old Man with a Stick*, 1986

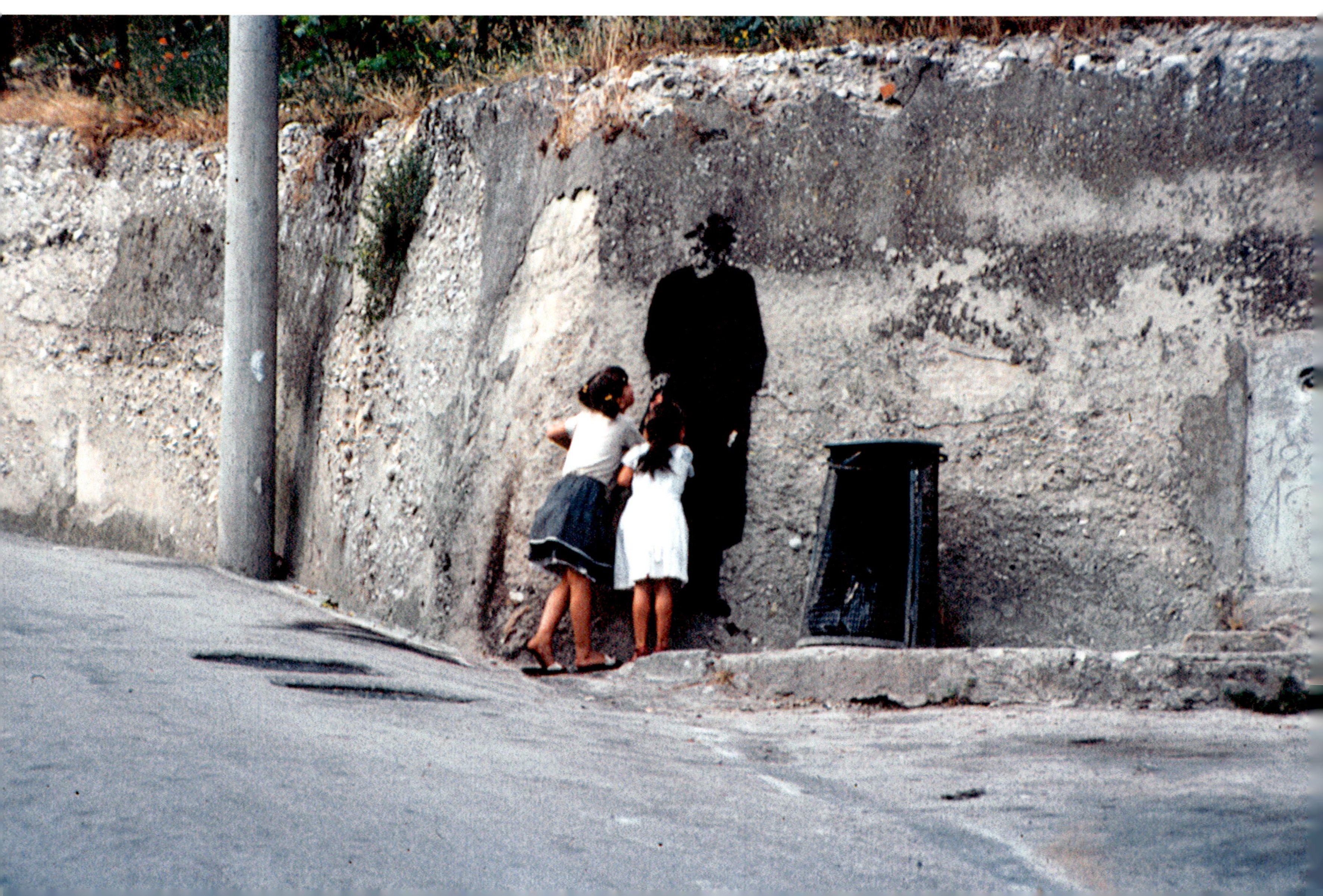

In this process, a motif is cut out of cardboard or a similar material and painted onto the wall at the desired location with spray paint or another form of pigment. At the beginning of the graffiti scene, especially in New York City, there was not much to see in regard to substance, except the names of the graffiti artists and their various slogans. That changed with the use of stencils, because with these, one could transfer more complex figures onto walls in a shorter amount of time thanks to the preparatory work done before in the studio. In some cases, pictures were made completely in the studio and then simply pasted to the walls as posters. Blek's best-known motif at the beginning was rats (hence his nickname), which were a major problem in Paris in the early 1980s. The rats were followed by life-size pictures of people, like his *Old Man*, which became his next trademark (fig. left). Time and again Blek painted him on walls, and passers-by took photographs with him because, in certain contexts, he was astonishingly lifelike.

With stencils one could work with light and shadow in a reduced fashion and thus bring more depth and vividness to pictures painted on walls, which in turn triggered a further development. An increasing number of new artists and new stencils could be seen in Paris and, like the first graffiti artists, a dialogue between these artists was also established that could be followed by everyone. The paintings became increasingly political, even if only their humour and poetry predominate today. "Personally, I think the colors of our sprays help the urban landscape to bloom with poetic intentions", says Blek le Rat.[48] His work has inspired many other artists to work in this way. The best known of all these is arguably Banksy (b. probably 1974), even though it is still not publicly known who is actually behind the name. He also uses the stencil technique for most of his work and admits to having Blek le Rat as his role model: "Every time I think I've painted something slightly original, I find out that Blek le Rat has done it as well. Only twenty years earlier" (see pp. 180 – 181).[49] Banksy repeatedly takes up socially and politically relevant themes in his pictures, usually with a dark humour. A result of his fame, he helped street art realise new possibilities in terms of content and also to the greater attention and recognition of critics and the public.

The French artist Pierre Delavie (b. 1956) has also garnered a great deal of attention with his large-scale 'urban lies', a term he prefers to 'trompe l'œil' as the latter traditionally refers to small-format works in 18th-century cabinets of curiosities (see pp. 63–64, 91). By contrast, Delavie covers entire buildings with gigantic printed canvases, lending these structures, often highly recognisable, a completely new and surprising look (see pp. 182–184).

Just as Delavie produces his own enormous architectural spaces, the British artist Slinkachu (b. 1979) creates a personal microcosm with his art. Moreover, it is a microcosm that, despite the enormous difference in size, seems very familiar to us: Just as with us 'big people', his 'little people' are looking for a little happiness, tranquillity and contentment, and are faced with problems and difficulties to overcome. Since 2006, Slinkachu has been staging his little world in our big one on a scale of 1:87. And yet, he himself is still often not clear on what his work should be called: "My work has different stages that encompass a few different mediums so it can be hard for me to nail down an exact definition of what I do. It's sculpture, photography and street art all at once".[50] His work usually comes with a sense of humour and a wink. After arranging and photographing his scenes, he abandons the figures to their own devices and the city. Some people have the good luck to come upon one or another of such scenes. Slinkachu's work is also an appeal to the inhabitants of cities to look more closely and pay more attention to their surroundings. His work can be seen figuratively or quite literally as an illustration of the struggle of the little guy. "I am trying to tell a story through the images and installations, or create an emotional response of some sort."[51] Some characters become heroes on the hunt for a bee, others miss their taxi (figs. right) or drown in a puddle. The world itself and life in big cities are often absurd enough, so why should a world like Slinkachu's not exist? – At least in his imagination and on our streets.

Sculptures play an increasingly important role in street art. Not least because the closeness of sculpture to things real can often lead to confusion between art and reality. That such things can also be staged on a grand scale was demonstrated in 2015 by the Argentinian artist Leandro Erlich (b. 1973) with a spectacular installation in the middle of Karlsruhe (see p. 185).

Another genre of street art, well worthy of the name, is chalk drawing on the ground. The form originated from the tradition of the Italian 'Madonnari' (i.e., Madonna painters), mostly untrained, non-professional

▶ Slinkachu, *Taxi!*, 2009

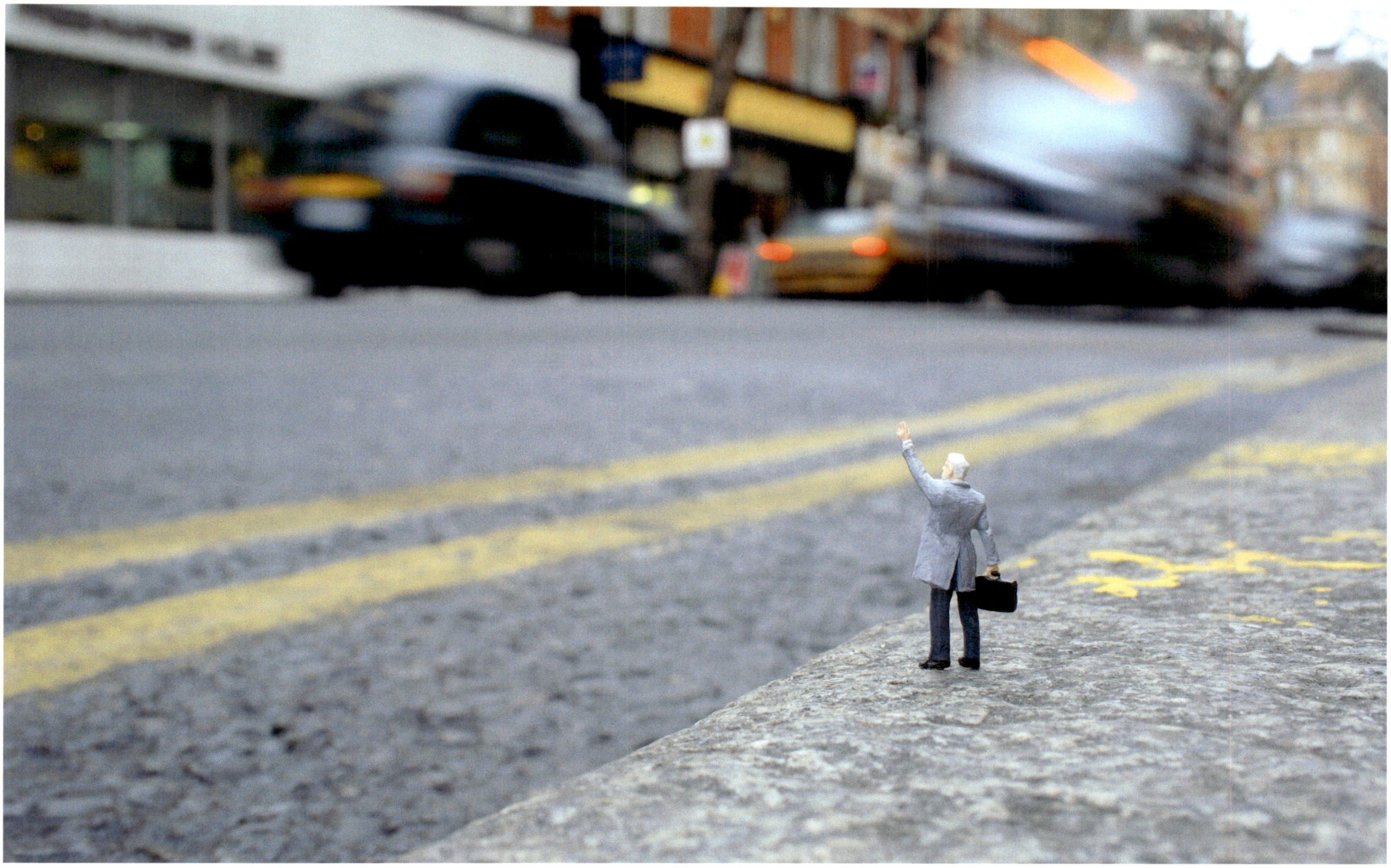

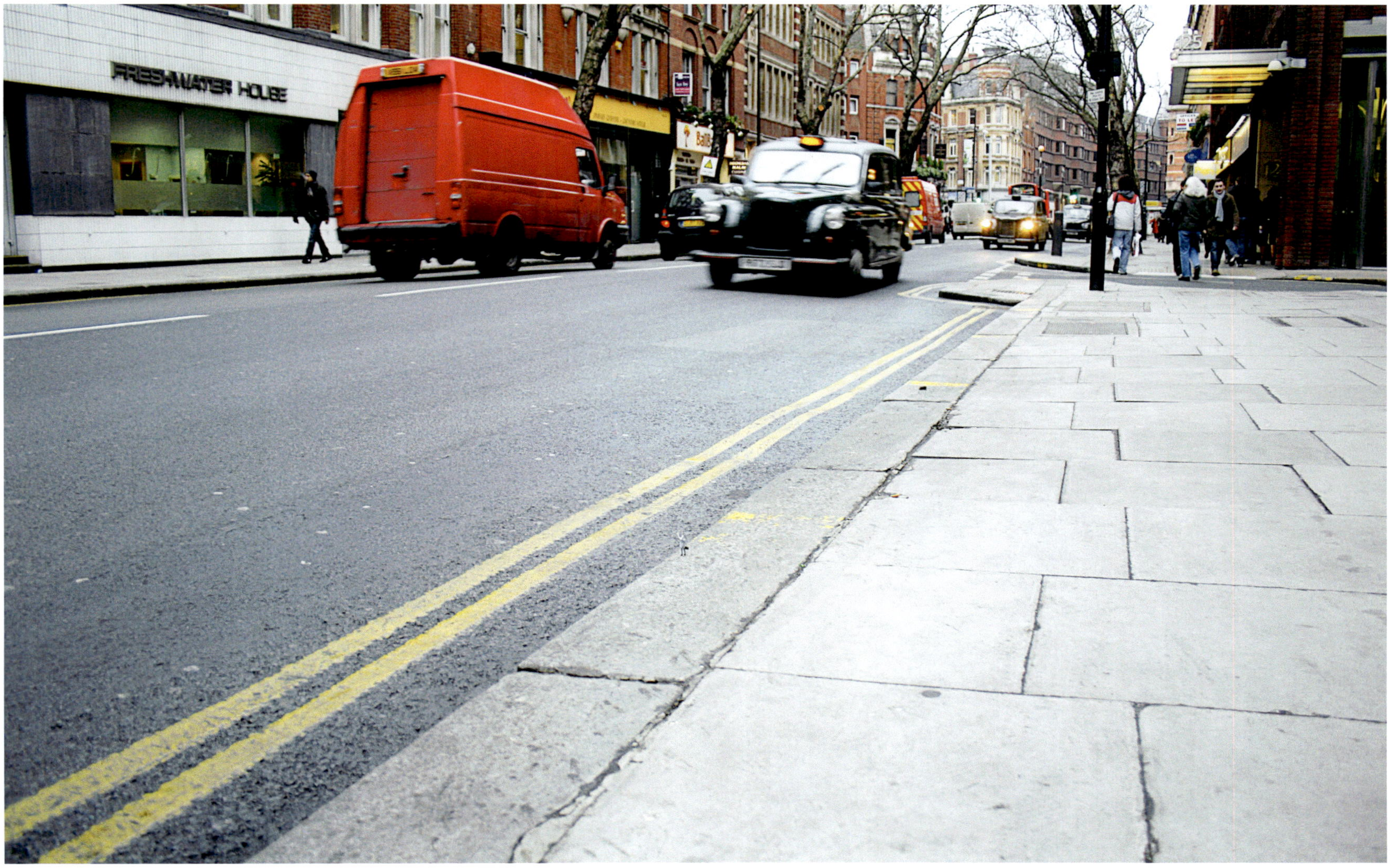

FRESHWATER HOUSE

artists who earned some money with images of the Saints along pilgrimage routes in Italian cities through donations from the faithful. Such street painting can still be seen in many pedestrian zones today, and the tradition has given rise to street painting festivals, which in turn came to inspire the American graphic artist Kurt Wenner (b. 1958) to develop his new way of painting. He was the first to create three-dimensional street happenings instead of simple chalk pictures. Wenner makes use of an old technique, anamorphosis, a kind of distorted perspective painting, which allows one to achieve an amazing and realistic three-dimensional effect when seen from a particular vantage point. Suddenly, a simple street turns into a chasm into which one fears to fall, if one sees it from the right spot. Seen from other viewpoints, the same paintings seem to make no sense at all. Kurt Wenner worked as a space illustrator at NASA before he quit one day and began to create street

▼ Kurt Wenner, *Dies irae*, 1983

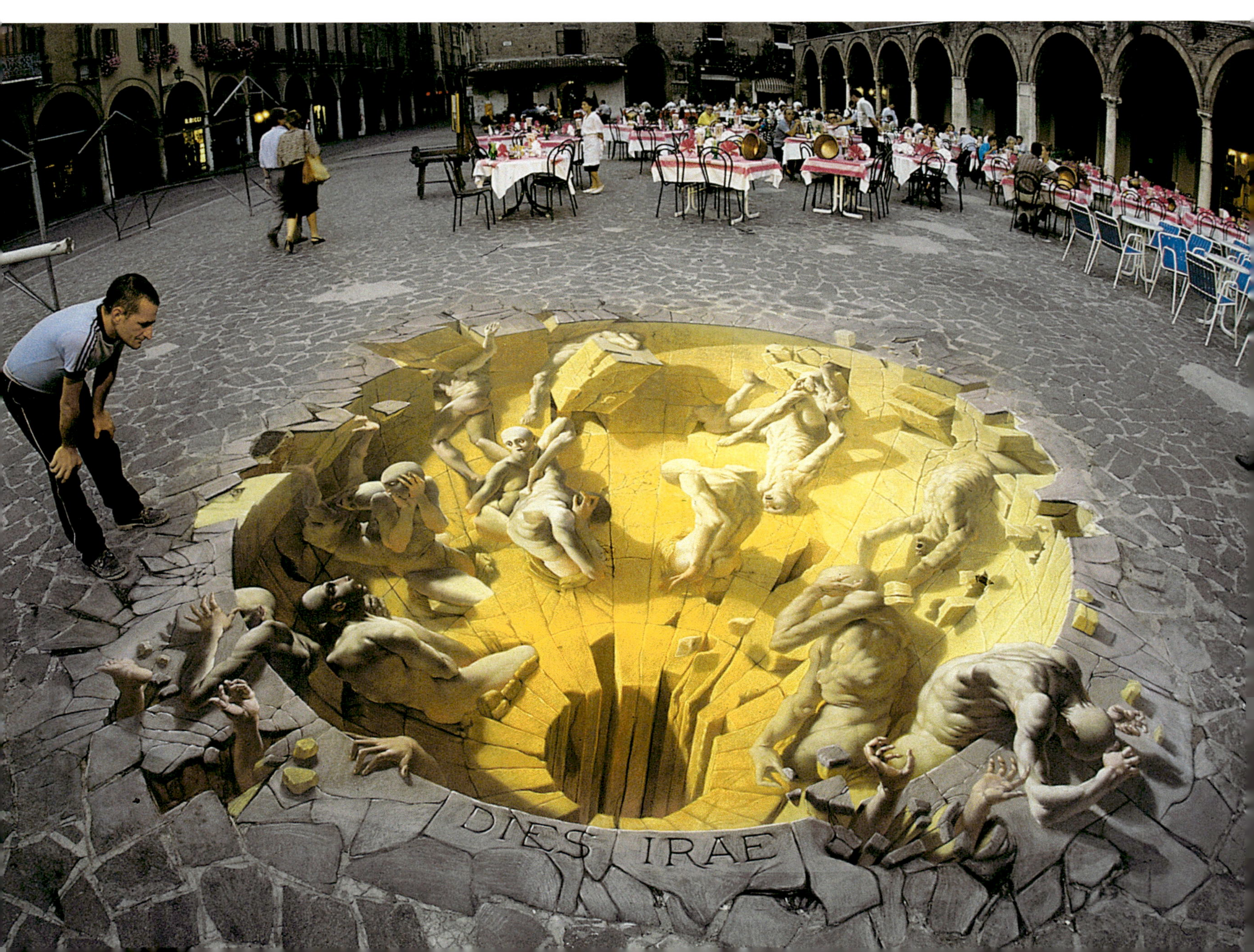

paintings of the highest quality. He is an admirer of classical drawing and painting and was curious how he could transfer the effect of faux domes, like the one created by Andrea Pozzo in Sant'Ignazio in Rome (see pp. 46–47), to the ground. The problem in this was the viewing angle, which in church ceilings rarely exceeds 90 degrees. If one stands on the street and looks at an image on the ground, the viewing angle is about 120 degrees and the distortions used to compensate for this must be correspondingly greater. Wenner thus used the technique of anamorphosis, as is seen, for example, in the painting *The Ambassadors* (1533) by Hans Holbein the Younger. In the foreground, in front of the two brothers, there is a strangely shaped mass, which, when viewed from the far-right side of the painting, turns into a skull. Wenner used this effect for his first work *Dies irae*, which he painted on the street in Mantua in 1983 (fig. left). The idea had come to him when he thought of church ceilings, where one feels one is looking up into the vastness of heavenly eternity. What would it be like, then, if one were to look down into the opposite, the abysses of hell?

One of his most well-known successors worldwide is the German painter and graphic artist Edgar Müller (b. 1968), who conjures up his huge distorted chasms on the streets of the world (fig. p. 176). As with all anamorphoses, even Edgar Müller's work seems strange when viewed from the wrong angle. This is why Müller sometimes installs a special lens at the vanishing point through which one can experience the perfect illusion.

The Dutch artist Leon Keer (b. 1980) also works at a high standard with anamorphosis. He makes use of well-known brands and figures from current popular culture such as Pac-Man, gummy bears (fig. p. 179 below) or Lego figures. He gained fame with a Lego version of the world-famous Terracotta Army of the Chinese Emperor Qin Shi Huang (259–210 BC). However, Keer has no intention of stopping at three dimensions, but is working on four-dimensional street art. In other words, he wants to advance into new regions with the virtual realities that are available to us anytime and anywhere with the use of our smartphones. Using the technology of augmented reality, he is making figures appear to come out of the ground in a highly realistic manner, although they can only be seen on a mobile phone.

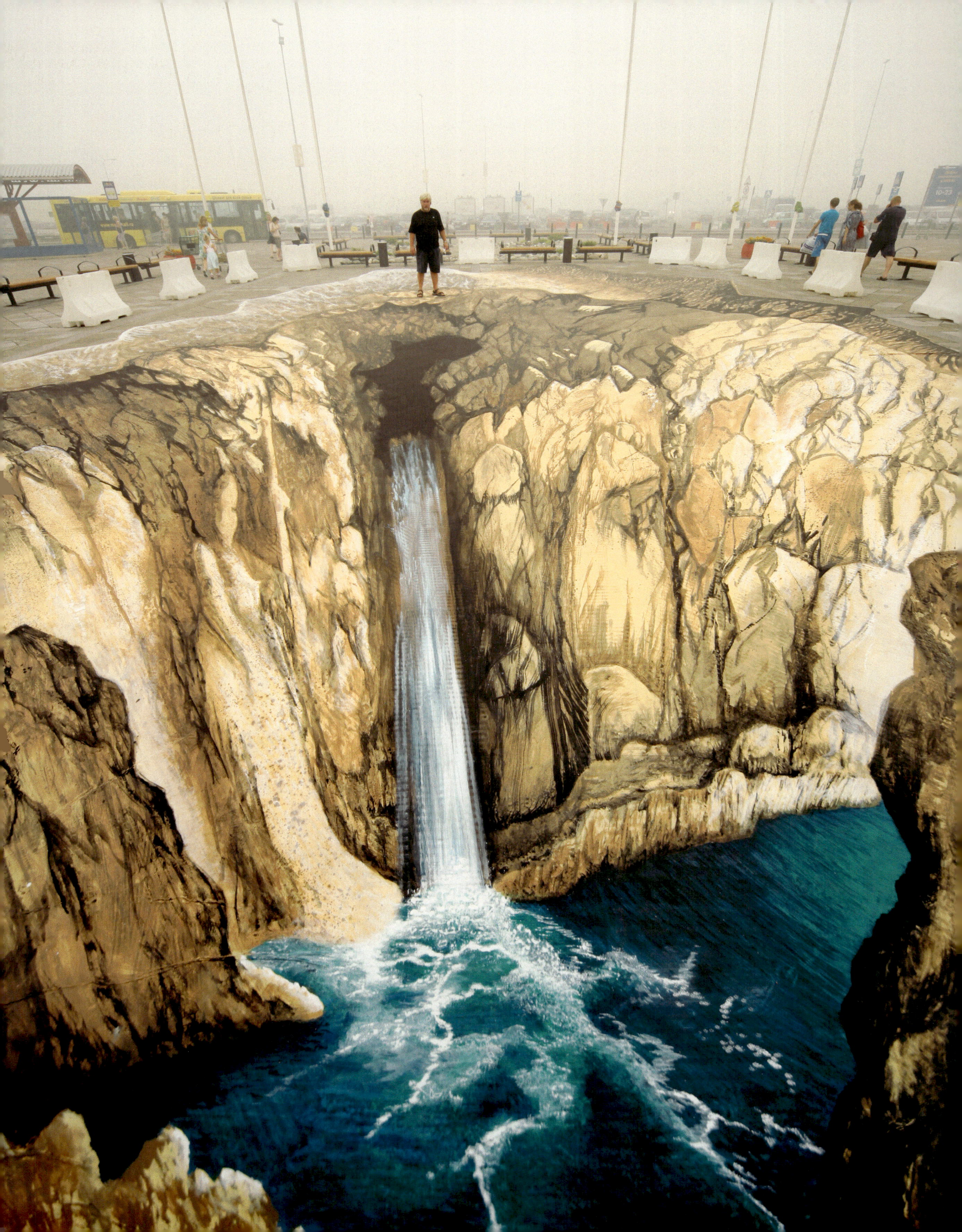

Rather traditional in the sense of art which deceives the eye, but no less fascinating, are the works that 1010 (pronounced 'ten ten') – the peculiar alias of a 1979-born Hamburg-based artist – paints on, or rather in the walls (fig. p. 178). Since 2010 he has been making holes in walls and flat surfaces offered to him around the world by using tiered amorphous forms. They are perfect works of trompe l'œil, where, even if one stares at them for a long time, it is simply impossible to comprehend that one is only looking at paint on a wall. Like Banksy and many other street artists, 1010 also values anonymity. The abysses and caves, created according to all the rules of illusionist art, seem sombre, but his use of harmonious colours also creates spectacular invitations into the unknown depths of space. In May 2018, 1010 created an 18,000 square metre chasm on the banks of the Seine in Paris that one almost dares not enter. *Stream* consists of coloured eddies that stretch for over two kilometres along the Seine's Left Bank from the Pont Royal to the Pont Alexandre III.

Abstract trompe l'œils of this quality are highlights of an art form that was once – and sometimes still is – forbidden. And who would have thought that this formerly illegal art could even help to regulate traffic. For some time now, agencies for road safety have been looking into the benefits of using three-dimensional street painting. The result has been zebra crossings, where one almost fears destroying one's vehicle if one does not slam on the brakes in time (fig. p. 179 above).

In everything that the artists of street art do, it pushes us pedestrians, just passing by, to take a closer look and to realise that everything around us can be a vast stage and a huge canvas in an infinitely large gallery for both small and large art.

◄ Edgar Müller, *Duality*, 2010

▼ 1010, *Tropfen und Ringe* (*Droplets and Rings*), 2017

▶ **Above**
The 3D zebra crossing on St John's Wood High Street, London, 2019

▶ **Below**
Leon Keer, *3D Gummy Bears*, 2015

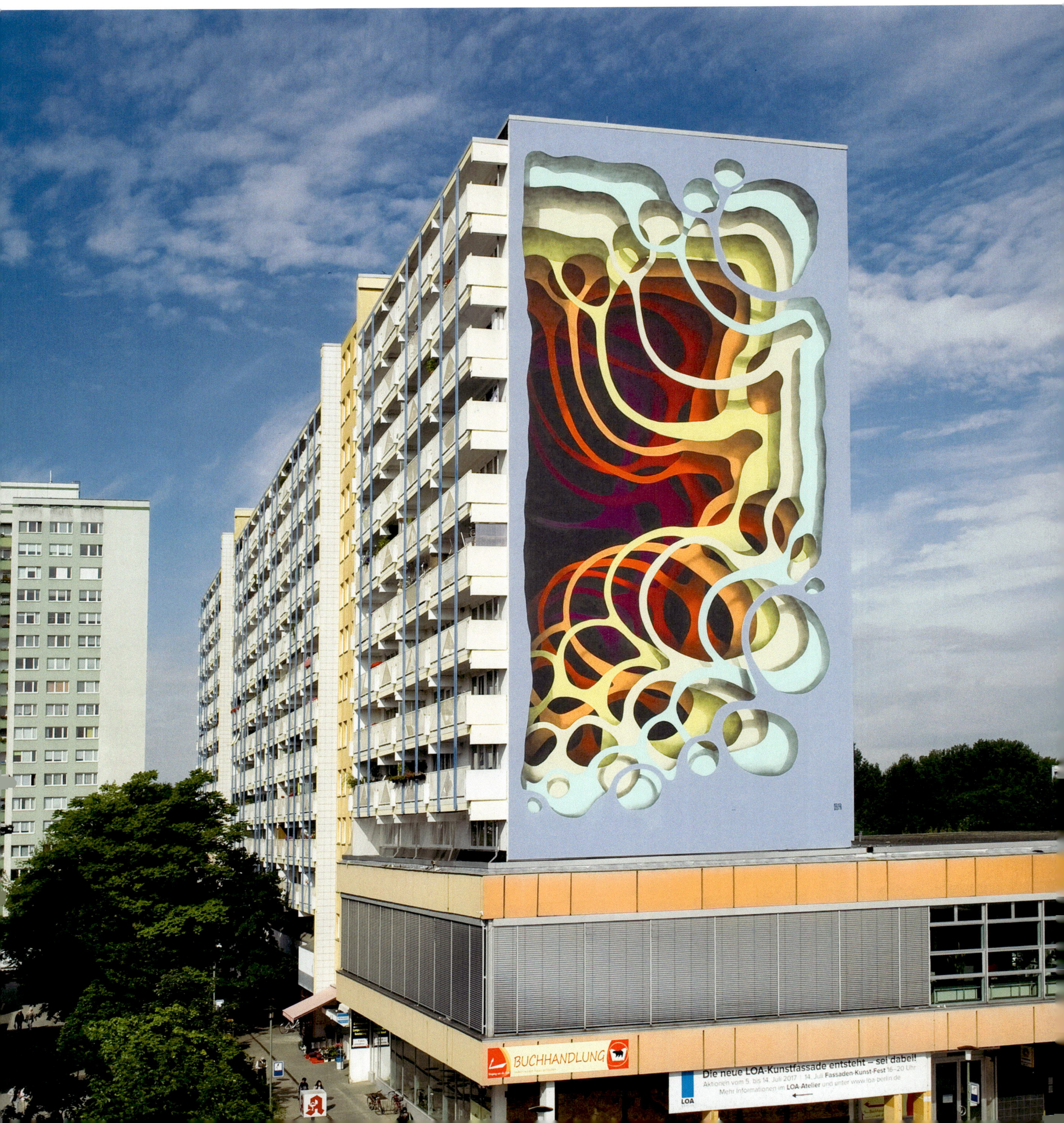

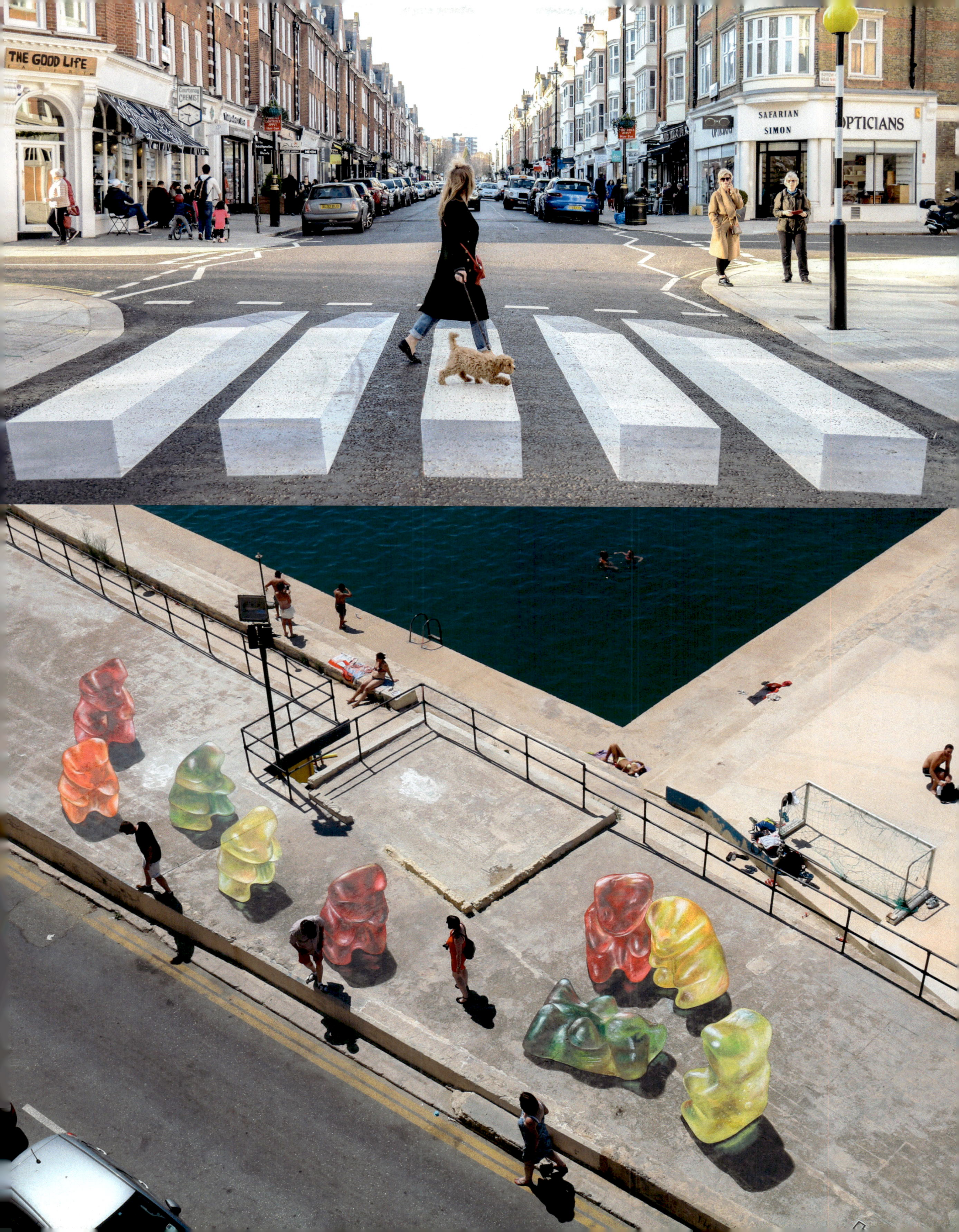
THE GOOD LIFE
SAFARIAN
SIMON

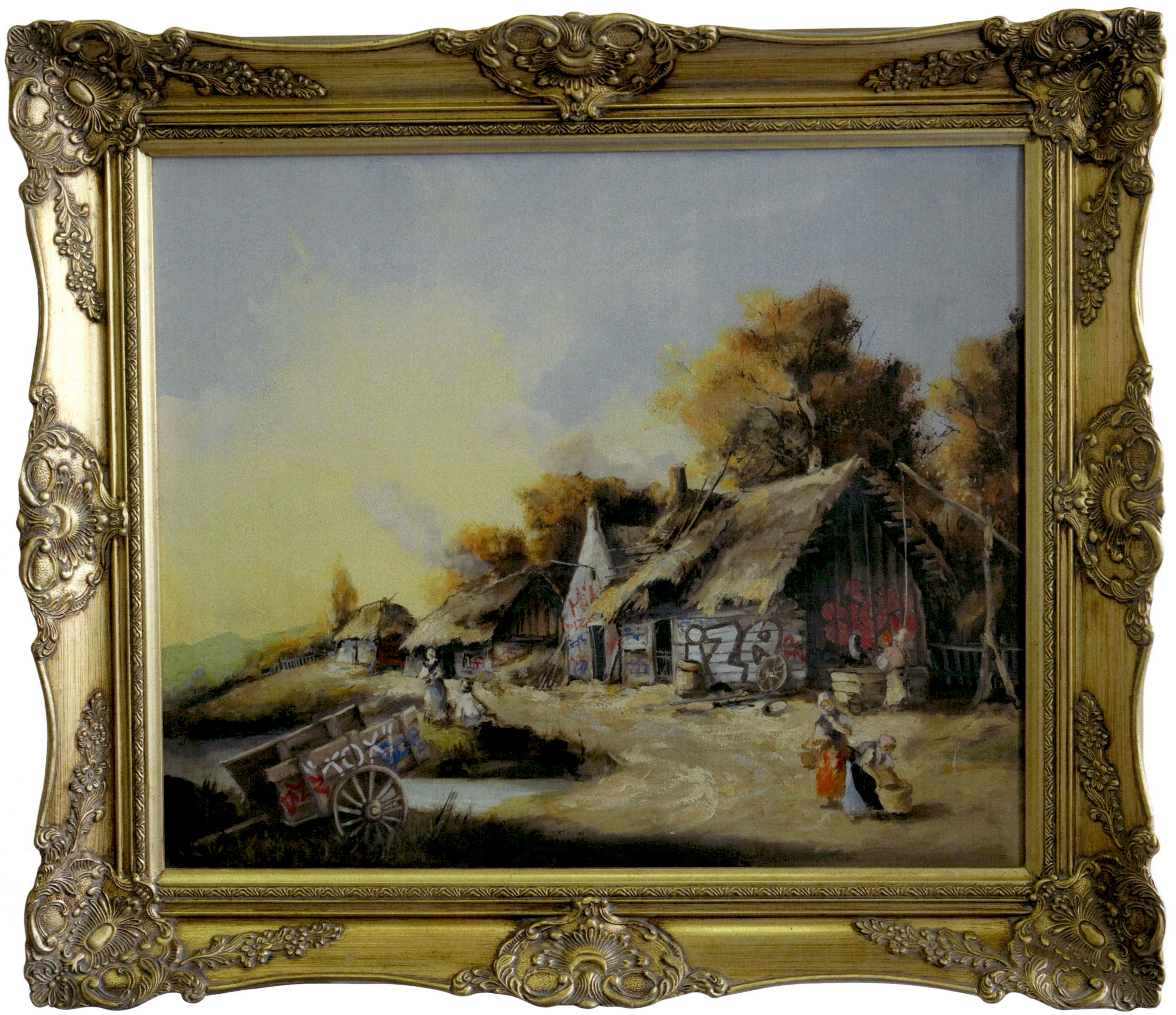

Banksy

Tox Cottage

Canvas

◀ **Facing page**

Naked Man, 2006

Mural

Bristol

Banksy does not only create graffiti. He has also become known for pictures that resemble classical paintings but have been given a few modern modifications, such as nuclear waste barrels or farmhouses decorated with graffiti (fig. left). He smuggled these works into museums, stuck them to the wall in frames and watched to see how long it took for the 'fake' paintings to stand out amongst the real ones. Sometimes, if the pictures did not fall off the wall themselves, it took days before the deception was discovered. Banksy once smuggled an alleged prehistoric rock painting into the British Museum, which was then added to the museum's collection without hesitation by the director, who obviously had a good sense of humour. Most of Banksy's pictures, like those of other street artists, were illegal and usually promptly removed. However, through h s actions, Banksy quickly gained considerable notoriety. In 2006, a picture of a naked man was painted in one night on the building wall of a sexual health clinic. The man is apparently trying to make a getaway from a rendezvous through the window, from which the cuckolded husband and his wife look, searching for him (fig. right). The largely illusionistic and humorous image is located directly opposite the Bristol City Council, putting the local authorities in a quandary: to preserve order or to let the city's most famous artist get away with something like this? The solution was a survey in which 93% of Bristol's residents voted not to remove the painting. It has since become one of the city's most famous tourist attractions. Working worldwide, as do most of his peers, the surprise factor inherent in Banksy's artistic activities has made him arguably the best-known anonymous artist internationally today. Works which he painted on the wall separating Israel from the West Bank present subverted idyllic images, both stunning and politically explosive, which draw attention to the separation barrier and the problems associated with it.

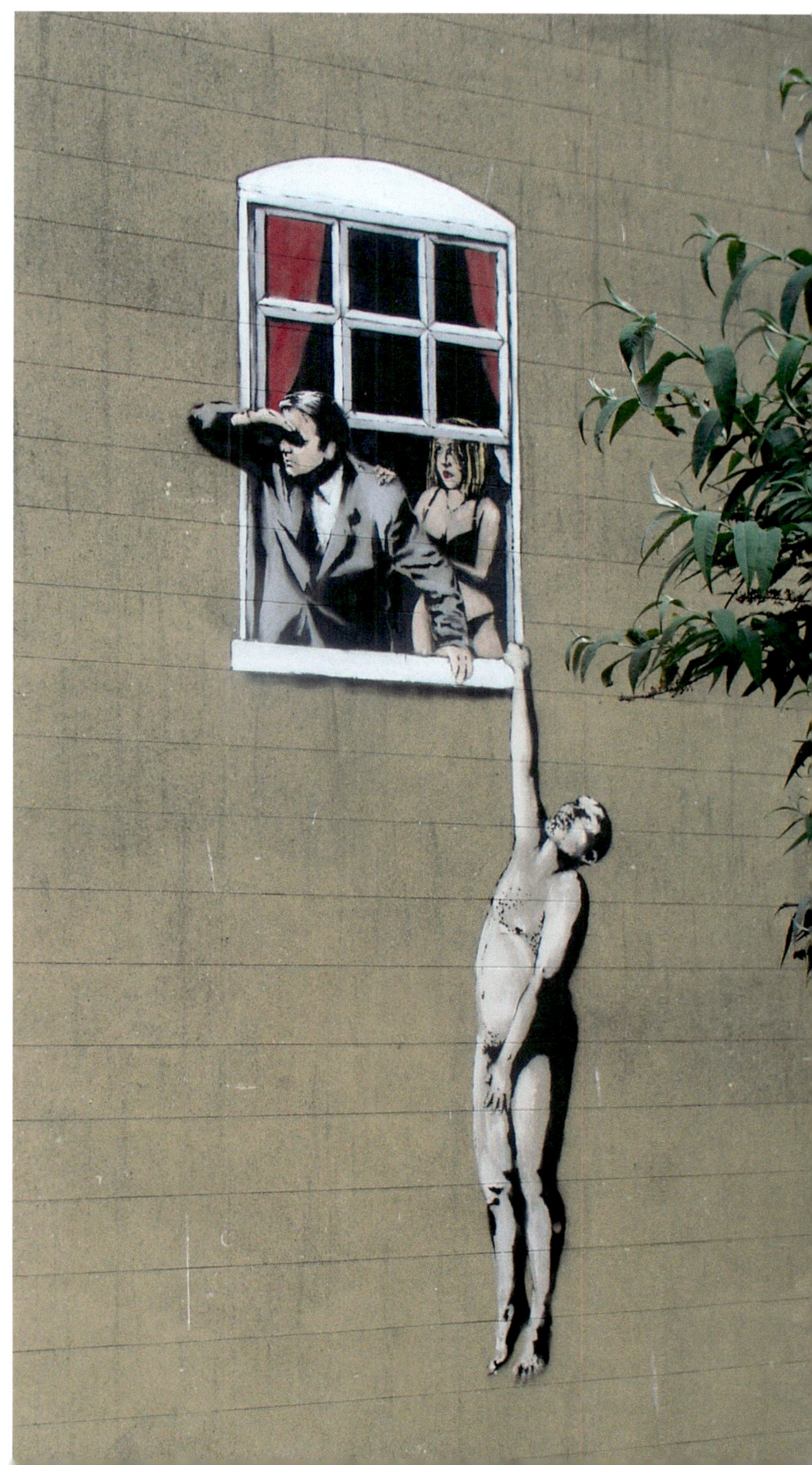

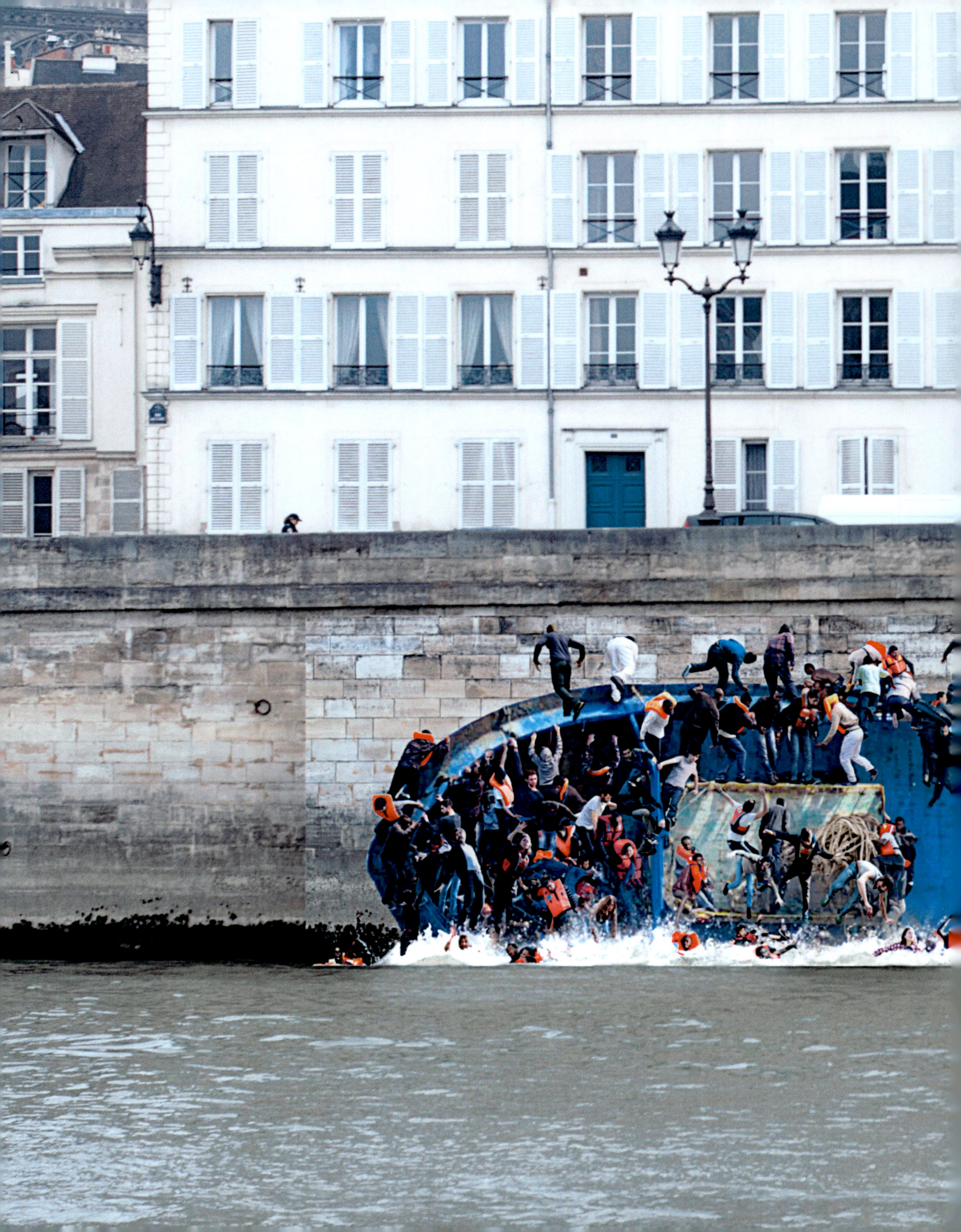

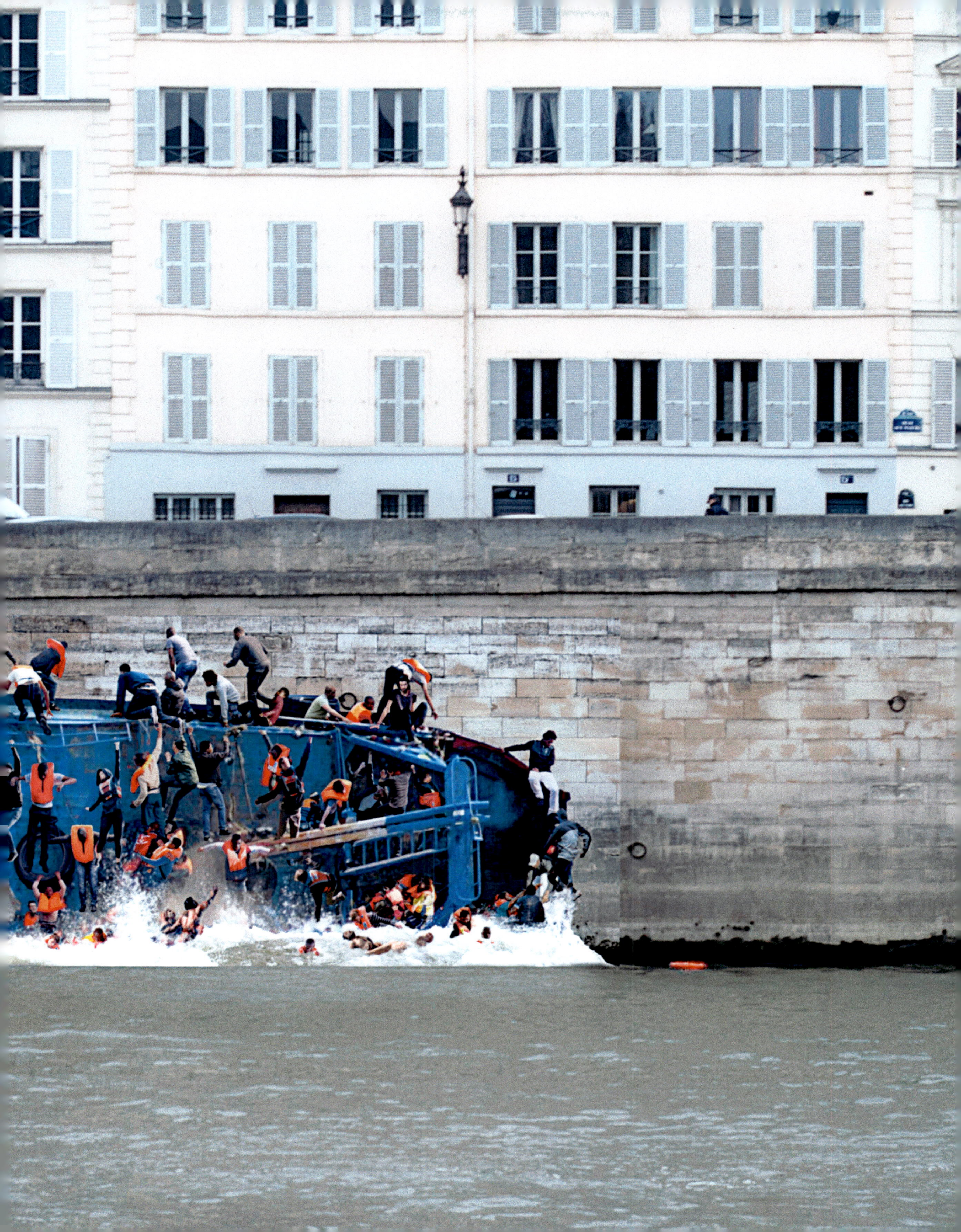

Pierre Delavie

Le Radeau de Lampéduse, 2017

Printed canvas
Paris
◀ **Previous spread**

The French artist Pierre Delavie (b. 1956) describes his works as 'urban lies'. In 2013, for example, he made it seem that he had diverted the historic high street of Marseilles, La Canebière, and extended it almost to infinity. To further enhance the effect of this 'lie', pedestrians were integrated into the work by means of projecting them as a video on the lower edge of the screen in the evening. In 2014, Delavie 'deconstructed' the Grand Palais in Paris by using architectural motifs printed on tarpaulins and panels which made the building appear as if it was on the verge of collapse. With his architectural interventions, Pierre Delavie tears people out of their aesthetic rut, breaking into the visual environment which his audience is accustomed to. He intervenes in reality and by doing so creates his 'urban lies'. "All my work is a game with reality, and it's necessary to doubt reality since it's not clear we are actually capable of perceiving it."[52]

In his *The Raft of Lampedusa* (*Le Radeau de Lampéduse*; fig. pp. 182/183) however, reality ceases to be a game and becomes instead a somewhat bitter blueprint for his artwork. On 11 January 2017, Delavie unveiled a life-size printed canvas on the quay walls of the Seine, which showed a capsizing refugee boat opposite Paris's city hall. It appears to be capsizing in real time, with its passengers falling into the river's water. In actual fact, the model for Delavie's work is a genuine photograph of this refugee boat which was taken by the Italian coastguard on 25 May 2016. With this rather spectacular action, carried out without official permission, Delavie wanted to draw attention to the current situation of refugees in the Mediterranean. The title *The Raft of Lampedusa* refers both to the island between Tunisia and Sicily, which is often the destination of refugees, and to the famous painting *The Raft of the Medusa* (*Le Radeau de la Méduse*), created by Théodore Géricault in 1819, a work which is familiar to all Parisians and indeed to French people as a whole. Géricault's work makes reference to a harrowing incident in 1816: "This tragedy shook the entire population, everyone felt themselves implicated; it provoked a real debate within society. Today, we are indifferent," said Delavie.[53] The artist wanted to dispel this indifference towards the refugee crisis with 'his' raft To confront the French people still more forcibly with the subject, Delavie added his own photos of Parisians, as if they were also refugees in distress at sea, "to remind everyone that They are Us, too".[54]

Until 2021, it is still possible to marvel at another of the French artist's huge 'urban lies': at Versailles, in an impressive piece, the artist has turned the palace's chapel inside out ...

Leandro Erlich

Pulled by the Roots, 2015

Outdoor installation with crane,
mixed media
Karlsruhe
ZKM - Center for Art and Media

Argentinean artist Leandro Erlich (b. 1973) continues to confuse and enchant people around the world with his installations and sculptures. Whether with obelisks, swimming pools that appear full or a section of house wall, which, accessible via ladder, seems to float in mid-air. In 2015, he tore a house out of the ground on Karlsruhe's market square with a crane and left it hanging (fig. right). At least that must have been how it seemed to the citizens of the city. The confusion must have been great, but these things can happen. Cranes have formed part of the city's skyline for a while now, because between 2010 and (probably) 2020 a tunnel for the city's light rail and tram system is being built. And, well, an overzealous crane operator with the wrong set of instructions ... What is more, the house on the hook was in the style of the important city planner Friedrich Weinbrenner (1766 – 1826) and thus seemed quite familiar. And to everyone's confusion, the house was well and truly uprooted, the roots still hanging from the underside of the two-storey townhouse. The ostensibly organic relationship between house and ground had been severed.

The house, ripped out, is not only a brilliantly carried out illusionistic joke, but also holds a deeper meaning. In times of great refugee movements, the house stands, on the one hand, for the idea of home and the organic relationship one has with it. On the other hand, it also stands for the possibility and threat of being uprooted and transplanted somewhere else, as happens so often to so many people. Here, too, despite all the amazement, exhilaration and the perfect illusion, street art (here in a rather literal sense) has once again created a space for questions and new approaches, and it has probably done so more effectively as a work of art than would have been possible using other means.

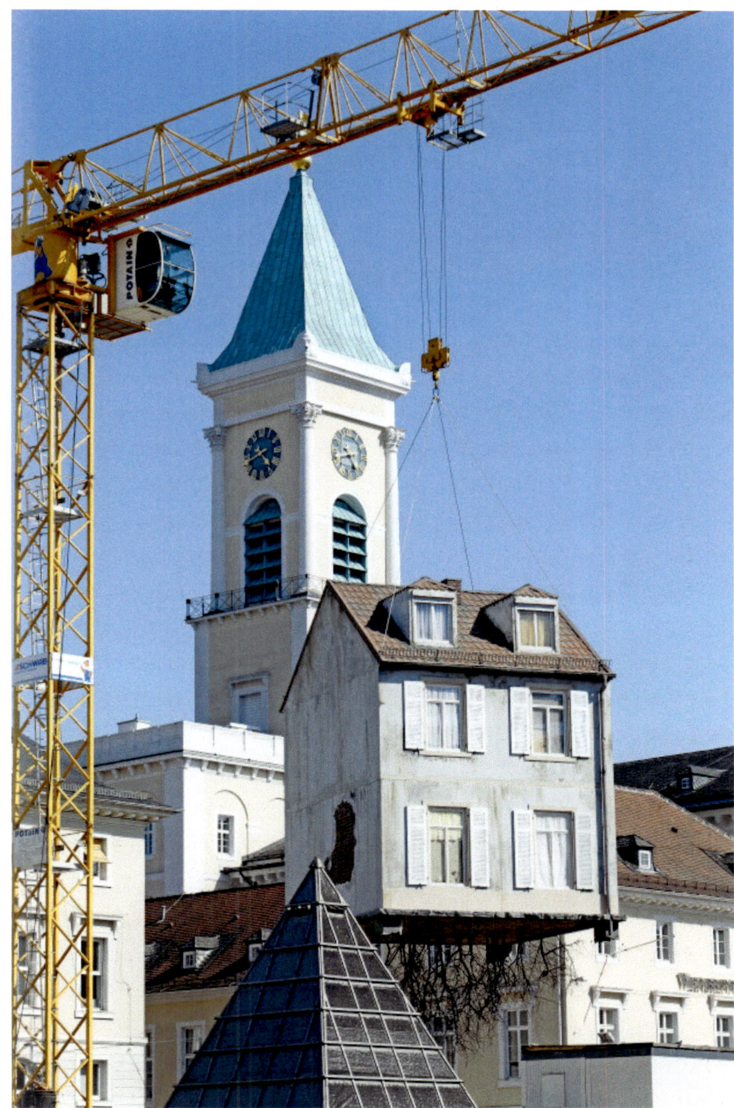

Mark Jenkins

Embed Series #1, 2006

Mixed Media
Washington, D.C.
▶ **Facing page**

Project 84, 2018

84 sculptures, mixed media
London
▶ **Overleaf**

Ordinary figures in ordinary places, whose behaviour, however, is unusual. This is how one could describe the sculptures of the American artist Mark Jenkins (b. 1970). Sometimes a woman sits in a dustbin, sometimes a man has a traffic cone on his head and sometimes a man is stuck with his head in the wall (fig. right). What is he doing there? Did he try to get through a wall and got stuck? It may seem unlikely, but it may not be impossible. Mark Jenkins often lets his characters, with their completely inconspicuous outfits, get into places or situations that range from peculiar to bizarre, when otherwise they appear completely normal. The figures often do not stand out, but if they do, it sometimes happens that passers-by may call the police for help. For example, when one of Jenkins's figures is floating, held over water by only a few balloons (Malmö, Sweden, 2008). And the rescue would be easy, because his figures are sculptures made of cling film and adhesive tape. The artist himself or his colleagues are wrapped with it and taped in a certain pose, and then cut out again. The resulting hollow forms are reassembled as sculptures. They are then dressed and sent on their mission. This is the confusion, the attention and the possible dialogue with the public that results.

Mostly the figures are found in rather comical situations, but not always. In 2018, Mark Jenkins drew attention to the issue of suicide with an impressive installation in London. Eighty-four male figures suddenly appeared out of nowhere, standing on the edge of the roof of the London Studios on the South Bank, as if they would collectively throw themselves off at any moment (fig. pp. 188/189). Suicide is the most common cause of death amongst British men under forty-five. The eighty-four very real-looking male figures stand for the number of weekly deaths. As part of a prevention and education project ("Project 84"), each figure was intended to remind us of a real person whose story was told as part of the campaign. Street art, which usually causes amusement, confusion or at least astonishment on the streets of the world, can also deal with very relevant and charged topics if it is created by artists who have developed an ability to do so – over and above the humour.

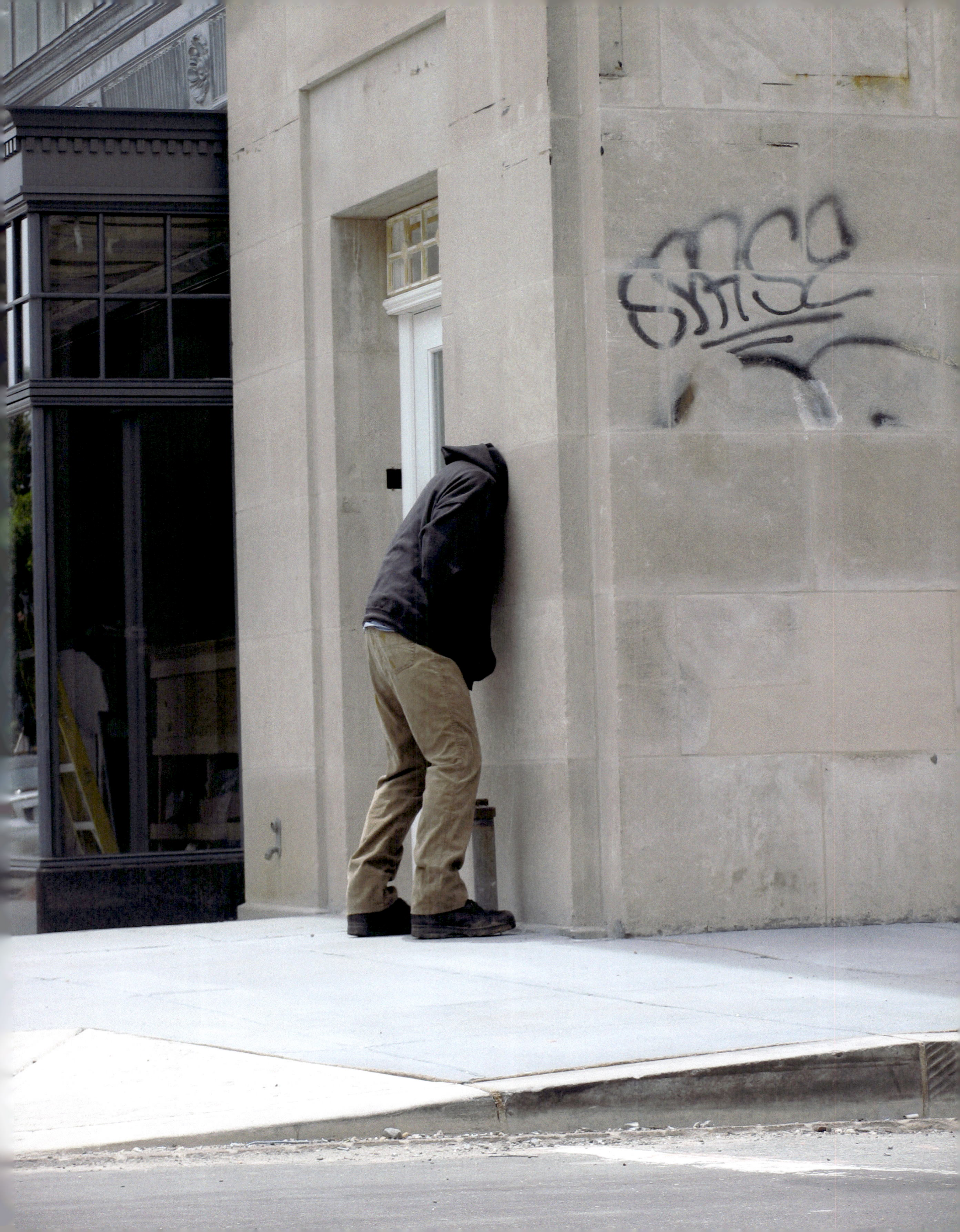

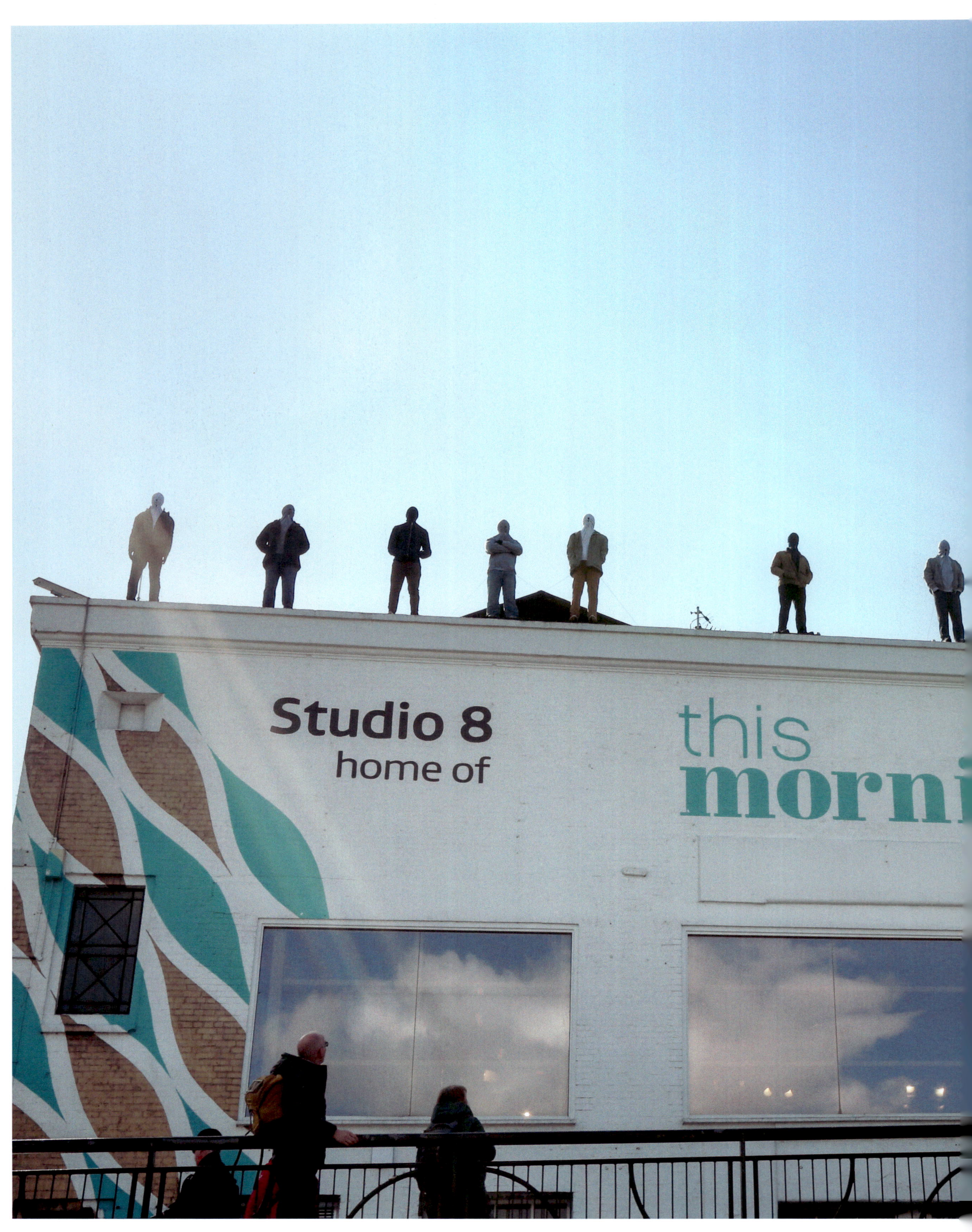
Studio 8
home of
this
morni

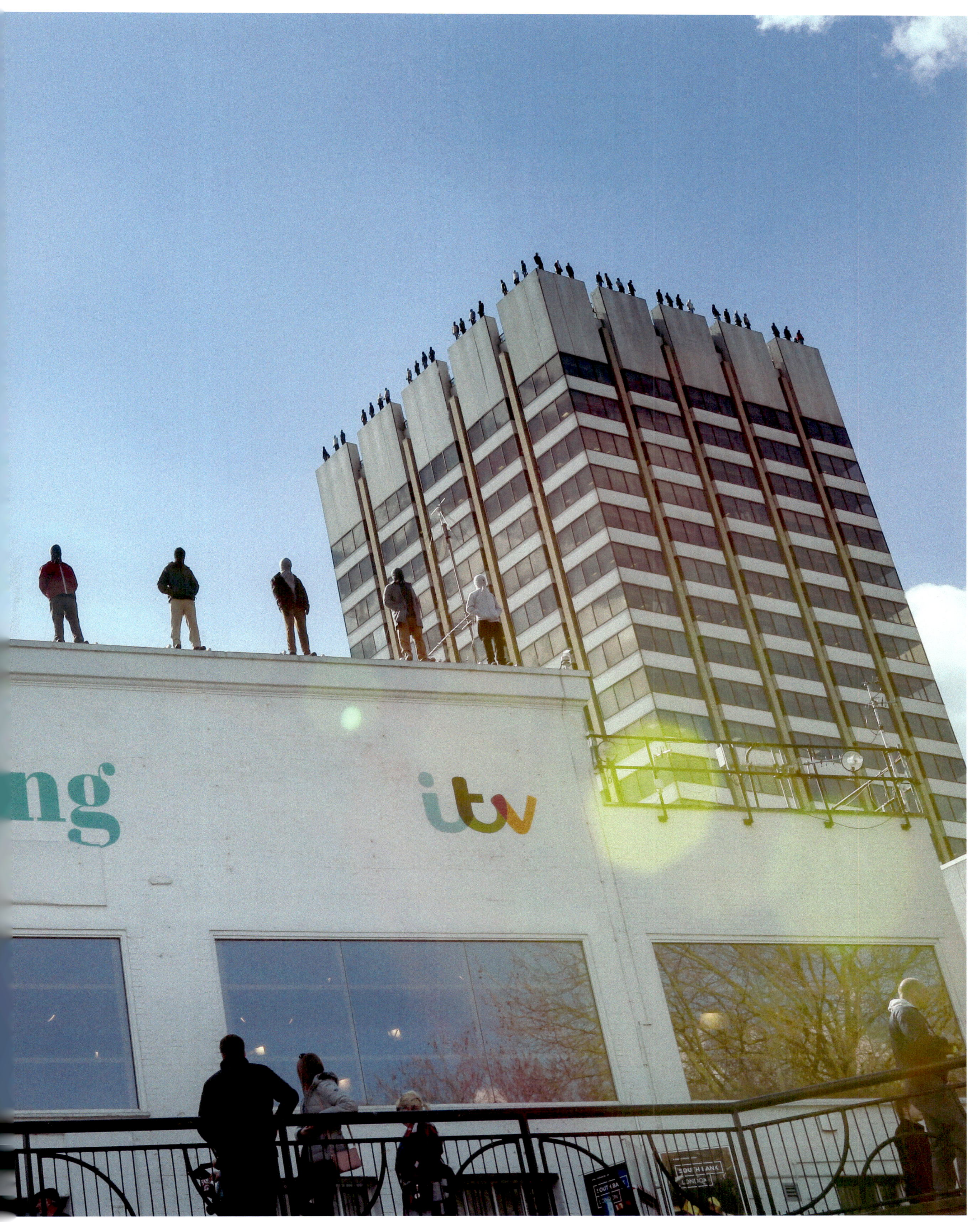

ng
itv

Notes

1 Theodor W. Adorno, *Minima Moralia: Reflections from Damaged Life* [1951], trans. E. F. N. Jephcott (London: Verso, 2005), p. 222.

2 Quoted in Florien Heine, *Mit den Augen der Maler. Schauplätze der Kunst neu entdeckt* (Munich: Bucher Verlag, 2009), p. 10; (translated by J. E. Macián).

3 Giorgio Vasari, *Lives of the Painters, Sculptors and Architects*, trans. Gaston du C. de Vere, vol. 1 (New York: Everyman's Library, 1996), p. 286.

4 Ibid., p. 811.

5 Ibid.

6 Quoted in Kevin Bruce, *The Murals of John Pugh: Beyond Trompe l'Oeil* (Berkeley, CA: Ten Speed Press, 2006).

7 Peeta: Spraycan Art and Beyond, "About Peeta", https://www.peeta.net/about/ (accessed 9 December 2019).

8 Vasari, *Lives of the Painters*, p. 320.

9 Giovanni Boccaccio, *Decameron*, trans. J. G. Nichols (New York: Everyman's Library, 2008), p. 374.

10 Ibid., p. 375.

11 William Martin Conway, *Literary Remains of Albrecht Dürer* (Cambridge: Cambridge University Press, 1889), p. 48.

12 William Dean Howells, *The Rise of Silas Lapham* (London: Penguin, 1986), p. 64.

13 Adrien Goetz, "Le siècle de l'illusion perdue : XIXe siècle", in *Le Trompe-l'œil de l'Antiquité au XXe siècle*, ed. Patrick Mauriès (Paris: Gallimard, 1996), p. 276; (translated by J. E. Macián).

14 Magritte: *Der Verrat der Bilder*, directed by Sylvain Bergère, written by Didier Ottinger and Sylvain Bergère, Schweizer Radio und Fernsehen, 23 December 2017, 18:24, https://www.youtube.com/watch?v=LDuWAoPJ7Xo (accessed 6 January 2020; translated J. E. Macián).

15 Philips Angel, *Praise of Painting*, trans. Michael Hoyle, in "Ten Essays for a Friend: E. de Jongh 65", ed. Xander van Eck et al., *Simiolus: Netherlands Quarterly for the History of Art* 24, no. 2/3 (1996), p. 244; see also Florien Heine, *Art: The Groundbreaking Moments* (Munich: Prestel, 2012), pp. 139f.

16 F. T. Marinetti, "The Founding and Manifesto of Futurism", in *Futurism: An Anthology*, ed. Lawrence Rainey et al. (New Haven, CT: Yale University Press, 2009), p. 51.

17 Victor Vasarely, *Vasarely*, trans. I. Mark Paris (New York: Alpine Fine Arts Collection, 1979), p. 15.

18 Josef Albers, "Op Art and/or Perceptual Effects", in *Yale Scientific Magazine* 40, no. 2 (November 1965), p. 8.

19 *Magritte: Der Verrat der Bilder*, 18:30; (translated by Noel Zmija-Maurice).

20 Karl Ruhrberg, *Painting*, vol. 1 of *Art of the 20th Century*, ed. Ingo F. Walther (Cologne: Taschen, 2000), p. 344.

21 Bridget Riley, interview by John Leighton, "Video Transcript", National Galleries of Scotland, 2019, https://www.nationalgalleries.org/sites/default/files/transcriptions/Video%20Transcript%20Bridget%20Riley.pdf, (corrected slightly, based on the video of the interview, cf. https://www.youtube.com/watch?v=Af3RgRRAGa4, accessed 6 January 2020).

22 Rudolf Arnheim, "Die Seele in der Silberschicht" [1925], in *Die Seele in der Silberschicht. Medientheoretische Texte. Photographie - Film - Rundfunk*, ed. Helmut H. Diederichs (Frankfurt am Main: Suhrkamp, 2004), S. 11; (translated by Noel Zmija-Maurice).

23 Roger Ballen, "Manchmal ist der Albtraum das, was wir brauchen", interviewed by Tobias Haberl, *Süddeutsche Zeitung Magazin*, 17 November 2014, https://sz-magazin.sueddeutsche.de/kunst/manchmal-ist-der-albtraum-das-was-wir-brauchen-80786; (translated by Noel Zmija-Maurice). See also Florian Heine and Brad Finger, *50 Contemporary Photographers You Should Know* (Munich: Prestel, 2016), p. 52.

24 Karl Ruhrberg, *Painting*, p. 336.

25 Linda Chase, *Hyperrealism* (New York: Rizzoli, 1973), pp. 9f; see also *Realismus. Das Abenteuer der Wirklichkeit. Courbet - Hopper - Gursky*, ed. Christiane Lange and Nils Ohlsen, exh. cat. Kunsthalle Emden, (Munich: Hirmer, 2010), p. 388.

26 Quoted in Heine, *Mit den Augen der Maler*, p. 157; (translated by Noel Zmija-Maurice)

27 Erik Johansson, "Impossible Photography", TED-Salon London, Fall 2011, https://www.ted.com/talks/erik_johansson_impossible_photography/transcript?language=en (accessed 4 February 2020).

28 Ibid.

29 Hans Werner Holzwarth, ed., *Art Now! Vol. 3*, (Cologne: Taschen, 2008), p. 120; see also *Realismus*, ed. Lange and Ohlsen, p. 173.

30 Quoted in "JR Makes The Louvre Invisible", *British Journal of Photography*, 2 June 2016, https://www.bjp-online.com/2016/06/jr-makes-the-louvre-invisible/ (accessed 4 February 2020).

31 Quotes in Lizzie Crook "Optical Illusion Added to IM Pei's Louvre Pyramid Then Immediately Destroyed", *Dezeen*, 2 April 2019, https://www.dezeen.com/2019/04/02/louvre-pyramid-jr-artist-paris-museum-optical-illusion/ (accessed 4 February 2020).

32 See Michael Zhang, "These Portraits Were Made by AI: None of These People Exist", *PetaPixel*, 17 December 2018, https://petapixel.com/2018/12/17/these-portraits-were-made-by-ai-none-of-these-people-exist/ (accessed 31 October 2019).

33 " 'big, bigger, biggest'. Die monumentalen überwirklichen Porträts des amerikanischen Künstlers Chuck Close", WDR, 20 May 2007, https://web.archive.org/web/20070927211410/http://www.daserste.de/ttt/beitrag_dyn~uid,n4y2n6zri17v4gif~cm.asp (accessed 4 December 2019; translated by J.E. Macián).

34 Quoted in Heine and Finger, *50 Contemporary Photographers*, p. 96.

35 Quoted in Florien Heine, *Photography: The Groundbreaking Moments* (Munich: Prestel, 2012), p. 175.

36 Quoted in Heine and Finger, *50 Contemporary Photographers*, p. 96.

37 Quoted in Zach Sokol, "Pelle Cass' Time-Lapse Photos Outsmart Even The Trickiest Photographers", *Vice*, 15 October 2013, https://www.vice.com/en_uk/article/4xqyvm/Video-pelle-cass-time-lapse-photography-explores-the-interconnectedness-of-daily-life (accessed 7 January 2020); quoted in Lucy Bourton, "How Pelle Cass Creates his Jarring 'Still Time-Lapse' Images", It's Nice That, 22 May 2019, https://www.itsnicethat.com/articles/pelle-cass-crowded-fields-photography-220519 (accessed 6 December 2019).

38 Ray Cummings, *The Girl in the Golden Atom* (London: Methuen, 1922), p. 34.

39 Felice Varini, interview with *International Design Network* 15, no. 5 (2008), http://www.varini.org/varini/presse-varini/01-dp-varini.pdf (accessed 4 December 2019).

40 Euripides, *Oedipus-Chrysippus and Other Fragments*, ed. and trans. Christopher Collard and Martin Cropp, Loeb Classical Library 506 (Cambridge, MA: Harvard University Press, 2008), p. 263.

41 Euripides, *Helen*, German trans. Oliver Primavesi, quoted in *Gods in Color: Painted Sculpture of Classical Antiquity*, ed. Vinzenz Brinkmann, exh. cat. Arthur M. Sackler Museum, Harvard University Art Museums (Munich: Biering und Brinkmann, 2007), p. 194.

42 Quoted in Ruth Skilbeck, "Simon Klose: Director, Benalla Art Gallery," *Australian Art Collector*, December 2008, p. 138, https://www.sullivanstrumpf.com/assets/Uploads/McDonald-John-Precious-and-Powerful-Australian-Art-Collector-Dec-2008.pdf (accessed 26 November 2019).

43 Lee Wohlfert, "At Duane Hanson's Strange New Show, Only the Artist Is Lying Down on the Job", *People*, 6 March 1978, https://people.com/archive/at-duane-hansons-strange-new-show-only-the-artist-is-lying-down-on-the-job-vol-9-no-9/ (accessed 6 January 2020).

44 Judith Palmer, "Eyeball to Eyeball with Mueck and His Works", Eye on Tuesday, *Independent*, 2 June 1998, https://www.independent.co.uk/life-style/eyeball-to-eyeball-with-mueck-and-his-works-1162363.html (accessed 6 January 2020).

45 J. B. S. Haldane, "Possible Worlds", *Possible Worlds and Other Essays* (London: Chatto & Windus, 1927), p. 286.

46 Patricia Piccinini, "The Bond", *Artist's Statements*, http://www.patriciapiccinini.net/writing/105/429/26 (accessed 26 November 2019).

47 Ibid.

48 Xavier Prou, "The Manifesto of Stencilism", https://blekleratoriginal.com/en/blek-le-rat-2/ (accessed 2 December 2019).

49 Quoted in "The Birth of Paris Street Art: Before Banksy, There Was Blek le Rat", Culture Trip, 23 December 2016, http://blekleratoriginal.com/en/the-birth-of-paris-street-art-before-banksy-there-was-blek-le-rat/ (accessed 2 December 2019).

50 Quoted in Alessandra Mattanza, *Street Art: Famous Artists Talk About Their Vision* (Milan: White Star, 2017), p. 207.

51 Ibid., p. 208.

52 Pierre Delavie, interview with Gaël Dupret, April 2017, https://www.gaeldupret.com/pierre-delavie/ (accessed 21 February 2020; translated by J. E. Macián).

53 Quoted in Charlotte Viguié, "Une œuvre montre un naufrage de réfugiés au bord de la Seine à Paris", France 24, https://www.france24.com/fr/20170112-une-oeuvre-montre-naufrage-refugies-bord-seine-a-paris (accessed 21 February 2020; translated by J. E. Macián).

54 Ibid.

Image credits

© 1010, www.instagram.com/1010zzz/ Photo: Miguel Ferraz: 4
© 1010, www.instagram.com/1010zzz/ Photo: Benjamin Pritzkuleit: 178
akg-images: 69, 75, 82/83, 88/89, 94/95, 105; Cameraphoto: 53; De Agostini Picture Lib./V. Pirozzi: 24/25; De Agostini Picture Lib./G. Barone: 27; Heritage Images/Fine Art Images: 54/55; Andrea Jemolo: 47, 48/49, 142; Les Arts Décoratifs, Paris/Jean Tholance: 56; Erich Lessing: 2, 18, 50; Liszt Collection: 7; Eric Vandeville: 14/15; Rabatti & Domingie: 17, 38
© Giacomo Balla: VG Bild-Kunst, Bonn 2020/Photo: akg-images/De Agostini Picture Lib./M. E. Smith: 74
© Banksy. Courtesy of Pest Control Office, Banksy: 180, 181
© Blek le Rat/Photo: Didier Moulin: 170
© Blue Sky: 32
bpk: Alinari Archives/Bencini, Raffaello: 58; Alinari Archives/Magliani, Mauro for Alinari: 41; DeA Picture Library: 10/11; RMN – Grand Palais/Gérard Blot: 151; Staatliche Kunsthalle Karlsruhe/Wolfgang Pankoke: 86/87
Bridgeman Images: 67, 148; Andrea Jemolo: 29; Luisa Ricciarini: 30; De Agostini Picture Library/G. Nimatallah: 62; Alinari Archives, Florence: 108
© Pelle Cass: 133, 134/135
© Maurizio Cattelan/Courtesy Maurizio Cattelan's Archive/Photo: Getty Images/Raphael Gaillarde/Gamma-Rapho: 146/147
© Chuck Close, courtesy Pace Gallery: 126
© John DeAndrea/Photo: Courtesy Denver Art Museum: 154/155
© Pierre Delavie: 182/183
© Thomas Demand: VG Bild-Kunst, Bonn 2020/Courtesy Sprüth Magers: 116/117
© Leandro Erlich Studio, 2015/ZKM | Zentrum für Kunst und Medien Karlsruhe, Photo: ONUK: 185
© 2019 The M. C. Escher Company, The Netherlands. All rights reserved. www.mcescher.com: 98
© Richard Estes, courtesy Marlborough Gallery, New York: 110/111
© Philippe Froesch: 153
© Generated Photos, https://generated.photos: 125
© Andreas Gursky: VG Bild-Kunst, Bonn 2020/Courtesy Sprüth Magers: 129, 130/131
© Richard Haas/Photo: Getty Images/Raymond Boyd: 33
© Duane Hanson: VG Bild-Kunst, Bonn 2020/Photo: © Christie's Images/Bridgeman Images: 161
Joachim Hiltmann/Stanislaw Rowinski/Andreas Torneberg: 144
© The J. Paul Getty Museum, Los Angeles: 107 l.
© Mark Jenkins: 187
© Mark Jenkins/Courtesy CALM charity (https://www.thecalmzone.net/) and Simon Vaughan: 188/189
© Sam Jinks/Photo: Murray Fredericks: 156
© Erik Johansson: 114
© JR-art.net: 122/123
© Leon Keer/instagram.com/leonkeer: 179 b.
© Liu Bolin. Courtesy: Boxart Galleria d'Arte, Verona: 138
© Alexey Kondakov: 120
Kunsthistorisches Museum, Wien: 61
Landesamt für Denkmalpflege Sachsen (Wolfgang Junius): 159
Liebieghaus Skulpturensammlung: 141
© René Magritte: VG Bild-Kunst, Bonn 2020/Photo: akg-images: 70/71
© René Magritte: VG Bild-Kunst, Bonn 2020/Photo: mauritius images/SuperStock/Fine Art Images: 96/97
mauritius images: Bildarchiv Monheim GmbH/Alamy: 149; Edouard Coleman/Alamy: 99; Dipper Historic/Alamy: 64 r., Claire Doherty/Alamy: 179 a.; Adam Eastland/Alamy: 43; The History Collection/Alamy: 106; Historic Images/Alamy 65; NMUIM/Alamy: 64 l.; Pictorial Press Ltd/Alamy: 107 r.; The Picture Art Collection/Alamy: 8 r., 44, 91, 92; Prisma Archivo/Alamy: 73; Universal Images Group North America LLC/Alamy: 85
© Ron Mueck/Courtesy McClelland Sculpture Park and Gallery, Langwarrin /Photo: Getty Images/Jeff J. Mitchell/Staff: 162;
© Ron Mueck/Courtesy Queensland Art Gallery Foundation, Collection: Queensland Art Gallery | Gallery of Modern Art, Brisbane. Purchased 2008. Installation view: Fondation Cartier, Paris / Photo: Getty Images/Alain Benainous: 164/165
© Edgar Müller: 176
© Tim Noble: VG Bild-Kunst, Bonn 2020/Photo: Florian Heine: 158
© PEETA/Photo: Alexander Krziwanie/Stadt.Wand. Kunst: 37
© Patricia Piccinini: Courtesy the artist, Tolarno Galleries and Roslyn Oxley9 Gallery: 166/167
Prestel-Archiv: 22/23
John Pugh (https://commons.wikimedia.org/wiki/File:Academe_Trompe-l'oeil_Mural_by_John_Pugh,_Taylor_Hall,_CSU_Chico.jpg), https://creativecommons.org/licenses/by-sa/4.0/legalcode: 34
© Lee Quiñones: 169
© Bridget Riley 2020. All rights reserved. Streak 2/Monsoon Art Collection: 102/103
© Bridget Riley 2020. All rights reserved. Blaze 1/National Galleries of Scotland. Private Collection: 101
Roemer- und Pelizaeus-Museum Hildesheim/archive photo: 8 l.
© Georges Rousses: VG Bild-Kunst, Bonn 2020: 118
© Slinkachu: 173
© Mark Tansey. Courtesy Gagosian/Foto: bpk/ The Metropolitan Museum of Art. Gift of Jan Cowles and Charles Cowles, in honour of William S. Lieberman, 1988: 80/81
© Felice Varini: VG Bild-Kunst, Bonn 2020/Photo: Kristof Vrancken: 136/137
© Sue Webster: VG Bild-Kunst, Bonn 2020/Photo: Florian Heine: 158
© 1986 Kurt Wenner: 174
© Victor Vasarely: VG Bild-Kunst, Bonn 2020/Photo: bpk/CNAC-MNAM: 78
© Victor Vasarely: VG Bild-Kunst, Bonn 2020/Photo: Carmen Thyssen-Bornemisza Collection: 77
All other templates come from the archives of the publishing house.

The Author

Florian Heine is a photographer, art historian, writer and editor. His work as a photographer spans the genres of fine-art, portrait, commercial and industrial photography, and along with multiple solo exhibitions his photographs may be seen decorating Munich's Feldmoching underground station. As an author, he has written numerous books on art, photography and architecture for both adults and children. For the ZDF/3SAT television series *Das erste Mal – Wie Neues in die Kunst kam* (*The First Time – Innovations in Art*), based on his book of the same title, Florian Heine served as the program's art expert co-host and provided the script. His book *WELTERBE – Deutschlands lebendige Vergangenheit* about Germany's UNESCO World Heritage Sites was presented with the 2018 ITB Book Award.

A member of Verlagsgruppe Random House GmbH
Neumarkter Strasse 28 · 81673 Munich

A CIP catalogue record for this book is available from the British Library.

Editorial direction Prestel: Constanze Holler
Copyediting: José Enrique Macián
Translation: Noel Zmija-Maurice
Picture research: Dorothea Bethke
Production management: Andrea Cobré
Design and layout: Sofarobotnik, Augsburg & Munich
Separations: Schnieber Graphik, Munich
Printing and binding: Graphisches Centrum Cuno GmbH&Co.KG, Calbe
Typeface: Gotham
Paper: 150g Profimatt

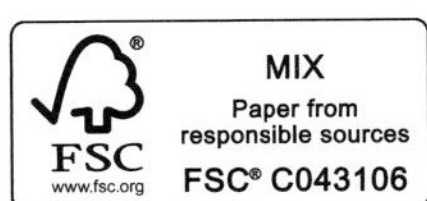

Verlagsgruppe Random House FSC® N001967

Printed in Germany
ISBN 978-3-7913-8678-2
www.prestel.com